D0764229

States of Confinement

Also by Joy James
and available from St. Martin's Press

Shadowboxing:
Representations of Black Feminist Politics

States of Confinement

Policing, Detention, and Prisons

Edited by Joy James

St. Martin's Press
New York

ISBN 0-312-21777-3

Library of Congress Cataloging-in-Publication Data

States of confinement : policing, detention & prisons / edited by Joy
    James.
        p. cm.
    Includes bibliographical references and index.
    ISBN 0-312-21777-3 (cloth)
        1. Discrimination in criminal justice administration—United
States. 2. Discrimination in juvenile justice administration-
-United States. 3. Discrimination in capital punishment—United
States. 4. Discrimination in law enforcement—United States.
5. Minorities—United States. I. James, Joy.
HV9950.S74 1999
364'.089'00973—dc21   99-28675
                                                                 CIP

Book design: Acme Art, Inc.

First edition: February 2000
10 9 8 7 6 5 4 3 2 1

CONTENTS

PART I
EXECUTIONS

PART II
BLACKS AND CRIMINAL JUSTICE

PART III

GENDER, SEXUALITY, AND CONFINEMENT

PART IV

POLICING

PART V

POLITICAL REPRESSION AND RESISTANCE

ACKNOWLEDGMENTS

Special thanks to those who helped in the development of this anthology: Maura Burnett, Shana Alfaro, Sabrina Hodges, Heather Larrabee, Leviticus Ra-Zamien, J. M. Lagrander, Anthony Papa, Alika Wong, Aliza Wong, Karen Moreira, Ana Sheffield, Deborah Hollis, Ward Churchill, and Jennifer Simington and Alan Bradshaw from St. Martin's production department.

Many individuals and organizations, too numerous to all acknowledge individually, assisted in the 1998 "Unfinished Liberation: Policing, Detention & Prisons" conference at the University of Colorado at Boulder that provided the foundation for this book. A few require special thanks for their unwavering support: Loretta Wahl, K. Kim Holder, Sirat Al Salim, Angell Perez, Christie Donner, the Rocky Mountain Peace and Justice Center Prisoners' Rights Project, Angela Davis, T. Denean Sharpley-Whiting, David Theo Goldberg, Janet Jacobs, Tom Mayer, Brother Jeff Fard, Sara Goering, Alison Jaggar, Steve Medina, Evelyn Hu-DeHart, Estevan Flores, Norberto Valdez, Lee Lew-Lee, Ashara Ekundayo, Francisco Martinez, Vivian Stromberg, William McIver, and KGNU. At the University of Colorado at Boulder, critical support was also provided by: the Office of the Dean of the College of Arts and Sciences, the Women's Resource Center, the Center for the Study of Values and Ethics, the Women's Studies Program, and the Department of Ethnic Studies.

PERMISSIONS

INTRODUCTION

States of Confinement: Policing, Detention, and Prisons explores the racial, sexual, and class inequalities tied to "criminal justice" in the United States. It raises such issues as inequities in prosecution and sentencing and exploitation and abuse in policing and imprisonment.

Currently, some 70 percent of the nearly 2 million imprisoned in U.S. jails, prisons, and detention centers are "minorities," or (poor) "people of color"; approximately 200,000 mentally ill people are incarcerated. The contributors to *States of Confinement*—progressive writers, activists, attorneys, and scholars—offer critiques of the death penalty, racism and the criminal justice system, confinement based on gender and sexuality, police misconduct and brutality, and the state's punitive responses to political radicalism and resistance. Here, twenty-six chapters explore the limits of a democratic society that has dedicated immense resources to policing and punishment. Nearly half of these chapters stem from papers presented at the March 1998 "Unfinished Liberation: Policing, Detention and Prisons" conference held at the University of Colorado at Boulder.[1]

The United States has the highest incarceration rate in the industrialized world. It is also one of the few "developed" countries that continues to deploy the death penalty. To talk about policing, imprisonment, and state executions, historically or in contemporary times, one must speak of race and class. Increasingly, new literature addresses the realities of our racialized, class-biased, and reactionary criminal and legal system.[2]

A few striking examples illustrate the gross inequality and abuse rampant in the current prison industry and the system of state policing. In March 1999 the Amnesty International Rights for All campaign issued a report, *Not Part of My Sentence: Violations of the Human Rights of Women in Custody,* documenting the abuses of women in U.S. prisons and jails. By June 1997 there were 138,000 women incarcerated in the United States; triple the number since 1985 and ten times the number of women imprisoned in Spain, England, France, Scotland, Germany, and Italy combined.[3] Most of the women incarcerated in the United States are nonviolent offenders convicted of economic crimes or drug-related offenses. Eighty percent are mothers, eighty percent are poor, and the majority are "women of color." The less common violent offenses are generally connected to domestic abuse. Racial bias in sentencing means that "minority" women charged with both nonviolent and violent crimes will increasingly make up the growing population of incarcerated females. (Sentencing bias is pervasive: African American or Latina women who kill their batterers are four times more likely than white women to be sentenced to prison even if the acts are defined as self-defense.) Serving time, this population of caged women find themselves subject to new forms of physical and sexual abuse. For instance, although the Convention Against Torture that the United States ratified in 1994 defines rape of women in custody by correctional officers as "torture," the United States government has engaged in virtually no monitoring of the conditions and situations of imprisoned women in respect to human rights violations.[4]

In government, the majority in Congress and the Supreme Court, as well as the president, Bill Clinton, have embraced the punitive rhetoric of punishment at least for the poor and racialized. Most politicians and elected officials support the death penalty, even though the American Bar Association has advocated a moratorium given the rampant and acknowledged racial bias in state executions. Race, of both the defendant and the victim, is the primary factor in capital punishment. Those convicted of killing a white person are four times more likely to receive the death penalty, particularly if they are not white themselves. On the eve of a new millennium, the Supreme Court has found this acceptable and state executions not cruel and unusual punishment in our democracy; even though in 1994 U.S. Supreme Court Justice Harry Blackmun noted: "Even under the most sophisticated death penalty statues, race continues to play a major role in determining who shall live and who shall die."[5] Over sixty-five percent of juvenile offenders sentenced to death since the reinstitution of the death penalty in 1976 have been either black or latino.[6] In addition, as one of the few democratic nations to execute minors, the United States has executed more youths than any other country.[7]

The contradictory and repressive nature of "democratic" law itself is striking. The Thirteenth Amendment to the Constitution codifies rather than abolishes slavery: Those duly convicted of a crime can be forced into involuntary servitude or slavery for the duration of their incarceration. A hundred years ago, more African Americans died in the convict prison lease system than they did during slavery, worked to death by a business venture coordinated by both state and private industry that replaced plantation labor with prison labor, a commodity that could always be replenished by sweeps arresting blacks because they were black. Today, according to the Washington, D.C.–based Sentencing Project, if a black person and a white person commit (or are convicted of) a similar offense, the black person is much more likely to be sentenced to prison. As prisoners' rights advocate Angela Y. Davis has noted, one is more likely to be incarcerated because of race (if he or she is black or brown) than for committing a crime.

Most men and women are in prison for nonviolent offenses, often related to the drug trade and addiction. As part of the state's ongoing "war on drugs," increased funds for policing (both domestically and internationally) and prisons have flowed generously. The United States is likely the world's largest nation-state consumer of illicit drugs; it has the most draconian and racialized drug laws among industrialized nations. European Americans are the majority of consumers of both crack (considered an urban drug for black and latino consumers) and powder cocaine (designated as the drug of choice for affluent white suburbanites).[8] Yet black and latino defendants disproportionately are policed, arrested, and incarcerated for drug use and sale.[9]

Racialized policing has also led the Congressional Black Caucus and progressives to adopt the phrase "DWB"—driving while black or brown—to denote the national prevalence of racial profiling in police harassment and arrests. In addition, human rights activists have noted the similarities between DWB and the Black Codes following the Civil War in which white patrollers could stop and question largely law-abiding African Americans solely because of their race and their ability or desire to move freely.[10] Similar repressive measures are used against Latinos and Chicanos by immigration police.

Prisons then exist as a central dilemma for a racially constructed and class-stratified democracy. This anthology explores the limits of conventional politics, extending its focus beyond the borders of the "free world" to study contracting democracy and the manifestations of expanding repression across the United States.

States of Confinement is organized into five sections: "Executions"; "Blacks and Criminal Justice"; "Gender, Sexuality, and Confinement"; "Policing"; and "Political Repression and Resistance." In "Executions," Part I, Robert Meeropol offers "Testimony" on the death penalty based on his childhood and adult perspectives on the executions of his parents, Ethel and Julius Rosenberg. Lee Bernstein, in "'. . . Give Me Death': Capital Punishment and the Limits of American Citizenship," presents a historical and theoretical analysis of the death penalty in the United States. Steven Hawkins documents the prevalence among death row inmates of African American and Latino youths, often juvenile offenders who were victims of physical or sexual abuse as young children. "The Ordeal of Mumia Abu-Jamal," by Daniel R. Williams, discusses the controversial case of the death row inmate-journalist considered by many to be a political prisoner falsely accused of killing a policeman.

Part II, "Blacks and Criminal Justice," begins with a chapter by Manning Marable that reviews the state of black America, its economic marginalization, and its vulnerability to the prison industrial complex. Angela Y. Davis's "From the Convict Lease System to the Super-Max Prison" examines the growing industries surrounding prisons and the disproportionate incarceration of blacks and Latinos by linking the emergence of nineteenth-century race-based incarceration to contemporary racism and involuntary servitude in prison. Marc Mauer argues in "Young Black Americans and the Criminal Justice System" against the racial disparities in sentencing that target African American males to such a degree that blacks who are convicted of the same offenses as whites are eight times more likely to be incarcerated. In "The New Black Leadership: Gang-Related?," Salim Muwakkil examines the policing, contradictions, and contributions of Chicago gangs that finance social services for their impoverished communities through an underground political economy based primarily on the drug trade. Focusing on black women in cities, Adrien K. Wing provides a critical view of African American women and the criminal justice system, in "Black Women and Gangs."

"Gender, Sexuality, and Confinement," Part III, examines different forms of social, sexual, and racial violence in relation to criminalization and incarceration. Joanne Belknap writes of the restricted access that imprisoned women have to medical attention in "Programming and Health Care Accessibility for Incarcerated Women." Juanita Díaz-Cotto's "Race, Ethnicity, and Gender in Studies of Incarceration" focuses on "women of color" in order to examine bias in social science studies of women's prisons. Luana Ross's "Imprisoned Native Women and the Importance of Native Traditions" discusses the impact of Native American religions on the self-esteem and identity of incarcerated native women in the West. In "Military Prostitution in Asia and the United States," Alexandra Suh writes about Korean women who marry U.S. servicemen only to be forced into the sex industry when they immigrate as "brides." Brenda Rodriguez provides in "HIV, AIDS, and Rape in Texas Prisons" an exposé of the adverse conditions that HIV-positive prisoners and prisoners with AIDS face. AnnJanette Rosga explicates the links between social homophobia and hate crimes in "Ritual Killings: Antigay Violence and Reasonable Justice."

Part IV, "Policing," studies different mechanisms of confining both subordinate and marginalized peoples and the general citizenry. In "All the Brother Wanted Was a Ride: Lynching and Police Powers in Texas," Larvester Gaither examines the historical relationship between extralegal violence, in the case of 1998 lynching victim James T. Byrd, and the resurgence of antiblack vigilantism and police brutality. David Theo Goldberg's "Surplus Value: The Political Economy of Prisons and Policing" critiques the profiteering and the privatization of U.S. prisons. Gabriel Torres and David A. Love outline a national campaign to increase recognition of the victims of police brutality in "The Militarization of the Police in the United States." Eric Tang's "State Violence, Asian Immigrants, and the 'Underclass'" focuses on the New York Police Department's misconduct toward Asian American youths. In "The INS and the Criminalization of Immigrant Workers," Julie A. Su details the criminalization of immigrant workers and the tactics employed by the

Immigration and Naturalization Service against largely Asian and Latina garment workers. Gary T. Marx, in "The New Surveillance," describes recent developments in electronic surveillance and the diminishment of privacy rights in contemporary society.

Part V, "Political Repression and Resistance," begins with Margaret Ratner and Michael Ratner's description of abuses of the grand jury system and its role in repressing and jailing activists. The selective policing and deportation of radicals is explored in Huessin Ibish's "At the Constitution's Edge: Arab Americans and Civil Liberties." José López's "Political Incarceration" discusses the use of prisons as tools in domestic "counterinsurgency." Donna Willmott speaks of her own experience as a political prisoner incarcerated for her activism with the Puerto Rican independentistas and the need to support U.S. political prisoners. Judi Bari's "Earth First! and the FBI" highlights the misconduct of police agencies in dealing with environmental activists, describing police harassment following her survival of a car bombing.

These are only a select few of the thousands of voices issuing critiques of what has been labeled the "prison industrial complex" and the rising abuse of police powers in the United States. (Some of the most incisive analyses remain those of the imprisoned struggling for humanity.) In this era, in the new century, prisons and policing pose the most visceral and unsettling juxtapositions between freedom and "slavery"; between citizenship and subjugation. This volume does not ignore the reality of social violence in U.S. culture and society. Rather it explicates the ways in which social myths and political demagoguery have joined with dehumanizing and often racist, (hetero)sexist, and classist speech and practices to create the "monster" that must be excoriated and exorcised. By demonizing marginalized social sectors and by obscuring complex social realities, such rhetoric and policies appear to confine all of us who abide in this punitive, national culture.

NOTES

1. Additional essays gathered from the conference were published in a special issue titled "Unfinished Liberation: Policing and Imprisonment" in *Radical Philosophy Review* vol. 3, no. 1 (Fall 1999).

2. See Mumia Abu-Jamal, *Live From Death Row: This is Mumia Abu-Jamal* (New York: Addison-Wesley, 1995); Daniel Burton-Rose, Dan Pens, and Paul Wright, *The Celling of America* (Monroe, ME: Common Courage Press, 1998); Jerome Miller, *Search and Destroy* (Cambridge: Harvard University Press, 1996); Elihu Rosenblatt, ed., *Criminal Injustice* (Boston: South End Press, 1996).

3. Amnesty International, Rights for All, *Not Part of My Sentence: Violations of the Human Rights of Women in Custody* (New York: Amnesty International, March 1999), 15-16. Amnesty documents that these European countries combined have a population of 150 million women, compared to 120 million women in the United States.

4. The United States was to submit a report on its compliance with the Convention Against Torture in 1995, but no report to date has been released. In response, a coalition of over sixty non-governmental organizations (NGOs) issued a report in October 1998 titled *Torture in the United States: The Status of Compliance by the U.S. Government with the International Convention Against Torture and Other Cruel, Inhuman or Degrading Treatment or Punishment.* See Morton Sklar, ed., *Torture in the United States* (Washington, D.C., World Organization Against Torture, October 1998).

   The report notes that the major areas of noncompliance in the United States center on: the death penalty; prison conditions and the treatment of refugee detainees; physical and sexual abuse of women in prisons; the return of refugees to situations of torture and persecution; and their long-term detention under abusive conditions. Other violations noted in the report are: the United States's failure to extradite or prosecute torturers who worked with the Central Intelligence Agency or were trained at the School of the Americas; the state's lack of adequate domestic implementation of the 1996 Illegal Immigration and Immigrant Responsibility Act; and arms sales and other assistance by the U.S. government that support torture in foreign countries (such as the sale of electronic stun gun equipment and some 10,000 shock batons to Turkey to be used against the Kurdish minority, the same equipment that Amnesty International has denounced in its use against U.S. prisoners).

5. Quote cited in Morton Sklar, ed., *Racial and Ethnic Discrimination in the United States: The Status of Compliance by the U.S. Government with the International Convention on the Elimination of Racial Discrimination* (Washington, D.C., The Coalition Against Torture and Racial Discrimination, October 1998), 5.

6. Ibid., 6.

7. See ibid, 5.

8. For state complicity in the drug trade see *Inside the Shadow Government,* Declaration of Plaintiffs' Counsel filed by the Christic Institut, U.S. District Court, Miami, Florida, March 31, 1988; and Gary Webb, *Dark Alliance* (New York: Seven Stories Press, 1998). See also: Dan Baum, *Smoke and Mirrors: The War on Drugs and the Politics of Failure* (New York: Little, Brown & Company, 1996).

9. See: Dan Baum, *Smoke and Mirrors.*

10. See George E. Curry, "Policing Police," and Marcia Davis, "Roadside Racism," in *Emerge,* June 1999.

I

EXECUTIONS

ONE

Testimony

ROBERT MEEROPOL

As far as I know my brother, Michael, and I are the only people to have both their parents executed by the government of the United States. After sharing the personal impact of that with you, I will go on to discuss tactical questions and later finish with some broader strategic concerns.

As a child I lived a nightmare. My parents, Ethel and Julius Rosenberg, were arrested by the Federal Bureau of Investigation (FBI) in the summer of 1950, shortly after my third birthday. They were charged with conspiracy to commit espionage, more specifically with conspiring in 1944 and 1945 to steal the secret of the atomic bomb and give it to the Soviet Union. They were tried, convicted, and sentenced to death the following spring, shortly before my fourth birthday. The executions took place on June 19, 1953, when I was six.

How much does a six-year-old understand about something like that and how much do I remember about it today? I remember quite a bit. I particularly remember the last week of my parents' lives. On Monday, June 15, 1953, when the Supreme Court adjourned for the summer, my parents were scheduled to die on Thursday. On Tuesday a special petition was presented to Justice William Orville Douglas as he left for vacation. On Wednesday Douglas stayed the execution and went on vacation. On Thursday the Supreme Court was recalled into special session. On Friday morning Douglas's stay was overturned by a 6 to 3 vote. My parents were executed that evening, Friday, June 19, one minute before sundown so as not to "desecrate" the Jewish Sabbath.

Although I couldn't read the newspapers, I saw this on TV and heard about it on the radio. As a six-year-old, my interpretation of these events was that prior to Monday, June 15, the Supreme Court Justices asked my parents' lawyer to give them ten reasons why my parents should not be killed and he did. So the Supreme Court stayed the execution. Then they reconvened the Court that Thursday to ask the lawyer for an eleventh reason. When he was unable to provide it, my parents were killed.

I pretended not to understand what was going on so adults would not fuss over me. While in some ways I did not understand, I got the essence.

As an adult I've come to terms with my nightmare. I founded the Rosenberg Fund for Children and work as its executive director to transform the destruction that was visited upon my family into something positive for other families. The Rosenberg Fund for Children is a public foundation that provides for the educational and emotional needs of children in this country whose parents have been targeted in the course of their progressive activities.

I've come to terms with my nightmare, but I haven't gotten over it. The pain is still there. Sometimes it comes out in small ways. I still feel the pain whenever I happen to see "6:19" displayed on the digital clock radio in my bedroom. It reminds me of June 19, the date my parents were killed. In fact, I inwardly cringe a little whenever I see the number 619. You'd be surprised at how often you can come across a number like that.

And the pain does not stop with me, it even affects my children. My older daughter, who graduated from college in June 1994, has given me permission to quote from the postscript of her senior thesis. The thesis was about the grandmother she never knew:

> On my wall hangs a picture of my grandmother and the subject of my thesis: Ethel Rosenberg. Her presence on my wall contrasts with her absence from my life. Yes, I have pictures of my grandmother drawn by artists as renowned as [Pablo] Picasso and [Fernand] Lèger, but I don't have any family photos of her, no happy images of the two of us together, lying on the beach or sitting down to a family Seder.

The photos which clutter my desk show other familiar faces: my parents, my younger sister, and my friends all gaze at me—captured, frozen images of times remembered and shared. But the picture of my grandmother stands apart. More formal, more professional, more impersonal; this picture is the only one which does not inspire memories of past time. . . . [T]here are no memories of my grandmother because she was killed before I was born.

I do not forgive the government for its state-sponsored killing of my parents. There is no way for the government, or for anyone else, to make good that loss to me and my family. I don't believe that the death penalty serves any positive purpose. It does not act as deterrent. It will not bring back murdered family members; it will not heal shattered families; but it will shatter the innocent families of those the state executes.

ARGUMENTS

A lot of people oppose the death penalty on moral grounds. There were people who worked to save my parents' lives (just as today there are those working to save Mumia Abu-Jamal's life), not because they believed in my parents' innocence but because they felt the death penalty was wrong. These beliefs are often religious or ethical, and I admit that I too believe that the death penalty is morally wrong.

I don't think, however, this is the track anti-death penalty forces should pursue. There are others who in their hearts do not believe capital punishment is immoral, and such core beliefs are often not susceptible to rational persuasion. This deeply divisive issue has fervent advocates on both sides, but there are also many who do not feel so strongly, one way or the other. These are the people we must reach, and I believe there are a number of arguments against the death penalty that can reach them.

One of the most effective arguments is to point out that the death penalty requires perfection. Obviously, there is no room to correct the execution of an innocent person, and because no human system is mistake free, mistakes are inevitable. That means innocent people will be killed, and most people don't want this to happen.

We should also expose the nature of many pro-death penalty zealots. These advocates don't care that it doesn't deter, that it isn't cheaper than incarceration, and that it won't make the nation safer. It doesn't bother them that it is racist or that it is used almost exclusively against the poor. While the class bias and racism of the use of capital punishment in this country is demonstrable, anti-capital punishment arguments based on these facts have relatively little impact on many audiences, a fact that probably reflects the class bias and racism rampant in America today. Nevertheless, despite the fact that many may not be swayed, the racist nature of capital punishment as it is employed in this country must be noted whenever possible. It is hoped that these efforts to educate ultimately will bear fruit, but for now they may not change many minds. And we must never forget that capital punishment, from the Haymarket Martyrs, through Nicola Sacco and Bartholomeo Vanzetti and my parents, to Mumia Abu-Jamal today, has been used repeatedly as an instrument of political repression.[*]

These facts, along with all other arguments, will be ignored by those who simply want revenge. Some of them like the idea of killing and derive gratification from it. These pro-death penalty fanatics are seeking an

---

[*] Ed.: Chicago police had violent clashes with trade unionists in the late nineteenth-century. On May 3, 1885, police fired on a gathering of striking workers and sympathizers who were fighting "scabs" (replacement workers that undercut the unions), wounding many and killing four. On the following day, three thousand assembled for a meeting in Haymarket Square. One hundred and eighty police arrived to end the meeting, a bomb exploded among them wounding sixty-six (seven died later); police fired into the crowd, wounding 200 and killing several people. Although it was not known who threw the bomb, the police arrested eight anarchist leaders in Chicago, four were later hung.

Nicola Sacco and Bartholomeo Vanzetti were Italian anarchists and workers living in Boston during the time of the U.S. government's violent confrontations with workers and radicals. A friend and fellow anarchist, Andrea Salsedo, was arrested by New York FBI agents in 1920. The FBI detained Salsedo for weeks, denying him contact with friends, family, or lawyers; when his body was found on the pavement below the building the FBI claimed he committed suicide by jumping from their fourteenth floor window. Responding to Salsedo's death, Sacco and Vanzetti armed themselves; soon after they were arrested and accused of a robbery and murder. Despite protests of their innocence, they were convicted. After extensive appeals and rallies charging that they were framed because of their political activities, Sacco and Vanzetti were electrocuted in 1927 as troops protected the prison and police forcibly broke up demonstrations. See Howard Zinn, *A People's History of the United States* (New York: Harper & Row, 1980).

outlet for the violence within themselves. They are the ones most likely to engage in violence on our streets and in their homes. They are a symptom of the sickness that is eroding our humanity. Pandering to their bloodlust will only increase the level of violence in our society. If we succeed in showing those we can reach the true nature of rabid death penalty proponents, we can turn the tide of public sentiment against the increasing number of executions.

There are other effective arguments as well. Some people follow a simple logical progression in determining that they favor capital punishment. They envision the most horrendous murderer, someone like Jeffrey Dahmer (who cannibalized his victims). They conclude that they support capital punishment because they would not object to his execution. But these same people can quickly grasp that supporting the execution of one murderer is not equivalent to supporting the general practice of capital punishment in this country. The logical sequence just described cannot be sustained once the death penalty is seen as an institution. Capital punishment is a nationwide system set in motion by thousands of county prosecutors and district attorneys. The decision to charge someone with a capital offense is left in the hands of these elected government officials. These days many citizens wouldn't even trust government officials to put up a traffic light. Realizing that capital punishment gives these types of people the power of life or death over others gives them pause.

There is also a more subtle, but still powerful, anti-capital punishment argument: It is antidemocratic and inevitably corrupting. One of the premises of the Constitution is that the people are sovereign. In other words, the only rights we the people cede to the government are those that are specifically enumerated in the Constitution. Americans' suspicion of concentrated governmental power is probably best summed up by the nineteenth-century British Lord Acton, who said: "Power tends to corrupt. Absolute power tends to corrupt absolutely."

The imposition of the death penalty, the power of life and death, is a form of absolute power. Give people in government that power and they will abuse it. The last week of my parents' lives provides a potent example of just how corrupting the death penalty can be. As I mentioned, on Monday, June 15, 1953, when the Supreme Court adjourned for the summer, my parents were scheduled to be executed that Thursday (June 18). On Tuesday morning as Justice Douglas, the Court's most liberal member, was leaving the Supreme Court building to start his vacation, he was confronted by two lawyers who were not previously involved in the case, who presented him with a novel argument that my parents' execution would be illegal. The attorneys reasoned that my parents, who were tried and sentenced for violating the Espionage Act of 1917, should instead have been charged with violating the Atomic Energy Act of 1947. This was significant because the latter act required a jury recommendation of death before a capital sentence could be imposed, and there had been no jury recommendation in my parents' case. The attorneys concluded that an execution under these circumstances would be illegal.

Justice Douglas agreed to postpone his vacation for one day to consider this contention. The next morning he stayed the execution so the entire Court would be able to consider it, then went on vacation. It looked like Douglas had given my parents a new lease on life, but it was not to be. According to FBI files not made public until more than twenty years later, that Tuesday evening, as Douglas was considering the request, Attorney General Herbert Brownell met secretly with Supreme Court Chief Justice Fred Vinson. The file states that at that meeting Chief Justice Vinson "said that if a stay is granted he will call the full Court into session Thursday morning to vacate it."

This file provides documentary evidence that the attorney general conspired with the chief judicial officer of the United States to vacate a stay of execution authored by another sitting Supreme Court Justice *before they had read the legal reasons for the stay.* They couldn't have known the legal basis of the stay because the stay wasn't written until the next morning. In other words, the Chief Justice of the Supreme Court and the Attorney General of the United States engaged in a conspiracy to obstruct justice. That is a felony.

It could be argued that, since FBI files sometimes contain inaccurate information, we can't be certain that this meeting actually took place. The events that unfolded belie this argument. The Chief Justice was true to his word. On Thursday morning he recalled the Supreme Court into special session. The justices heard arguments that afternoon and on Friday morning announced that Douglas's stay had been overturned by a 6 to 3 vote. The executions were scheduled and carried out that evening.

STRATEGY

Personal testimony from those affected by the death penalty and these arguments can be very persuasive. It is possible to expand the national campaign for abolishing the death penalty. However, we face a difficult strategic challenge. How do we relate our anti-capital punishment efforts to broader questions of mass imprisonment, the prison industrial complex, slave labor and brutality in prisons, the racist imprisonment of a significant portion of young African American males, the creation of Third World enclaves in our cities and their repression by semicolonial occupation forces that feed the prisons with the people they arrest, the obscene accumulation of astounding wealth by the giant corporations and their control of the economy that produces even more poverty, and on and on? Isolating capital punishment from these questions may maximize the chances of producing a "liberal" single-issue mass movement with a significant chance of achieving one important, but very limited, victory for humanity—the elimination of capital punishment. Yet placing this effort in the context of these other issues seems essential in dealing with a problem that is rapidly assuming holocaust proportions. Doing so, however, may drastically narrow the base of support for anti-capital punishment work. There must be compromise. And because those who will not abandon the broader questions are some of the most vigorous anti-capital punishment activists, achieving successful compromise is critical to ending both capital punishment and confronting many of the other issues raised.

TWO

"... Give Me Death": Capital Punishment and the Limits of American Citizenship

LEE BERNSTEIN

If a stranger, completely disabled, disarmed, strengthless, throws himself on the mercy of a warrior, he is not, by this very act, condemned to death; but a moment of impatience on the warrior's part will suffice to relieve him of his life. In any case, his flesh has lost that very important property which in the laboratory distinguishes living flesh from the dead—the galvanic response. If you give a frog's leg an electric shock, it twitches. If you confront a human being with the touch or sight of something horrible or terrifying this bundle of muscles, nerves, and flesh likewise twitches. Alone of all living things, the suppliant we have just described neither quivers nor trembles. He has lost the right to do so. As his lips advance to touch the object that is for him of all things most charged with horror, they do not draw back on his teeth—they cannot.

—Simone Weil, *The Iliad; or, The Poem of Force*[1]

During the height of World War II, philosopher Simone Weil argued in her brilliant essay, *The Illiad; or, The Poem of Force,* that the threat of force by the powerful served to paralyze and silence resistance by those who were targeted. Weil implied that the terror of violence goes beyond the pain of a blow or the end of a life. An additional terror lies in the way violence inflicted by the powerful creates an inability to react, to protest, or to critique. Since the early years of the U.S. republic, the death penalty has raised crucial questions about the meaning of citizenship, particularly along lines of race and class. Of course, killing people for crimes— whether against fellow citizens or against the state itself—was nothing new. Ancient also were the protests that preceded and the outrage that followed the deaths of the celebrated or anonymous among the condemned. But enlightenment concepts like "natural rights" and "equality" gave rise to a new debate over capital punishment. Benjamin Rush, signer of the Declaration of Independence and professor of medicine at the University of Pennsylvania, and Robert Turnbull, author of the widely read *A Visit to the Philadelphia Prison* (1796), joined Thomas Jefferson in seeking to shift criminal justice away from corporal and capital punishment and toward imprisonment and rehabilitation. As the meaning of citizenship shifted, so did the treatment of those who violated the "natural rights" of life, liberty, and property. In the last thirty years, and particularly during the 1970s, those debating the desirability of capital punishment have returned to the meaning of citizenship and the role of state-sponsored violence—including police brutality, corporal punishment, and capital punishment—in a republic shaped around the principle that all people share "natural" rights. During the post-Revolutionary period, death penalty opponents joined slavery abolitionists in arguing that capital punishment, like slavery, called into question the national commitment to the principle that all are created equal. By the 1970s, a shift had occurred that deprived anti-death penalty advocates of this line of argument: Citizenship had been rewritten so that defenders of capital punishment could call into question the patriotism of those who blocked executions. This shift had a particularly devastating effect on those who sought to show the links among race, rights, and capital punishment by depriving them of what had been the most successful legal and political challenge to the death penalty.

In the decade prior to the Revolution, Italian philosopher Cesare Beccaria called for an abolition of capital punishment. Beccaria's argument centered on the ineffectiveness of capital punishment in deterring violent crime. But the implications of his argument also raised issues that spoke directly to the shifting meaning of citizenship in post-Revolutionary America: "The penalty of death is a war of the nation against a citizen. The death of a citizen can only be thought necessary for two reasons. First, that although he has been deprived of liberty, he still has such connexions [*sic*] and such power that the safety of the nation is endangered; and that he can provoke by his existence a revolution dangerous to the settled form of government. The death of such a citizen, then, becomes necessary when a nation is regaining or losing its freedom."[2] The implications of the death penalty for all citizens were such that it should be used only in those cases when that one individual threatened the stability of the state. Translations of Beccaria's works quickly appeared in the nascent nation across the Atlantic, influencing Thomas Jefferson, when governor of Virginia, to call for a new criminal code that emphasized punishments in proportion to the crime. At the time of his writing, Virginia law provided for the death penalty in cases of manslaughter, rape, and robbery as well as murder. The language of this bill echoed the first draft of the Declaration of Independence, which Jefferson had penned just three years earlier:

> Whereas it frequently happens that wicked and dissolute men resigning themselves to the dominion of inordinate passions, commit violations on the lives, liberties and property of others, and, the secure enjoyment of these having principally induced men to enter into society, government would be defective in it's principal purpose were it not to restrain such criminal acts, by inflicting due punishments on those who perpetrate them; but it appears at the same time equally deducible from the purposes of society that a member thereof, committing an inferior injury, does not wholly forfeit the protection of his fellow citizens, but, after suffering a punishment in proportion to his offense is entitled to their protection from all greater pain, so that it becomes a duty in the legislature to arrange in a proper scale

the crimes which it may be necessary for them to repress, and to adjust thereto a corresponding the gradation of punishments.[3]

As in his critique of slavery, Jefferson sent a mixed message: He questioned capital punishment but stopped short of calling for its repeal. Whereas Beccaria called for life in prison for murder, Jefferson's bill called for execution in cases of treason, for a husband who murdered his wife, for a child who murdered a parent, or for a parent who murdered a child. Except for cases of murder and treason, Jefferson felt that capital punishment deprived the commonwealth of the labors of fellow citizens who could be reformed. Jefferson sought to restore people to society, except in those cases where doing so would mean a direct threat to the public. In the end, Jefferson believed that the frequent use of capital punishment would weaken rather than preserve the new commonwealth. Jefferson's bill failed, but by placing the idea within the context of "natural rights," he showed how Beccaria's views were in keeping with the rhetoric of the new republic. Several of Jefferson's contemporaries embraced Beccaria's call for total abolition of capital punishment, acknowledging that his reasoning derived from a shared devotion to the Enlightenment principles that gave rise to the United States. Benjamin Rush was among the most influential of the abolitionists. In two essays, Rush critiqued criminological and theological arguments that favored the death penalty. The major criminological argument then and now was that the punishment of murder by death deterred similar crimes by raising the cost of the crime so high as to eliminate its attractiveness. Rush critiqued this view using Beccaria's idea that the death penalty reduced the horror of taking away a human life and therefore multiplied murders. But Rush's argument centered on what he saw as the more important values of the new republic:

> [C]apital punishments are the natural offspring of monarchical governments. Kings believe that they possess their crowns by a *divine* right: no wonder, therefore, they assume the divine power of taking away human life. Kings consider their subjects as their property: no wonder, therefore, they shed their blood with as little emotion as men shed the blood of their sheep or cattle. But the principles of

republican governments speak a very different language. They teach us the absurdity of the divine origin of kingly power. . . . The United States have adopted these peaceful and benevolent forms of government. It becomes them therefore to adopt their mild and benevolent principles.[4]

Rush raised serious questions about U.S. dedication to the principles that he held so dear by showing that the new nation's use of the death penalty aped the monarchical practices of the colonial empire. This view implied that citizens are not subjects to a higher earthly authority but reside in a community of equals in which the stated purpose of government is to promote shared rights. Rush's view did not only raise questions of the treatment of convicts. In showing that the early republic explicitly guaranteed these shared rights only for free white men and established a voting role only for white men of some economic independence, the death penalty abolitionists raised questions about the government's role in establishing the practical meaning of citizenship. Robert Turnbull, in an essay originally published in the *Charleston* (South Carolina) *Daily Gazette* in 1796, praised the newly opened Walnut Street Jail in Philadelphia as a benevolent alternative to corporal and capital punishments. Turnbull saw imprisonment as a racially integrated alternative to corporal and capital punishment when he pointed out that "about one-eighth of the number of convicts compose the negroes and mulattoes, between whom and the whites, in this country, are none of those shameful distinctions you are daily accustomed to in the Southern States."[5] Writing not only during a time when some African American residents of Pennsylvania still struggled against their own enslavement and publishing in a Charleston newspaper, Turnbull optimistically felt that black people and white people eating, working, and praying together—albeit behind bars—marked a significant advance in U.S. race relations. Turnbull reserved his most impassioned criticism for the death penalty, which he saw as fundamentally destructive of the relationship between one person and another in a republic.[6] The punishment of death, like the presence of slavery and racial hierarchy, worked against the health and happiness of the community, particularly one that celebrated natural equality.

The immediacy and finality of capital punishment continued to make it a suitable subject to define the meanings and limits of citizenship throughout the nineteenth and twentieth centuries. I want to hint at the contours of this larger pattern by looking closely at the 1970s, another watershed era in the history of capital punishment in the United States. In the years following the assassinations of Martin Luther King, Jr., and Robert F. Kennedy, civil rights organizations such as the Urban League and the National Association for the Advancement of Colored People (NAACP) Legal Defense and Educational Fund (LDF) joined Amnesty International and the American Civil Liberties Union (ACLU) in condemning the death penalty. In insisting that the application of the death sentence—particularly when applied to black men in cases involving the rape of a white woman—constituted an arbitrary and racist double standard, these organizations succeeded in overturning the death sentences of every death row inmate—regardless of race—in a series of cases between 1967 and 1972, when the case of *Furman v. Georgia* resulted in a flurry of activity in state and federal legislatures.[7] The debate that preceded the shaping of bills by elected representatives once again rearticulated the language of citizenship. Rather than arguing that "natural rights" trumped calls for capital punishment, this time those in favor of the most extreme forms of state-sponsored violence appropriated the language of citizenship to argue for the death penalty.

More than the other organizations already named, the LDF placed capital punishment at the center of its civil rights agenda in the late 1960s and early 1970s. In some ways, this was nothing new. One of the first national campaigns the young NAACP waged in the 1920s sought to bring to light southern lynchings. One recent book provocatively suggests that NAACP efforts served only to regularize and institutionalize these informally sanctioned death sentences carried out in the name of white supremacy.[8] Furthermore, following the 1955 lynching of fourteen-year-old Emmett Till, the NAACP was instrumental in making clear the racist context for punishing transgressions with death. Jacqueline Goldsby argues that the rise of television and photo-magazines, such as *Life, Look, Ebony,* and *Jet,* provided a visual record that subjected "the lynchers . . . to public judgment and repudiation," even if this did not result in convictions.[9] When the all-white, all-male jury failed to convict

Till's killers, it was clear to their supporters and critics alike that the application (or absence of application) of the penalty of death reinforced racial hierarchies.[10]

In the late 1960s and early 1970s, the LDF added an absolute rejection of capital punishment to its previous commitment to defending African Americans facing death in cases of rape. During its fall term of 1969, the Supreme Court heard the case of *Maxwell v. Bishop* (later called *Maxwell v. Arkansas*), then the latest in a string of postconviction challenges to capital punishment. Starting in 1967, the LDF provided attorneys with what came to be called the "Last Aid Kit" of seventeen different petitions, orders, briefs, and applications that would stall the execution of condemned prisoners.[11] This stopgap strategy resulted in the inability of any state to carry out an execution, but it put off the fundamental question of whether the death penalty would continue. To many in the media and legal community, the pending execution of William Lee Maxwell in Arkansas appeared to be, as the title of a *New York Times Magazine* feature indicated, "The Case that Could End Capital Punishment."[12] Maxwell, a twenty-two-year-old African American with a string of convictions for petty crimes, was sentenced to death in 1962 for raping a Hot Springs white woman, a crime for which he maintained his innocence. Between 1930, the first year such statistics were collected, and Maxwell's 1969 appeal, state governments executed 445 men for rape. Of these, 40 were white, the rest African American.[13] LDF lawyers and the Supreme Court justices were well aware of these statistics, but the likelihood of the Court buying these arguments as evidence of wrongdoing in any one trial seemed slim. In fact, the Court had refused to hear cases where lawyers presented this argument. Instead, the Supreme Court agreed to hear this case because Anthony Amsterdam, lead attorney for the LDF, argued that the use of a single, standardless jury put undue pressure on defendants to take the stand in the conviction stage of the trial, thus violating the constitutional provision against self-incrimination. While the Court seemed sympathetic to this argument and ordered a new trial for Maxwell, as it had in the previous session's ruling against the widespread use of "death qualified juries"—juries made up only of people willing to agree to a sentence of death—this case would not provide the broad-based elimination of the death penalty that the

NAACP lawyers sought.[14] It was clear that the Supreme Court remained uncomfortable with capital punishment, but it would use neither racial discrimination nor procedural claims as the basis for abolition. *Furman v. Georgia*, the 1972 case that ultimately commuted the sentences of over 600 death row inmates in thirty-two states, did not rule on the procedural questions of earlier cases. Instead, the Supreme Court ruling in *Furman* seemed to center on the racist application of the death penalty. *Furman* involved four cases: two African American men convicted of raping white women and two African American men convicted of murdering white people. The Court agreed with the LDF argument that capital punishment as then practiced constituted cruel and unusual punishment, an Eighth Amendment argument it had previously rejected.[15] However, rather than ruling that the death penalty unfairly targeted African Americans convicted of crimes against whites or that the state killing people was unacceptably cruel, the Court found the process of prosecutorial selection arbitrary. The idea that states executed people "arbitrarily" rather than in a racially discriminatory fashion both acknowledged and rejected the underlying motivation of the LDF's efforts.[16] Thus, at the same time that this ruling saved the lives of those on death row, it also signaled to lawmakers that they could write new statutes and procedures to nullify race-based challenges to capital punishment.

Following this cue, states scrambled to create new provisions that would pass Eighth Amendment muster.[17] While the Supreme Court did overturn the use of the death penalty, most of the concurring and all of the dissenting opinions rejected the claim that the practice denied "equal protection" for people of color. In denying the centrality of race in the race-neutral (or racially coded) word "arbitrary," the Supreme Court marked the emergence of a new public discourse that condemned racist practices but also eliminated the ability of people targeted because of their race to react, protest, or critique on racial grounds. Ostensibly protecting those on death row from capricious juries, *Furman v. Georgia* also eliminated a crucial route of defense for the future.

When federal and state legislatures again returned to the question of capital punishment, most limited the discussion to the areas proscribed by Cesare Beccaria in the 1760s. Virtually all of the new bills left out the racially suspect category of rape, focusing instead on crimes directed against the state or its representatives. For example, a federal bill focused on treason and espionage; escapes from custody that involved a death; blowing up government buildings; killing of law enforcement or corrections officers, heads of foreign governments, high elected officials, or, in a gesture seemingly aimed at an expected constitutional challenge, Supreme Court justices.[18] On the state level, early bills and laws often created mandatory death sentences for those convicted of murdering police officers and prison workers, in the ultimately false hope that such sentences would avoid charges of "arbitrariness." After two Black Muslim inmates killed the warden and deputy warden of Philadelphia's Holmesburg Prison in 1973, Pennsylvania promptly passed a new death penalty law for cases involving the murder of police officers or prison officials.[19] Only rarely was rape included in the list of punishable crimes, and even then it was only in cases where a death occurred.

While all of these early statutes failed in the face of constitutional challenges, they show that a shift had occurred. Where the LDF and other challengers to capital punishment argued that the death penalty violated the rights of poor people and people of color, state legislatures now argued that the lack of such a penalty posed a threat to state officials and national stability. The fact that most death row inmates remained poor and/or people of color seemed incidental. Challenges on the basis of race continued. In North Carolina, which in 1974 had the largest death row in the country, at forty-five prisoners, a 5,000-person rally brought together the National Alliance Against Racism and Political Repression (cochaired by Angela Y. Davis) and civil rights veteran Reverend Ralph David Abernathy.[20] The Abernathy-led chant of "Let my people go" made sense considering the continued importance of race in the application of capital punishment, but the earlier Supreme Court decision and the new seemingly race-neutral laws (and the racially charged language of "law and order" popularized by President Richard Nixon) served to undermine the power of race-based critiques within the criminal justice system. Many of the new challengers similarly evaded the questions of race by returning to religious arguments or to the ineffective deterrence value of capital punishment.[21]

The 1976 decision *Gregg v. Georgia* reestablished the constitutionality of capital punishment when the Supreme Court approved laws that provided for a separate sentencing hearing and automatic judicial review in capital convictions. Hoping to increase prosecutorial restraint, the Court mandated that "aggravating factors" were required for people convicted of first-degree murder to be eligible for the death penalty. Despite these protections, the simultaneous racist application and denial of race-based critiques continued. Of the first six people executed after the *Gregg* decision, five were white.[22] While it is difficult to prove that these cases represented a conscious process of prosecutorial and judicial selection, it is clear that these executions pre-empted race-based challenges even while the nation's death rows remained largely poor and African American. In Benjamin Rush's Philadelphia, African American people convicted in a death eligible case are 38 percent more likely than other defendants to receive a death sentence. Nationally 98 percent of all prosecutors responsible for seeking the death penalty are white.[23] "Give Them Death," a 1990 *U.S. News and World Report* article, reported that 80 percent of those polled supported capital punishment, double the figure for 1966, which marked the height of the NAACP's race-conscious campaign against capital punishment.[24] In the face of continued frustration, lawyers once again rely on the "Last Aid Kit" techniques of the pre-*Furman* era as virtually all other avenues are exhausted.[25] The rhetoric and reality of violent retribution gained new prominence as the argument that the death penalty is applied in a racially discriminatory fashion fell out of favor. Our nation's death rows continue to grow and the number of executions increases, but, as Simone Weil warned, as our lips advance to touch the object that is most charged with horror, they do not draw back on our teeth—they cannot. Supreme Court decisions that limit or eliminate arguments based on the racially discriminatory practice of executions make the rapid increase in the rate and number of executions more alarming. As we lose avenues of protest and critique, our silence intensifies the horror of the execution chamber.

NOTES

1. I am grateful to Sam Thonet for introducing this essay to me a decade ago. Simone Weil, *The Iliad; or, The Poem of Force* (Wallingford, PA.: Pendle Hill, 1956).
2. Cesare Beccaria, "Of Crimes and Punishments" (1764), in Alessandro Manzoni, *The Column of Infamy*, trans. Kenelm Foster and Jane Grigson (New York: Oxford

University Press, 1964), 45. The first English translation of this essay appeared in New York in 1773, but it did not achieve much circulation until after the Revolution.

3. Thomas Jefferson, "A Bill for Proportioning Crimes and Punishments" (1779), reprinted in Bryan Vila and Cynthia Morris, eds., *Capital Punishment in the United States: A Documentary History* (Westport, Conn.: Greenwood Press, 1997), 17.

4. Benjamin Rush, "On Punishing Murder By Death," in Dagobert D. Runes, ed., *The Selected Writings of Benjamin Rush* (New York: Philosophical Library, 1947), 52-53.

5. Robert J. Turnbull, *A Visit to the Philadelphia Prison* (Philadelphia: Budd and Bertran, 1796), 45.

6. Using a common metaphor of the period, Turnbull compared the body politic to a human body: "crimes may be called disorders of a state, perpetrators of them the parts affected, and legislatures the prescribing physicians. How surprising, that no other remedy should be applied to eradicate the complaint than an *amputation* of the infected limb!" Ibid., 80.

   Regarding the penalty of death for treason, Turnbull relied on an impassioned sarcasm: "Does the existence of one poor delinquent endanger the security of a government or nation? If so, alas, my country, how art though fallen! Weak in condition indeed! Where is they *boasted strength and energy,* those expressions the infant lips of thy citizens have so often uttered, and to which we would all attend with the sweetest rapture?" Ibid., 79.

7. For a broad discussion of this movement, see Herbert H. Haines, *Against Capital Punishment: The Anti-Death Penalty Movement in America, 1972-1994* (New York: Oxford University Press, 1996).

8. James W. Marquart, Sheldon Edland-Olson, and Jonathan R. Sorensen, *The Rope, the Chair, and the Needle: Capital Punishment in Texas, 1923-1990* (Austin: University of Texas Press, 1994), 18. In 1969 the Urban League issued a statement calling for the abolition of the death penalty on grounds that "the death penalty did not deter crime, was discriminatory as applied to Negroes and the poor and might be in violation of the Constitution. . . . The Board said the death penalty was most often applied in cases involving crimes by blacks against whites." See: "Abolition of Death Penalty Is Urged by Urban League," *New York Times,* March 4, 1969, 19.

9. Jacqueline Goldsby, "The High and Low Tech of It: The Meaning of Lynching and the Death of Emmett Till," *Yale Journal of Criticism* 9, no. 2 (1996): 275.

10. Ibid., 251; see also Stephen J. Whitfield, *A Death in the Delta: The Story of Emmett Till* (New York: Free Press, 1988), 24-25.

11. NAACP Legal Defense and Educational Fund, Inc., "Documents for Proceeding in Federal Habeas Corpus in a Capital Case in Which Execution Is Imminent," Vila and Morris, eds., *Capital Punishment in the United States,* 131-32.

12. Richard Hammer, "The Case that Could End Capital Punishment," *New York Times Magazine,* October 12,1969, 46. See also Sidney E. Zion, "Court Faces Test on Death Penalty," *New York Times,* March 3, 1969, 63. Anthony Amsterdam of the LDF revealed to Zion that "our aim is the total abolition of capital punishment in the United States."

13. Hammer, "The Case that Could End Capital Punishment," 55. In cases of murder, states executed 1,664 whites and 1,630 African Americans. Despite compromising 13 percent of the total population African Americans constituted roughly 50 percent of the people executed.

14. Fred P. Graham, "Court Postpones Death Row Ruling," *New York Times,* June 2, 1970, 1. On "death qualified juries" see *Witherspoon v. Illinois.* 391 U.S. 510 (1968).

15. Haines, *Against Capital Punishment,* 37. *Furman v. Georgia,* 408 U.S. 238 (1972), reprinted in Vila and Morris, eds., *Capital Punishment in the United States,* 142-43.

16. Justice Douglas did write that "imposing the death penalty enables the penalty to be selectively applied, feeding prejudices against the accused if he is poor and despised, and lacking political clout, or if he is a member of a suspect or unpopular minority, and saving those who by social position may be in a more protected position." In contrast, Justice Stewart did not agree that racial discrimination had been proved but concurred that the death penalty was "wantonly and so freakishly imposed." *Furman v. Georgia,* 408 U.S. 238 (1972).

17. By 1973 half of all states had considered death penalty legislation. By May of that year thirteen states passed death penalty laws, two legislatures passed legislation that awaited the signature of noncommittal governors, and one governor vetoed a law. "Death Penalty Has Been Restored by 13 States," *New York Times,* May 10. 1973, 18.

18. Warren Weaver, Jr., "Death Penalty Restoration Is Voted by Senate," *New York Times,* March 14, 1974, 1.

19. Francis X. Clines, "Governor Signs Measure to Restore Death Penalty," *New York Times,* May 18, 1974, 1; "Philadelphia Warden and Aide Stabbed to Death by Two Inmates," *New York Times,* June 1,1973, 70; "Philadelphia Prison Shifts 235 After Slaying of Two Officials," *New York Times,* June 17, 1973, 49.

20. "Justice Assailed in North Carolina," *New York Times,* July 5, 1974, 16.

21. In 1973 Representative Robert F. Drinan (D-MA), a Roman Catholic priest, called for the abolition of the death penalty. "Bill Is Introduced in House to Abolish Death Penalty," *New York Times,* March 15, 1973, 25. In his opinion in *Furman v. Georgia* (408 U.S. 238 [1972]) Justice Marshall made it clear that he rejected capital punishment on grounds that it held no deterrence value, an idea that some mainstream media outlets thought might serve as a convincing argument. See, for example, "Thou Shalt Not Kill," editorial, *New York Times,* March 13, 1973, 38.

22. Haines, *Against Capital Punishment,* 59.

23. Richard C. Dieter, *The Death Penalty in Black and White: Who Lives, Who Dies, Who Decides* (Washington D.C.: The Death Penalty Information Center, 1998), 20. This report is available through the DPIC, 1320 18th St. NW, 5th Fl., Washington D.C. 20036. See also D. Baldus et al., "Race Discrimination and the Death Penalty in the Post-Furman Era: An Empirical and Legal Overview, with Preliminary Findings from Philadelphia," *Cornell Law Review* 83 (September 1998): 1638-770.

24. Steven V. Roberts and Ted Gest, "A Growing Cry: Give Them Death: Legal Changes Will Speed the Pace of Executions," *U.S. News and World Report,* March 26, 1990, 24; "Gallup Poll Sees Concern on Crime," *New York Times,* February 16, 1969, 47. Perhaps the strongest indicator that race-based critiques have been silenced and redirected is that now over half of all African Americans polled support capital punishment.

25. For a vivid picture of this frustration and the use of habeas corpus petitions to slow the process that leads to executions, see Michael Mello, *Dead Wrong: A Death Row Lawyer Speaks Out Against Capital Punishment* (Madison: University of Wisconsin Press, 1997).

THREE

Sentencing
Children to Death

STEVEN HAWKINS

[O]ffenses by the young also represent a failure of family, school, and
the social system, which share responsibility for the development of
America's youth.

—*Eddings v. Oklahoma*

INTRODUCTION

The issue of youth crime and violence has risen in the nation's
consciousness as a result of a recent wave of gun-related fatalities
committed in schools by youths. In 1997 there were four reported
multiple shootings involving children as both perpetrators and victims.
In 1998 and 1999 incidents of young people using handguns on their
peers were reported in Tennessee, Pennsylvania, Texas, Arkansas, Oregon, and Colorado.[1] This recent pattern of fatal shootings in schools
across the nation by children as young as eleven years old has resulted in
a clamor for more draconian judicial measures, with politicians increasingly calling for capital punishment as a means of social redress.

: Control Act of 1997 would
federal death penalty from
rnors in California and New
the death penalty could be
In 1998 Texas State Repre-
d his intention to propose a
ng age to eleven years old,
id a message to our kids that

tougher on juvenile crime,
ight of the discriminatory
n sought and applied against
olation of the United States
iment. Even a cursory glance
h row as juvenile offenders
rved almost exclusively for
ny of whom were victims of
ysfunctional environments.
ist alone in the world as a
ted States currently has the
the world and has executed

USE OF THE DEATH
PENALTY AGAINST U.S. CHILDREN

In 1642, at Plymouth Colony, Massachusetts, Thomas Graunger became the first person executed for a crime he committed as a child; he was a child when killed. Since then 355 people have been executed for childhood offenses.[3] The youngest child executed in the United States was James Arcene, a Cherokee Indian hanged in Arkansas in 1885 for his participation in a robbery and murder that he committed at age ten. In the twentieth century, Fortune Ferguson was only thirteen when he was executed in 1927 in Florida for rape.[4] As of 1999, thirteen persons had been executed for childhood offenses in the modern era of the death penalty, following the U.S. Supreme Court's reinstatement of capital punishment in 1976. All were sixteen or seventeen at the time of their crimes; seven were white, five were black, and one was Latino.[5]

Twenty-three of the thirty-eight states that authorize capital punishment allow for children to be sentenced to death.[6] Eighteen of these states allow sixteen-year-olds to be eligible for the death penalty: Alabama, Arizona, Arkansas, Delaware, Idaho, Indiana, Kentucky, Louisiana, Mississippi, Missouri, Nevada, Oklahoma, Pennsylvania, South Carolina, South Dakota, Utah, Virginia, and Wyoming. The remaining five states— Florida, Georgia, New Hampshire, North Carolina, and Texas—set seventeen years old as the minimum age. While federal and military jurisdictions also have the death penalty, neither currently imposes capital punishment on persons for childhood offenses. The military and the following states execute eighteen-year-olds: California, Colorado, Connecticut, Illinois, Kansas, Maryland, Nebraska, New Jersey, New Mexico, New York, Ohio, Oregon, Tennessee, and Washington.

Over the years, the methods of execution have evolved, but the horror of the state taking the lives of young offenders remains. On June 16, 1944, George Stinney was strapped into an electric chair in Clarendon County, South Carolina. He was a fourteen-year-old African American boy who stood five feet one inch tall and weighed ninety-five pounds. He had been convicted just two months earlier of the murder of an eleven-year-old white girl. Stinney was so slight that the guards had difficulty strapping him into the chair and attaching electrodes to his leg. A mask was placed over his face, but after the first jolt of 2,400 volts, the mask slipped off, revealing his wide-open, tearful eyes and saliva coming from his mouth. The next two surges of electricity ended his young life.[7]

Despite the penetrating stare which Stinney cast upon his executioners and the society that condemned him, today the practice of sentencing children to death continues in the United States. A total of 173 death sentences have been imposed upon youths since 1973, some only a year older than George Stinney.[8] In 1999 in twelve different states, seventy persons were on death rows waiting to die for offenses they committed as minors. All were sixteen or seventeen years old at the time of the crimes. The greatest number of these youths can be found in Texas, the state that leads the nation in sending children to death row.

At the federal level, the Juvenile Crime Control Act of 1997 would have lowered the minimum age for the federal death penalty from eighteen to sixteen. At the state level, governors in California and New Mexico favored lowering the age at which the death penalty could be applied to fourteen and thirteen years old. In 1998 Texas State Representative Jim Pitts (Republican) announced his intention to propose a bill that would lower the death-sentencing age to eleven years old, proclaiming that the law was needed to send a message to our kids that they cannot do these kinds of crimes.[2]

ᴋ In their scramble to see who can be tougher on juvenile crime, politicians and constituents alike lose sight of the discriminatory manner in which the death penalty has been sought and applied against children as well as the increasing global isolation of the United States in carrying out this barbaric form of punishment. Even a cursory glance at the inmates who were placed on death row as juvenile offenders reveals that the ultimate penalty is reserved almost exclusively for African American and Latino children, many of whom were victims of physical or sexual abuse and raised in dysfunctional environments. Moreover, the United States stands almost alone in the world as a country that executes its young. The United States currently has the highest juvenile death row population in the world and has executed the largest number of juvenile offenders.

USE OF THE DEATH
PENALTY AGAINST U.S. CHILDREN

In 1642, at Plymouth Colony, Massachusetts, Thomas Graunger became the first person executed for a crime he committed as a child; he was a child when killed. Since then 355 people have been executed for childhood offenses.[3] The youngest child executed in the United States was James Arcene, a Cherokee Indian hanged in Arkansas in 1885 for his participation in a robbery and murder that he committed at age ten. In the twentieth century, Fortune Ferguson was only thirteen when he was executed in 1927 in Florida for rape.[4] As of 1999, thirteen persons had been executed for childhood offenses in the modern era of the death penalty, following the U.S. Supreme Court's reinstatement of capital punishment in 1976. All were sixteen or seventeen at the time of their crimes; seven were white, five were black, and one was Latino.[5]

Twenty-three of the thirty-eight states that authorize capital punishment allow for children to be sentenced to death.[6] Eighteen of these states allow sixteen-year-olds to be eligible for the death penalty: Alabama, Arizona, Arkansas, Delaware, Idaho, Indiana, Kentucky, Louisiana, Mississippi, Missouri, Nevada, Oklahoma, Pennsylvania, South Carolina, South Dakota, Utah, Virginia, and Wyoming. The remaining five states— Florida, Georgia, New Hampshire, North Carolina, and Texas—set seventeen years old as the minimum age. While federal and military jurisdictions also have the death penalty, neither currently imposes capital punishment on persons for childhood offenses. The military and the following states execute eighteen-year-olds: California, Colorado, Connecticut, Illinois, Kansas, Maryland, Nebraska, New Jersey, New Mexico, New York, Ohio, Oregon, Tennessee, and Washington.

Over the years, the methods of execution have evolved, but the horror of the state taking the lives of young offenders remains. On June 16, 1944, George Stinney was strapped into an electric chair in Clarendon County, South Carolina. He was a fourteen-year-old African American boy who stood five feet one inch tall and weighed ninety-five pounds. He had been convicted just two months earlier of the murder of an eleven-year-old white girl. Stinney was so slight that the guards had difficulty strapping him into the chair and attaching electrodes to his leg. A mask was placed over his face, but after the first jolt of 2,400 volts, the mask slipped off, revealing his wide-open, tearful eyes and saliva coming from his mouth. The next two surges of electricity ended his young life.[7]

Despite the penetrating stare which Stinney cast upon his executioners and the society that condemned him, today the practice of sentencing children to death continues in the United States. A total of 173 death sentences have been imposed upon youths since 1973, some only a year older than George Stinney.[8] In 1999 in twelve different states, seventy persons were on death rows waiting to die for offenses they committed as minors. All were sixteen or seventeen years old at the time of the crimes. The greatest number of these youths can be found in Texas, the state that leads the nation in sending children to death row.

Texas took the life of Joseph Cannon for a crime he committed when he was seventeen. Cannon's entire childhood was scarred by sexual and physical abuse. At age of four, he sustained a brain injury when hit by a truck. His education ended in first grade because of learning disabilities. By the age of ten, Cannon was the victim of sexual abuse by his grandfather. He tried to commit suicide on many occasions. After one such attempt, Cannon told a psychiatrist that "Nothing good had ever happened in my life." He turned to drugs for comfort, inflicting further brain damage upon himself. At trial, the jury was never told about the horrors he experienced as a child. When this information was finally disclosed after he was sentenced to death, Texas officials showed no mercy. Despite pleas from individuals and organizations, including Pope John Paul II, Archbishop Desmond Tutu, the Children's Defense Fund, and the Child Welfare League of America, Joseph Cannon was executed on April 22, 1998.

In other areas of the law, society clearly excludes children from certain activities deemed appropriate only for adults. People cannot vote or serve on a jury until the age of eighteen. Nor can people be drafted into military service before that age. Buying alcohol and cigarettes is likewise strictly governed, with anyone under twenty-one years old now excluded from purchasing in most states.

Yet perversely, the law does not make exceptions for children when it comes to the death penalty. Here we allow minors to be eliminated from the human community. At the same time, we lower the age at which the death penalty and other punishments can be imposed. We sentence sixteen-year-olds to death; impose life sentences on fourteen-year-olds; and expel eleven-year-olds from school forever.

THE CHILDREN WE SENTENCE TO DEATH

At present, all seventy persons under sentence of death for childhood offenses are male. One-quarter of them were sixteen years old at the time of their crimes; two-thirds of them are of color. The typical child sent to death row is a seventeen-year-old African American or Latino boy whose victim was a white adult. Of the seventy youths, sixteen are sixteen years old, fifty-four are seventeen years old. Thirty-two are African American

(46 percent); fourteen are Latino (20 percent); and twenty-four are white (34 percent).

A cursory examination of the lives of those persons sentenced to death as children has revealed that a disproportionate number suffered brain injuries or were victims of sexual and physical abuse. A 1988 study published in the *American Journal of Psychiatry* examined all of the offenders sent to death row for childhood crimes in four states.[9] The results showed that *every one* of the fourteen persons studied had suffered serious head injuries as children, and *all* had serious psychiatric problems. Twelve of them had been severely abused; five had been sodomized by older male relatives; and only two had IQ scores above ninety. Few of these vulnerabilities were revealed at trial; indeed, only five had received pretrial psychiatric evaluations.

Although this study is now a decade old, its observations still accurately describe the lives of those persons currently sitting on death rows across the nation for childhood offenses. Dwayne Allen Wright, for example, was sentenced to death in Virginia for an offense he committed at seventeen. His early life was scarred by deprivation and tragedy. His mother was frequently unemployed and his father was constantly in jail. His brother was murdered when Dwayne was ten years old, and shortly afterward he began to suffer from serious depression. By the age of fifteen, he had been admitted into a psychiatric hospital.

Heath Wilkins was sentenced to death in Missouri for a crime he committed at the age of sixteen. As a child he was brutally beaten and sexually abused. He was given drugs by an uncle at age six, and at age ten he spent six months in a psychiatric institution. At trial, he pled guilty, waived his right to a jury trial, and asked for the death penalty, claiming that for someone who was in so much pain that they were hurting others, death seemed like an escape.

RACISM AND THE DEATH SENTENCE

Race discrimination in the application of the death penalty has been well documented. Studies conducted over the years confirm that race continues to be a decisive factor in determining who will live and who will die. A 1990 report by the United States General Accounting Office found "a pattern of evidence indicating racial disparities in the charging, sentencing and imposing [of] the death penalty. . . ."[10]

Children have not been immune to this racial bias. Between 1642 and 1899 approximately 52 percent of those who were executed for childhood offenses were African American. That proportion has risen to nearly 75 percent in the twentieth century.[11] In southern states, people of color make up *over* 90 percent of those put to death for crimes committed in childhood.[12]

Moreover, when rape was still a capital offense in the United States, *all* forty-three persons put to death for either committing or attempting to commit this act as a minor were African American. In every case but one, the victim was white.[13]

This racial bias also crosses gender lines. While it is rare for female juvenile offenders to be executed in the United States, eight of the ten who were put to death for crimes committed under age eighteen were black, and one was American Indian. All were executed for a crime against a white person.[14]

Since reinstatement of the death penalty in 1976, over 65 percent of those persons sentenced to death for crimes they committed as children have been either African American or Latino, respectively 12.7 percent and 11.2 percent of the population. As previously noted, nearly two-thirds of those under the sentence of death for childhood offenses are members of these racial groups. The tragic message this fact conveys is that society deems these youths' lives to be less capable of redemption; children of color who kill are generally considered beyond rehabilitation.

CONDEMNATION BY
THE INTERNATIONAL COMMUNITY

In the 1990s only six countries are known to have executed persons for childhood offenses. In this area the United States is not only aligned with Iran, Nigeria, Pakistan, Saudi Arabia, and Yemen, but it is the world leader, having executed more persons (ten youths) for crimes they committed as children than all other countries combined. (Iran has executed four children and Nigeria, Pakistan, Saudi Arabia, and Yemen each have executed one child or youth.)

International human rights instruments are unequivocal in their prohibition of the application of the death penalty on persons for childhood crimes. The International Covenant on Civil and Political Rights (ICCPR), for example, plainly states in Article 6(5) that *the death sentence shall not be imposed for crimes committed by persons below eighteen years of age.*[15] The U.S. State Department has praised the covenant as the most complete and authoritative articulation of international human rights law that has emerged in the years following World War II.[16] Nevertheless, upon ratifying the ICCPR in 1992, the United States entered the following reservation: "The United States reserves the right, subject to its Constitutional constraints, to impose capital punishment on any person (other than a pregnant woman) duly convicted under existing or future laws permitting the imposition of capital punishment, *including such punishments for crimes committed by persons below eighteen years of age.*"[17] No other nation ever entered such a reservation. Taking this as an affront to core obligations under the ICCPR, eleven European nations (Belgium, Denmark, Finland, France, Germany, Italy, the Netherlands, Norway, Portugal, Spain, and Sweden) took the unusual step of filing formal objections.[18]

Article 4(5) of the American Convention on Human Rights also prohibits use of the death penalty against persons for childhood crimes. In the case of Terry Roach, an application protesting the U.S. violation of this article was brought before the Inter-American Commission for Human Rights. After a hearing on the matter, the commission ruled that the proscription on executing persons for offenses they committed as children was a matter of *jus cogens,* meaning that no country could derogate from this fundamental human rights norm.[19]

Finally, the United Nations Convention on the Rights of the Child, in Article 37(a), proscribes imposing the death penalty on persons for offenses they commit when still children. No other human rights treaty has ever gained acceptance as quickly as this convention, a strong indication of its universal principles. The United States, however, is only one of two countries (the other is Somalia) in the world that has yet to ratify the convention, in large part because of its problems with Article 37(a).

U.S. DOMESTIC LAW

There are strong indications that the execution of juvenile offenders violates contemporary standards of decency: a majority of States decline to permit juveniles to be sentenced to death; . . . respected organizations with expertise in relevant areas regard the execution of juveniles as unacceptable, as does international opinion.

—Justice William Brennan Jr.,
in his dissent to *Stanford v. Kentucky*

In *Thompson v. Oklahoma*,[20] the U.S. Supreme Court in 1988 first addressed the constitutionality of applying the death penalty against persons for crimes they committed as children. After being certified to stand trial as an adult pursuant to an Oklahoma state statute, William Wayne Thompson was convicted and sentenced to death for a homicide he committed at the age of fifteen. The statute under which he was sentenced, however, set no minimum age at which the commission of murder could lead to imposition of the death penalty. In her controlling concurrence, the decisive fifth vote for a judgment, Justice Sandra O'Connor reasoned that because of considerable risk that the state legislature had not considered that its actions would make fifteen-year-olds eligible to be put to death, under the circumstances it would be unconstitutional to allow Thompson's death sentence to stand.[21] The critical issue here is that the Court left the moral issue of whether fifteen-year-old offenders were eligible to be put to death to be decided by state legislatures.[22] Therefore, there is no indication how the Court would view a state statute that expressly authorized imposition of the death penalty on persons who commit crimes at the age of fifteen.

In 1989, in *Stanford v. Kentucky* and *Wilkins v. Missouri*,[23] the Court ruled that it was constitutional to impose the death penalty on persons who commit crimes at sixteen and seventeen years of age. In writing the Court's opinion, Justice Anthony Scalia reasoned that since twenty-five of the thirty-seven states that did impose the death penalty at that time permitted imposition of capital punishment on persons who commit crimes at these ages, there was no violation of the Eighth Amendment's ban against cruel and unusual punishment.[24]

In reaching this conclusion, however, the Court did not take into account those states that did not impose capital punishment on *any* age group. If the Court had considered non–death penalty states in determining whether evolving standards of decency banned imposition of the death penalty against children, it would have found, by its own count,[25] an even split among state legislatures. Thus the constitutional question would have been far more difficult to answer. The Court also refused, in evaluating evolving standards of decency under the Eighth Amendment, to consider the sentencing practices of other countries.[26] Yet, as the dissent noted, in earlier opinions the Court already had recognized legislation in other countries as objective indicators of contemporary standards of decency.[27] Over fifty nations had abolished the death penalty and a majority of countries that retained it prohibited its use against persons for childhood crimes. Based on this and other criteria, the dissent reasoned that the global community appeared overwhelmingly to disapprove of the imposition of the death penalty for juvenile offenders.[28]

Finally, the Court ignored its earlier decisions that emphasize that the Eighth Amendment forbids punishment wholly disproportionate to the offender's blameworthiness.[29] Adults recognize that they should not respond to the actions of a child in the same way as they would respond to similar actions of an adult. Children often give less thought to ultimate consequences; they are more vulnerable, more impulsive, and less self-disciplined than adults.[30] While these developmental characteristics are not an excuse for illegal action, they have a direct bearing on the appropriate punishment for children.

WHAT ABOUT THE "JUVENILE CRIME WAVE"?

Crime, and murder in particular, has been decreasing in the United States over the past few years. Considerable concern, however, has arisen about the higher level of violent crime by juveniles. This fear has been compounded by demographic predictions that the proportion of the U.S. population in the crime-prone years of young adulthood will be increasing over the next decade. Tragically, many politicians respond to such predictions by increasing the severity of punishments for juveniles, including the expansion of the death penalty. Aside from concerns about whether threats of increased punishment will have any effect on juvenile offenders, it appears that the fear of a juvenile crime wave has been an overreaction.

A *USA Today* poll found that while Americans believe that 43 percent of all crime in the United States is attributable to juveniles, the actual amount is only 12.8 percent.[31] In 1996 FBI crime statistics showed that homicide arrests for youths ages ten to seventeen had *fallen* by 23 percent since 1993. Overall juvenile arrests for violent crimes, including assault, robbery, rape, and murder, dropped almost 3 percent in 1995 alone.[32] Moreover, the majority of crimes committed by children occur in a few large cities. The Center on Juvenile and Criminal Justice found that 80 percent of the nation's counties did not record a single homicide by a teenager in 1994. Chicago, Detroit, Los Angeles, and New York have eight times the juvenile homicide arrest rate as the rest of the country.[33] Such figures call for more carefully crafted solutions aimed at the problems of the inner city rather than extending the death penalty's reach to more minors.

Evidence from one large city, Boston, Massachusetts, indicates that there are programs that work to reduce teenage violence; not a single teenager under the age of seventeen was murdered in the sixteen months between July 1995 and November 1996.[34] Homicide rates for the twenty-four and under age group were down by two-thirds from the early 1990s. The marked decline in violence is attributed to coordinated efforts by local, state, and federal law enforcement agencies against gang violence and gun trafficking in the city.[35] Among the interventions that were introduced by authorities in Boston since the early 1990s are the following: a focus on gun trafficking to and from gang-involved youth; a comprehensive and immediate interagency response to gang violence; urging gangs to explore nonviolent means of resolving conflicts; and preventing outbreaks of gang violence before they become deadly.

David M. Kennedy of Harvard University, one of the developers of the program known as "Ceasefire," has stated that these interventions have resulted in extraordinary homicide reductions.[36] In other effective programs, even earlier age- and gang-related interventions are key to reducing youth crime. According to research by the National Council on Crime and Delinquency, successful programs for delinquent youths include: continuous case management of delinquent youths; opportunities for youth achievement and involvement in program decision making; clear and consistent consequences for misconduct; enriched educational and vocational programming; and a variety of forms of counseling for youths and their families.

CONCLUSION

The abolition of the death penalty for children in the United States is long overdue. Rather than expend time and valuable resources on an outmoded and ineffective form of punishment, we should be placing our energies on viable solutions to violent youth crime. By refusing to kill children for their worst transgressions, we can focus on rebuilding and restoring their lives and treating all children with the priority, dignity, and respect of which they are deserving.

U.S. courts have turned their backs on compelling constitutional and moral arguments against the death penalty for children, while politicians continue to rely on quick-fix solutions to deeply entrenched problems that lead to criminality and violent crimes. As a result, the United States stands alone among Western nations in its practice of killing children. A national movement that directs its efforts exclusively toward the goal of the abolition of the death penalty for children is required.

NOTES

1. Tamar Levin, "Experts See Shift in the Nature of School Violence," *The New York Times,* May 22, 1998. The 1999 deaths at Colorado's Columbine High School received international attention.

2. Sam Howe Verhovek, "Texas Legislature Proposes the Death Penalty for Murderers as Young as 11," *The New York Times,* April 18, 1998, A7.

3. See V. Streib, *The Juvenile Death Penalty Today,* 1998, 3. (Claude W. Pettit College of Law, Ada, Ohio). Online: www.law.onu.edu/faculty/streib/juvdeath.htm.

4. "Key Events in U.S. Juvenile Executions," *Roanoke Times & World News,* August 9, 1998.

5. In 1976, Texas executed Charles Rumbaugh, Jay Pinkerton, Johnny Garret, Curtis Harris, Ruben Cantu, Joseph Cannon, and Robert Carver. Carter and Harris were black, Cantu was Latino, all others executed were white. That year, South Carolina put to death J. Terry Roach (white); while Louisiana executed Dalton Prejean (black);

Missouri executed Frederick Lashley (black); and Georgia put to death Chris Burger (white).
In 1998 Virginia executed Dwayne Wright (black); in 1999 Oklahoma killed Sean Sellers (white).

6. Thirteen jurisdictions remain without the death penalty: Alaska, District of Columbia, Hawaii, Iowa, Maine, Massachusetts, Michigan, Minnesota, North Dakota, Rhode Island, Vermont, West Virginia, and Wisconsin.

7. D. Bruck, "Executing Teenage Killers Again," *Washington Post,* September 15, 1981, D1.

8. Streib, *The Juvenile Death Penalty Today,* 14-21.

9. Dorothy Otnow Lewis, "Neuropsychiatric, Psychoeducational and Family Characteristics of 14 Juveniles Condemned to Death in the United States," *American Journal of Psychiatry* 145:5, May 1988.

10. United States General Accounting Office, Report to Senate and House Judiciary Committees, *Death Penalty Sentencing: Research Indicates Pattern of Racial Disparities,* (Washington, D.C.: February 1990).

11. See V. Streib, "Imposing the Death Penalty as Children," in K. Haas et al., eds., *Challenging Capital Punishment: Legal and Social Science Approaches* (Newbury Park, CA: Sage Publications, 1988).

12. See J. Coburn, "Growing Up on Death Row," *Washington Post,* July 19, 1988. The article states that only 13 of 169 juvenile executions in the South involved whites; since 1988, seven more juvenile offenders were executed in southern states, three of whom were white.

13. Amnesty International, *United States of America: The Death Penalty and Juvenile Offenders* (London: Amnesty International: October 1991), 62.

14. T. Gillman, "Koslow Jury Could Add to History," *Dallas Morning News,* June 30, 1994, 25A.

15. International Covenant on Civil and Political Rights, adopted December 16, 1966, entered into force March 23, 1976, G. A. Res. 2200, 21 U. N. GAOR. Supp. (No. 16) 52, U. N. Doc. A/6316 (1966).

16. U.S. Department of State, *Civil and Political Rights in the United States: Initial Reporting of the United States of America to the U.N. Human Rights Committee under the International Covenant on Civil and Political Rights,* July 1994, at I (Introduction).

17. Ibid., 66 (emphasis added).

18. International Commission of Jurists, *Administration of the Death Penalty in the United States: Report of the Mission,* June 1996, 92-93.

19. Inter-American Commission on Human Rights, Res. 3/87, Case No. 9647, OAS/ Serv.L./VII.71/Doc. 9 (1987).

20. 487 U.S. 815 (1988).

21. 487 U.S. at 857 (O'Connor, J., concurring).

22. 487 U.S. at 858.

23. 492 U.S. 361 (1989).

24. 492 U.S. at 370-73.

25. The dissent, finding fault with the majority's reading of the number of non–death states, found that twenty-seven states (including the District of Columbia) had concluded that no one under eighteen years of age should be subjected to the death penalty. With respect to the issue of death eligibility for sixteen-year-olds, the dissent found that thirty states were opposed. 492 U.S. at 384.

26. 492 U.S. at 369 n. 1.

27. 492 U.S. at 389-90.

28. 492 U.S. at 390.

29. 492 U.S. at 393.

30. 492 U.S. at 395.
31. P. Edmonds, "To Some, Ultimate Penalty is Ageless," *USA Today*, September 28, 1994, 11A.
32. "Juvenile Crime Seen in Short-Term Lull," *Law Enforcement News*, September 30, 1996, 6.
33. Ibid.
34. See F. Butterfield, "In Boston, Nothing Is Something," *New York Times*, November 21, 1996, A20.
35. Massachusetts does not have a death penalty.
36. "Youth Gun Deaths in Boston: Little More Than a Hill of Beans," *Law Enforcement News*, January 15,1997, 1.

FOUR

The Ordeal of Mumia Abu-Jamal

DANIEL R. WILLIAMS

Mumia Abu-Jamal is the most celebrated death row inmate in the country today. It is quite possible, depending on the outcome of his fight to secure a new trial, that he may become the most prominent in our country's shameful history of killing its own citizens. He has written two well-received books (*Live from Death Row* and *Death Blossoms*).[1] He also has written numerous articles (published in such venues as *The Nation* and the *Yale Law Journal*) addressing topics ranging from prison conditions to U.S. foreign policy, and has even recorded commentaries for National Public Radio (which were canceled after conservatives and right-wing politicians objected). That Abu-Jamal still has the resiliency and focus to speak out for the voiceless and the oppressed from within the depths of death row is a testament to this man's fighting spirit and evolved humanity as a human rights advocate.

Abu-Jamal landed on death row after one of the most remarkable trials in recent history. He was charged with the murder of a police officer after being arrested at the scene where the officer lay mortally wounded. The incident occurred shortly before 4:00 A.M. on December 9, 1981. The slain officer, Daniel Faulkner, had stopped a Volkswagen driven by

Abu-Jamal's brother, Billy Cook, ostensibly for a traffic-related offense. Witnesses saw Officer Faulkner beating Cook for reasons that have never been clear. By chance, Abu-Jamal was across the street as this was happening, and he ran toward the scene. As he approached, the officer fired, and the bullet entered in a downward trajectory through Mumia Abu-Jamal's lung, liver, and diaphragm, ultimately lodging in his spine. The bullet trajectory turns out to be significant, as it exposes the falsity of the only testimony linking Abu-Jamal directly to the death of Officer Faulkner, who was shot at about the same time as Abu-Jamal. Wounded, Abu-Jamal stumbled a few feet and collapsed on the curb.

At least five witnesses saw someone flee in the direction of a nearby alleyway immediately after the shooting. But upon their arrival the police, without any meaningful investigation, immediately concluded that Abu-Jamal was the cop killer. Well known in Philadelphia as an outspoken critic of police brutality, Abu-Jamal alleges he was brutally beaten by police once he was arrested; in a 1995 hearing witnesses testified that they saw police kicking and punching him. Officers at one point slammed his head into a traffic post as if he were a human battering ram. Abu-Jamal was then transported to a nearby emergency room, where he alternated between minimal consciousness and unconsciousness while police officers attempted to disrupt the medical attention he was receiving. Abu-Jamal was beaten so severely that his family could not recognize him, and his gunshot wound left him virtually unable to speak for some time. Six months later Abu-Jamal, who had recovered from his injuries, was in a Philadelphia courtroom before a mostly white jury, again fighting for his life.

My first involvement in Abu-Jamal's legal defense involved reading his trial transcripts. As a lawyer I've read many trial transcripts, and I've handled many criminal trials and appeals. But nothing in my legal education or experience prepared me for what those pages contained. Abu-Jamal was unlike any criminal defendant I had ever encountered. He sparred repeatedly with the trial judge, Albert Sabo (often called the "King of Death Row" for having presided over more death verdicts than the vast majority if not all the other judges in the country). The primary point of contention was Abu-Jamal's insistence that he be allowed to conduct his own defense. Abu-Jamal was outraged that Judge Sabo stripped him of his constitutional right to act as his own lawyer during the jury selection phase of the case on the dubious pretext that members of the jury panel were frightened of him. Then the judge literally compelled an unprepared and ill-equipped attorney to pick up the case from that moment on.

I don't use the word "compelled" lightly. Abu-Jamal's "court-appointed" attorney did not want to handle this trial and, in fact, begged to be relieved of this obligation. Not only was his plea rejected, he was held in contempt and threatened with a six-month jail sentence unless he stopped his "whining" and represent Abu-Jamal. (This attorney argued to be released from his obligations before the Pennsylvania Supreme Court, only to be told to go back and do his best.) In a 1995 evidentiary hearing, this lawyer testified for three days, explaining that he never talked to a single witness before trial, that he never mastered the details of the case, and that he never prepared a strategy for dealing with the prosecution's evidence against Abu-Jamal.

Abu-Jamal, a man on trial for his life, recognized that his "defender" was begging to be relieved from the obligation of representing him at trial and was admitting to being totally unable to handle the responsibility. Nevertheless, the system expected Abu-Jamal to be silent. Most criminal defendants are poor, inarticulate, and thoroughly demoralized by the oppression associated with poverty and educational deprivation. They sit in court silently, often barely understanding the legal wranglings going on around them. They do not protest as the assembly line carries them to the human warehouses that we call prisons.

As I reviewed the trial transcripts, I realized that Abu-Jamal was no ordinary criminal defendant. This was a man who was saying "no" to injustice, a man who knew *how* to say "no" to injustice. In fact, he had devoted his entire life to saying "no" to injustice, from his youthful experiences as a Black Panther to his rise as a recognized radio journalist in Philadelphia.

Each time a witness would testify for the prosecution, Abu-Jamal would await the defense's turn to cross-examine. When he himself rose to question a witness rather than acquiesce in the ineffective questioning by his court appointed lawyer, Judge Sabo would order him to sit down, and the sparks would fly. Abu-Jamal was banished from the trial so often for protesting the proceedings that he missed over half of the trial as he sat in a jail cell. When I read this remarkable spectacle of injustice in an American courtroom, I thought of Albert Camus's philosophical ruminations about the genesis of human rights. Camus, without doubt one of the most articulate opponents of capital punishment, paints a picture in his book *The Rebel* of a lowly slave saying "no" to his master, as if to draw a line across which even the slave will not be forced to go. That line, that "slave's 'no,'" is the true source of human rights. All the academic discourse about the universality of human rights, all the political rhetoric that uses "human rights" as a club to secure economic advantage in a competitive global marketplace, is mere adornment to the "slave's 'no.'" Abu-Jamal's protestations in his trial—there, in a courtroom where "rights" are supposed to reign supreme—were the repeated utterances of that "slave's 'no.'" That's why Abu-Jamal's case deserves our attention.

From the moment Abu-Jamal was charged with the murder of Officer Faulkner, his case became a lightning rod of controversy. From the outset, many rallied to his defense, as he was a well-known outspoken journalist and committed spokesperson for the urban poor. In late 1980, at age twenty-six, Abu-Jamal was elected chair of the Philadelphia Chapter of the Association of Black Journalists. The January 1981 issue of *Philadelphia Magazine* named him "one of the people to watch in 1981." He had been a target of police repression (as evidenced by over 800 pages of FBI files) from the late 1960s, when, as a teen, he was a founding member of the Black Panther Party, through 1981, when he was an award-winning journalist critical of police brutality. At the very first hearing of the case in 1982, the judge noted that it had "explosive tendencies in the community." The prosecutor described the 1982 trial as "one of the biggest events in the criminal justice system in the city of Philadelphia for a quarter of a century."

Although Abu-Jamal's court-appointed attorney was a highly reluctant and unprepared participant in the trial, one must wonder whether the skill and dedication of even the best defense lawyer would have been enough to overcome the limited resources available to the defense. With a police officer dead, law enforcement pulled out all the stops to mount a case against Mumia Abu-Jamal, conducting over 125 witness interviews and a battery of scientific tests. The court allotted the princely sum of

$150 to the defense to investigate the case. Only two eyewitnesses were contacted by a defense investigator, which is remarkable in view of the fact that subsequent defense investigation has revealed no less than five eyewitnesses who saw the perpetrator fleeing the scene. None of these five eyewitnesses knew or communicated with each other when they reported their observations to the police; and they all saw the perpetrator flee in the same direction and on the same side of the street. In a noteworthy display of lack of preparation, at one point in the trial the attorney used the judge's phone in a desperate attempt to convince one of the eyewitnesses to appear; meanwhile the jury was left waiting.

The defense lacked the funds to retain a pathologist or a ballistician, the services of both of whom were vital. With no pathologist the defense was unable to show that the trajectory of a bullet that struck Abu-Jamal was inconsistent with the testimony of the prosecution's star eyewitness. This witness, a prostitute named Cynthia White, testified that she saw the fallen officer shoot in an *upward direction* as Abu-Jamal was standing over him. We now know that the trajectory of the bullet that hit Abu-Jamal's chest was going in a *downward direction*; hence Cynthia White's purported eyewitness account must be a complete fabrication. A downward trajectory is consistent with the fact that Abu-Jamal was shot as he ran toward the scene of his brother's arrest, with the officer elevated on the curb and Abu-Jamal leaning slightly forward as he ran.

As for the ballistics evidence, Abu-Jamal's attorney failed to present to the jury the medical examiner's report, which states that the slain officer was "shot by .44 cal." The supposed murder weapon was a .38 caliber gun linked to Abu-Jamal, which cannot be mistaken for a .44 caliber weapon. Moreover, a copper bullet jacket was found on the sidewalk near the slain officer; the bullet to which it belonged did not come from any of the guns discovered at the scene (the supposed murder weapon and the officer's gun). No evidence was discovered indicating that the supposed murder weapon had been fired recently; and there existed no gunshot residue evidence indicating that Abu-Jamal had fired a gun. Yet none of this evidence was considered by the jury.

Cynthia White's testimony, though damaging to Abu-Jamal, was ripe for discrediting. She had provided police with different accounts of what she allegedly saw; as the trial grew nearer and the police pressure more intense, each of her versions was more incriminating than the last. Fourteen years after White gave her perjurious testimony, we on the defense team have been able to present evidence showing why White falsely incriminated Abu-Jamal. A key piece of this newly discovered evidence comes through the testimony of a former prostitute, Veronica Jones, who was near the scene of the shooting. Jones explained that Philadelphia cops told her and White that they could "work" the streets without fear of arrest so long as they helped the prosecution's case. Yet another former prostitute and close associate of White's, an FBI informant named Pamela Jenkins, testified in a 1997 hearing that White had confided to her that she testified falsely at the trial only after police threatened her.

Veronica Jones provided more information to the defense. Within a week of the shooting, detectives visited her at her home to secure a statement. Jones told the detectives, in graphic detail, that she saw two men run from the scene after the shooting stopped. When summoned to the stand at the trial, she stunned the defense by retracting her statement about the fleeing men. What happened? The answer came when Jones testified in an evidentiary hearing in 1996. She explained that, shortly before the trial, she had been arrested on gun charges and faced a ten-year prison term. Frightened and vulnerable, Jones listened when two detectives visited her in the jail and offered her a way out. Jones testified that these detectives told her that she would be released from jail so long as she did not help Abu-Jamal's defense in the upcoming trial. Both sides kept up their end of the bargain, and Jones was soon released from jail.

After announcing that she no longer wanted to live a lie, Jones told the court in 1996 that her original statement to the police about the fleeing men was the truth and that her retraction was due to police coercion. After hearing this testimony, a visibly angry Judge Sabo ordered Jones immediately jailed on a stale, unresolved, and petty bad check offense that had been of no interest to anyone until she stepped forward to tell the truth. As law enforcement authorities seized her from the witness stand, Jones tearfully exclaimed that this shameful tactic would not cause her to lie again.

Two other eyewitnesses testified at the 1982 trial that they had seen Abu-Jamal run to the scene (a fact that was never disputed). But they

skeptical about every other aspect of the prosecution's case. Writing in the prestigious *American Lawyer* magazine after reviewing the court record, a leading conservative American journalist (who is also a lawyer) concluded that the confession was a police fabrication.

With no funds, with no dedicated and qualified defense attorney (in short, with no meaningful defense mounted on his behalf), and with an onslaught of manufactured evidence, Abu-Jamal's fate was preordained. The sequestered jury began deliberating on a Friday of a Fourth of July weekend. Within hours they returned a guilty verdict. All that remained was fixing the appropriate sentence. In a capital case, this is done in a separate phase of the trial—appropriately called the "penalty phase"—wherein the same jury hears evidence concerning whether the imposition of death is warranted.

Abu-Jamal's trial attorney admitted in the 1995 hearing that he never considered how to handle this delicate phase of the trial. Although Abu-Jamal was well-known and highly recognized as a conscientious journalist who was committed to social justice, his attorney did not call a single witness in the penalty phase to testify on his behalf. Instead, the virtually all-white, law-and-order jury was treated to a sorry exhibition of political red-baiting. After Abu-Jamal declared his innocence and castigated the judge for presiding over a farcical trial, the prosecution launched into an illegitimate attack on his past political beliefs and associations. The centerpiece was a twelve-year-old newspaper article about the Black Panther Party containing an interview of Abu-Jamal when he was sixteen years old.

When the prosecutor questioned Abu-Jamal about his assertion that "political power grows out of the barrel of a gun," he explained that the quotation was borrowed from Mao Ze-dong and that U.S. history bears out the truth of that maxim. The prosecutor continued with the political attack, confronting Abu-Jamal with the fact that he endorsed the slogan "All power to the people" and that he was an active member of the Black Panther Party. In this assault on Abu-Jamal's ideological stance as a young man, the prosecutor's earlier efforts to secure a nearly all-white jury paid enormous dividends, as Philadelphia's racial divide ensured that these jury members would be inflamed by the specter of Abu-Jamal as a black militant. Death was the appropriate sanction, the prosecutor argued, because Abu-Jamal's lifelong disdain for police and governmental authority prompted his cold-blooded killing of a police officer on December 9, 1981. This argument, as distorted from reality as it was, undoubtedly eclipsed the fact that until this arrest Abu-Jamal had never run afoul of the law and was an award-winning journalist and compelling "voice of the voiceless."

As a death row inmate, Abu-Jamal had an automatic right to take an appeal to the Pennsylvania Supreme Court. Nevertheless, he could not take any appellate action for a year after his trial because of Judge Sabo's failure to formally enter the judgment of conviction and sentence for that period of time. Then Abu-Jamal's newly assigned appellate attorney literally did nothing for an additional year, leading to his removal from the case. His replacement counsel took a year to prepare the briefs and other papers that were ultimately filed with the Pennsylvania Supreme Court. When it came time for Abu-Jamal's case to be decided, two of the six justices on the court inexplicably removed themselves.

The February 27, 1997 written decision by the Pennsylvania Supreme Court rejecting the appeal is a disgraceful piece of work. It expresses no concern that the prosecution intentionally removed African Americans from the jury panel, in blatant violation of the United States Constitution; nor was the fact that Abu-Jamal was denied his absolute right to represent himself and to be present at his own trial considered. The decision also failed to reveal the fact that the prosecutor told the jury that Abu-Jamal would have "appeal after appeal" to review the jury's verdict, notwithstanding an earlier court decision, mandated by a U.S. Supreme Court case, that held that this very same argument, by the very same prosecutor as in Abu-Jamal's case, was improper.

Efforts to have his case examined by the United States Supreme Court were unceremoniously rebuffed, as that Court simply refused even to consider his appeal. Remarkably, the U.S. Supreme Court agreed to consider an appeal by a member of the Aryan Brotherhood, a white supremacist organization, who argued that the prosecutor's use of his political affiliation in the penalty phase of his capital trial violated his First Amendment rights. Abu-Jamal's request to have his case joined with this appeal was denied. The Supreme Court ultimately overturned the death sentence of the white racist, while Abu-Jamal's death sentence, secured by exactly the same illegitimate means, has remained in force for nearly two decades.

This appalling spectacle of injustice continues. In 1996 Abu-Jamal filed suit against prison authorities for opening his mail related to his trial. A federal judge agreed, finding that prison authorities wrongfully invaded the sanctity of the attorney-client relationship. It turns out that prison authorities in 1995 intercepted legal correspondence, including sensitive materials containing legal strategies and litigation plans indicating that the defense intended to file a petition for a new trial on June 5, 1995. That correspondence found its way into the governor's office. Forewarned, the governor issued the death warrant that called for Abu-Jamal's execution in mid-August, before he had a chance to file his legal papers. As a result of this death warrant, Judge Sabo hastily conducted an evidentiary hearing in order to meet this deadline of death. Fortunately, as a result of intense international pressure, Judge Sabo capitulated and ordered a stay of execution as the deadline approached.

In 1998, the legal team presented Abu-Jamal's case again to the Pennsylvania Supreme Court. The legal team mounted a devastating attack on the prosecution's case, dismantling every meaningful aspect of the trial to reveal that not only was guilt not proven, but the evidence strongly points towards innocence. It is doubtful that any other capital case has been so thoroughly discredited. The legal team has exposed the systematic suppression of exculpatory evidence, including the manipulation of witnesses through crude techniques ranging from overt intimidation to petty secret deals. It debunked the so-called confession. It shone light on the outrageous bias of Judge Sabo. It presented evidence of discrimination in the jury selection, of inadequacy of defense counsel, and of improper inflammatory argumentation by the prosecutor. It showed that the so-called murder weapon did not match the ballistics findings contained in the medical examiner's report. It showed that at least five eyewitnesses, none of whom knew or consulted with each other, saw the perpetrator run along the same side of the street and in the same direction toward a nearby alleyway. The list goes on.

The legal team was never optimistic about its chances with the Pennsylvania judicial system, although from a narrow legal standpoint, hope seemed reasonable, given how discredited was the prosecution's case. But, the Pennsylvania Supreme Court decision denying a new trial proved how right we were to be pessimistic. Remarkably, as the defense team was poised to enter federal court to secure a new trial—only a step toward thwarting a continuation of a monumental injustice—the "counter-movement" waged against Abu-Jamal's supporters has requisitioned another disreputable piece of evidence to prop up this false conviction. Quite fittingly, it is another account of an alleged confession, bringing the tally to three.

The first two "confession" accounts have been thoroughly discredited. The first account—that Abu-Jamal confessed in a police van to an admittedly corrupt high-ranking member of the Philadelphia Police Department—was too implausible for even the prosecution to use at Abu-Jamal's trial. The second account—discussed earlier in the essay—is so patently absurd that even a leading conservative legal commentator with *American Lawyer* magazine denounces the evidence as manufactured and, in large measure based upon the prosecution's use of that evidence, concurs that Abu-Jamal's trial was unfair.

The most recent account of a confession—reported for the first time in the August 1999 issue of *Vanity Fair*—is perhaps the most outlandish. As reported in that magazine, Abu-Jamal implied his guilt to an obscure prison volunteer some seven years earlier. According to Philip Bloch, Abu-Jamal responded with a terse, "yes," when asked if he had any regrets over killing Faulkner. Bloch suggests that, of all people, Abu-Jamal used him as a repository for his heavy conscience. (Abu-Jamal acknowledges he and Bloch discussed a variety of topics, including the legitimacy of political violence, but characterizes this latest revelation as an effort by Bloch to secure notoriety and as so absurd as to be laughable). Bloch never memorialized this stunning admission; nor did he report it to anyone.

Bloch insists that he phrased the question in such a way as to leave no doubt that Abu-Jamal's affirmative response implied his guilt in the killing of police officer Faulkner. Seven years later, Bloch resists the possibility that he might have asked a question worded slightly differently, but carrying a whole new meaning. Could he have asked, "do you regret *the* killing of police officer Faulkner?," as opposed to asking Abu-Jamal if he regretted "killing police officer Faulkner"? Could he have asked Abu-Jamal if he felt sorrow over the killing of police officer Faulkner? Bloch insists that his question was never framed to leave any doubt that Abu-Jamal's answer was an implied admission of guilt. Yet, with the passage of years, how easily can a passing exchange of no real moment be transformed into a momentous confession of guilt? The answer is, quite easily.

But there is more to this belated account of a confession by a celebrated death row inmate who has never wavered in his proclamation of innocence. Bloch claims that he was prompted to break his own silence because he was upset over the intensity of the pro-Mumia movement. This is a rather curious claim, however, in view of the fact that back in August of 1995, the defense team vigorously attacked the prosecution's claim that Abu-Jamal had confessed in 1981, calling that evidence manufactured in order to ensure a much-needed conviction. It would seem, if this revelation were true, that August of 1995 was the most propitious moment for Bloch to have come forward, supplying a confession that the prosecution desperately needed to produce.

The primary fact of this revelation's timing is not, as Bloch suggests, the status of the pro-Mumia movement; rather, it is the vindictive state of affairs in the counter-movement launched by the Fraternal Order of Police (FOP), which has cynically deployed police officer Faulkner's widow to advocate immediate execution with no review of judicial malfeasance that could lead to a new trial. Bloch's ridiculous account of a confession—which he admits surfaced only after he saw the FOP's anti-Mumia web site—is simply the latest aspersion the FOP has cast upon Abu-Jamal to strip him of his international stature. So, what was Abu-Jamal's response to all of this? Anger, and then laughter. Bloch wants his moment in the spotlight, and Abu-Jamal graciously hopes he receives it—particularly in a federal courtroom under the unforgiving klieg lights of blistering cross-examination. In fact, weeks after the media uncritically reported Bloch's statements Abu-Jamal located a letter written to him by Bloch three months after the alleged confession. In the letter, Bloch writes that he believes it's possible for Abu-Jamal to receive justice if he were to be granted a new, fair trial.

Efforts now are directed toward the upcoming battles in the federal court system: The legal team filed a petition for habeas corpus in federal district court in Philadelphia on October 15, 1999. The Bible states that it is easier for a camel to go through the eye of a needle than it is for a rich man to pass through the gates of heaven. That description captures the difficulties in litigating death penalty cases in federal court in the late 1990s: it is easier to squeeze a camel through a very small hole than to convince a federal judge to overturn a state court determination that a death row inmate must die.

Americans have President Bill Clinton and Congress to thank for restricting the ability of death row inmates to litigate their cases in federal court. In April of 1996, Congress passed into law the Anti-Terrorism and Effective Death Penalty Act of 1996, legislation that arose out of the outrage over the Oklahoma City bombing. As it applies to death penalty cases, this statute is designed to make the assembly line of death operate more smoothly. It limits the ability of death row inmates to get meaningful treatment of their cases.

The nuances of the new death penalty statute are too complicated to explain here. Lawyers and judges are still scratching their heads over what this new law means in practical terms. But some things are relatively clear. Federal courts must now "defer" to the findings by the state courts in ways that were unheard of earlier. Thus the federal court must accept Judge Sabo's findings, as flawed as they are, unless the defense team can show that they are wholly unsupported. As noted above, for the past three years evidentiary hearings on the case have been held before Judge Sabo, who must assess what "facts" have been established. While the legal team established a vast array of facts supporting the bid for a new trial, Sabo's "findings of fact" virtually negate everything proved in court. The task ahead is to convince a federal judge that Sabo's "findings of fact" don't hold water.

That is only the first hurdle. The new law even restricts the ability of federal courts to evaluate whether state courts have made errors on the law. It is no longer sufficient to show that the state courts misapplied the law in a case. Even if a federal court disagrees with a state court's legal ruling, it still must uphold that decision. A federal court may overturn a state court's conviction or sentence only if it finds that a state court's application of a federal constitutional principle is "unreasonable." In other words, Congress is telling us that the assembly line of death will not be stopped simply because a state court has made a mistake, even where the evidence suggests a death row inmate may be innocent. Only in the rarest of circumstances, where the state court's legal evaluation of a federal constitutional claim is so outside the realm of acceptability as to be deemed "unreasonable," can a state court's ruling be overturned.

The only thing that is truly "unreasonable" is the death penalty itself. Capital punishment in the United States has its roots in racial violence, particularly the hideous practice of lynching. A United Nations Human Rights investigator recently confirmed what most of us already know—namely, that the death penalty in the United States is racially and economically discriminatory and politically driven. The fifty-three member nations of the United Nations Commission on Human Rights recently passed a resolution calling for a worldwide moratorium on executions; the United States voiced its opposition, as did such countries as China and Pakistan. Even Russia and South Africa—historically bastions of human rights violations—voted in favor of the moratorium. And even the American Bar Association, an organization that could never be accused of being politically progressive, has called for a moratorium in this country. Yet our politicians and judges tell us that this assembly line of death must proceed still faster. Mumia Abu-Jamal's case is a flashpoint for the death penalty and for the progressive movement generally. If we cannot defeat the forces of repression in this case, we must take stock of whether our struggles for justice will ever amount to much.

NOTES

1. Mumia Abu-Jamal, *Live from Death Row* (New York: Addison-Wesley, 1995); and *Death Blossoms* (Farmington, PA: Plough Publishing, 1997).

BLACKS AND CRIMINAL JUSTICE

FIVE

Black Radicalism and an Economy of Incarceration

MANNING MARABLE

The poet Langston Hughes once suggested years ago that the black American's search for democracy in the United States was "a dream deferred." Perhaps we should now add that this dream has been so long delayed, corrupted, and compromised that many black folk question the viability of the entire political project called "American democracy."

Any understanding of U.S. society and history must begin with the study of the black American experience in this country. This is because the status and existence of black people, the quality of our lives, and the range of possibilities that we can realistically achieve through our own endeavors, is the essential litmus test for the viability of U.S. democracy. It is the distance between America's rhetoric and its reality, between what America says about itself and what it actually is.

The reality of "blackness" has all too often been the criteria for determining a series of questions about the relationship among the people, the state, and society: Who is a citizen, and who is not? Who has voting rights, and who does not? Who rides in the Jim Crow section of the bus, and who does not? Who lives in the ghetto, and who does not? Who is the first person to get a job, and who is the last?

The basic paradox one must confront in any consideration of the role of race in the U.S. political economy is the tension between "marginalization" and "inclusion." Historically, African American culture has been central to the construction of the cultural and the aesthetic contours of America. Politically, the issue of race has been absolutely central to the major conflicts in the American experience, from the Civil War to the civil rights movement. Economically, black labor was essential in the construction of this nation, from the unpaid exploitation of slavery to the underpaid labor of African Americans in central cities in the 1990s. Nevertheless, despite our centrality, we continue to be marginalized by the mainstream dominant social order. We are perpetually unequal members of the household, but never members of the national family. In the language of "hip-hop" culture, we are "dissed" in the very house we have helped to construct.

From the vantage point of African American history, from the depths of our sorrow and anger, we ask ourselves, why do we continue to be marginalized? Who benefits from this marginalization? Who is responsible for maintaining the structure of power and privilege that makes this marginalization an enduring fact of American life?

African Americans understand that race is not a valid biological concept; that it has no genetic validity. Stripped of the rhetoric of superiority and inferiority, the science of race is nothing but a fraud, grounded in power, privilege, and violence against those who are oppressed. Yet our lives are defined and circumscribed by the brutal reality of racism, a system that denies the humanity of millions of people, limiting their education, employment, health, housing, and future.

How has this racial crisis affected the state of black America? We can best measure the destructiveness of racism in the lives of our own children. Growing up black in white America has always been a challenge, but never more so than today. To be young and black in the 1990s means that the basic context for human development—education, health care, personal safety, the environment, employment, and shelter—is increasingly problematic. To be young and black today means fighting for survival in a harsh and frequently unforgiving urban environment.

In short, capitalism is killing our children. Ample evidence is provided by Marian Wright Edelman who heads the Children's Defense Fund. Today, in comparison to white children, black children are one and one-half times more likely to grow up in families whose household head did not graduate from high school. They are twice as likely to be arrested for property crimes, to be unemployed as teenagers and later as adults, and to become teenage mothers. African American infants are two and one-half times as likely to die in the first year of life and to be born at low birthweights. They are three times more likely than white young people to live in group quarters (such as orphanages or foster homes) and/or to be suspended from school or be subjected to corporal punishment. African American young people are four times as likely to be born of mothers who have had no prenatal care, mothers who died during childbirth, or mothers dying from HIV infection. They are five times more likely to be arrested by the police for violent crimes than are white youth. And they are nine times more likely to become victims of homicide.

The root of the racial crisis is found within the U.S. economy, which is characterized by the concentration of wealth among a small minority of American households and the rapid expansion of social misery, falling incomes, and inequality for the majority of the population of the country. As of 1993, the top 1 percent of all income earners in the United States had a greater combined net wealth than the bottom 95 percent of all income earners. In short, a small number of individuals—2 to 3 million at the most—control the overwhelming majority of the resources. This massive inequality also can be measured in our cities. Between 1973 and 1989, the overall average of all wage earners living in the cities fell by 16 percent. In the New York borough of Manhattan, where I live, the poorest one-fifth of the population in 1990 earned an annual average income of $5,237. The richest one-fifth earned an average income of $110,199 annually. In individual neighborhoods less than three miles apart, the vast income gap between affluence and poverty can only be described as obscene. In West Harlem, for example, a predominately African American and Dominican community, the average annual family income was $6,019. The average incomes for affluent families in one district of Manhattan's upper East Side was $301,209. In other words, for every dollar that the wealthy households have, the poorest have two cents. The identical profile of inequality exists in every American city. In Los Angeles, the median annual incomes of the poorest fifth and the wealthiest fifth in 1990 were $6,821 compared to $123,098. In Chicago, the median annual income gap was $4,743 compared to $86,632. In Detroit, the difference was $3,109 compared to $63,625. And in Orleans Parish of the city of New Orleans, Louisiana, the rich made thirty times as much as the poor, $83,389 compared to $2,793. Millions of median-income households are forced to have three or more income earners, just to stay even. Millions more have been pushed into unemployment and poverty, while for America's privileged and powerful elites, things have never been better.

There are many ways to measure the political economy of racism. For example, a 1994 study of the Office of Personnel Management found that African American federal employees are more than twice as likely to be dismissed as their white counterparts. Blacks are especially likely to be fired at much higher rates than whites in jobs where they comprise a significant share of the labor force: For example, black clerk typists are 4.7 times more likely to be dismissed than whites, and black custodians are 4.1 times more likely to be fired. Discrimination is also rampant in capital markets. Banks continue policies of "redlining," denying loans in neighborhoods that are largely black and Hispanic. In New York City in 1992, for instance, blacks were turned down for mortgage applications by banks, savings and loans, and other financial institutions about twice as often than whites. And even after years of affirmative action programs, blacks and Latinos remain grossly underrepresented in a wide number of professions. For example, African Americans and Latinos represent 12.4 percent and 9.5 percent respectively of the U.S. adult population. But of all American physicians, blacks account for barely 4.2 percent and Latinos, 5.2 percent. Among engineers, blacks represent 3.7 percent, Latinos, 3.3 percent; among lawyers, blacks account for 3.3 percent, Latinos, 3.1 percent; and for all university and college professors, blacks made up 5 percent, Latinos, 2.9 percent. As the Reverend Jesse Jackson observed in a speech before the National Press Club, while native-born white males comprise only 41 percent of the U.S. population, they are 80 percent of all tenured professors, 92 percent of the Forbes 400 chief executive officers, and 97 percent of all school superintendents.

How does the U.S. system cope with this vast polarization between wealth and poverty? The primary response by the U.S. government, elected officials, and the corporate elite to the growing crisis of inequality has been the massive expansion of public and private security forces and the incarceration of literally millions of black, Latino, and poor people. Between 1980 and 1990 the number of police in the United States doubled. As of 1995, local and state police forces employed 554,000 officers. An additional 1.5 million private security officers currently are employed to guard office buildings, stores, affluent neighborhoods, and corporate headquarters all over the country. Private patrol cars now cruise entire communities of upper- to middle-class Americans, with their streets closed off to outside traffic. Much of the new suburban housing being built today in "planned communities" is surrounded by walls and gates, wired for electronic surveillance, and guarded twenty-four hours a day by private security personnel.

It was in this context in 1994 that the U.S. Congress passed President Bill Clinton's $30 billion Omnibus Crime Bill. The bill's "draconian" provisions included: $10.8 billion in federal matching funds to local governments to hire 100,000 new police officers over the next five years; $10 billion for the construction of new federal prisons; an expansion of the number of federal crimes to which the death penalty applies from two to fifty-eight (the bill also eliminated an existing statue that prohibited the execution of mentally incapacitated defendants); a so-called three strikes proposal that mandates life sentences for anyone convicted of three "violent" felonies; a section that allows children as young as thirteen to be tried as adults; and the creation of special courts able to deport noncitizens alleged to be "engaged in terrorist activity" on the basis of secret evidence.

Even more striking has been the massive expansion in recent years of the U.S. prison system. In the last two decades, the U.S. prison population more than tripled, from about 550,000 in 1980 to 1,700,000 today. In the state of California alone, between 1977 and 1992, the prison population soared from under 20,000 to over 150,000.

The racial oppression that defines U.S. society as a whole is most dramatically apparent within the criminal justice system and the prisons. Today, about one-half of inmates, or over 800,000, in federal and state prisons and jails are African Americans. About one-third of all black men in their twenties today are in prison or jail, are on probation or parole, or are awaiting trial. As of 1990, one in twelve black males between the ages of eighteen and fifty-four were confined in federal, state, or local penal institutions.

The racist character of the U.S. prison system should not obscure the equally important class dimensions of mass imprisonment. According to a 1991 survey of the U.S. Department of Justice, about one-third of all prisoners were employed at the time of their arrests. Only 55 percent held full-time jobs. About two-thirds of all prisoners have less than a high school–level education and enough marketable skills to permit them to be competitive in the labor market. The study that surveyed 14,000 inmates in 277 state prisons throughout the United States found that 70 percent of prisoners legally earned less than $15,000 in the year prior to arrest, with 32 percent earning less than $5,000. The prisons of the United States are vast warehouses, for the poor and unemployed, for low wage workers and the poorly educated, and, most especially, for Latino and African American males.

What are our priorities, when this country devotes billions of dollars to confine millions of Americans in prisons, rather than investing in schools, hospitals, child care centers, and the environment? In June 1998 I spent an entire day in Sing Sing prison in New York State, giving lectures to prisoners who were enrolled in a professional degree program. I met dozens of intelligent young black and Latino men who want to make a productive contribution to their families, community, and society. But how can they accomplish this, when the government's priorities and policies are designed not to address problems but simply to warehouse human beings in prisons?

The prison industrial complex has become America's most profitable growth industry. Between 1979 and 1990 prison construction nationwide increased 612 percent. With the exception of General Motors, there are more full-time employees at work in the prison industry than in any Fortune 500 corporation. Everyday we are building in the United States over one hundred new jail and prison cells. We must have the courage to challenge this massive waste of resources and the immoral destruction of human lives. We must demand public investments in decent housing, elementary and secondary schools, colleges, jobs, and health care, so that all people can be productive rather than being confined on the outside, at the margins.

So, what is to be done? There can be no compromise with capitalism, when millions of black Americans are unemployed, when our children are dying, when toxic waste dumps are poisoning us. There can be no compromise with capitalism, when the average black man dies before he can collect Social Security, or when reactionary politicians demonize African American women on public assistance. There can be no compromise with racism, patriarchy, homophobia, and imperialism.

We need to build a Black Radical Congress that is broad, inclusive, and democratic—not top down, but bottom up. We need to acknowledge the honest differences among us, but we must unite to fight the common enemy. We need to build a radical movement for black power in this society. We need all perspectives—lesbians and gays, trade unionists, Pan Africanists, feminists, Communists, revolutionary nationalists—to build the BRC or Black Radical Congress.

In the words of the BRC call: "We stand at the edge of a new century. The moment for a new militancy and a new commitment to the liberation of all black people, at home and abroad, has arrived." Now is the time to build a national campaign, setting into motion a renewed struggle to reclaim our historic role as the real voice of democracy in this county. Now is the time to overcome our differences, to unite. "Spread the word: 'Without struggle there is no progress!' Now is the time!"

NOTE

This chapter is the edited text of a keynote address at the June 1998 Black Radical Congress convention in Chicago, Illinois.

SIX

From the Convict Lease System to the Super-Max Prison

ANGELA Y. DAVIS

Albert Wright, Jr., is a fifty-year-old African American man who is serving a forty-year term in the Western Illinois Correctional Center. In this prison of 2,000 men, of whom some 66 percent are black, he wrote in an impassioned plea to readers of *Emerge*, a black monthly magazine: "[T]here is seldom a positive response to the cries for help in combating the inhuman treatment that we are subjected to daily. Few of you know what the treatment is like. What prison administrators tell you is not anything near the truth." Wright makes it very clear that he is not asking for financial support or material goods. "I am talking about genuine interest in what is happening to your people. We are still people. We just happen to be in prison."[1] But like many of the hundreds of thousands of black men currently trapped in a political web of state and privately run prisons, Wright's humanity—and that of the imprisoned youth on whose behalf he made his appeal—goes unrecognized by a penal system that has abandoned the goals of individual rehabilitation and social reintegration in favor of increasingly harsh forms of punishment and retribution. Because the racist-informed discourse on criminality goes largely unchallenged, black male bodies are treated as dispensable by communities in the "free world" that have all but forsaken those who are marked as criminal. Albert Wright obviously was concerned that middle-class black communities are among those guilty of distancing themselves from the plight of prisoners; by submitting his piece to *Emerge,* he was simultaneously criticizing and reaching out to these communities.

Black men are now the primary targets of what prison reform advocate Jerome Miller calls the "search and destroy"[2] mission of a criminal justice system that, we must remember, also trains its sights on black women and other men and women of color as well as on poor white people. African American males, who comprise less than 7 percent of the U.S. population, constitute nearly half of the people in jail and prison.[3]

I do not intend to suggest that most imprisoned people have not committed a crime of some sort. In fact, studies repeatedly have found that a vast majority of most populations have engaged at one point in their lives in some type of behavior that is proscribed by law. However, only a small percentage of these acts is ever examined within the context of the criminal justice system.[4] Considering the fact that in the late 1990s, approximately one-third of all young black men are either in prison or directly under the control of a correctional system, it is not entirely far-fetched to argue that one has a greater chance of going to jail or prison if one is a young black man than if one actually has committed a crime. While most imprisoned young black men also may have broken a law, it is more the fact of their race and gender than of their guilt or innocence that tends to bring them into contact with the criminal justice system.

The staggering numbers of imprisoned black men should not, however, eclipse the fact that black women—a majority of whom are arrested for drug-related offenses—constitute the most rapidly expand-ing of all imprisoned populations.[5] This phenomenon is attributable to the fact that poor black women are increasingly targets of police surveillance for similar reasons as their male counterparts as well as for reasons related directly to their gender. The dismantling of welfare, for example, and the attendant demonization of single black mothers—who are represented as procreators of crime and poverty—contributes to a problem that is leading large numbers of poor black women into prison. Moreover, differential criminalization of drug use means that those unfortunate enough to become addicted to crack cocaine can be arrested and thrown in jail, while their middle-class counterparts who have access to legal drugs like Valium or Prozac are free to indulge their drug habits. In fact, the current rise in the numbers of imprisoned black men and women can hardly be justified by any recent increase in the crime rate among black people. Author Steven Donziger points out that "there are so many more African Americans than whites in our prisons that the difference cannot be explained by higher crime among African Americans—racial discrimination is also at work, and it penalizes African Americans at almost every juncture in the criminal justice system."[6] Yet black people and people of color in general are increasingly the main human raw material being used for the expansion of the U.S. penal system. I believe that the peculiarly racialized and gendered history of punishment in the United States has, in part, facilitated the structural and ideological transformation of the penal system into a prison industrial complex that imprisons, dehumanizes, and exploits ever-increasing numbers of people, the vast majority of whom are poor and black.

It is not a coincidence that rehabilitation, the historical goal of the prison, has receded theoretically and practically as U.S. prisons have come to house spiraling numbers of black men. The current notion that the "criminals" with which prisons are overcrowded are largely beyond the pale of rehabilitation—that "nothing works"—is very much connected with the fact that in the contemporary era, the terms "black" and "male," when combined, have become virtually synonymous with "criminal" in the popular imagination. This is not to ignore the complex historical evolution of the rehabilitative ideal, from a moral and religious to a medicalized framework, or the problematic category of recidivism, which has figured prominently in measurements of the success of rehabilitation.[7] However, narratives of rehabilitation have been so informed by the racial assumptions that have shaped moral and religious frameworks on one hand and medical frameworks on the other that an examination of these relationships may yield insights about the current construction of imprisonment as the inevitable destiny of young black men. It also may assist us to understand why the rather small proportion of women imprisoned recently has begun to rise to unprecedented heights, with black female bodies increasingly subjected to a process of criminalization paralleling that of their male counterparts.

Given the recent emergence of supermaximum prisons and the increasingly punitive character of U.S. prisons in general—which, in the 1990s, were being divested of educational, recreational, and other programs historically associated with rehabilitation projects—it is important to recall that in their early history, prisons were proposed as radical alternatives to the bodily pain that then comprised the dominant mode of punishment. The penitentiary—the historical manifestation of the prison as a site for punishment (rather than as a holding facility for people awaiting trial and punishment)—was conceived architecturally and theoretically as a plan for the moral reformation of the individual. As such it expressed the overarching Enlightenment-age assumption that reason formed the core of every human being. It also expressed modernity's vision of inevitable progress. However, as philosopher David Goldberg points out, the "defining of humanity in relation to rationality clearly prefaces modernity's emphasis on rational capacity as a crucial differentia of racial groups."[8] In fact, modernity's construction of rational humanity was not only racialized, it was gendered as well.

Although it has been argued that the origin of the term "penitentiary" is related to a plan in England to incarcerate "penitent" prostitutes,[9] the penitentiary as an institution for the reformation of criminals was aimed largely at white men. In the United States this is significant in that the birth of the penitentiary occurred during the last half-century or so of slavery, a period that also witnessed intense contestations over the future of women's rights.

Reflecting modernity's relegation of women of all racial backgrounds, and men of color, to reason's antithesis—nature, instinct, and the senses—the putative universality of reason masked strong racial and gendered assumptions about the bodies in which universal reason resided. During much of the nineteenth century, white women had no autonomous juridical status, and they were punished largely within the domestic sphere. As daughters, they were subjected to corporal punishment by their fathers, and as wives, by their husbands. White women deemed "criminal" and brought into the criminal justice system were considered "fallen" and, as such, beyond the pale of moral rehabilitation.

Until the abolition of slavery, most black men and women were under the authority of their slave masters, who developed punishment regimes designed simultaneously to inflict severe bodily pain and to safeguard the body as a laboring and thus profitable commodity. An example of this was the digging of holes in which pregnant women could lay their stomachs in order to protect their unborn children—who were grist for the mills of slave labor—while being flogged.[10] In this context, punishment was entirely detached from the goal of moral reformation. Because slave laborers were valued largely in relation to their size and strength, the value of male slaves was generally higher than that of female slaves, a probable consequence of which was the privileging of the male body for labor and punishment. This is not to dismiss the horrors to which women were subjected under slavery, which included sexualized forms of punishment such as rape as well as gendered forms of punishment related to the control and preservation of women's reproductive labor.

During the post–Civil War era, extralegal lynching along with the legalized Black Codes identified the bodies of black people as the loci of punishment. In this way, black men and women continued to be excluded, on the grounds of both race and gender, from the moral realm within which punishment in the penitentiary was equated with rehabilitation. Black men were barred from the individuality and masculinity with which even the criminal citizen was imbued. Black women, on the other hand, were barred from the femininity that tended to protect many white women from imprisonment.

The birth of the English and American penitentiaries, whose most ardent advocates were passionately opposed to harsh corporal punishment, had little impact on the punishment regimes to which slaves were subjected. Neither did they effectively alter the ways in which white women were punished. As such they were implicitly racialized and gendered as new and less cruel modes of white male punishment.

The most widely publicized penitentiary design was the panopticon engineered for total observation and proposed by utilitarian philosopher Jeremy Bentham. Although few prisons actually were constructed according to its strict standards, its discursive impact was such that it was linked closely to the project of prison rehabilitation. Between 1787 and 1791 Bentham published a series of letters describing in detail a new architectural design for prisons and other institutions requiring the surveillance and control of large numbers of people. Bentham's panopticon was supposed to guarantee the ubiquitous monitoring and the imposition of discipline he thought criminals needed in order to internalize productive labor habits.

According to Bentham's plan, which he hoped would win him a contract with the government to build and operate a penitentiary, prison inmates would be housed in solitary cells situated on circular tiers, all of which would face a multilevel guard tower. Bentham suggested the use of Venetian blinds, combined with a rather complex interplay of light and darkness, to guarantee that the prisoners—whose cells were arranged so that they could not see each other—also would be unable to see the warden in the guard tower. The warden's vantage point, on the other hand, would allow him a clear view of all the prisoners. However—and this was the most significant aspect of Bentham's mammoth panopticon—because each individual prisoner would never be able to determine where the warden's gaze was focused, each one would be compelled to behave as if he were being watched at all times.

The most consistent attempt to implement Bentham's panopticon design took place in the United States at the Stateville Penitentiary, located hear Joliet, Illinois, which officially opened on March 9, 1925. It took shape as a direct result of a reform movement, begun in 1905, that exposed the state of Illinois for maintaining "brutal and inhumane conditions" at the old Joliet prison, built in 1860.[11] When a legislative committee returned from a trip to Europe to examine prison planning abroad, they announced that they were most impressed by Bentham's panopticon. Although Stateville was partially constructed as a panopticon, by the time construction was entering its last phase, the state had given up on the circular plan and completed the prison with rectangular cell houses. For the first twenty-five years of its history, Stateville held a majority white prison population. However, by the mid-1950s, the prison population was majority black.[12]

As theorist Michel Foucault later pointed out, the prisoner of the panopticon "is seen, but he does not see; he is the object of information, never a subject in communication . . . [a]nd this invisibility is a guarantee of order."[13] Moreover, the crowd, a compact mass, a locus of multiple exchanges, individualities merging together, a collective effect, is abolished and replaced by a collection of separated individualities. From the point of view of the guardian, the crowd is replaced by a multiplicity that can be numbered and supervised; from the point of view of the inmates, by a sequestered and observed solitude.[14]

This process of individualization via the panopticon assumed that the prisoner was at least a potentially rational being whose criminality merely evidenced deviation from that potential. This architecture and regime also assumed that the individual to be reformed panoptically was in possession of mental and moral faculties that could be controlled and transformed by the experience of imprisonment. White women were theoretically exempt from this process, since in Britain and in the United States at the turn of the nineteenth century the overdetermining ideology of the "fallen woman" constructed female criminals as having no prospect of moral rehabilitation. Black men and women, on the other hand, were ideologically barred from the realm of morality and, unlike white women, were not even acknowledged as ever having been epistemological subjects and moral agents. Thus, they could not even fall from grace, a state they were deemed incapable of attaining in the first place.

Slaves were not accorded the social status of individuals. If they were granted any individuality at all, it was corporal in nature, defined by their value on the market, their laboring potential, and the punishment they received. As a consequence, they often were not even subject to the gender differentiation operative in the dominant culture. Women's quotas in the plantation fields, for example, where their tasks were essentially the same as men's, were established in connection with their size and weight, rather than with their gender. Women also were targets of the whip and the lash, the major weapons of punishment during slavery.

As black people began to be integrated into southern penal systems in the aftermath of the Civil War—and as the penal system became a system of penal servitude—the punishment associated with slavery became integrated into the penal system. "Whipping," as author Matthew Mancini has observed, "was the preeminent form of punishment under slavery; and the lash, along with the chain, became the very emblem of servitude for slaves and prisoners."[15] Many black people were imprisoned under the laws assembled in the various Black Codes of the southern states, which, because they were rearticulations of the Slave Codes, tended to racialize penality and link it closely with previous regimes of slavery. The expansion of the convict lease system and the county chain gang meant that the antebellum criminal justice system, which focused far more intensely on black people than on whites, largely defined southern criminal justice as a means of controlling black labor. According to Mancini:

> Among the multifarious debilitating legacies of slavery was the conviction that blacks could only labor in a certain way—the way experience had shown them to have labored in the past: in gangs, subjected to constant supervision, and under the discipline of the lash. Since these were the requisites of slavery, and since slaves were blacks, Southern whites almost universally concluded that blacks could not work unless subjected to such intense surveillance and discipline.[16]

Scholars who have studied the convict lease system point out that in many important respects, convict leasing was far worse than slavery; the title of Mancini's study is *One Dies, Get Another* and the title of David Oshinsky's work on Parchman Prison *Worse Than Slavery*. The concern slave owners necessarily expressed for individual slaves because of their particular individual value no longer applied to convicts, who were leased out en masse and could be worked literally to death without affecting the profitability of a convict crew. According to descriptions by contemporaries, the conditions under which leased convicts and county chain gangs lived were far worse than those under which black people had lived as slaves. The records of Mississippi plantations in the Yazoo Delta during the late 1880s indicate that

> the prisoners ate and slept on bare ground, without blankets or mattresses, and often without clothes. They were punished for "slow hoeing" (ten lashes), "sorry planting" (five lashes) and "being light with cotton" (five lashes). Some who attempted to escape were whipped

"till the blood ran down their legs"; others had a metal spur riveted to their feet. Convicts dropped from exhaustion, pneumonia, malaria, frostbite, consumption, sunstroke, dysentery, gunshot wounds, and "shackle poisoning" (the constant rubbing of chains and leg irons against bare flesh).[17]

The U.S. penitentiaries as they developed according to the Pennsylvania and Auburn systems envisioned labor as a rehabilitative activity; convict labor in the South, overwhelmingly black, was designed to reap the largest possible profits. Rehabilitation had little or nothing to do with the punishment industry as it developed there. Thus the theory of punishment associated with the new U.S. penitentiaries and with the Benthamian conception of the panopticon was entirely at odds with the forms of punishment meted out to newly freed black people.

In the contemporary era, the emergent prison industrial complex, which is fueled increasingly by privatization trends, recalls the early efforts to create a profitable punishment industry based on the new supply of "free" black male laborers in the aftermath of the Civil War. Steven Donzinger, drawing from the work of Norwegian criminologist Nils Christie, argues that

> companies that service the criminal justice system need sufficient quantities of raw materials to guarantee long-term growth. . . . In the criminal justice field, *the raw material is prisoners,* and industry will do what is necessary to guarantee a steady supply. For the supply of prisoners to grow, criminal justice policies must ensure a sufficient number of incarcerated Americans regardless of whether crime is rising or the incarceration is necessary.[18]

Just as newly freed black men and a significant number of black women constituted a virtually endless supply of raw material for the embryonic southern punishment industry and provided much-needed labor for the southern states as they attempted to recover from the devastating impact of the Civil War—so in the contemporary era do unemployed black men, along with increasing numbers of black women, constitute an unending supply of raw material for the prison industrial complex.

According to 1997 Bureau of Justice Statistics, African Americans as a whole now represent the majority of state and federal prisoners, with a total of 735,200 black inmates—10,000 more than the total number of white inmates. As the rate of increase in the incarceration of black prisoners continues to rise, the racial composition of the incarcerated population is approaching the proportion of black prisoners to white during the era of the southern convict lease and county chain gang systems. Whether this human raw material is used for its labor or as the forced consumers of commodities provided by corporations directly implicated in the prison industrial complex, it is clear that black male bodies are considered dispensable within the "free world." They are also a major source of profit in the prison world. This relationship recapitulates in complicated new ways the era of convict leasing.

The privatization characteristic of convict leasing also has its contemporary parallels, as companies like Corrections Corporation of America and Wackenhut literally run prisons for profit. In the late 1990s the seventeen private prison companies operating in the United States (and sometimes also abroad) have constructed approximately one hundred jails and prisons in which 50,000 inmates are incarcerated. Private prisons have multiplied at four times the rate of expansion of public prisons. Observers of the private prison phenomenon have estimated that there will be three times as many private facilities by the turn of the century and that their revenues will be more than $1 billion.[19] In arrangements reminiscent of the convict lease system, federal, state, and county governments pay private companies a fee for each inmate; thus private companies have a stake in retaining prisoners as long as possible and in keeping their facilities filled.

In the state of Texas, there are thirty-four government-owned, privately-run jails in which approximately 5,500 out-of-state prisoners are incarcerated. These facilities generate about $80 million annually for Texas.[20] Capital Corrections Resources, Inc., operates the Brazoria Detention Center, a government-owned facility located forty miles outside of Houston, Texas. Brazoria came to public attention in August 1997 when a videotape broadcast on national television showed prisoners there being bitten by police dogs and viciously kicked in the groin and stepped on by guards. The inmates, forced to crawl on the floor, also were being shocked with stun guns as guards—who referred to one black prisoner as "boy"—shouted "Crawl faster!"[21] After the tape's release, the state of Missouri withdrew the 415 prisoners it housed in the detention center. Although accompanying news reports made few references to the indisputably racialized character of the guards' behavior, in the section of the Brazoria videotape that was shown on national television black male prisoners were seen to be primary targets of the guards' attacks.

The thirty-two-minute Brazoria tape, which jail authorities stated was a training tape showing corrections officers "what *not* to do" was made in September 1996. Important evidence of the abuse that takes place behind the walls and gates of private prisons came to light in connection with a lawsuit filed by one of the prisoners who was bitten by a dog; he was suing Brazoria County for $100,000 in damages. The Brazoria jailers' actions—which, according to prisoners there, were far worse than depicted on the tape—were indicative not only of the ways in which many prisoners throughout the country are treated but of generalized attitudes toward people locked up in jails and prisons; it is believed that, by virtue of their imprisonment, they deserve this kind of severe corporal punishment. According to an Associated Press news story, once the Missouri inmates had been transferred back to their home state from Brazoria, they told the *Kansas City Star* that ". . . guards at the Brazoria County Detention Center used cattle prods and other forms of intimidation to win respect and force prisoners to say, 'I love Texas.'" "What you saw on tape wasn't a fraction of what happened that day," said inmate Louis Watkins, referring to the videotaped cellblock raid of September 18, 1996. "I've never seen anything like that in the movies."[22]

It is interesting that this prisoner compared what he saw during the detention center raid to cinematic representations of prison experience. One of my arguments is that prison experience, in popular representational practices, is a quintessentially black male experience. Whether brutal punishment within penal settings is inflicted on white, Latino/a, Asian, Native, or African American men or women, the typical prisoner—and the target of this brutality—is generally considered to be a black man. The gross violations of prisoners' civil and human rights, in this sense, are very much connected with the generalized equation of "criminal" or "prisoner" with a black male body.

The current construction and expansion of state and federal super-maximum security prisons, whose purpose is to address disciplinary problems within the penal system, draws on the historical conception of the panopticon. Again, black men are vastly overrepresented in these super-max prisons and control units, the first of which emerged when federal correctional authorities began to send prisoners whom they deemed to be "dangerous" to the prison in Marion, Illinois. In 1983 the entire prison was "locked down," which meant that prisoners were confined to their cells twenty-three hours a day.[23] Today there are at least fifty-seven supermaximum security federal and state prisons located in thirty-six states.[24] A description of super-maxes in a 1997 report of Human Rights Watch sounds chillingly like Bentham's panopticon. What is different, however, is that all references to individual rehabilitation have disappeared:

> Inmates in super-maximum security facilities are usually held in single cell lock-down, what is commonly referred to as solitary confinement. . . . [C]ongregate activities with other prisoners are usually prohibited; other prisoners cannot even be seen from an inmate's cell; communication with other prisoners is prohibited or difficult (consisting, for example, of shouting from cell to cell); visiting and telephone privileges are limited. The new generation of super-maximum security facilities also rely on state-of-the art technology for monitoring and controlling prisoner conduct and movement, utilizing, for example, video monitors and remote-controlled electronic doors. These prisons represent the application of sophisticated, modern technology dedicated entirely to the task of social control, and they isolate, regulate and surveil more effectively than anything that has preceded them.[25]

Some of these super-max prisons house inmates in cells with solid steel gates rather than bars—an arrangement that recalls the railroad cars used in the past to house leased convicts—so that prisoners literally can see nothing. They are fed through a slot in the gate, unable even to see the guards who bring their food. According to Jerome Miller, "[t]he disproportionate percentage of black men in the general prison populations is outstripped by the much greater percentages of black men housed in super-max prisons."[26] Miller refers to a study by researcher William Chambliss, who found that on one day in 1993, 98 percent of the inmates confined in the super-max prison in Baltimore, Maryland, were African Americans.[27]

The danger of super-max prisons resides not only in the systematically brutal treatment of the prisoners confined therein but also in the way they establish standards for the treatment of all prisoners. They solidify the move away from rehabilitative strategies and do so largely on the backs of black men. Moreover, as prisons become more repressive and as this repression becomes more remote from—and, by default, accepted within—the "free world," they promote retrograde tendencies in educational institutions that serve the populations most likely to move from schools into prisons. These educational institutions begin to resemble prisons more than schools. In poor black communities, for example, schools tend to direct resources needed to address educational crises toward security and discipline. Rather than preparing students for college, middle and high schools in these communities are fast becoming prep schools for prison, molding black children into raw material for punishment and coerced labor.

The extent to which black men today function as the main human raw material for the prison industrial complex only highlights the many ways in which the prison system in the United States in general resembles and recapitulates some of the most abhorrent characteristics of the slavery and convict lease systems of the late nineteenth century. As mentioned earlier, the rampant exploitation of prison labor in an increasingly privatized context is a modern-day form of convict leasing. While black men are not the only population vulnerable to this exploitation, the overwhelming numbers of black men imprisoned in the United States makes them by far the most threatened members of our society when it comes to the new form of enslavement being implemented through the prison system.

The fact that we can draw these connections between latter-twentieth-century imprisonment practices in the United States and various systems and practices in place a century ago is largely a result of the racism woven into the history of the prison system in this country. The ultimate manifestation of this phenomenon can be found in the super-max prison. Its main function is to subdue and control "problematic" imprisoned populations—again, comprised largely of black men— who, having been locked away in the most remote and invisible of spaces, are no longer thought of as human. The absolute authority exercised over these disappeared populations[28] by super-max administrators and staff— and the lick of accountability on the part of private corporations in the prison business and/or benefit from prison labor—is reminiscent of the impunity with which slave owners, overseers, and, later, patrons of the convict lease system routinely disregarded the humanity connected with the black bodies they systematically abused.

In this sense, the super-max draws on, even as it also serves to feed, the perpetuation of racism at every level of our society. This is true, in fact, of the entire prison system; the continued practice of throwing away entire populations depends on the popular imagination viewing those populations as public enemies. It is precisely this relationship between racism and imprisonment that requires antiracist activists and prison activists to work together; on the eve of the twenty-first century, these two movements are inseparable.

NOTES

1. Albert Wright, Jr., "Young Inmates Need Help, From Inside and Out," *Emerge*, October 1997, 80.
2. See Jerome G. Miller, *Search and Destroy: African American Males in the Criminal Justice System* (Cambridge: Cambridge University Press, 1996).
3. Steve Donziger, ed., *The Real War on Crime: The Report of the National Criminal Offenders* (New York: Harper Perennial, 1996), 102.
4. Edgardo Rotman, *Beyond Punishment: A New View on the Rehabilitation of Criminal Offenders* (New York: Greenwood Press, 1990), 115.
5. According to John Irwin and James Austin, "African-American women have experienced the greatest increase in correctional supervision, rising by 78 percent from 1989 through 1994." See: John Irwin and James Austin, *It's About Time: The Imprisonment Binge* (Belmont, Calif.: Wadsworth Publishing Co., 1997), 4.
6. Donziger, *The Real War on Crime*, 99.
7. Richard Hawkins and Geoffrey Alpert point out that: "Right now there is no uniformly accepted definition of recidivism. It generally refers to a return to crime, but in operation refers only to those detected in crime. Given that many crimes go undetected (some of which are committed by former offenders), virtually any official measure of recidivism is a *conservative estimate* of the failure rate among persons released from treatment. One reviewer of various recidivism definitions notes thirteen different indicators of 'failure,' ranging from a recorded police contact to being returned to prison." See Richard

Hawkins and Geoffrey P. Alpert, *American Prison Systems: Punishment and Justice* (Englewood Cliffs, NJ: Prentice-Hall, 1989), 198-99.

8. David Theo Goldberg, *Racist Culture: Philosophy and the Politics of Meaning* (Cambridge, Mass: Blackwell Press, 1993), 23.

9. Hawkins and Alpert, *American Prison Systems,* 30.

10. Angela Y. Davis, *Women, Class and Race* (New York: Random House, 1981), 9.

11. See James B. Jacobs, *Stateville: The Penitentiary in Mass Society* (Chicago: University of Chicago Press, 1977), 15-16.

12. Ibid, 58.

13. Michel Foucault, *Discipline and Punish: The Birth of the Prison* (New York: Vintage, 1979), 200.

14. Ibid., 201.

15. Ibid.

16. Matthew Mancini, *One Dies, Get Another: Convict Leasing in the American South, 1866-1928* (Columbia: University of South Carolina Press, 1996), 25.

17. David Oshinsky, *Worse Than Slavery: Parchman Farm and the Jim Crow Justice System* (New York: The Free Press, 1996), 45.

18. Donzinger, *The Real War on Crime,* 87.

19. Kristin Bloomer, "Private Punishment," *San Francisco Chronicle,* May 10, 1997, A3.

20. Sue Anne Pressley, "Texas County Sued by Missouri Over Alleged Abuse of Inmates," *Washington Post,* August 26, 1997, A2.

21. Madeline Baro, "Video Prompts Prison Probe," *Philadelphia Daily News,* August 20, 1997.

22. "Beatings Worse Than Shown on Videotape, Missouri Inmates Say," Associated Press, August 27, 1997, 7:40 P.M. EDT.

23. "Cold Storage: Super-Maximum Security confinement in Indiana," A Human Rights Watch Report (New York: Human Rights Watch, October 1997), 13.

24. Ibid.

25. Ibid, 14. Citation from Craig Haney, "Infamous Punishment: The Psychological Consequences of Isolation," *National Prison Project Journal* (ACLU)(Spring 1993):3.

26. Miller, *Search and Destroy,* 227.

27. Ibid.

28. My usage of this term follows Terry Kuper's suggestion that entire populations are being "disappeared" from U. S. society via the prison system.

SEVEN

Young Black Americans and the Criminal Justice System

MARC MAUER

In 1990 The Sentencing Project released a report that documented that almost one in four (23 percent) African American males in the age group twenty to twenty-nine years old was under some form of criminal justice supervision—in prison or jail, on probation or parole.[1] That report received extensive national attention and helped to generate much dialogue and activity on the part of policymakers, community organizations, and criminal justice professionals.

Despite these efforts, many of the factors contributing to the high rates of criminal justice control for African American males remained unchanged or worsened during the succeeding five years. Public policies ostensibly designed to control crime and drug abuse had in many respects contributed to the growing racial disparity in the criminal justice system while having little impact on the problems they were aimed to address.

Thus, by 1995 we saw the following:

- Almost one in three (32.2 percent) young black men in the age group 20 to 29 was under criminal justice supervision on any given day—in prison or jail, on probation or parole.
- The cost of criminal justice control for these 827,440 young African American males was about $6 billion a year.
- In recent years African American women have experienced the greatest increase in criminal justice supervision of all demographic groups, with their rate of criminal justice supervision rising by 78 percent from 1989 to1994.
- Drug policies constitute the single most significant factor contributing to the rise in criminal justice populations in recent years, with the number of incarcerated drug offenders having risen by 510 percent from 1983 to 1993. The number of black (non-Hispanic) women incarcerated in state prisons for drug offenses increased more than eightfold—828 percent—from 1986 to 1991.
- While African American arrest rates for violent crime—45 percent of arrests nationally—are disproportionate to their share of the population, this proportion has not changed significantly for twenty years. For drug offenses, though, the African American proportion of arrests increased from 24 percent in 1980 to 39 percent in 1993, well above the African American proportion of drug users nationally.
- African Americans and Hispanics constitute almost 90 percent of offenders sentenced to state prison for drug possession.

These new criminal justice control rates are even more disturbing than the earlier rates. Combined with the potential impact of current social and criminal justice policies, they attest to the gravity of the crisis facing the African American community. The current high rates of criminal justice control are also likely to worsen considerably over the next several years. In addition to the steady twenty-five year increase in criminal justice populations, the impact of current "get-tough" policies in particular suggests continuing increases in criminal justice control rates and increasing racially disparate impacts.

THE "WAR ON DRUGS"
AND INCREASED ARRESTS

While debate will continue on the degree to which the criminal justice system overall contributes to racial disparities, there is increasing evidence that the set of policies and practices contained within the phrase "war on drugs" has been an unmitigated disaster for young blacks and other minorities. Whether these policies were designed consciously or unconsciously to incarcerate more minorities is a question that may be debated. In essence, though, what we have seen are policy choices that have not only failed to reduce the scale of the problem but have seriously eroded the life prospects of the primary targets of those policies. The following text discusses the main elements of these policies.

Arrest policies beginning in the 1980s have disproportionately affected African Americans and other minorities: first, through greatly increased numbers of drug arrests; and second, through an increased rate of minority drug arrests. Drug arrests increased dramatically in the 1980s, rising from 471,000 in 1980 to 1,247,000 by 1989.[2] As the number of arrests grew, so did the proportion of African Americans, from 24 percent of all drug arrests in 1980 to 39 percent by 1993.[3]

Some persons would contend that African Americans are arrested in larger numbers because of their higher rates of drug use and sales. There are no reliable data on the overall composition of drug sellers in the total population, but we have reasonably good data available on drug possession through the annual household surveys of the National Institute on Drug Abuse (NIDA). Data for 1993 reveal that African Americans comprised 13 percent of monthly drug users, compared to the 1993 drug arrest proportion of 39 percent. Even if we only consider arrests for drug possession, which should be reflective of drug use, African Americans still constitute 34.7 percent of such arrests. Although the NIDA surveys have some limitations,[4] the degree of disparity between drug use and drug possession arrests is of such magnitude that it clearly points to disproportionate arrest practices.

A recent analysis by criminologists James Lynch and William Sabol points to additional significant racial effects of law enforcement practices.[5] Lynch and Sabol analyzed data on incarceration rates, race, and class during the period 1979 to 1991. They identified inmates as either being "underclass" or "non-underclass" (working class or middle class) based on educational levels, employment history, and income and concluded that the most significant increase in incarceration rates was for working-class black drug offenders, whose rates increased six-fold, from 1.5 per 1,000 in 1979, to match that of underclass blacks at 9 per 1,000 in 1991. The trends for whites, on the other hand, were just the opposite, with the underclass drug incarceration rate being double that of the non-underclass by 1991.

Lynch and Sabol suggest several factors that may explain these trends. The "spillover" effect of residential racial segregation, along with law enforcement targeting of black neighborhoods, may sweep more non-underclass blacks into the criminal justice system than is the case in the more stratified white housing patterns. They conclude that:

> All of the processes described . . . lead to the same result, an increased targeting of black working and middle class areas for discretionary drug enforcement and ultimately increased incarceration for drug offenses. The immunity that working and middle class status used to bring in the black community (and still does among whites) may have been lost. While the processes that produced these outcomes may not have been racially motivated in intent, they have resulted in racially disparate outcomes.[6]

PROSECUTION AND SENTENCING POLICIES

Aggravating the racial disparities in arrest patterns are decisions made by prosecutors that can increase the severity of the impact of drug policies on minorities. A 1995 survey of prosecutions for crack cocaine offenses conducted by the *Los Angeles Times* revealed that not a single white offender had been convicted of a crack cocaine offense in the federal courts serving the Los Angeles metropolitan area since 1986, despite the fact that whites comprise a majority of crack users.[7] During the same period, though, hundreds of white crack traffickers were prosecuted in state courts. While federal prosecutors contend that they target high-level

TABLE 7.1
DRUG OFFENDERS IN PRISON AND JAIL,
1983 AND 1993

	TOTAL NO. OF INMATES		% DRUG OFFENDERS		NO. DRUG OFFENDERS	
Year	1983	1993	1983	1993	1983	1993
Jail	223,552	459,804	9.3%	23.0%	20,790	105,755
Federal Prison	31,926	89,586	27.6%	60.8%	8,812	54,468
State Prison	405,322	859,295	7.0%	22.5%	28,373	193,341
Total	660,800	1,408,685	8.8%	25.1%	57,975	353,564

traffickers, the *Times* analysis found that many African Americans charged in federal court were low-level dealers or accomplices in the drug trade. The consequences of this prosecutorial discretion are quite serious because federal mandatory sentencing laws require five- and ten-year minimums even for first offenders. The study found that whites charged with crack offenses and prosecuted in California state courts received sentences as much as eight years less than in the federal courts.

Compounding the higher arrest rates for drug offenses have been changes in sentencing policies that also have affected African Americans disproportionately. The advent of a renewed generation of mandatory minimum sentencing statutes, now in place in all states and in the federal system, has led to dramatic increases in the number of incarcerated drug offenders.

The impact of these policies can be seen in several ways. First, the risk of incarceration per drug arrest increased more than 400 percent from 19 per 100,000 in 1980 to 104 per 100,000 by 1992, far greater than for any other offense during that period.[8] As will be seen, this has led to a 510 percent increase in the number of incarcerated drug offenders between 1983 and 1993, with one out of four inmates now serving time or awaiting trial for a drug offense.

The full impact of these policies has yet to be seen, since many of the mandatory sentences only began to be applied in large numbers in the late 1980s and 1990s. In state prison systems, therefore, while average time served in prison has not changed appreciably in recent years, we can expect it to rise in the future due to the impact of mandatory sentencing and other harsh policies.

In the federal system, the impact of these changes is already being felt, with the average time served by drug offenders increasing 50 percent, from twenty-two months in 1986 to thirty-three months by 1992. Compounding this has been the much-discussed disparity in sentencing between crack cocaine and powder cocaine, whereby those persons convicted of crack possession receive a mandatory prison term of five years by possessing only one one hundredth of the quantity of crack cocaine as those charged with powder cocaine possession. Fourteen states also have statutes that distinguish between crack and powder cocaine in sentencing.[9] The U.S. Sentencing Commission found that blacks accounted for 84.5 percent of federal crack possession convictions in 1993 while comprising 38 percent of those who report using crack in the past year.[10] The Sentencing Commission also has calculated that a person convicted of trafficking in five grams of crack with a maximum retail value of $750 will receive the same sentence as an offender charged with selling 500 grams of powder cocaine retailing for $50,000.[11]

Thus, the cumulative impact of arrest and sentencing policies on African Americans has led to severe disproportions in rates of incarceration. Looking at minorities overall, we find that African Americans and Hispanics represented almost 90 percent of all sentences to state prison for drug possession offenses in 1992. While we have no available data regarding other factors that often correlate with a higher likelihood of incarceration, particularly prior criminal record, these findings are of such magnitude that they raise serious questions about the racial implications of current drug policies.

AFRICAN AMERICAN MALES
AND ECONOMIC OPPORTUNITY

As we have seen, increasingly larger numbers of African American males have come under criminal justice supervision as a result of drug offenses. Despite the national concern about drugs, the nature of the drug distribution process and the individuals involved in it remain poorly understood.

Several recent studies provide insight into the lives of young men who become involved in the drug trade. A 1990 study by Peter Reuter and colleagues at RAND examined the criminal histories and demographic characteristics of groups of young black males arrested for drug distribution in Washington, D.C.; black males represent the overwhelming majority of persons arrested for that offense.[12] The researchers documented the extent to which drug dealing has become a source of income for this group, with fully one-sixth of the black males born in 1967 having an arrest for drug distribution by the age of twenty; it is projected that one-quarter would have an arrest by the age of twenty-nine. Somewhat surprisingly, though, the study found that about two-thirds of the offenders had been employed at the time of arrest, primarily at low-wage jobs with a median income of $800 a month. Thus, drug dealing became a type of "moon-lighting" for some of these young men, with the daily sellers achieving median earnings of $2,000 a month in drug sales.

Similarly, Samuel Myers, Jr., of the University of Minnesota, has examined the potential for increasing legitimate wages earned by drug sellers as a means of reducing criminal activity.[13] Analyzing data from inmate surveys, Myers found that whites incarcerated for drug dealing had significantly higher legal wages than blacks relative to their illegal earnings. He concludes that "the dominant factor contributing to drug selling, especially among black males, is unattractive labor market opportunities."[14]

Finally, research by criminologist John Hagedorn of the University of Wisconsin-Milwaukee on African American and Latino gangs and drug dealing in Milwaukee has found great variation both in the extent to which gang members were involved in drug dealing and in their orientation toward conventional lifestyles.[15] While a small proportion of gang members were committed to drug dealing as a career, the majority "were not firmly committed to the drug economy." The main character-istics that they shared were: working regularly at legitimate jobs, with occasional drug dealing; conventional aspirations toward economic security; and conventional ethical beliefs about the immorality of drug dealing, even while justifying their drug sales as necessary for survival.[16]

The findings of these studies reveal the potential effectiveness of various responses to drug dealing. The RAND researchers found that

despite the actual and perceived risks of drug dealing in Washington—
the chances of arrest or physical harm being significant—"such risks
failed to deter substantial numbers of young males from participating in
the trade."[17] They speculate that the lure of immediate rewards combined with adolescents' lesser concern for physical harm and/or their
future prospects combined to make drug selling very appealing and
conclude that: "The prospects for raising actual and perceived risks
enough to make for markedly more deterrence through heavier enforcement against sellers do not appear promising."[18] Noting that many drug
sellers are also users who feel compelled to sell drugs to support their
addiction, the researchers suggest that reducing demand is critical if the
rewards of the legitimate labor market are to be viewed as attractive.

Hagedorn asks whether current drug policies are actually producing
criminogenic effects by reducing the prospects of these young gang
members for productive employment and life experiences, since the "key
to their future lies in building social capital that comes from steady
employment and a supportive relationship, without the constant threat
of incarceration."[19] He concludes that:

> Long and mandatory prison terms for use and intent to sell cocaine
> lump those who are committed to the drug economy with those who
> are using or are selling in order to survive. Our prisons are filled
> disproportionately with minority drug offenders . . . who in essence
> are being punished for the "crime" of not accepting poverty or of being
> addicted to cocaine. Our data suggest that jobs, more accessible drug
> treatment, alternative sentences, or even decriminalization of nonvio-
> lent drug offenses would be better approaches than the iron fist of the
> war on drugs.[20]

CONCLUSION

If the goal of public policy in recent years had been to incarcerate record
numbers of black Americans, then that policy would have been a
tremendous success. But if the goal was to make our streets safer and to
build strong families and communities, then public policy has been a
dramatic failure. In order to move public policy along, it would be useful

to ask ourselves how the nation would react if nearly one in three young white men were under some form of criminal justice control. We can only speculate, of course, but there are some historical examples to inform us. In the 1960s and 1970s, for example, the country experienced substantial changes in both marijuana use and public policy regarding its use. As white middle-class Americans began to use marijuana in large numbers, public attitudes and policy changed, generally becoming much more tolerant. In some jurisdictions, personal possession of marijuana was either decriminalized or essentially ignored by the police. Nothing about the drug itself had changed, only the composition of the "offenders" using it.

Rescuing a generation of young black men and women from the various social ills that confront them will not be easy, quick, or accomplished without many pitfalls along the way. But if the task is to be completed eventually, it would behoove us to learn from the mistakes of recent years and to begin implementing a strategy that will ensure that the next generation of children will face a future filled with greater opportunity and promise.

NOTES

This essay is excerpted from Marc Mauer and Tracy Huling, "Young Black Americans and the Criminal Justice System: Five Years Later," The Sentencing Project, 1995. Washington, D. C.

1. Marc Mauer, "Young Black Men and the Criminal Justice System: A Growing National Problem," The Sentencing Project, February 1990. Washington, D. C.
2. "Drugs and Crime Facts, 1990," Bureau of Justice Statistics, 1991. Department of Justice, Washington, D. C.
3. FBI, *Uniform Crime Reports,* various years. Department of Justice, Washington, D. C.
4. As a household survey of drug abuse, the NIDA data do not include institutionalized persons, homeless people not living in a shelter, and people with less stable residences generally. Therefore, low-income African Americans may be undercounted in these surveys.
5. James P. Lynch and William J. Sabol, "The Use of Coercive Social Control and Changes in the Race and Class Composition of U.S. Prison Populations," Paper presented at the American Society of Criminology, November 9, 1994.
6. Ibid., 30.
7. Dan Weikel, "War on Crack Targets Minorities Over Whites," *Los Angeles Times,* May 21, 1995, 1.
8. Allen J. Beck and Peter M. Brien, "Trends in U.S. Correctional Populations: Recent Findings from the Bureau of Justice Statistics," in Kenneth C. Haas and Geoffrey P. Alpert, eds., *The Dilemmas of Corrections* (Waveland Press, 1995). Project Heights, IL.

9. United States Sentencing Commission, *Cocaine and Federal Sentencing Policy,* February 1995, 129-34. Washington, D. C.

10. Ibid., 156.

11. Ibid., 175.

12. Peter Reuter, Robert MacCoun, and Patrick Murphy, "Money from Crime: A Study of the Economics of Drug Dealing in Washington, D.C.," RAND, June 1990. Santa Monica, CA.

13. Samuel L. Myers, Jr., "Crime, Entrepreneurship, and Labor Force Withdrawal," *Contemporary Policy Issues* 10, no. 2 (April 1992).

14. Ibid., 96.

15. John M. Hagedorn, "Homeboys, Dope Fiends, Legits, and New Jacks," *Criminology* 32, no. 2 (May 1994): 197-219.

16. Ibid., 209.

17. Reuter, MacCoun, and Murphy, *Money from Crime,* xiii.

18. Ibid.

19. Hagedorn, "Homeboys, Dope Fiends, Legits, and New Jacks," 215.

20. Ibid., 216.

EIGHT

The New Black Leadership: Gang-Related?

SALIM MUWAKKIL

One warm October morning in 1993, an event happened that shook Chicago's civic leaders to the marrow of their bones. An orderly but enthusiastic crowd of at least 10,000 protesters, mostly African American youths, descended on the city's Loop to demand a permanent solutions to the problem of funding Chicago's public schools. The huge protest literally shut down city business for the day—except, of course, the police department, which was out in all of its glowering glory. The city of big shoulders was virtually quaking in its boots, stymied and stunned by two pressing questions: Where did these people come from? And, more important, who was in control? Both of those questions zero in on what is one of the most important, although rarely acknowledged, issues for the African American community in the twenty-first century: the problem of leadership.

The crowd was not just orderly, it was disciplined. That was unusual in itself for such a massive gathering, but considering the fact that most of the protesters were black, inner-city youth, it was downright eerie. "Gang-related" is the tag usually affixed to such people in the media. They routinely are portrayed as feral, larcenous, and lethal and usually are greeted with disdain and disgust by mainstream America. But that day they provoked awe and perhaps some respect. For many of these youths, that was a lot more appealing than the scornful stares they usually faced.

Chicago's shaken city fathers—and mothers—quickly realized their need to get to the bottom of the protest and prevent a repeat performance. Progressive theorists and activists were rubbing their eyes in astonishment at the unexpected spectacle of grass-roots organizing success; it seemed to have sprung from nowhere. Veteran community organizers also were taken aback by the sudden swarm of new allies in the struggle for education funding equity. They were grateful but wary. While many activists found it difficult not to be delighted by a spurt of youth activism, they also were suspicious of the neophyte protesters— with their baggy pants and surly expressions.

The police, on the other hand, were unequivocal in their distaste for the demonstration. It was gang initiated, gang led, and nothing but a sleazy attempt to legitimize the gang's criminal activities, as they saw it. The gang the police blamed was the Gangster Disciples, or GDs, Chicago's largest street gang. The GDs' ranks have extended far beyond Chicago's borders. According to police officials, GDs can claim thousands of members, and a significant percentage of the inmates currently in Illinois prisons are GDs. The "chairman" of this expanding empire is a middle-age man named Larry Hoover who currently is incarcerated in a federal facility. In fact, Hoover has been in Illinois jails since 1974, during which time he's managed to solidify his leadership. When he entered prison on a murder charge at twenty-three, he was illiterate. During his incarceration he has earned several degrees and a reputation as a street soldier who rose to the top of the murderous gang underground by dint of his own personality. He has enhanced his leadership even in prison and has evolved into an authentic ghetto philosopher propounding a new message. In the mid-1980s he composed a manifesto that he titled "The Blueprint," which originally was distributed among his followers within the Illinois prison system but promptly spread beyond. The ambitious work is an idealistic mixture of metaphysics, black nationalism, and community activism.

Part of Hoover's blueprint was to create a "legitimate" political arm of the GDs, and in 1990 he created a group called 21st Century VOTE

(Voters Organized for Total Empowerment). And it was the work of 21st Century VOTE that put the fear of God into those Loop denizens that day in 1993. Without a doubt, the spectacular display of civic concern helped accelerate negotiations regarding school funding. A smaller protest of about 4,000 people turned out a few weeks later to demonstrate their concern about the state legislature's attempt to cut healthcare benefits for welfare recipients; the bill stalled in committee. Although many activists were uneasy with the group, there was wide agreement that the tactic of deploying thousands of organized human bodies was an important new weapon in the progressive arsenal. During the campaigns for the 1994 elections, 21st Century VOTE troops were busy registering voters and working for some of the candidates. Two candidates for alderman with explicit GD ties (Hal Baskin in the Sixteenth District and Wallace "Gator" Bradley in the Third) ran against two black incumbents. Those races were watched closely to determine if 21st Century VOTE's influence extended from the streets into the voting booth. It didn't; both GD-connected candidates lost. But the group continued to demonstrate its influence, implementing block clean-up campaigns and other community-oriented activities.

Within a year after the election, the group branched out to concert promotion and brought a number of high-profile entertainers to Chicago. It created a small-scale apparel business called "Ghetto Prisoner." Hoover made a guest appearance on the 1996 album entitled *The Resurrection* by the rap group Geto Boys; in it he outlined his new philosophy and the group touted his clothing line. The Ghetto Prisoner company employed hundreds of Chicago's unemployed youth in legitimate enterprises until the feds shut it down, partly in an attempt to control the GDs economic power.

But the GDs also control the distribution and availability of marijuana, crack cocaine, and heroin in a large swatch of Chicago's South Side. Unfortunately, that drug commerce is the most vital sign of market capitalism in many of the blighted neighborhoods in which the GDs ply their trade. The underground economy employs a high proportion of the community youth; after their invariable busts and incarcerations they enter a cycle of gang affiliations that are relentlessly reinforcing. With 21st Century VOTE, Hoover sought to interrupt that cycle—gently. In

"The Blueprint," he urged his acolytes to get knowledge and become community builders. Of course he knew it was not that easy. We all know it is not easy, but that is not the point. The point is: What is the alternative?

Law enforcement officials refuse to grant any legitimacy to movements like the one exemplified by Hoover's 21st Century VOTE. And while it is clear that police have a vested interest in exaggerating the danger gangs pose, seldom is that interest publicly acknowledged. In the Associated Press, where I got my start in journalism, we were taught that a crime did not really happen unless we added the phrase "police said" to ensure credibility. One of the things that helped me understand the structural biases of mainstream journalism was my own hard-earned knowledge that police I grew up knowing were as apt to lie as anyone else. They were hardly arbiters of veracity. But often the police are required to mend ruptures in the social fabric and to perform other tasks for which they are spectacularly ill-equipped. For that I have some sympathy for them. While reporting on the gang truce movement I have had some conversations with Chicago police gang unit commander Robert Guthrie. This was his assessment of that nationwide movement to end the carnage of gang violence: "We're impeding the flow of narcotics and these gangbangers just want us out of Dodge City, that's all." Commander Guthrie thought that 21st Century VOTE was merely an attempt to intimidate political officials into granting Hoover parole. The commander completely dismissed any claim that the group had wholesome civic motives. It was financed by drug money, he said; the young people who gathered at the varied protests were ordered to attend or get beat down, he insisted.

As police often do (indeed, must do), Gunthrie excluded the context. The context includes what we do to frame the choices of these young African Americans. We confine black youth to resource-poor, postindustrial moonscapes, we then woefully miseducate them with undemanding teachers so that they have no marketable skills and even less self-esteem; we then imprison them for plying their trade in the underground economy. They are virtually compelled to seek fortune in illegitimate commerce and then punished for making the most logical economic decisions. With few groups like the Boy Scouts or

Boys Clubs or, like in my day, the Police Athletic League or PAL, available in many inner city neighborhoods, black youths are being criminalized for associating in the only fraternal options available: street gangs. It is a classic bind. Urban black youths are tracked into social marginality by structural economic forces and then are condemned for not picking themselves up by their bootstraps.

The injustice of such a system really is quite obvious to anyone who impartially examines the data. So, the question is: Why do we tolerate it? Well, we are culturally inclined to accept the idea that African Americans are disproportionately criminal. Since the end of the Civil War black people, men especially, have been relentlessly criminalized. Even before slavery's end white doctors diagnosed blacks' desire for freedom as psychologically deviant. The word "draptomania" was coined to describe an ailment of which the symptoms were repeated attempts to escape slavery. A survey of the popular media from 1901 to 1912 conducted by historian Rayford Logan found that the words "brutes," "savages," "imbecile," and "moral degenerates" were routinely used in popular media to describe African Americans. If you peruse contemporary writing on streetgangs, you would discover many of the same words.

But this historical twinning of blacks and crime is even more fundamental than we commonly think. The Thirteenth Amendment of the Constitution reads: "Neither slavery nor involuntary servitude, except as punishment for a crime whereof the party shall have been duly convicted, shall exist within the United States, or any place subject to their jurisdiction." Although this law purportedly abolished slavery, it simply took the peculiar institution of chattel slavery out of the hands of the individual white entrepreneur and made it an exclusive government monopoly. And after the Emancipation Proclamation freed anyone who was a slave, the Thirteenth Amendment required the southern states to catch the former slave involved in a crime; then they were permitted to enslave the person again, even if they had to invent a crime. Thus, imprisonment was a method southern states used to defy the imperial dictates of the abolitionist North.

In a real sense, this meant that to be free and black in the South was a criminal offense. But the equation of melanin with criminality was and is not limited to that region below the Mason and Dixon line; it is a national phenomena. It was common for Americans to think of African Americans as inherently inclined toward criminality, and that image still dominates. That was one reason for the tremendous unease inspired by 21st Century Vote's protest march. In fact, city officials were so uneasy that they pushed through an "antiloitering" ordinance that allowed police to arrest any gathering of youth they chose. This blatantly unconstitutional piece of legislation has since been struck down on constitutional grounds. But, encouraged by their fearful constituents, many city officials remain convinced that such stringent law enforcement tactics are absolutely appropriate. Chicagoans, like most Americans, are fed a consistent media diet of black crime and depravity because the media's job is to help mold a cultural consensus that rationalizes the status quo. For example, landmark studies of television published by communications scholar Robert Entman concluded that Chicago television news programs promote racial anxiety and antagonism by treating black and white criminal suspects in markedly different ways.[1] These striking differences in treatment demonstrated a clear media bias. Initially, media commentators lauded Entman's work and bemoaned its dismal conclusion. Then they ignored it. Most African Americans could have provided a critique that echoes Professor Entman's findings, but their complaints increasingly are falling on deaf ears. The mainstream media, reflecting the sentiments of society in general, are losing patience with complaining black folks. "Stop whining!" shout commentators, when African Americans or Latinos complain of race-specific insults and injuries.

The parallel between slavery and this current incarceration epidemic also manifests itself in prison labor. Despite international opposition to (and hypocritical congressional denouncement of) prison labor, the U.S. Justice Department flagrantly indulges in the practice and currently is pushing for a bigger share of the prison labor market. The government earns $500 billion per year producing products from paint brushes, to prescription eyewear, to Patriot missile parts from prison labor for a fraction of what it would cost to have these items produced through a "free" or nonprison enterprise. Since 1990 thirty states have legalized the contracting out of prison labor to private companies.

In Arizona, 10 percent of all inmates work for private companies and make less than minimum wage. Prisoners test blood for major medical firms and raise hogs for John's Meats. In New Mexico, prisoners take hotel reservations by phone. In Ohio, inmates do data entry; they made Honda parts as well, until political pressure from labor unions forced an end to that particular arrangement. Spalding golf balls are packed by imprisoned labor in Hawaii. In Texas, inmates held in a private prison owned by the Wackenhut Corporation build and fix circuit boards for L.T.I., a subcontractor that supplies companies such as Dell, IBM, and Texas Instruments. Toys R Us occasionally uses prison labor to restock its shelves.

Clearly the economic incentives to institutionalize these labor benefits are growing. Already the budget to construct this prison industrial complex has grown to $32 billion, and that means big profits for many businesses. The hiring and training of correctional workers is one of the fastest growing areas in government.[2] More than 600,000 full-time employees worked in corrections in 1995, more than in any Fortune 500 company except General Motors. And the numbers continue to rise.

In addition, private prisons are a flourishing growth industry. One of the hottest stocks on Wall Street is that of the aforementioned Wackenhut Corrections Corp., the country's largest private prison management firm. The company's stock soared 203 percent in 1995 over 1994's earnings; the company continues to expect strong profits for future years. The stocks of other private prison firms also have undergone healthy growth; most even have outperformed the cybercentric, high-tech stocks that are fueling the stock market. Young African Americans and Latinos are the chief raw materials for this burgeoning growth industry. And as they are siphoned into this corrections complex, they are being extracted from their communities at the primary age of family formation. Their possibilities for gainful employment are reduced considerably, thereby making them less attractive as marriage partners and unable to provide for children they father. This in turn contributes to the deepening of poverty in low-income communities. They are politically disenfranchised and thus are less likely to take an interest in political affairs.

The incarceration epidemic accelerates community decay in other ways as well. As prison becomes a common experience for young males, its stigmatizing effect is diminished. That already was beginning to happen during my coming-of-age in the 1960s. From how a person held his hands or assumed his boxing stance, we could tell from what detention facility he had "graduated." It was a mark of distinction in my 'hood to box as if you went to Annandale reform school in southern New Jersey or Warwick in upstate New York. Just the assumption of a particular fighting posture was sometimes enough to bluff your way out of an actual fight. Reform school alumni were accorded extra deference. And that was thirty-five years ago. But further, gang or crime group affiliations on the outside may be reinforced within the prison only to emerge stronger as the individuals are released back to the community. Listen to a rap record these days, especially gangsta rap—the subgenre that focuses on life in the underground economy made possible and profitable by the war on drugs— and you will find that most of the slang is based on prison vernacular. The term "one love" the popular saying "It's all good," and many other slogans and by-words of hip-hop culture get their start in the yard. The baggy-jeans style of dress was born in the prisons of southern California. In fact, hip-hop culture offers us an extraordinary glimpse into the shared expectations and aspirations of urban black youth, and it is a culture saturated with jail signifiers.

With jobless communities increasingly becoming the norm, as pointed out in sociologist William Julius Wilson's *When Work Disappears,*[3] there are few males in these inner city neighborhoods with stable ties to the labor market, so ex-inmates (and the culture they represent) tend to serve as role models for community youth whether we like it or not. That's why self-righteous fulminations against their attraction tend to be ineffective. That's why many of us who stay in touch with the streets appreciate the new thinking of Larry Hoover and other folks, like Sanyika Shakur—also known as "Monster" Kody Scott. With so many black youth matriculating from penitentiaries, it is better that their royalty profess positive ideals than do not.

Unfortunately, 21st Century VOTE was deeply crippled by a federal sting operation that wound up charging Hoover with narcotics trafficking from jail. Although none of the group's principals was ever charged with a crime, the organization was deemed a gang front, monitored, and harassed virtually out of business. Although Tom Harris, the titular president, insists the group soon will be resurrected, prospects look dim.

21st Century VOTE represented one shining moment of possibility for African American organizers. In Chicago organizers are attempting to bring the leadership of 21st Century VOTE into the activist orbit, as they learn more effective ways of reaching the hardcore youth traditionally attracted to street gangs to tap their crucial energy.

This is the youthful energy that was captured so effectively by the early Black Panther Party, particularly by Fred Hampton's Chicago branch.* Now this energy is being siphoned away from the black community by an ever encroaching jail-industrial complex that epitomizes the scavenger ethic at the heart of capitalism. That insatiable complex requires the raw material of young black and brown bodies, and society continues to track our precious resources into its gaping maw. Without intervention—effective, not theoretical intervention—that dynamic will persist. Hoover and others like him represent the possibility of effective intervention, and we would be fools not to exploit that resource.

NOTES

1. See Robert Entman, "Representation and Reality in the Portrayal of Blacks on Network Television News," *Journalism Quarterly* 71 no. 3 (Fall 1994): 509; and Entman, "Blacks in the News: Television, Modern Racism and Cultural Change," *Journalism Quarterly* 69 no. 2 (Summer 1992): 341-361.
2. See "Correctional Populations," Washington, D. C., U. S. Census Bureau and Bureau of Justice Statistics, 1996 update.
3. William Julius Wilson, *When Work Disappears: The World of the New Urban Poor* (New York: Random House, 1996).

---

* Ed.: Twenty-one-year-old Fred Hampton and fellow Panther leader Mark Clark were executed in a COINTELPRO operation in December 1969 by Chicago police assisted by the FBI. The U. S. government later awarded over $1 million to their families for their wrongful deaths.

NINE

Black Women and Gangs

ADRIEN K. WING

The gang phenomenon has become synonymous with black male criminality, and societal solutions have emphasized increased incarceration of these men. The gang problem cannot be resolved unless policymakers, academics, and the media provide more balanced attention to these affected groups. This chapter contributes to this process by focusing on black women, using an innovative legal jurisprudence known as critical race feminism (CRF) that emphasizes the theoretical and practical concerns of women of color under the law.

ROLES OF BLACK WOMEN IN THE GANG REALM

Black women's association with gangs can be conceptualized in eight different ways, falling into two different categories: women as gang members and women who affect gang members. Within the first category there are four identifiable roles: (1) females who are members of female gangs; (2) females in auxiliaries to male gangs; (3) females in sexually integrated gangs; and (4) females who are not actual gang members but want to be. In the second category there are also four roles: (1) girlfriends and wives of male gang members; (2) mothers of gang members' children; (3) blood relatives of gang members; and (4) concerned women in the gang-affected community. These roles are representative of the multiple identities of black women and often occur simultaneously. While female gang members are in the minority, they are a significant component of the total gang problem.[1] The female gang members commit acts equally as violent as their male counterparts, and such violence is expected to increase.[2]

Initiations begin the violent episode of gang life for females. Many girls are jumped-in, which means they must prove themselves by fighting multiple gang members simultaneously.[3] Another possible violent initiation occurs when girls scar their own faces using a razor blade.[4] Equally as damaging are the initiations in integrated or auxiliary gangs that involve being sexed-in; during such initiations the girls have no choice as to which male gang members or how many of them they will have sex with.[5] In some instances there is no consent and the girl is gang raped. This physical and sexual abuse often results in increased violence as the girls respond by becoming even more violent in an effort to regain some control over their lives.

Another response to the subordination that occurs within integrated and auxiliary gangs is the growth of all-female gangs.[6] Independent, autonomous female gangs do exist[7] and function separately from males and male gangs. More common, however, is the auxiliary female gang that is affiliated with and takes its name from an existing male gang.[8] One researcher found that it is the "male gang that paves the way for the female affiliate and opens the door into many illegitimate opportunities."[9] The Sex Girls, a female auxiliary to a male group, even went to rumbles and fought alongside the men.[10] Black females also participate in sexually integrated gangs. These "coed" gangs are predominantly male; usually females are excluded from decision-making roles;[11] however, in rare instances females have achieved leadership status over the males. On the periphery of each of these gangs are the "wannabes," who aspire to gang membership. These may be children who are pretending to be gang members, by wearing certain clothing and using gang hand signs, with no real intention of joining the gang, or they may be recruits who are or will become active in the gang.[12]

In all three types of female gangs, girl gang members are committing crimes, including murder, felonious assault, armed robbery, and even rape or sexual battery. The rate at which females are committing violent crimes is rising at approximately twice the rate as for males.[13] The arrest rates for females committing property crimes also has increased more than the rate for males.

In light of the increasing violence and number of crimes perpetrated by female gang members, their affiliation with gangs must be examined more thoroughly. Similarly, the environment and the families of these black female gang members must be analyzed for a more comprehensive approach to developing preventive measures.

African American females can exert influence and affect the lives of gang members in any of four main roles: as mothers and blood relatives of both male and female gang members, as the wives and girlfriends of male gang members, as the mothers of male gang members' children; and as other women within the community who are concerned for the well-being of these gang-affected youth and for their communities. African American females in each of these roles have the potential to affect the gang members' activities and to alter the negative impact of gangs on their communities.

Mothers have the potential of playing the most important role in a gang member's life. As mothers, these women are primarily responsible for nurturing, supervising, and educating their children. Given the shortage of males within the black community, due to over-incarceration, a majority of these women are single parents who are struggling at the poverty level in a violent environment. Many of these mothers are doing everything possible to give their children the emotional, financial, and spiritual attention they need, and they are shocked, appalled, and then finally resigned when street life claims their children. Some mothers may be unable to provide such nurturing for their children because they themselves are involved in criminal behavior and drug use; they may be too over-whelmed by their own circumstances to deal with the problems their children face. Yet these women still can be a positive influence and aid in preventing gang violence whether through parent-based community groups or by exerting individual control over their own children.

Other blood relatives of gang members also can play positive roles in preventing and discouraging gang affiliation and gang violence. Sisters, daughters, aunts, and cousins can provide support and a sense of family to gang members, emotional ties that will help diminish dependency on gang association and may induce gang members to leave the gang life.[14]

Girlfriends and wives of male gang members can be influential in convincing them to leave the gang and lead traditional, noncriminal lifestyles as well. Such women often have been called both the cause and the cure of much gang violence. Many fights within and between gangs are attributable to women, who are often seen as the "property" of the gang and as the "prize" for which they are fighting. Yet these women can and have used their influence to affect gang members in a more positive way. As one gang member stated, "If it wasn't for [his wife] . . . , [he would] be dead or in the penitentiary, or a whole lot of other people would be dead."[15]

In addition, black women can exert influence over the lives of gang members as the mothers of gang members' children. Many male gang members have multiple children by one or more women and see procreation as an indicator of masculinity. Some mothers of gang members' children are gang members themselves. The rapper Ice-T describes his daughter's mother as a "Criplette" who was "down" with the Hoover Crips (Los Angeles) when they met.[16] These women can affect their children's fathers by encouraging them to take responsibility for their actions, to provide for their children, and to be good fathers.

One other role that black women play in relation to the gang realm is that of concerned citizens. These are the women who live in or work in these communities and are affected by the negative impact that gangs can have. Other women are not physically connected with the gang problems of the inner city but nonetheless care what happens to these areas and to the children and families living there. Many women such as educators, scholars, and journalists are genuinely concerned about the problems associated with gang violence. These women can affect gang members by helping to find better solutions to the gang problem and by implementing such solutions within the gang-affected communities.

Thus far gang literature has ignored the multiple roles that black women play with respect to gang members. Researchers seldom mention gang members' mothers and or children. Yet these are the women who will have the greatest affect on the lives of gang members.

Their significance should not be ignored; rather these women should be utilized to create more effective approaches to restoring gang-affected communities.

TOWARD A CRITICAL RACE FEMINIST THEORY OF GANG INVOLVEMENT AND CRIMINALITY

The classic theoretical explanations of gang involvement and criminality have focused primarily on males. This male-centered analysis is purportedly a result of the predominance of males in gangs and criminal activity. Theories that do focus on females tend to ignore racial and ethnic factors. Thus no theoretical explanation addresses the multiple perspectives of the black female gang member.

Since Frederick Thrasher's classic study of gangs in Chicago,[17] sociologists and criminologists have devoted much of their efforts to researching and analyzing the gang phenomenon. Many theories focus on juvenile delinquency. One of the most prevalent theories addresses the concept of subculture. Robert Merton's strain theory provides a foundation for the subculture theories by recognizing that within the lower social and economic classes, there exist structural impediments to success that result in criminal activity.[18] Albert Cohen extended this idea to subcultures, stating that delinquent gang activity was a group solution to the frustrations experienced by lower- class males.[19] Walter B. Miller posits that the gang is a normal aspect of lower-class life and is a norm within that subculture.[20] Modern structural-behavioral theorists, such as William Julius Wilson, argue that factors such as unemployment, poverty, and in some cases racial or gender oppression are the basis for the problems in black communities and have resulted in the development of an "underclass."[21] Some have argued that "underclass" African American males have adapted to structural oppression by modifying their values and their culture.[22] A related theory is Edwin Sutherland's differential association theory, based on cultural transmission. His thesis is that delinquency is learned through association and interaction with lawbreakers.[23] Similarly, social learning theory suggests that juveniles learn delinquent behavior and that their behavior is reinforced through social interaction.[24]

All of these theories could be applicable to females but most researchers have chosen to focus on males. One researcher, Ruth Morris, did apply the structural strain theory to female delinquents and surmised that a deviant subculture did not exist for females.[25] Other applications of traditional theories to females have resulted in flawed biological and sex-role theories.[26] Some more recent theories have argued that increased opportunities for and the "liberation" of women has resulted in increases in female criminality.[27] Similarly, researchers Dorie Klein and June Kress contend that economic factors and the historical social position of women must be examined to explain female crime. They claim that "women's lack of participation in 'big time' crime highlights the larger class structure of sexism that is reproduced in the illegitimate marketplace."[28]

After surveying the traditional and more recent sociological and criminological theories, it becomes apparent that no one theory has attempted to explain criminality based on multiple factors. The various theories essentialize the criminal experience, focusing on only one factor, race, class, or gender, and fail to be applicable to the multiple identities of a black female gang member. Thus I propose the creation of a comprehensive, multifactored analysis that integrates and synthesizes the existing theories.

Using a multidisciplinary critical race feminism approach, a comprehensive analysis should combine elements of subculture, structural strain, cultural deficiency, learning, and feminist theory. Black female gang members' social class, culture, family, friends, peers, opportunities, and victimization are all factors that impact on their criminality and gang involvement.[29]

Black female gang members are triply burdened by class, race, and gender. Often these gang members live in the poor inner city regions of large cities and come from a poor family, usually headed by a single female. They feel their choices are limited, and they strive to overcome economic and gender repression. They turn to the subculture of the gang to fulfill their needs for power and status and take the gang's values for their own, becoming increasingly involved in violence and crime.[30] Theirs becomes a subculture of deviance, "a subcultural life of poverty and crime."[31]

These females turn to the gang to protect them from violence and to provide them with family-like relationships.[32] Often their fathers are absent, and these females are deprived of the kind of stable family environment every child needs.[33] They also are deprived of positive role models and mentors, since most of the people they come into contact with are criminals or their victims.[34]

Due to all of these and other contributing factors, the needs of females within these communities are not being met. African American females must turn elsewhere to fulfill them. In the gang they hope to find love, protection, acceptance, belonging, guidance, and support. Yet in the gang they also find violence and crime. For African American females, a variety of factors intertwine and produce an inner-city "market" for gang involvement. The prevalence of factors such as poverty, lack of opportunity, and lack of a stable family environment within the inner-city explains the high rates of gang membership in those communities. Through the integration of existing sociological and criminological theories, these and other causal factors can be identified; such factors will provide a basis to develop more effective solutions to gang violence and crime.

PRAXIS: STRATEGIES AND PROGRAMS

Suppression is the most commonly used strategy to combat the gang problem.[35] Federal agencies, law enforcement, and prosecutor's strategies are aimed at suppressing and punishing gang activity. Police departments have developed specialized programs to conduct street-sweeps or dragnets, intensify gang surveillance, and increase pressure and control of gang members.[36] Some prosecutors' offices also have established specialized gang units.[37] These offices often use vertical prosecution, in which one prosecutor handles a particular case from beginning to end, in gang-related cases.[38]

New laws and statutory enactments have aided law enforcement and prosecutors in their suppression efforts. California's Street Terrorism Enforcement and Protection Act is one example of state statutory responses to gang violence and has served as a model for many other states.[39] This act subjects gang affiliated criminals to sentence enhancements.[40] In addition, parents of gang members may be prosecuted under the act.[41] The 1994 Violent Crime Control and Law Enforcement Act also provided for sentence enhancements of gang-affiliated offenders.[42] This act also provided for adult prosecution of certain juvenile offenders in relation to gang activity.[43] These statutes and provisions are designed to increase the suppression and punishment of gang activity; they have had limited success at combating gang violence.[44]

Prevention and intervention strategies may be more effective, but they are less common and often are insufficiently funded.[45] Nonetheless, some programs do attempt to implement a prevention or intervention strategy.[46] One such program is the Safe Streets program in Pierce County, Washington, which focuses on high-risk youths and targets communities with high rates of school dropout and delinquency.[47]

One prevention-oriented program was designed for youths currently in gangs, ex-gang members, and at-risk youths. This program, Amer-I-Can, is a life skills management curriculum, founded by football Hall of Fame recipient, actor, and activist Jim Brown. The program and its facilitators assist in the development of personal skills such as problem solving, emotional control, goal setting, and employment retention. The Amer-I-Can program has proven effective for all types of people and is one of few programs that involves African American females as participants, facilitators, administrators, and consultants.

Other contemporary prevention programs are community based. The Youth Outreach program in Columbus, Ohio, and the Alternative to Gang Membership program in Paramount, California, stress prevention through early intervention and provide alternative recreational and educational activities for youths.[48] Some of these programs focus on gang violence reduction and feud mediation.[49] Most programs combine a variety of components and provide a mix of services, including family intervention, employment assistance, and conflict mediation.[50]

Prevention programs that specifically address the needs of females are exceptionally rare. Although Congress did allocate funding for such programs, only twelve programs were devoted to at-risk females.[51] Existing programs do not specifically address the needs and difficulties of the African American female.

A new approach to developing prevention and intervention programs is needed to ensure that black females are not excluded or ignored. By centering upon the black female within the gang-affected community more effective programs can be developed that will benefit her and the entire community.

A more effective and comprehensive approach to developing solutions to the gang problem must address the differing roles of the African American female in the gang realm. Drawing on critical race feminism, solutions must be crafted that are sensitive to the multiple experiences and perspectives of these women. Such solutions and the resulting programs must be targeted at improving the status of black women in all their roles. By uplifting these women we will, in turn, be uplifting the entire community.

A new approach based on critical race feminism would incorporate all of the factors leading to gang affiliation for black females and also would enlist the aid of all those women who affect gang members. Such an approach should include assistance programs to aid mothers and families and to meet such needs as child care, health care and employment assistance.[52] Such assistance will help to ensure that African American females have a stable family environment and can provide such an environment for her children.

The program's approach should also attempt to increase educational and vocational opportunities for African American females. Early intervention educational programs, like the Perry Preschool Project,[53] target children at risk for school failure; such programs will ensure that African American females have a solid educational base that will increase their employment opportunities. Any new program also should incorporate other elements, such as providing positive role models, life skills management, and parenting skills training.

The new CRF approach to the African American female would be multidisciplinary. While my recommendations are intended to produce comprehensive, multidimensional strategy, my efforts in this chapter should be considered as introductory and as an invitation for further research and development in this area. Such a vast problem cannot be solved through these suggestions alone. Yet, I believe that my approach provides a solid base upon which to build.

CONCLUSION

Effective solutions to gang violence and crime involve placing black women at the center rather than at the margins of the analysis. As I have discussed, these women have multiple identities and many roles that inextricably link them to the problems and also to the solutions of gang association. By taking a critical race feminism approach to the formulation of solutions, programs can be developed that consider the African American woman in all of her roles, including gang member, girlfriend, wife, and mother. A CRF approach will ensure that programs are more comprehensive in scope and are better able provide a variety of resources for the diverse group they serve. Such a strategy will benefit the entire community by providing women within the community with the resources they need to improve their lives and the lives of their children and their families. By placing the African American woman at the center of the theory, she will become the center of the praxis, and the center of solutions to the gang problem.

NOTES

1. Estimates of female gang participation have ranged from 10 to 30 percent of the total gang population. See Irving A. Spergel, *The Youth Gang Problem: A Community Approach* (New York: Oxford University Press, 1995), 57.
2. Malcolm W. Klein, *The American Street Gang* (New York: Oxford University Press, 1995), 111. Klein expects that increases in male gang violence "will be matched by proportional increases in female gang violence."
3. Gini Sikes, "Girls in the Hood: Violent Crime Among Teenage Girls," *Scholastic Update* (February 11, 1994): 20.
4. The members of an all-female gang in Brooklyn, New York, signal their membership by cutting themselves from ear to mouth with a razor blade so as to leave a large and visible scar. Ruaridh Nicoll, "Gang Babes Love to Kill, Scar-Faced Girls of Brooklyn Show Passion for Mayhem," *The Guardian,* November 12, 1995, 24.
5. Carla Marinucci et al., "Girls Gangs Growing in Numbers, Escalating Violence," *Houston Chronicle,* January 1, 1995, 38. This type of sexual initiation puts girls in danger of contracting the AIDS virus.
6. One female joined an all-female gang because she felt "like a secondary player in her boyfriend's gang." Marego Athans et al., "Girls Getting More Active, More Violent Inside Gangs," *Sentinel,* December 17, 1995, 1A.
7. A National Institute of Justice Survey found ninety-nine independent female gangs in thirty-five different jurisdictions. G. David Curry et al., "Gang Crime and Law Enforcement Recordkeeping," *National Institute of Justice Research in Brief* (August 1994): 8.

8. Anne Campbell, "Female Participation in Gangs," in C. Ronald Huff, ed., *Gangs in America* (Newbury Park, Calif.: Sage Publications, 1990), 163, 177.

9. Anne Campbell, *The Girls in the Gang* (New York: Basil Blackwell, 1984), 32.

10. 10. Ibid., 159.

11. Lee Bowker and Malcolm Klein, "Female Participation in Delinquent Gang Activity," *Adolescence* 15 (1980).

12. Irving Spergel et al., "National Youth Gang Suppression and Intervention Program," *Juvenile Justice Bulletin* 2 (1990): 84.

13. See Yvette Craig and Stephen G. Michaud, "More Girls into Killing, Experts Say," *Fort Worth Star-Telegram,* February 8, 1997, 1.

14. "Monster" Kody Scott, a former Crip in Los Angeles, stated in his autobiography, "To continue banging would be a betrayal first of my children, who now depend on me for guidance, morals, and strength." Sanyika Shakur, *Monster: The Autobiography of an L.A. Gang Member* (New York: Atlantic Monthly Press, 1993), 357.

15. Yusuf Jah and Sister Shah' Keyah, *Uprising: Crips and Bloods Tell the Story of America's Youth in the Crossfire* (New York: Scribner, 1995) at 139 (interviewing "General" Robert Lee and his wife of twenty-one years, Shelia).

16. Ibid. (foreword by Ice-T).

17. Frederick Thrasher, *The Gang: A Study of 1,313 Gangs in Chicago* (Chicago: University of Chicago Press, 1963).

18. Robert Merton, "Social Structure and Anomie," *American Sociological Review* 3 (1938): 672.

19. Eileen B. Leonard, *Women, Crime and Society* (New York: Longman, 1982), 118-20 (citing Albert K. Cohen, *Delinquent Boys: The Culture of the Gang* [Glencoe, Ill.: Free Press, 1955]) and Herman Mannheim, *Comparative Criminology* (Boston: Houghton Mifflin, 1965).

20. See Walter B. Miller, "Lower Class Culture as Generating Milieu of Gang Delinquency," *Journal of Sociology. Issues* 14 (1958): 5.

21. See William Julius Wilson, *The Truly Disadvantaged* (Chicago: University of Chicago Press, 1987).

22. See Richard Majors and Janet Mancini Billson, *Cool Pose: The Dilemma of Black Manhood in America* (New York: Lexington Books, 1992).

23. Barri Flowers, *The Adolescent Criminal: An Examination of Today's Juvenile Offender* (Jefferson, N.C.: McFarland, 1990), 130 (citing Edwin H. Sutherland, *Principles of Criminology* [Chicago: J.B. Lippincott Company, 1939]).

24. Ibid., 131.

25. Ruth R. Morris, "Attitudes Toward Delinquency by Delinquents, Non-Delinquents and Their Friends," *British Journal of Criminology* 5 (1965): 249, 251.

26. See Carolene Gwynn, "Women and Crime: The Failure of Traditional Theories and the Rise of Feminist Criminology," *Monash University Law Review* 19 (1993): 92.

27. See Freda Adler, *Sisters in Crime: The Rise of the New Female Criminal* (New York: McGraw-Hill, 1975).

28. Dorie Klein and June Kress, "Any Woman's Blues: A Critical Overview of Women, Crime, and the Criminal Justice System," *Crime & Social Justice* (Spring-Summer 1976): 41.

29. Recent researchers have found that a combination of factors, such as economic instability, childhood victimization, and peers, are all criminogenic influences. See Deborah Baskin et al., "The Political Economy of Female Violent Street Crime," 20 *Fordham Urban Law Journal* 20(1993): 404, 406.

30. See Carl Taylor, *Girls, Gangs, Women and Drugs* (East Lansing, Mich.: Michigan State University Press, 1993), 7-11.

31. Campbell, *The Girls in the Gang,* 267.

32. Ibid., 175.
33. See James Garbarino, *Raising Children in a Socially Toxic Environment* (San Francisco: Jossey-Bass, 1995), 47-62.
34. Alison Abner, "Gangsta Girls," *Essence* (July 1994): 64.
35. Irving Spergel et al., "National Youth Gang Suppression and Intervention Program," *Juvenile Justice Bulletin* 2 (Washington, D.C.: U.S. Department of Justice, Office of Juvenile Justice and Delinquency Prevention, 1990).
36. See Spergel, *The Youth Gang Problem,* 197, and Klein, *The American Street Gang,* 161.
37. Claire Johnson et al., "Prosecuting Gangs: A National Assessment," *National Institute of Justice Research on Brief* (February 1995): 5.
38. Spergel, *The Youth Gang Problem,* 210 (citing Richard M. Daley, "Gang Prevention Unit," *Cook County State's Attorney's Office Report* [1985]).
39. David R. Truman, "The Jet and Sharks Are Dead: The State Statutory Responses to Criminal Street Gangs," *Washington University Law Quarterly* 73(1995): 683, 688.
40. Ibid., 686.
41. Spergel, *The Youth Gang Problem,* 211 (citing Susan Burrell, "Gang Evidence: Issues for Criminal Defense," *Santa Clara Law Review* 30(1990): 739, 745).
42. Pub. L. No. 103-322, 108 Stat. 1796, sec. 15001 (codified as amended at 42 U.S.C.A. Ch. 136).
43. Pub. L. No 103-322, 108 Stat. 1796, sec. 15002 (codified as amended at 42 U.S.C.A. Ch. 136).
44. Spergel, *The Youth Gang Problem,* 177.
45. The 1994 crime bill allocated less than a third of its $30 billion to prevention programs. Limited resources are often cited as one of the obstacles to effective prevention programs. See Spergel, *The Youth Gang Problem,* 296.
46. For more information on such programs see ibid., 247-96.
47. Ibid., 257.
48. Klein, *The American Street Gang,* 154-55.
49. See ibid. (describing these and a variety of other community programs).
50. Catherine H. Conly, et al., "Street Gangs: Current Knowledge and Strategies," U.S. Department of Justice, Office of Justice Programs, National Institute of Justice, no. 6 in the Issues and Practices in Criminal Justice series (1993): 30.
51. G. David Curry, "Gang Related Violence," *Clearinghouse Review* (Special Issue 1994): 443, 447.
52. An example of this type of program was created under New Jersey's Hispanic Women's Demonstration Resource Centers Act and provided a variety of services directed at providing relief to women and families. See Gloria Bonilla-Santiago, "Legislating Progress for Hispanic Women in New Jersey," *Social Work* (May 1989): 270.
53. Jane Watson, "Crime and Juvenile Delinquency Prevention Policy: Time for Early Childhood Prevention," *Georgetown Journal on Fighting Poverty* 2 (1995): 245-251.

I I I

GENDER, SEXUALITY, AND CONFINEMENT

TEN

Programming and Health Care Accessibility for Incarcerated Women

JOANNE BELKNAP

INTRODUCTION

Although prisoners in general have been a forgotten and neglected portion of the population, this situation has been particularly apparent for incarcerated females. While these women have received little attention, they also have benefited from few programs. The justification for the paucity of programs in women's prisons is that women are not the "major breadwinners" and, given that there are fewer female than male prisoners (women constitute just over 6 percent of U.S. prisoners), programs for women are too expensive per capita: in short, the penal system in the United States was developed by males and for males.[1] These problems are particularly troubling given that the increase in women's incarceration rates in the United States has exceeded men's every year since 1981, tripling during the 1980s, while the number of incarcerated men about doubled.[2]

The increase in women's imprisonment can be accounted for largely by increases in minor property crimes (mostly larceny-theft) and by drug and public order offenses. There appears to be an increased willingness both to incarcerate women and to give them longer sentences. A number of factors are relevant to understanding women's imprisonment: race and racism, the likelihood and effects of surviving male violence, chemical dependency, and parenting issues. Each of these is briefly discussed in the following text.

Although the United States has given significant play (as it should) to the disproportionately high rates of incarcerated African American males (for example, more young black men are in U.S. prisons than in its colleges), a similar yet worse pattern in women's prisons has been overlooked. Often even higher rates of African Americans exist in women's than in men's prisons,[3] and the percent of women of color in U.S. prisons has been increasing over time.

Recent research on incarcerated women also has uncovered the significantly high likelihood that incarcerated women and girls are survivors of male violence: incest, rape, and battering.[4] This fact is significant not only in terms of programs and counseling for these survivors; growing research links surviving abuse with chemical dependency.[5] Furthermore, although a sizable amount of the increase in women's incarceration rate has been attributed to drug offenses, little has been done to evaluate the availability and effectiveness of alcohol and drug programs for incarcerated women.[6]

Another significant concern for imprisoned women is parenting. Incarcerated women are far more likely than incarcerated men to be the emotional and financial providers for children and to have custody of their children before imprisonment. Even if incarcerated men have custody of their children, they are usually secure in the fact that the children's mothers will provide for them during the males' imprisonment. Women, on the other hand, are far less likely to be able to rely on fathers to take over parenting during their incarceration. Moreover, children are more likely to be negatively affected by the incarceration of their mothers than their fathers, given gender differences in parental responsibilities in society at large. The average number of dependent children per incarcerated woman is between two and three, and the percent of incarcerated women with children is growing.[7]

The purpose of the current study is to examine incarcerated women's program opportunities (including health care). This study analyzes a one-page survey completed by inmates in a U.S. women's prison. In addition to questions regarding personal characteristics, the survey included asked about access to recreational, vocational, educational, and health programs at the institution.

PRISON PROGRAMMING FOR INCARCERATED WOMEN

Historically, incarcerated women have been viewed as incapable or unworthy of education or training in prison. According to prison scholars Robert R. Ross and Elizabeth A. Fabiano: "In general, treatment and training programs for female offenders are distinctively poorer in quantity, quality, and variety, and considerably different in nature from those for male offenders."[8] Both the prisoners and the staff rank education as the most valuable resource for women during incarceration, a fact that is not surprising given that less than one-third of all incarcerated females hold a high school degree at intake. A study on coed prisons found that the women were more likely than the men to request academic programs, while women and men were equally likely to request vocational programs. One study found, however, that the women with more education prior to incarceration were the most likely to participate in prison educational programs.[9]

Research has also found sex discrimination in the availability of activities for incarcerated men and women. A study in Scotland found that male prisoners were allowed to play darts, cards, Ping-Pong, dominoes, and so on, activities unavailable to imprisoned women.[10] Another study reported, as if this were perfectly normal and acceptable, that the activity called the "Hen House" provided an opportunity for the women in a coed prison to get together with the staff wives to make Christmas cookies and spend the evening sewing, knitting, and talking.[11] Men's prisons have vastly better recreational facilities and programs, based on the myth that men need more physical exertion than women.[12]

Apparently there is a related assumption that men are more in need of heterosexual contact than women, given that some states allow male prisoners conjugal visits while no such opportunities are provided for female prisoners.[13]

Additionally, women often are excluded from halfway house programs, work release programs, and furloughs. Predictably, the programs that do exist have tended to push women into the "gender-appropriate" roles of wife and mother. Such programs deny the large and growing number of single women who head households as well as the obvious sexist assumptions about who "deserves" jobs and programs. There is also some indication that women's access to programs in jails is significantly more limited than their access in prisons.[14]

Perhaps most disturbing is the finding that women who attempt to combat the sexism in educational and vocational prison opportunities are often punished—sometimes with long periods in solitary confinement. Although some federal court cases have determined that sex discrimination is occurring in prison vocational and educational programming, these decisions have made little impact in improving such programming for incarcerated women.[15]

Similar to the limited access to recreational, educational, and vocational programming, incarcerated women also suffer from extremely limited access to medical and health care,[16] care that is inferior even to what is available to their male counterparts. Not surprisingly then, the majority of lawsuits filed by or on behalf of incarcerated women are for inadequate medical services.[17] Research, such as that by S. Mahan, on women's health access in prison has found that they often have difficulty in obtaining necessary prescribed medications and in receiving transportation and being scheduled to see physicians. Although it may be easier for female prisoners to have access to social workers than to physicians, often social workers are unable to provide useful counseling due to the structure of their position in the prison, according to prison researchers Russell P. Dobash, R. Emerson Dobash, and Sue Gutteridge.[18]

Thus, regardless of the type of program (educational, vocational, recreational, or health), female prisoners appear to be disadvantaged. This fact is particularly significant given the recent increase in women's incarceration rates and the growing acceptance of the extraordinarily high rates of female prisoners who have survived male violence; this is a population in need of better programs.

METHOD

The study reported here was designed to assess program opportunities and needs for females incarcerated in a state prison. In return for keeping the prisoners' identities and the name of the state prison confidential, the researcher was allowed to distribute a one-page survey to sixty-eight female prisoners enrolled in a self-esteem course in 1992. All of the women participating in this course chose to complete the survey. The course leader estimated that drug-addicted prisoners may have been overrepresented in the sample because about half of the prisoners were referred from existing prison drug and alcohol programs.

Ideally, a random sample and a more extensive survey format should have been used, but this option was not available. Given that so little is known about programs in women's prisons, however, this study provides some new information and helps highlight some of the issues that should be explored regarding programs for and future research on incarcerated women.

The research instrument was designed to allow the women to respond with their own ideas and experiences, and thus was mostly open-ended. In addition to questions about access and needs concerning educational, vocational, recreational, and medical programming, the survey also asked for some personal information; specifically, the respondents recorded their ages, race/ethnicity, number and ages of children, information about drug and alcohol addictions, amount of the current sentence served, and the amount left to serve. It was believed that these factors might influence program requests and experiences. The researcher tabulated all of the programs listed by the respondents for each question and created a codebook to quantify the data. These quantitative data are combined with some of the respondents' lengthier written comments from the survey to formulate the findings reported in this chapter.

FINDINGS

The sample ranged in age from twenty to fifty-five-years-old, and almost one-third of the sample was thirty-six to forty-years-old. As expected, the sample was over half African Americans and about two-fifths Anglo. Two of the women identified themselves as American Indian. (The racial composition was reflective of the prison population as a whole). One-fifth of the women had no children and ten percent had five or more. The average number of children in this sample was 2.3. This is consistent with prior research on incarcerated women.[19] Almost two-thirds of the women reported having dependent children. About one-quarter of the dependent children were cared for by grandparents and less than one-fifth were cared for by their fathers. Seven percent were cared for by child services or foster care. Others were cared for by other family members and friends, while over one-quarter were cared for by a combination of people. Some of the women reported being upset about having their children separated from each other (as well from them).

Two-fifths of the sample reported addictions to alcohol and almost two-thirds reported addictions to drugs. This rate may be due to the fact that drug-addicted women may have been oversampled into the class in which the survey was distributed. The length of time served in the prison ranged from two months to more than twelve years, with an average of 25.8 months. The sample was fairly evenly distributed between those serving less than one year, those serving one to two years, and those having served more than two years. It also was fairly evenly divided between those who had two or fewer years left to serve and those who had more than two years left.

The survey asked which programs and activities the women participated in, existing programs and activities they would like to participate in (but have not had access to yet), and programs and activities they wish were offered. Two-thirds of the women reported participating in high school or G.E.D. courses, and over one-third had taken at least one college course. Slightly over one-quarter had participated in vocational training, over half had participated in recreational activities, and four-fifths reported participating in other types of programs (e.g., twelve-step, self-awareness, parenting, domestic violence, and stress management).

The most popular recreational activities were exercise programs, including aerobics, weight lifting, and gym. Almost two-fifths of the sample had participated in one of these. The next most popular recreational activity, a class on current events, was listed by 15 percent of the sample. Ten percent of the sample took part in team sports (e.g., volleyball and basketball), about 8 percent took part in church or Bible study, and about 8 percent participated in arts and crafts.

Information on other types of programs in which the women participated emphasizes the need for drug programs for incarcerated women. Almost half were active in twelve-step programs such as Alcoholics Anonymous or Narcotics Anonymous, and one-quarter took part in other drug programs. Over half had participated in self-help or self-awareness programs, over one-third in parenting programs, and over one-fifth in a domestic violence program. Three women also reported participating in a support group for prisoners with life sentences.

The survey also asked the women which programs they would like to participate in but could not get in to. The drug programs, self-help/self-awareness, and domestic violence were programs with limited access. Sixteen percent wanted access to twelve-step programs and over one-quarter wanted access to other drug programs. Twelve percent wanted access to self-help/self-awareness programs, and one-fifth wanted access to domestic violence programs. Almost one-tenth reported wanting access to college courses. (This statistic might be misleading since perhaps some women who wanted access to college courses did not consider educational programs as an option in these open-ended questions specifically asking about programs, not classes or courses). Eight percent wanted access to secretarial programs, and 6 percent wanted to take part in programs to stop smoking cigarettes.

One-fifth of the respondents requested more self-help/self-awareness programs, and a significant number wanted new programs in the following areas: reintegration into society after sentence completion (16 percent); nurses' training (15 percent); incest counseling (12 percent); coping and stress management (12 percent); and vocational training (9 percent). Six percent wanted more college courses, and 5 percent wanted family counseling programs. Some respondents wrote that a policy prohibiting participants in college programs from taking substance abuse or self-help programs was unfair. Others claimed that no one (including the staff) even knew which programs were available, and another stated, "You must be five years from your [parole] board [date] to participate in furthering your college education." The findings reported thus far are consistent with prior research findings.

Treatment for female offenders, whether in the community or in jail or prison, often consists of attending drug education classes and Alcoholics Anonymous or other twelve-step meetings. Where more intensive treatment exists, the programs frequently have been established by men or modeled after programs intended for men. Such programs often do not meet the special needs of women, which in addition to treatment for substance abuse include services related to physical and sexual abuse, physical and mental health problems, limited educational and vocational skills, and care for their children.[20]

Three open-ended questions in the survey asked how easy it was to see doctors, counselors, and dentists respectively. The responses were coded as "easy," "medium," and "difficult"; "don't know" was added for the responses regarding access to counseling and the dentist. Presumably, there were no "don't know" responses for physicians because everyone had tried to see a doctor, but not everyone had tried to see a counselor or dentist. These findings suggest that it is most difficult to see a doctor and least difficult to see a dentist. Some of the responses may highlight the difficulty in seeing a doctor: "It's not easy at all unless your [sic] dying. Because it took me 8 and + months to get into [sic] see the doctor, and by then I was over my illness"; and "Its [sic] hard as heck, you could easily die here." Responses about the difficulty in getting counseling in the women's prison suggested that one had to be "in a serious state of mental anguish, such as suicidal" or "just about to lose your self-control," and even then, the "services weren't effective." A small minority of respondents, however, reported that counseling was "there for you."

The data suggest that the dentist was easier to make an appointment with than doctors or counselors but that the dentist's services were limited to pulling teeth. These were some of the most harrowing responses to read: ". . . when he does dental work most people get infections and are in so much pain. His equipment isn't very sterile, he doesn't change his gloves, talks on the phone while pulling your teeth.

He's very negligent." Woman after woman wrote something like "you can eventually get in to see the dentist, but he does not clean or fill teeth, he only pulls them." In short, it appears that preventive medicine is rare, for physical, dental, or mental health care. In fact, these findings, which are consistent with prior research, indicate a serious lack in effective health care for incarcerated women.

The final data analysis was conducted to determine whether characteristics about the prisoners were related to their responses about programs and activities. Eight variables were significantly related to the women's responses on program experiences and needs. The characteristic most frequently associated with the responses on programs was whether the women reported having a drug problem. This was followed by race and time served, respectively. Age, whether the woman reported an alcohol problem, whether she reported having dependent children, and time left to serve also were occasionally related to responses on programming. These significant relationships are discussed next.

Sixty-one percent of women reporting a history of drug addiction participated in self-help/self-awareness programs as compared to 35 percent of those not reporting drug addiction. Fifty-nine percent of women reporting drug addiction histories participated in twelve-step programs compared to 26 percent reporting no drug addictions; 36 percent of women reporting drug additions participated in non–twelve-step drug programs while no women reporting drug problems did so. These findings are not surprising; we would expect women reporting drug addictions to be more likely to take part in drug programs. Notably, women who did not report a drug addiction history were more likely than those reporting drug addiction to participate in domestic violence programs (39 percent with no drug problem, 14 percent with a drug problem), vocational programs (42 percent with no drug problem, 19 percent with a drug problem), and arts and crafts (17 percent with no drug problem, 2 percent with drug problem). These findings suggest that those women with a reported drug addiction were more focused on the drug problem than on anything else. Similarly, women reporting an alcohol problem (39 percent) were more likely to participate in non–twelve-step drug programs than women with no reported alcohol problems (10 percent), and women with alcohol problems (0 percent) were less likely to participate in arts and crafts than their counterparts with no alcohol problems (13 percent).

After drug addiction status, race/ethnicity was the characteristic that had the greatest impact on women prisoners' program expectations and experiences. (Native American women were left out of the analysis because there were only two in the sample, making cross-tabular analysis difficult to accurately interpret.) African American women were more likely than Anglo women to participate in high school and G.E.D. programs (50 percent of blacks, 25 percent of Anglos) and non–twelve-step drug programs (34 percent of blacks, 11 percent of Anglos), and to request more vocational programs (16 percent of blacks, 0 percent of Anglos). Eighteen percent of Anglo women participated in arts and crafts while no African American women did.

The third most influential characteristic was the amount of time served. The more time a woman had served, the more likely she was to report having participated in a domestic violence program. Perhaps this is because women who have killed their batterers receive some of the longest sentences. Similarly, women who had served more than one year were twice as likely to have participated in self-help/self-awareness programs; women who had served one to two years were more likely than women who had served less than a year and than those who had served more than two years to report wanting to participate in more self-help/self-awareness programs. Notably, women who had served one to two years were more likely than those women who had served more or less than this amount to request more self-help programs.

Prisoners' age was a factor in whether they participated in exercise programs and whether they would like to see a nursing program implemented in the prison. Women younger than thirty (55 percent) and older than thirty-nine (50 percent) were more than twice as likely as thirty- to thirty-nine-year-old women (23 percent) to participate in exercise programs. While no women forty and over reported interest in a nursing program, 10 percent of women under thirty and 25 percent of the women in their thirties wanted a nursing program to be implemented.

Predictably, women with dependent children (52 percent) were more than four times as likely as women without dependent children (12 percent) to report participating in parenting programs. For no known reason, however, women with dependent children (2 percent) were also far less likely to report playing a team sport (i.e., volleyball or basketball) than women without dependent children (24 percent). The only remaining variable that was significantly related to programming access and desires of prisoners was the amount of time left to serve in the sentence. Prisoners with less than one year to serve were about half as likely (27 percent) as those with one or more years left (60 percent) to report participating in self-help or self-awareness groups.

It is equally important to examine what is not significant. The characteristics describing the prisoners (race, age, drug problem, alcohol problem, dependent children, time served, and time left) were never significantly related to their reports of access to doctors, dentists, and counselors, nor to whether they would like to participate in domestic violence, drug programs, or twelve-step programs, and whether they went to church or took college classes.

CONCLUSION

The findings from this study suggest that the female prisoners took part in a variety of programs and activities but would like to have had easier access to many of the existing programs and desired new program offerings. The findings also imply that access to healthcare was problematic in this prison. Furthermore, even when access to health- care was obtained, the care provided often was reported as inadequate or even questionable.

The bivariate analysis was useful for determining relationships between prisoners' characteristics and their programming participation and desires. Notably, the characteristic most consistently related to responses about programming was whether prisoners reported addiction to drugs; this was followed by the prisoners' race, which was followed by the amount of time served. (Age, whether the prisoner had an alcohol problem, whether she had dependent children, and amount of time left to serve were less influential but still related to some responses on programming.) These results suggest that programming needs might be very different for women depending on whether they have a chemical dependency, their race, and time spent in prison. It appears that many female prisoners with drug problems are very focused on trying to deal with this problem while in prison, and that not enough chemical dependency programs are available. Additionally, the diversity of female prisoners points to the need for a diversity in programs available to them. That African American women were twice as likely to report participation in G.E.D. programs, three times as likely to participate in non–twelve-step drug programs, and far more likely to request vocational training programs than their Anglo counterparts suggests that societal structures related to race outside of prison influence racial differences in programming needs in the prison. Finally, this study indicates the need for more prison programs to help women respond to prior victimizations, such as incest and battering.

NOTES

An earlier version of this chapter originally appeared as "Access to Programs and Health Care for Incarcerated Women" in *Federal Probation* 60, no. 4 (1996).

1. See: Christopher J. Mumola and Llen J. Beck, "Prisoners in 1996," Bureau of Justice Statistics, Office of Justice Programs, U.S. Department of Justice, NCJ 164619 (June 1997); and L. W. Flanagan, "Meeting the Special Needs of Females in Custody: Maryland's Unique Approach," *Federal Probation* 59 (1995): 49-53.

2. See: C. Smart, *Women, Crime and Criminology: A Feminist Critique* (London: Routledge and Kegan Paul, 1976); J. Belknap, *The Invisible Woman: Gender, Crime, And Justice* (Belmont, Calif.: Wadsworth, 1996); and S. Kline, *Female Offenders: Meeting the Needs of a Neglected Population* (Laurel, Md.: American Correctional Association, 1993), 1-6. In a recent review of U. S. prison statistics two prison scholars, Leslie Acoca and James Austin (1996), noted that women's incarceration rates almost *quadrupled* between 1980 and 1994 (while the rate for men "only" doubled). Furthermore, they reported that 1 out of every 130 women in the U. S. (almost 800,000 women) were in prison or jail, or on probation or parole in 1994. See: Leslie Acoca and James Austin, *The Crisis: Women in Prison.* The National Council on Crime and Delinquency, February, 1996.

3. D. Binkley-Jackson, V. L. Carter, and G. L. Rolison, "African-American Women in Prison," in B. R. Fletcher, L. D. Shaver, and D. B. Moon, eds., *Women Prisoners: A Forgotten Population* (Westport, Conn.: Praeger, 1993), 65-74; and A. Goetting and R. M. Howsen, "Women in Prison: A Profile," *The Prison Journal* 63 no. 2 (1983): 27-46.

4. American Correctional Association, *The Female Offender: What Does the Future Hold?* (Arlington, Va.: Kirby Lithographic Company, 1990); R. Arnold, "Processes of Victimization and Criminalization of Black Women," *Social Justice* 17 (1990): 153-66; P. Carlen, *Women's Imprisonment: A Study in Social Control* (London: Routledge and Kegan Paul, 1983); M. Chesney-Lind, "Patriarchy, Prisons, and Jails: A Critical Look at Trends in Women's Incarceration," *The Prison Journal* 71 (1991): 51-67; M. E. Gilfus, "From Victims to Survivors to Offenders: Women's Routes of Entry and Immersion into Street Crime," *Women and Criminal Justice* 4 (1992): 63-90; R.

Immarigeon, "Women in Prison," *Journal of the National Prison Project* 11 (1987): 1-5; and E. Sargent, S. Marcus-Mendoza, and C. H. Yu, "Abuse and the Woman Prisoner," in Fletcher, Shaver, and Moon, eds., *Women Prisoners*, 55-64.

5. P. Carlen and N. Rodriguez, "Women Under Lock and Key," *The Prison Journal* 63 (1983): 47-65; Gilfus, "From Victims to Survivors to Offenders"; B. Owen and B. Bloom, "Profiling Women Prisoners: Findings From National Surveys and a California Sample," *The Prison Journal* 75 (1995): 165-85.; and Sargent, Marcus-Mendoza, and Yu, "Abuse and the Woman Prisoner."

6. R. R. Ross and E. A. Fabiano, *Female Offenders: Correctional Afterthoughts* (Jefferson, N.C.: McFarland, 1986).

7. R. Sarri, "Unequal Protection Under the Law: Women and the Criminal Justice System," in J. Figueira-McDonough and R. Sarri, *The Trapped Woman: Catch-22 in Deviance and Control* (Newbury Park, Calif.: Sage, 1987), 394-426.

8. See Ross and Fabiano, *Female Offenders*, 5.

9. See: R. M. Glick and V. V. Neto, "National Study of Women's Correctional Programs," in B. R. Price and N. J. Sokoloff, eds., *The Criminal Justice System and Women* (New York: Clark and Boardman, 1982), 141-54; R. I. Mawby, "Women in Prison: A British Study," *Crime and Delinquency* 28 (1982): 24-39; N.K. Wilson, "Styles of Doing Time in a Co-Ed Prison: Masculine and Feminine Alternatives," in. J. O. Smykla, ed., *Coed Prison* (New York: Human Services Press, 1980), 150-71.

10. See Carlen, *Women's Imprisonment.*

11. C. F. Campbell, "Co-corrections- FCI Fort Worth After Three Years," in Smykla, ed., *Co-ed Prison*, 83-109.

12. A. Goetting, "Racism, Sexism, and Ageism in the Prison Community," *Federal Probation* 49 (1983): 10-22.

13. J. Boudouris, *Prisons and Kids* (College Park, Md.: American Correctional Association, 1985).

14. See Carlen, "Women Under Lock and Key," and T. Gray, L. G. Mays, and M. K. Stohr, "Inmate Needs and Programming in Exclusively Women's Jails," *The Prison Journal* 75 (1995): 186-202.

15. See Sarri, "Unequal Protection Under the Law."

16. See: J. M. Pollock-Byrne, *Women, Prison, and Crime* (Pacific Grove, Calif.: Brooks/Cole, 1990), and J. Resnick and N. Shaw, "Prisoners of Their Sex: Health Problems of Incarcerated Women," in I. P. Robbins, ed., *Prisoners' Rights Sourcebook*, vol. 2 (New York: Clark Boardman, 1980), 319-413.

17. See: American Correctional Association, *The Female Offender*, and A. Aylward and J. Thomas, "Quiescence in Women's Prison Litigation," *Justice Quarterly* 1 (1984): 253-76.

18. The citation for this book is these authors (1986). *The Imprisonment of Women.* Oxford: Basil Blackwell.

19. See Gray et al., "Inmate Needs and Programming in Exclusively Women's Jails," 186-202.

20. M. L. Prendergrast, J. Wellisch, and G. P. Falkin, "Assessment of Services for Substance-Abusing Women Offenders in Community and Correctional Settings," *The Prison Journal* 75 (1995): 240-56.

ELEVEN

Race, Ethnicity, and Gender in Studies of Incarceration

JUANITA DÍAZ-COTTO

Social science studies on women's prisons tend to focus primarily on interpersonal relationships between prisoners and on the ways in which gender socialization prior to imprisonment influences the way prisoners respond to their incarceration.[1] With few exceptions, these studies either ignore racial and ethnic factors in women's prisons or make but token reference to them. This chapter critiques the major literature on women's prisons in regard to race and ethnicity.

Women of color tend to be overrepresented in penal institutions throughout the United States.[2] Despite this overrepresentation, social scientists (overwhelmingly heterosexual Anglo/European, middle-class, Judeo-Christians) have barely acknowledged the impact of racism and/or ethnocentrism on imprisoned women. A look at some brief references from social science literature is illuminating.

David Ward and Gene Kassebaum's 1965 groundbreaking study of the California Institution for Women merely acknowledged that "some inmates are Negro, and some are white."[3] The following year Rose

Giallombardo's major study of the Federal Reformatory for Women in Alderson, West Virginia—where 42 percent of the prisoners but only 7 of the 102 guards were African American—simply observed that "while racial barriers undoubtedly obscured sensitive areas of interrelationship, they were not as pervasive as expected."[4] Giallombardo also indicated that some white prisoners found the physical proximity of African American women distressing. Esther Heffernan's 1972 study of the Women's Reformatory at Occoquan, Washington, D.C., in which 79 percent of the prisoner population was African American, briefly mentioned that "the nucleus for politicizing was present in the articulate inmate understanding, particularly on the part of two Black Muslim women, of the class and race bias of the criminal justice system."[5] The study also mentions the existence of conflicts between the white rural and the urban African American staff. Edna Chandler's 1973 study of the California Institution for Women refers to the existence of three strong "ethnic prisoner organizations"—the Self-Help Afro-American Cultural Organization, the Mexican American Research Association, and the United Indian Tribes—that coexisted with "a group of nationalistically identified women"[6]—the Daughters of Italy) and a host of other prisoner groups. Chandler also observed that Preventers, an interracial/interethnic program created by prisoners, had been able to head off a number of racial conflicts. She also mentioned that African Americans, who composed one-third of the prisoner population were particularly unhappy that none of the members of the California parole board were African American. Historian Estelle Freedman points out how prison administrators used interracial lesbian relationships as an excuse to segregate prisoners in New York's Bedford Hills women's facility until the 1950s.[7]

Candace Kruttschnitt's 1983 study of the Minnesota Correctional Institution for Women in Skakopee found that Native American and African American prisoners felt discriminated against by the overwhelmingly white staff.[8] While Kruttschnitt stated that this perception might be based on the fact that almost one-quarter of the women of color were housed in solitary confinement, she concluded that "the correctional facility cannot be characterized as a racially hostile environment."[9] Her conclusion was based partly on interviews she conducted with white prisoners who argued that imprisoned women of color felt more discriminated against because they assumed a priori that such discrimination would take place. Kruttschnitt's study did not include an evaluation of how decisions to place prisoners in solitary confinement were arrived at. The author also observed that African American prisoners were more likely to associate with white prisoners than vice versa.

It was partly in reaction to the neglect of racial issues in women's prison literature as well as its "relative omission of the staff and their participation in the creation and maintenance of the social system within the prison"[10] that Elouise Spencer wrote a doctoral dissertation in 1977 on the social system of a medium-security women's prison.

Spencer found that African American and white prisoners who engaged in interracial relationships were ostracized by their peers. Interracial bonding between prisoners was also threatening to prison authorities. According to Spencer, "When expedient to do so, race consciousness is maneuvered to a heightened level as a further means of keeping inmates from engaging in meaningful relationships with each other on the basis of their collective status as inmates."[11] This strategy of "divide and conquer" led staff to deliberately interpret nonracial incidents, such as arguments and fights between African American and white prisoners, as racial. Staff also instigated conflicts between prisoners by "telling the whites one thing and the blacks another."[12]

Interracial tensions were worsened by the administrators' practice of discriminating against both African American prisoners and staff. Administrators granted special privileges, responsibilities, housing, and work assignments primarily to white prisoners. The "trusties" used their privileges to grant other prisoners desired goods and services in return for compliance with prison rules. When tensions increased, a few African American prisoners were granted special favors to demonstrate that discrimination did not exist. However, African American prisoners were more likely to be assigned to the kitchen and the laundry areas. As a result, their wages were lower than those of their white peers. Furthermore, African American prisoners received harsher punishment for rule infractions. Spencer also noted that while white prisoners were allowed to organize an antiblack group, African American prisoners were not allowed to form a group along racial lines.

African American staff, on the other hand, were discriminated against in the areas of promotion, work schedules, and work assignments. Staff who seemed to identify with prisoners, particularly African American prisoners, were harassed by white coworkers. They could also be denied promotion and/or subjected to continual demotions by administrators. Some were given difficult work-shift assignments. Others were accused of wrongdoing, such as having an affair with a prisoner.

In spite of the role racism played within the facility, Spencer concluded that she "did not observe the blatant racism which had been reported by inmates in male institutions throughout the United States."[13] For Spencer, the most important measure of racism was the extent to which physical force was used to subdue prisoners and whether the racist recognized that he or she was being racist. Because Spencer did not believe physical force was used in women's facilities to the extent that it was used in men's prisons, she minimized both the impact racism had on women prisoners and the levels of physical violence actually used in women's prisons.

Nicole Hahn Rafter is a social scientist who examined the historical impact of racism on the evolution of women's reformatories and prisons.[14] She found that in New York, Ohio, and Tennessee racism played important roles in determining the overrepresentation of African American women within the penal population, particularly after the end of the Civil War.

In southern states where prisoners were leased out as laborers, white women were seldom leased; they were sent more often to central state prisons or prison farms (plantations). African American women (and men) were leased to work on farms, in mines, and in railroad gangs. Later, when African American women in southern states were sent to penitentiaries and prison farms in increasing numbers, they lived in segregated quarters, often of lesser quality than those of white prisoners. In these settings, African American women were more likely to be assigned to laundry and fieldwork while white women were assigned to sewing, housekeeping, gardening, and taking care of animals.

In those states with reformatories and separate penitentiaries for women and men, African American women were more likely to be sent to custodial prisons for women or to women's sections of male institutions. Southern reformatories were reserved for white women. Outside the South, most African American women imprisoned in reformatories were segregated from white prisoners. In reformatories with educational programs and jobs that paid (even if meager) wages, whites were channeled into clerical positions and other assignments while African Americans were assigned to laundry work and nonpaying jobs. Moreover, the programs and services offered by institutional staff and outside volunteers, who tended to be white, were more likely to cater to white prisoners. Even where African American prisoners were allowed limited access to recreational activities, they were "encouraged to conform to racial stereotypes,"[15] such as participation in prison glee clubs.

Another researcher who observed racism in women's prisons throughout the country was Kathryn Watterson.[16] At the State Correctional Institution for Women in Muncie, Pennsylvania, for example, where 53 percent of the prisoners were African American, tensions between prisoners was fueled by the fact that white prisoners were assigned to the better-paying jobs, were more likely to be given a warning than a disciplinary write-up, and were less likely to be sentenced to the maximum security cottage.

Watterson also observed that until the 1990s, Latinas imprisoned in institutions throughout the country were not officially allowed to read or write letters in Spanish, speak in Spanish with visitors and friends, or subscribe to Spanish-language newspapers and magazines. The justification given for this was the lack of bilingual staff to censor written material and monitor conversations between prisoners.

In 1998 Barbara Owen published her study of the Central California Women's Facility (CCWF), which focused primarily on how gender roles learned prior to imprisonment affected the manner in which prisoners related to one another, to staff, and to significant others on the outside.[17] Owen was aware that women of color were disproportionately represented in the state's women's prison population. As a result, she wondered whether racial division affected the manner in which women "do time." Owen found that female prisoners did not divide into the racially and geographically based gangs found in male prisons. While she acknowledged that "race and ethnic identities form a subtext that mediates relationships among the women and between the workers,"

Owen concluded that they are "not a primary element of prison social organization."[18] This was so, she argued, because there was little "overt segregation" as women tended to mix racially (and ethnically) in the gym, yard, and dayrooms. Prisoners also participated in interracial and interethnic same-sex relationships and prison family networks. Overt racism, in Owen's view, was also prevented by the fact that regulations, while not always enforced, mandated a "mixture of ethnicities in a given room or job assignment."[19] When race and ethnic issues emerged it was, according to Owen, only ". . . during times of special confrontations, such as interpersonal conflict or competition over scarce resources, or in cultural expressions (songs, movies or slang) where racial context was brought out from its background."[20] Although at least one-fourth of the prisoners were Latinas, Owen's only reference to the impact of ethnic factors within the prison setting was that Spanish-monolingual prisoners had other prisoners translate for them. In spite of Owen's observations, several of the prisoners she interviewed continued to insist that racial frictions created a lot of tensions and that, as a result, prisoners tended to stick to their own kind. Interviews conducted by the author with former CCWF prisoners confirm these observations. Furthermore, according to African American and white prisoners interviewed by Owen, some of the guards promoted racism by telling African American and white prisoners conflicting things about one another. Imprisoned women of color also argued that white prisoners were assigned to the better-paying jobs, particularly those in Prison Industry sector.

Futhermore, as Owen's study documented, at times white guards' hostility to prisoners of color took the form of verbal and physical abuse. As Chicago, an African American prisoner, declared, ". . . here the staff will call you 'nigger'. . . . Or they will tell you to get up on the wall and be rough with you and kick your legs open with their knees. Like they did to me. . . . They said, 'You fucking nigger, I ought to body slam you.'"[21] Prisoners' frustrations with such situations sometimes led them to vent their anger on other prisoners.

It was partly in response to the lack of literature on the role played by ethnic and racial factors in penal settings that I published a study in 1996 comparing the impact of state policies on Latina(o) prisoners in New York State, the manner in which prisoners sought to reform prison conditions, and the response of penal staff and third parties to prisoners' calls for support.[22]

Findings indicated that while it was not uncommon to find female prisoners participating in interracial/interethnic formal and informal prisoner groups, rifts continued to exist along racial, ethnic, and class lines. Most prisoners continued to socialize primarily with members of their own ethnic or racial group. Latina prisoners further subdivided according to their nationality, language spoken, and sometimes skin color. Those most likely to mix with African American and/or white prisoners were those who spoke English, could pass for either "black" or "white," and/or participated in "homegirl" networks formed by prisoners who came from the same neighborhoods.

During the 1970s and 1980s, it was not uncommon for Latina and African American prisoners to have verbal and physical confrontations with one another. While prison authorities were aware of these incidents, little was done to discourage them. The conflicts between Latina and African American prisoner leaders led the former to create what became known as the Hispanic Committee to address issues specific to Latinas.

Language barriers, the lack of an adequate number of bilingual personnel, and the lack of disciplinary records and charges written in Spanish meant that Latinas, particularly those with little or no knowledge of the English language, were more likely than their English-speaking counterparts to be penalized for violating rules and regulations they were unaware of. It was only as the result of a class action suit won by prisoners (*Powell v. Ward*, 542 F. 2d 101 [1976]) that translations of disciplinary records and charges were mandated as of 1979. However, both Latina prisoners and staff continued to be reprimanded for speaking in Spanish without authorization.

The lack of an adequate number of bilingual personnel and outside volunteers meant that Latinas were less likely to be provided with vocational and rehabilitation programs deemed necessary for early parole release. Equally serious was the lack of bilingual personnel in the medical department. Few bilingual staff members could be called upon for medical emergencies or could understand prisoners' descriptions of symptoms and medical histories. Confidentiality was compromised when nonmedical personnel and/or other prisoners were asked to translate. Moreover, a significant number of Latina prisoners were not properly informed of their diagnoses, provided instructions for proper use of medication, and/or provided appropriate follow-up treatment. As a result, 50 percent of the prisoners who died at Bedford Hills for medical reasons between 1977 and 1985 were Latinas.[23] During that time, Latinas comprised less than 25 percent of the prisoner population.[24]

Due to their overrepresentation within the prisoner population and the prejudices of the predominantly white staff, Latina and African American prisoners were also more likely than white prisoners to suffer physical abuse at the hands of guards.

While the literature on imprisoned women seldom mentions how prisoners have sought to reform prison conditions, my study found that when outside sources of support were available, for example, in the form of prisoners' rights attorneys, prisoners were more than willing to join together to engage in litigation efforts against the facility.

In 1998 Native American scholar Luana Ross published a ground-breaking study comparing the conditions encountered by Native American and white women imprisoned at the Women's Correctional Center in Montana.[25] Ross found that while prisoners as a group "experienced violence in the form of sexual intimidation, the overuse of mind-altering drugs, lengthy stays in lockup," and "separation from children," Native American prisoners were subjected to further discrimination based on cultural and religious practices.[26] (Chapter 12 presents Ross's research.)

CONCLUSION

Mainstream social scientists studying women's prisons have tended to focus their research on emotional and sexual relationships among female prisoners to the almost total exclusion of others types of alliances. With few exceptions, studies have highlighted gender issues while ignoring the importance, of racism, ethnocentrism, and class biases within prison settings. By discussing the experiences of imprisoned women as if devoid of significant influences from penal personnel, state policies, and social movements, prisoners' experiences have been portrayed as taking place within a social vacuum. As a result, social scientists have distorted the experiences not only of prisoners of color but also of white prisoners and staff. Given the racial and ethnic diversity present in women's prisons, homogeneous descriptions of female prisoners appear to be the result of researchers' own racial, ethnic, gender, and class biases more than a reflection of reality.

While a number of studies on women's prisons provide information about how gender socialization prior to imprisonment affects the manner in which female prisoners will relate to one another, to staff, and to significant others, studies that take into account racial and ethnic factors demonstrate that gender analysis is not sufficient to understand the experiences of imprisoned women. Furthermore, it is not enough to say that racism, for example, had an adverse impact on the lives of female prisoners prior to their incarceration. For women of color, their history of colonization, forced immigration to the United States, and slavery also must be considered to understand how the treatment and conditions they confront in prison are part and parcel of the genocide their communities have been subjected to since the process of European colonization began. In fact, as Ross and I have argued, imprisonment is part of the process by which the dominant white majority imposes its will on people of color. Social scientists who ignore such histories of oppression contribute, even if unwillingly, to the continued propagation of distortions and stereotypes about the experiences of all people.

Students of women's prisons must be willing to analyze how their own multiple privileges and biases distort their analysis. To accomplish this task, they also must be willing to study the oppressive role the United States government has played in maintaining the continued oppression of people of color, particularly through the use of penal institutions. Such analysis requires us to assign at least as much responsibility to economic and political factors as on the individual actions of prisoners. Prisons must be studied as what they are, institutions that are used to control the behavior of certain social groups and communities.

NOTES

This chapter is part of a larger project analyzing mainstream social science conceptions of imprisoned women. I would like to thank Rosalind Ruth Calvert for her editing suggestions.

1. See Kathleen A. O'Shea and Beverly R. Fletcher, *Female Offenders: An Annotated Bibliography* (Westport, Conn.: Greenwood Press, 1997).

2. As of June 30, 1991, women of color constituted 61.4 percent of women held in state institutions and 64.5 percent of women in federal prisons. *American Correctional Association, Juvenile and Adult Correctional Departments, Institutions, Agencies and Paroling Authorities* (Laurel, Md.: American Correctional Association, 1992).

3. David Ward and Gene Kassebaum, *Women's Prisons: Sex and Social Structure* (Chicago: Aldine-Atherton, 1965), 58.

4. Rose Giallombardo, *Society of Women: A Study of a Women's Prison* (New York: John Wiley & Sons, 1966), 195.

5. Esther Heffernan, *Making It in Prison: The Square, the Cool, and the Life* (New York: John Wiley & Sons, 1972), 29.

6. Edna Walker Chandler, *Women in Prison* (Indianapolis: Bobbs-Merrill, 1973), 69.

7. Estelle Freedman, *Their Sisters' Keepers: Women's Prison Reform in America, 1830-1930* (Ann Arbor: University of Michigan Press, 1981). See also Eugenia Cornelia Lekkerkerker, *Reformatories for Women in the United States* (Batavia, Holland: Bij J.B. Wolters' Uitgevers-Maatschappij, 1931).

8. Candace Kruttschnitt, "Race Relations and the Federal Inmate," *Crime and Delinquency* 29 (October 1983): 577-92.

9. Ibid., 577.

10. Elouise Junius Spencer, "The Social System of a Medium Security Women's Prison," Ph.D. diss., University of Kansas, 1977, 61.

11. Ibid., 158.

12. Ibid., 147.

13. Ibid., 182-83.

14. Nicole Hahn Rafter, *Partial Justice: Women in State Prisons, 1800-1935* (Boston: Northeastern University Press, 1985).

15. Ibid., 155.

16. Kathryn Watterson, *Women in Prison* (Boston: Northeastern University, 1996).

17. Barbara Owen, *"In the Mix": Struggle and Survival in a Women's Prison* (Albany: State University of New York Press, 1998).

18. Ibid., 152.

19. Ibid.

20. Ibid., 154.

21. Ibid., 157.

22. Juanita Díaz-Cotto, *Gender, Ethnicity, and the State: Latina and Latino Prison Politics* (Albany: State University of New York Press, 1996).

23. Luz Santana, "Address before the Hispanic Inmate Needs Task Force," Hispanic Inmate Needs Task Force Awards Banquet, Albany, New York, November 20, 1985.

24. See State of New York Department of Correctional Services, Division of Program Planning and Evaluation, "Ethnic Distribution of Inmates Under Custody of New York State Correctional Facilities As of 9/1/82" (loose sheet); and ibid., Division of Hispanic and Cultural Affairs, Hispanic Inmate Needs Task Force, Final Report, "A Meeting of Minds, An Encounter of Hearts" (Action Plan), 1986, 205-206.

25. Luana Ross, *Inventing the Savage: The Social Construction of Native American Criminality* (Austin: University of Texas Press, 1998).

26. Ibid., 107.

TWELVE

Imprisoned Native Women and the Importance of Native Traditions

LUANA ROSS

Many imprisoned Native women struggle with the importance of Native traditions, the destruction of Native cultures, and the criminalization process. Therefore, any discussion of the value of Native traditions for women prisoners must begin with the criminalization of Native cultures by the federal government.

Native nations have been shattered by the course of their relationships with Euro-Americans and their laws. Aside from laws, the federal government actively pursued policies designed to suppress Native worlds. For instance, in 1901 all agents and superintendents of Indian reservations were notified to enforce the "short hair" order.[1] To the federal government, long hair signified a "primitive" culture, and those who had long hair were seen as "deviant" and subsequently criminalized.

Early "crimes" of resistance by indigenous people further depict their criminalization by Euro-America. As I have argued in *Inventing the Savage,* these acts came in the form of warfare, protecting their homelands, and the continuation of cultural traditions.[2] Crimes of resistance by courageous Natives are noticeable in the number imprisoned in Montana during the late 1800s and early 1990s for vagrancy, stealing horses and cattle from white men, the burning of Euro-American jails, and not sending children to Euro-American schools. The cultural oppression of Native people remained blatant, and cultures of resistance emerged. For example, on June 13, 1894, the *Weekly Missoulian* reported that despite a law against Native religions, "renegade Cree Indians" of Montana were preparing for an important ceremony—the Sun Dance. According to the newspaper, the governor had issued a proclamation against the Sun Dance, stating that it was "inhuman and brutalizing, unnatural and indecent, therefore abhorrent to Christian civilization." Prohibitions against Native religions, whether actual laws or merely federal government orders, were not lifted until 1934 with the passage of the Indian Reorganization Act. Religious freedom was supposedly strengthened in 1978 with the American Indian Religious Freedom Act.

One of the most oppressive institutions in the United States is the criminal justice system. Euro-American prisons always have operated to keep Native people in a colonial situation. As in the past, in the 1990s Native people encounter overwhelming odds at every stage of the Euro-American criminal justice system. Hence, high incarceration rates of Native people must be seen in the context of racist federal policy and an oppressive societal structure. The immense number of jailed Native Americans is depressing. For example, in 1995 Native Americans made up 6 percent of the total state population in Montana while Native men comprised 17 percent of the state's total male prisoner population and Native women comprised 25 percent of the state's total female prisoner population.[3] Currently, Native women are 40 percent of the total female prisoner population in Montana, according a May 10, 1998, report in the *Billings Gazette.*

Federal policy, specifically Public Law 280, creates an additional complication in the interpretation of incarceration rates. Reservations that fall under PL 280 are subjected to state jurisdiction; that is, Natives arrested on those reservations are sent to state prisons, not federal prisons. In Montana, out of seven Indian reservations, only one (Flathead) is a PL 280 reservation. The data for Native prisoners in Montana State

Prison includes only those arrested on Flathead or off-reservation; it does not include Natives from Montana incarcerated in federal prisons.

RACISM IN MONTANA STATE PRISONS

Many prisons, including Montana's, are now deleting the word "rehabilitation" from their list of goals. Nevertheless, when I conducted the study on imprisoned women at the Women's Correctional Center (WCC) in the early 1990s, the notion of rehabilitation was offered as a supposed healing process from being labeled "criminal" with no thought to discrimination in the criminal justice system or differing worldviews.[4] Authorities on Native Americans and depression caution against generalizing depressive symptoms, as defined by Western medicine, to other cultures.[5] What may be a symptom of depression in Euro-American culture may be a spiritual dilemma in Native culture, a facet of everyday life, or quite possibly a reaction to colonialism.

Many Native women at the WCC responded to the harsh prison environment by being detached, by observing how things were conducted. Prison counseling staff misinterpreted their behavioral reaction as a suppression of anger, which led to the overprescribing of a variety of mind-altering drugs. The women believed that because the counseling staff did not know how to relate to them as Native Americans, they tried to control them with drugs, which they were forced to take.

Critical of the WCC's rehabilitative programs, Native women sought culture-specific programming. When one woman tried to secure relevant programming, prison staff labeled her a troublemaker. This "troublemaker" is a traditional Native American, who was raised immersed in her culture. She has little knowledge of Euro-American culture and fluently speaks her native tongue. She said that white society always has made her feel "ashamed"; thus she does not communicate well with most white people. She added that because Natives are surrounded by white people in prison, they must learn to "walk stronger."

Enduring the same racialized experiences as Native women at the WCC, imprisoned Native Canadians Fran Sugar and Lana Fox discuss the impact of racism on their ability to heal in prison: "For Aboriginal women, prison is an extension of life on the outside, and because of this it is impossible for us to heal there. . . . For us, prison rules have the same illegitimacy as the oppressive rules under which we grew up. . . . Physicians, psychiatrists, and psychologists are typically white and male. How can we be healed by those who symbolize the worst experiences of our past?"[6]

Many scholars and activists argue that without Native traditions, imprisoned Natives cannot be rehabilitated effectively.[7] The director and spiritual advisor for the Navajo Nation's Corrections Project, Lenny Foster, believes that a spirit-based model of rehabilitation is the sole solution for imprisoned Natives.[8] Foster argues that prison programs based on Native American traditions have been extremely successful in changing negative behavior and that the released prisoners take the positive changes back to Native communities. In fact, because Native traditions are seen as healing, many prisoners who either fell away from their Native cultures or never knew traditional Native ways seek out their traditions while imprisoned.[9]

Medical anthropologist James Waldram conducted a study on the struggle of imprisoned Native Canadian men to practice Native traditions freely behind prison walls.[10] Waldram examined the affects of various traumas—including Indian boarding schools and racism—on the lives of Native people. He argues that Native people have experienced a kind of trauma that is directly related to colonialism. Extending existing theories of trauma to imprisonment and emphasizing the importance of culture in prison programming, Waldram warns that assimilationist programs are especially damaging to Native people. In the spirit of true rehabilitation and survival, Waldram suggests, and I agree, that historical Native traditions present the highest hope for imprisoned Natives.

According to Waldram, a Native spiritual path involves respect for one's self and others, a life free of substance abuse, and nonviolence. The most dedicated prisoners, according to Waldram, refuse to participate in the prison's subculture. I found this statement true in my work with imprisoned Native women in Montana. Traditional Native women were particularly bewildered by the prison's subculture. As a result, they refused to participate in it; for example, they would not use prison language ("kite," "roll-over," "snitch," etc.). Another example is that of a traditional prisoner who struggled with her testimony against her codefendants.[11] She was unable to make an immediate decision regarding her testimony. Family members prayed with her in jail and instructed her on honesty—a virtue in her tribe. Her relatives told her: "We always taught you never to lie; we taught you to be honest. This is how you were raised. You were raised in the Indian way and that's one of the things is that when you are Indian, you should not lie. If you know something, you'd better say something." She was still confused about her testimony and the label "snitch." That night she had a dream that helped her decide what to do. Divinely inspired, she made the decision to tell the truth about the crime. While some interpreted her actions as "snitching," to her she was telling the truth. Furthermore, as her instructions to do so came in the form of a vision, the label "snitch" is sacrilegious.

Similar to other imprisoned Natives, Native American prisoners at the WCC (re)turned to their cultures as a way to survive and resist imprisonment. Tim Giago, a well-known Native journalist and editor of *Indian Country Today,* reported that Native Americans told him that wardens often perceived their return to their traditions while imprisoned as "a step backward, a return to the 'savage ways' rather than a true religious awakening."[12]

Because racism is active outside prison walls, we can expect that it thrives inside prison. At the WCC, relationships between Native and white prisoners were strained and racism spilled over into their interactions. One Native woman who shared a cell with three white women said her situation was particularly difficult because her cell-mates ridiculed her religion. White prisoners and prison staff illustrated their ignorance of Native cultures by referring to Native religion as "voodoo." Although voodoo is an acceptable religion, white prisoners and staff used the term as an insult.

One Native prisoner sent a memo to prison staff stressing the importance of sweetgrass and sage to Native peoples. Because the staff believed these sacred items were drugs, and thus banned these items, she asked them to offer a cultural-awareness workshop. Fran Sugar clarifies the meaningfulness of sweetgrass to her as an imprisoned Native:

> At times when I'd burn my medicine, when we had sweetgrass smuggled in to us because sometimes it was seen as contraband, the

sweet smell of the earth would create a safe feeling, a feeling of being alive even though the cage represented a coffin, the prison a gravestone, and my sisters walking dead people. Those medicines were what connected me as a spirit child. One time when I was close to suicide I was told by Mista Hiya [spiritual leader] that my spirit was alive and it was housed in my physical shell. And from that hard time I learnt that my spirit was more important than my body because my body was controlled by the routine of life in prison. It was then the connectedness to being an Aboriginal Woman began. I began feeling good about myself even though I had only a few reasons to feel good. I understood there was a spirit within me that had the will to live.[13]

When Native women at the WCC finally won the right to burn sweetgrass at prayer meetings, white prisoners told the guards that Native prisoners were smoking marijuana. The Native women were insulted by the accusation, because the mixing of prayers with drugs or alcohol is sacrilegious. Several searches of cells occupied by Native women followed, increasing the racial tension between Natives and whites. During the investigations, the guards handled the sweetgrass and medicine bundles disrespectfully. One traditional Native woman had this to say about the careless treatment of sacred items:

I tell them [the guards], "These items are sacred to us. We have respect for them; that's all we ask from you—show a little respect. Is it any different from you going in there and jerking the Protestant's Bibles and throwing them around? Is it any different from you running in there and telling the Catholics or jerking their rosaries away? Don't Protestants have their own sacred items? Do you dump the Catholic's holy water out just to check if they have chemicals in them?"[14]

Because of the racialized conflict between white and Native prisoners, Native prisoners sought out relationships with other Native women. To Native prisoners, especially traditional women, culture was of primary importance to friendship. Recognizing the significance of culture as well as the racism in prison, one Native woman said:

If there's a bunch of white women in the dayroom, we don't really care to sit there because, you know, like Agnes said, "They talk too much." So, what we do is find a corner and sit and visit. Although it offends some of the white women in here when we do that, but sometimes we just like time to ourselves. We can relate to one another and be ourselves—be Indian. . . . in here [prison], you have to compose an image with these white women.[15]

CONSEQUENCES OF CULTURAL ALIENATION

Many prisoners are traumatized prior to incarceration. The trauma is then extended inside prison in a way that is unique to institutions of punishment. Trauma caused from such institutions can have drastic psychological consequences. For instance, a former director of a prerelease center in Montana remarked that Native women frequently attempted suicide prior to their release.[16] This person placed the blame directly on depression caused from cultural and social isolation.

Imprisoned Native Canadian women disproportionately attempt and complete suicide.[17] Social isolation is critical in the analysis of incarcerated Native Canadian women and custodial suicides, researchers have argued. Whether the isolation is caused by separation from families, or removal from the general population to maximum security, ultimately it is the result of incarceration. In addition, racism is an added burden to the distress caused by the separation from family and culture. It intensifies a poisonous environment that is already conducive to severe depression as defined by Euro-American and Native cultures.

In the context of colonialism, suicide can also be an act of defiance rather than the result of internalized oppression:

It reflects the hopelessness of trapped and imprisoned souls. It is an unwillingness to continue suffering. . . . According to many American Indians, whose lives have been affected by the government goal of assimilating them into the general ethos of American life, suicide could be construed as the ultimate act of freedom. It is an act that defies governmental control and challenges the dominant society to face up to its irresponsibility in meeting treaty agreements for health, education, and welfare.[18]

A CULTURE OF RESISTANCE

In the WCC, traditional Native women who were serving long sentences felt disassociated from their cultures and worried about being alienated from their communities. Culture was vital to these women, and they regularly requested from the prison administration cultural activities tailored for Natives. They particularly wanted permission to form a group that would allow them to express their respective Native cultures.

On February 20, 1991, the Native women presented a proposal to the prison administration to establish a Native women's society. The goals of the society included: culture-specific counseling, instilling of cultural pride, and availability of spiritual leaders. There was no reply from the prison administration. A month later the prisoners resubmitted the proposal, which led to the establishment of a Native women's group.

This spiritual group was not perceived positively by most white prisoners, prison staff, and prison authorities. For example, the prison allowed the Native women to meet for one hour every Sunday. Although that was not long enough for group prayer, prison staff would not extend the time. Oddly enough, various Christian groups were allowed more than one hour for their prayer meetings. The prison administration also allowed Native women to burn sweetgrass and sage during prayer time, *if* they resided in the general-population building. Native women in maximum security were not afforded this privilege.

The denial of culture and racism continued, and in 1993 the Native women issued a position paper to prison authorities. They requested access to Native spiritual leaders, a sweat lodge, and an end to a racialized prison system. Because of the inhumane conditions, in April of 1993 the American Civil Liberties Union (ACLU) filed a class action lawsuit. Based on information from the prisoners, the lawsuit regarding Native women prisoners and religion read: "No Spiritual Leader is available for Native American women and they do not have a Sweat Lodge. Male prisoners have the opportunity to participate in weekly religious services and Montana State Prison has a Sweat Lodge."[19]

After a long battle with the prison administration, Native men incarcerated in Montana have had permission to have a sweat lodge since 1983. Yet this same institution refuses to allow imprisoned Native women to practice the sweat lodge ceremony, despite their formal proposal. This fact reveals the gendered nature of incarceration.

PRISON REPRISAL

The oppressive prison environment at the WCC, including the denial of culture, prompted acts of resistance by imprisoned Native women that included: unity as Native women; maintenance of culture; letters to the ACLU, the Native American Prisoners Rehabilitation Research Project, local newspapers, and political figures; deliberate disobeying of prison rules, resulting in time in spent in maximum security; and escape (as two Native women did in 1994 and 1995).

According to former prisoner L. R. Reed, many imprisoned Native Americans would like to relate their experiences and file lawsuits because of the discriminatory treatment they face in prison. Nevertheless, they are intimidated by prison officials; hence, many stories go untold and Native prisoners continue to remain invisible. Furthermore, Reed says that prisoners who fall out of favor with prison authorities inevitably encounter reprisal.[20]

Prisoners at the WCC involved in activism suffered a range of retaliation by prison officials. Several Native women, who were documenting the prison's treatment of Native prisoners and sending the information to the ACLU, remarked that the prison staff were alarmed that they were affiliated with legal groups. Their actions proved threatening to prison staff, and one Native woman said she was told to "Either knock it off or you're going to be here for the rest of your life."[21] In fact, the warden told me that as long as he is the warden, this particular woman would serve her full forty years.

Many Native prisoners wrote letters to local newspapers criticizing the prison system and offering cost-effective alternatives to imprisonment.[22] These women were seen as "troublemakers" and were penalized by prison staff. For instance, they said that guards purposely baited them in order to confine them in maximum security or put them in lockup on bogus charges. Many times this was done to break the unity of the Native women. Another woman wrote letters to Native American newspapers and organizations expressing the intolerable treatment imprisoned Native women were receiving. She described the prison's reaction to her: "So I was labeled a radical; like I discriminate against white people. And, of course, they don't even understand that term, yet they hear someone else say it so they say it. They say I'm prejudiced because I want to help Native Americans."[23] This prisoner said that because she was negatively labeled by key prison personnel, other prison staff would not speak to her. Indeed, prison staff warned me about this prisoner. One described her as "a manipulator" and as a person who "hates white people." This prisoner was keenly aware that she was designated "a racist." Expressing her bewilderment over the label, she said: "They call me a racist and here I am in a white prison, run by white people, based on white values."[24]

These examples of retaliation—the danger of parole denial, lockup, and being falsely labeled as racist—illustrate the threatening environment that prison staff produce when prisoners practice Native cultures and actively support other prisoners. It should not puzzle anyone that Native women serve long stretches in maximum security for "behavioral" problems

CONCLUSION

In the new millennium, Native women imprisoned in Montana continue to be denied full religious autonomy. The denial of religious freedom continued at the WCC until 1995 when Ben Pease, a respected Crow elder, was permitted access to the women's prison. Prior to this, although the prison supposedly aimed at rehabilitative programming, the rejection of Native cultures was rampant.

One of the primary problems with the prohibition of religious freedom for Native women at the WCC is that it is illegal. The American Indian Religious Freedom Act of 1978 specifically states that imprisoned Natives have the right to fully practice their Native traditions. Imprisoned Native men are permitted the sweat lodge, while Native women are not, and white women have full access to their (Judeo-Christian-based) religions. Hence, there are separate rules for men and women and for Native Americans and white people, although having separate rules is illegal according to federal law.

Most important to the use of Native culture for rehabilitation is the acknowledgment of the strengths of Native cultures and their respective healing qualities. The practice of Native traditions has eased the burden of colonization and imprisonment. Regarding the healing aspect of culture, author James Gilligan suggests that "An intact culture can provide people with a powerful means by which to bolster their self-esteem and protect themselves from what could otherwise be overwhelming, soul-murdering intensities of shame and humiliation."[25]

Native Nations must practice their sovereign rights. One way tribes can maintain sovereignty is to regain control over their citizens by operating rehabilitative programs based on traditional philosophies and concepts of interdependence and reintegration. A positive move in Canada was the opening of the Okimaw Ohci Healing Lodge, designed for Native Canadian female offenders, in August of 1995. The concept underlying this alternative prison is true rehabilitation and healing through programming based on Native traditions. The Healing Lodge offers an environment conducive to the empowerment of Native women. It would be advantageous for all people, regardless of race/ethnicity, to adopt a similar program.

The Native women with whom I spoke believed that they had been involved in illegal activities because they were removed from their cultures. These women maintain that a return to Native cultures is the way to survive imprisonment because Native traditions are healing as well as empowering.

Imprisoned Native American women continue to resist domination and marginalization, as indigenous people have done for centuries. Passionately engaged in a struggle to remain Native, by maintaining their traditions within a repressive institution, these women are true revolutionaries. They should be commended for their efforts, especially since this overwhelming struggle of decolonization is in itself an important aspect of true rehabilitation. One of the greatest strengths imprisoned Native women have—which emerges from their cultures and histories of colonialism—is their vision: a vision for themselves, each other, Native communities, and Native nations.

NOTES

1. See F. Prucha, *The Great Father: The United States Government and the American Indians* (Lincoln: University of Nebraska Press, 1984).
2. See Luana Ross, *Inventing the Savage: The Social Construction of Native American Criminality* (Austin: University of Texas Press, 1998).
3. Ibid.
4. Ibid.
5. See E. Duran and B. Duran, *Native American Postcolonial Psychology* (Albany: State University of New York Press, 1995); and J. H. Shore and S. M. Manson, "Crosscultural Studies of Depression Among American Indians and Alaska Natives," *White Cloud Journal* 2 (1985): 5-11.
6. Fran Sugar and Lana Fox, "Nistum Peyako Seht'wawin Iskwewak (First Nations Women): Breaking Chains," *Canadian Journal of Women and Law* 3, no. 2 (1989-1990): 476-77.
7. See E. Grobsmith, *Indians in Prison: Incarcerated Native Americans in Nebraska* (Lincoln: University of Nebraska Press, 1994); L. R. Reed, "Rehabilitation: Contrasting Cultural Perspectives and the Imposition of Church and State," *Journal of Prisoners on Prison* 2, no. 2 (1990): 3-28; Ross, *Inventing the Savage*; and J. Waldram, *The Way of the Pipe: Aboriginal Spirituality and Symbolic Healing in Canadian Prisons* (Peterborough, Ontario: Broadview Press, 1997).
8. See Reed, "Rehabilitation."
9. See I. Cardozo-Freeman, ed., *Chief: The Life History of Eugene Delorme Imprisoned Santee Sioux* (Lincoln: University of Nebraska Press, 1993); *The Great Spirit Within the Hole,* prod. and dir. Chris Spotted Eagle, 50 min., Spotted Eagle Productions, 1983, videocassette; Grobsmith, *Indians in Prison*; Ross, *Inventing the Savage; To Heal the Spirit,* dir. by B. Barde, 40 min., Why Not Productions, 1990, videocassette; Waldram, *The Way of the Pipe.*
10. Waldram, *The Way of the Pipe.*
11. See L. Ross, "Punishing Institutions: The Story of Catherine (Cedar Woman)," in Susan Lobo and Steve Talbot, eds., *Native American Voices* (New York: Addison Wesley Longman).
12. See Tim Giago (Nawica Kjici), *Notes From Indian Country,* vol. 1 (Pierre, S.D.: State Publishing Company, 1984), 327.
13. Sugar, "Nistum Peyako Seht'wawin Iskwewak (First Nations Women)," 467.
14. Ross, *Inventing the Savage,* 165-66.
15. Ibid., 156-57.
16. See Ibid.
17. See K. Faith, *Unruly Women: The Politics of Confinement and Resistance* (Vancouver, B. C.: Press Gang Publishers, 1993); M. G. Grossmann, "Two Perspectives on Aboriginal Female Suicides in Custody," *Canadian Journal of Criminology,* 34, nos. 3-4 (1992): 403-16; *To Heal the Spirit.*
18. LaFromboise and Bigfoot 1988, quoted in R. Bachman, *Death and Violence on the Reservation: Homicide, Family Violence, and Suicide in American Indian Populations* (New York: Auburn House, 1992), 109.
19. See *Many Horses et al. v. Racicot et al.* 1993, 18.
20. See Reed, "Rehabilitation."
21. Ross, *Inventing the Savage,* 165.
22. Ibid.
23. Ibid., 164.
24. Ibid., 164-65.
25. James Gilligan, *Violence: Reflections on a National Epidemic* (New York: Random House, 1996), 205.

THIRTEEN

Military
Prostitution in Asia
and the United States

ALEXANDRA SUH

Kyung Richards spent seven years in a North Carolina prison on a murder charge.[1] She grew up in an economically devastated region in rural Korea. As a teenager, she was raped. Not long after that incident, and after the death of her father, she began working in a bar close to a U.S. military base. Kyung began a relationship with a U.S. serviceman while still in her teens. They married and came to the United States, but her husband, who was an addict, became abusive and Kyung found herself on her own. Later she became involved with another man, also a former serviceman and also an addict who also became very abusive; and, after several years Kyung moved herself and her two young children to a motel. She found work at a local bar, but unable to afford child care, she left her children alone in the motel with the television on while she went to work. One day Kyung came home to find one of her children dead: Apparently her two-year-old son had tried to use a drawer in the bureau as a step in an attempt to reach the television, and both bureau and television fell on top of him. She called someone she knew, who advised her to call the police. Unaware of investigatory proceedings, she tidied up the motel room before police arrived; she was afraid that if the police saw an untidy room, they would take away her other child. When police arrived, Kyung was still extremely upset, and cried that she had killed her son, overcome by the anguish of a mother who held herself ultimately responsible for her children's well-being. To this day she feels guilty for her son's death, blaming herself that she was unable to afford a baby-sitter. Although the outcome of this tragedy is striking, the conditions that led up to it—a lack of economic opportunities, services, and resources for racialized immigrant women with limited English fleeing domestic violence—are common.

The difficulty of Kyung's loss was redoubled by her treatment in the hands of a criminal justice system quick to judge an Asian woman who could not speak English, who lived at a motel and left her children alone while she went to work in a bar. Although the death was an accident, Kyung was charged with second-degree murder for killing her son. Prosecutors argued that her first grief-stricken cries that she had killed her son were a confession to murder. Even though Kyung's English abilities were severely limited at that time, she was not provided with a translator at her trial. The prosecutor, G. Dewey Hudson, interviewed in *The Women Outside,* described her crying on the stand during the trial as "shrill noises" which were "more animal-like, and so foreign to me; it was frightening to me,"[2] indicating ways in which Kyung was racialized through the trial. She was convicted and sentenced and lost custody of her daughter.

After Kyung had been in prison several years, a group of Korean women activists learned of her predicament. They began a campaign for her release, and eventually the governor of the state in which she was incarcerated granted clemency and Kyung was freed on parole. But Kyung had already served seven years. After leaving prison, she moved to New York, where the women involved in the campaign, along with others, founded the Rainbow Center. The center provided her with shelter, counseling, advocacy, and community support. In the years that followed, though, Kyung had to struggle with mental illness and periods of homelessness and never regained custody of her child.

In *Immigrant Acts*, scholar Lisa Lowe describes the historical contradictions that "have placed Asians 'within' the U.S. nation-state, its workplaces, and its markets, yet linguistically, culturally, and racially marked Asians as 'foreign' and 'outside' the national polity."[3] Through legal definitions of citizenship, the process has historically constituted citizenry not only as white but also as male. While many immigrant women facing poverty must work in the informal labor market and contend with labor law violations and immigration restrictions, those who are working or have worked as prostitutes face even more severe circumstances. Nominally discrete mechanisms of state policing—the criminalization of prostitution, the law enforcement and the criminal justice systems, and immigration legislation— operate to control, incarcerate, and exclude women from a polity seeking to consolidate itself not only as white and male but also as morally righteous, drug-free, and sane. Applicants for naturalization must state whether they have ever been a "habitual drunkard," "a prostitute," "an illicit trafficker in narcotic drugs or marijuana," "declared legally incompetent or confined as a patient in a mental institution," or "knowingly committed any crime for which [they] have not been arrested," all of which may not only exclude them from citizenship but also place them in deportation proceedings. To the degree to which involvement in prostitution and drugs and enforcement of laws that relate to those areas are racialized processes, immigrants of color are disproportionately impacted. In this chapter I consider the experiences of Korean immigrant women sex workers and former sex workers within the broader context of global labor migration and the racialized and gendered processes shaping citizenry and national culture. I seek to show how the legacy of U.S. imperialism and neoimperialism in Asia, operating together with the contradictory logics of global capital and the U.S. nation-state, combine systemically to produce and repress in the United States a class of criminalized Asian women sex workers, women whose vulnerability to abuse from husbands, employers, and clients in the private sector is reinforced in the public sector through state control and persecution. This situation enables the continued exploitation of Asian immigrant women sex workers.

PROSTITUTION

Prostitution is defined primarily through laws that criminalize it. Such laws render it illegal to offer to exchange particular services deemed sexual (whether one's own services or another's) for remuneration. But criminalization of prostitution must be placed in its historical and cultural context; in the United States, prostitution was listed as an occupation in the official census in the late nineteenth century. Significant among the forces that originally led to the criminalization of prostitution was the xenophobic drive to exclude Chinese from this country. In the late nineteenth century, U.S. mining and railroad companies recruited from China men who were not permitted to bring their families. Through the activities of recruiters who lured or kidnapped women and brought them to the United States, Chinese women in prostitution became institutionalized. They became targets of rhetoric about Asians' lack of morality, and antitrafficking and other laws were passed to protect white laborers against the establishment of permanent Chinese communities in the United States.[4] Thus the social construction of Asian women as prostitutes can be traced both to the process of U.S. economic globalization that brought labor from Asia and to the gendered exclusion of Asian permanent residents.

Analyses of women's or men's reasons for entering prostitution pathologize them as individuals. Those that do not focus on individual "deviance" generally follow one of two lines of thought. One tends to exalt Western liberal notions of choice and free will and risks leading to a libertarian glorification of prostitution as sexual and/or economic liberation, ignoring the fundamentally exploitative conditions under which much prostitution operates in our society, especially for nonwhite prostitutes. The other focuses exclusively on external forces in women's lives, such as sexual assault or economic conditions, and risks stripping women of agency and subjectivity, sometimes to the point of insisting that any woman who claims she has chosen prostitution is brainwashed. In any situation where physical force is not a factor, people make decisions based on circumstances and available options. In the case of women denied access to well-paying jobs, with little or no family financial support, prostitution is usually the only way to make a significant income. According to research done by Saewoomtuh, a center in Tongduchon, Korea, for women working in the clubs and bars near the U.S. bases, 70 percent of women working around the bases in Korea who were not lured into it cite financial need as the main reason for entering military prostitution, or prostitution in which the customers are mainly or exclusively military service personnel.[5]

THE UNITED STATES IN
KOREA AND MILITARY PROSTITUTION

From the Spanish-American War to World War II, the Korean War to the Vietnam War, and with the occupations, security treaties, political advisors, economic development policies, and cultural legacies that followed in their wake, neoimperialism in Asia has been crucial to the emergence of the United States as a superpower in the twentieth century. Asia scholar and policy specialist Walden Bello suggests, "[P]erhaps the best way to comprehend the U.S. presence in the Pacific is to describe it as a transnational garrison state that spans five sovereign states and the vast expanse of Micronesia. The U.S. Pacific Command is an integrated and extremely secretive complex composed of mobile forces and fixed bases over which the host states exercise merely nominal sovereignty."[6]

This discussion focuses on the relationship between the United States and one northeast Asian nation, Korea. Prostitution as such was not introduced to Korea by the United States. The *kisaeng* (women entertainers linked to prostitution in pre-modern Korea) tradition existed long before contact with Western powers. However, the emergence of U.S. military base prostitution as a distinct and significant economic and social institution can be traced to two interconnected phenomena: the sexual slavery of over 100,000 women in Asia, mostly Koreans, often referred to as "comfort women," under the Japanese Imperial Army during World War II; and the history of U.S. military engagement in Asia. Coming into Korea on the heels of the vanquished Japanese colonizers, after U.S. atomic bombs dropped on Japan precipitated the end of the war, the United States has played a long-standing and preponderant role in shaping conditions in South Korea.[7]

Today approximately one hundred U.S. military installations are scattered throughout South Korea. They have transformed economies and cultures at the local and national level. A significant part of this transformation was the rise of military prostitution around the bases and the shift in local economies to dependence on this prostitution. Adjacent to each base is a neighborhood or town centering on bars and clubs—off-limits to Korean nationals who do not work at the clubs—where servicemen meet prostitutes. Historically, militarized prostitution played an important economic role as a source of foreign currency for Korea and sustenance for countless families. Disparities in income between GIs and prostitutes were such that even up through the late 1980s, when South Korea's "economic miracle" began to touch some parts of the working poor, a "short time" cost the serviceman $5, and $10 got him an entire night with a woman. This was just a small fraction of the monthly salary of a serviceman—himself most likely from America's urban or rural underclass—whose lodging, meals, clothing, and accessories are provided for him.[8] In the 1950s annual per capita income for Koreans was under $100. Although it climbed in each succeeding decade, a majority of the population continued to live in poverty. For women, the situation was worse. As recently as 1995, women's nonagricultural wages in Korea were only 53.5 percent of men's. While an improvement over previous decades, this statistic indicates the great gender disparity that underlies the gross national product (GNP) average.[9] For women who needed to support themselves or their families, the possibility of earning $10 in one night was a rare opportunity, even if the lion's share went to club owners. U.S. military presence and economic dominance in Korea has been a driving force, combined with traditional Korean patriarchal and stratified society, in the production of a class of women criminalized and stigmatized in Korea and the United States as U.S. military base prostitutes.

Millions of Korean women facing economic crisis in the context of transformations of Korea's economy from a largely rural one to a largely urban, state capitalist economy, the gender imbalance in wages and employment opportunities, the accompanying political and cultural influence of the United States on Korea, and the particular culture of militarized masculinity within the U.S. Armed Forces, have been forced into prostitution in the past five decades. Patriarchal traditions in Korea combine with the contemporary reality of U.S. domination to place severe stigmas on the women who work as prostitutes. Even families that take money from these women often ostracize them. In the meantime, the United States continues to be renowned for its economic opportunities and social freedoms. A move to America seems to be a way for a woman to improve her situation, a way out of a culture that has rejected her, through marriage with a serviceman she is involved with and in many cases cares for. Since 1945 an estimated 150,000 or more Korean women have married U.S. citizens and immigrated to the United States.[10]

DOMESTIC VIOLENCE AND THE STATE

Although a comprehensive survey has not been done, anecdotal evidence indicates that a 70 to 80 percent rate of abuse, neglect, and abandonment exists in marriages between U.S. servicemen and Korean women. While some of these marriages do turn out well, this is not true in most cases. Women facing domestic violence in their marriages with U.S. servicemen are extremely vulnerable. Their husbands occupy positions of privilege and enfranchisement: They are male, often white, English-speaking, and familiar with the laws and customs of the country; they can easily converse with law enforcement officials, usually have a social and family network, benefit from greater access to financial resources, and enjoy the rights of citizenship. Frequently the husbands carry socially reinforced notions of superiority vis-à-vis their wives on the basis of race, gender, and nationality, in an ideological system where racialized women are subordinated and Korea is seen as feminized and weak. Their Korean wives often are geographically isolated, have difficulty with English, are underinformed about their rights and the law, often lack a Korean community that is supportive of them, and frequently have not had access to education or job training. The fact that the women are immigrants places them at greater risk, since their husbands are their immigration sponsors and they risk deportation if they leave the marriage. Although the 1994 Violence Against Women Act provides some protection for immigrant women battered by their spouses/

sponsors, claimants must be able to document their injuries. In many cases, Korean immigrant women do not have independent access to medical or legal services or information about their rights.

Violent discord in the marriage often brings on criminal prosecution for internationally and interracially married Asian immigrant women who are not from elite backgrounds. Yeon-ah Atkins was married to a former serviceman who abused her throughout the many years they lived together, and she raised his children from a previous marriage. On one particularly bad occasion, according to Yeon-ah, her husband tried to shoot her, and a bullet hole remains in the wall of her former home. When her husband got involved with another woman, he ignored her and left her alone at home, isolated and distressed. One day Yeon-ah set a fire in a garbage can in front of the house of her husband's lover, where her husband was at the time. Although she had set the fire in order to get his attention and force him to come outside of the house for a confrontation, the fire grew larger than she had intended. She ran away but the next day went to the police station. She was arrested and charged with arson. During the year that it took to get her charges down to a misdemeanor for setting the fire, her husband effectively threw her out of the house, placing all her belongings in storage under his name. She never recovered her home or her belongings. When she came to live at the Rainbow Center, she was homeless and severely depressed. She now lives on public assistance.

Since women working near the military bases generally have not graduated from high school or often even middle school in Korea,[11] they know that their employment prospects in the United States are limited. A number of women who are abandoned or forced to flee violent homes end up in massage parlor prostitution, homeless, or in the mental health departments of public hospitals, in some cases cycling through all three. One woman, Misook Lee, was abused physically and emotionally for many years by her husband, who was also Korean. She fled and ended up working in Korean massage parlor prostitution for seven years. Most of the women she met there had been married to U.S. servicemen and had worked as prostitutes near the U.S. bases in Korea. Many bases in the United States are bordered by bars and clubs staffed by Asian women married or formerly married to servicemen. In the Rainbow Center's six years of experience, domestic violence and sexual abuse, along with a lack of access to a supportive community or services, have without exception been factors in the lives of Korean women who have later ended up in prostitution, homeless, and in mental institutions. Ironically but not coincidentally, while the great majority of homeless men in the United States are veterans of its wars in Asia, most homeless Korean immigrant women in the United States are former military base prostitutes who had been married to U.S. military servicemen.

KOREAN MASSAGE PARLOR PROSTITUTION IN THE UNITED STATES

Korean massage parlor prostitution is generally not physically forced prostitution. Brothels do exist in which Asian women are physically detained and forced to serve men sexually. What goes on in these brothels should not be classified as prostitution but as sexual slavery.[12] The distinction between physical and other types of coercion can be dicey. The factors that impel women to go into massage parlor prostitution are not dissimilar to those that bring women to stay with an abusive partner or to work at a garment factory sweatshop for a $2 hourly wage. These factors may include debt bondage, economic dependence, social bonds, threats, and uncertainty about the future and alternatives. Structurally, the massage parlor operates like an agency, with the workers as independent contractors.[13] Women are generally not guaranteed work and are not paid by management. The massage parlor provides rooms, collects approximately $50 per customer, and sometimes provides security, with any specific services and fees to be negotiated between the worker and the customer. Management also sometimes loans money to workers. Massage parlor clients consist of men of all races and class backgrounds who at the individual level range from sympathetic and lonely to violent and brutal. Often clients are police officers. Misook states that she was astonished to recognize a large number of her clients at the police precinct one of the first times she was arrested.

In the 1980s and continuing today, there was a crackdown on Korean massage parlor prostitution. The crackdowns, whatever the intent behind them, result in extraction of profit from the women. The

Women Workers Project of CAAAV has found that police raids, mounted on grounds ranging from building code violations to prostitution, can sometimes occur more than once a week. Each time women are arrested, they must pay fees to lawyers and sometimes also serve the state in the form of community service. Because women often work extremely long shifts, they are obliged to carry large amounts of cash on them, sometimes amounting to thousands of dollars per person, which renders them vulnerable to theft by the police officers. At an arrest, the cash the women have on them is confiscated; whether the individual officer takes it for himself or turns it over to the precinct, the women never see the money again. Prostitutes' rights activist and scholar Priscilla Alexander has pointed out that many arrests of street prostitutes occur just after officers' shifts end. Arrest procedures going on past the end of a shift qualify the officer for overtime pay at a higher rate. In these and other ways, the state, its agents, and the private individuals running the parlors directly profit from prostitution. As CAAAV's Women Workers Project has noted, crackdowns drive women further underground, often into escort services, which, because women must meet customers at their locations, expose them to a far higher risk from violent customers. In one 1997 case on which CAAAV provided advocacy, Miyoung Taylor, a Korean woman working as an escort, was robbed, brutally beaten, raped, and left for dead in a Manhattan office building over the weekend. The beating was so severe that she was in a coma and might have died if a security guard had not found her. Fortunately, Miyoung recovered and was able to participate in the conviction of the perpetrator, a white male in his early twenties and a self-described martial arts expert.

SUBSTANCE ABUSE
AS AN OCCUPATIONAL HEALTH HAZARD

Substance abuse is overwhelmingly perceived in our society as an individual weakness or failing. While individuals can and must take responsibility for addressing problems posed by their abuse, I seek here to contribute to analyses of structural forces that contribute to addiction to "controlled substances." In Korean massage parlor prostitution in the

United States, workers' substance abuse must be seen not as an individual failing but rather as an occupational health hazard.

In many, though not all, parlors, management not only permits the use of drugs but sells them. A large number of clients use freebase cocaine, and selling small quantities to them for use at the parlor is an additional way to profit from them. The owners of some parlors encourage women workers to use drugs provided by the parlor on credit. This impacts women in a number of ways. Because it continually increases their debt to the owner, regular users are forced to work much longer hours at the parlor to support the ongoing expense, thereby increasing the available supply of labor. Then, according to one former worker, the addiction itself, in addition to the debt, makes it much harder to leave the parlor for those who might wish to do so.

Drugs enable some women to continue their work. While prostitution may not be a necessarily and essentially degrading or dehumanizing form of work, the particular conditions and the social stigma placed on Asian prostitutes today make it a difficult experience for many. In a survey conducted by Saewoomtuh, 92 percent of the women surveyed described themselves as having a "drug habit." There are no such studies of Korean or Asian immigrant women prostitutes in the United States, but since many women in Korean massage parlors have worked as U.S. military base prostitutes in the past, we can assume a good deal of overlap in the responses. The top reasons cited for drug use in the survey are to (1) forget physical and mental pain arising from prostitution; (2) fall asleep or relieve stress; (3) recuperate from fatigue; (4) eliminate feelings of shame and fear; and (5) accommodate pressure from customers or friends.[14]

The economic logic of the massage parlor as an institution encourages and fosters substance abuse (although this cannot be generalized to all parlors), and it is on this basis that substance abuse can be seen as an occupational health hazard. Because the drug prices are marked up, workers' substance abuse also significantly increases profits for the owner. In addition, many clients ask women to freebase with them, another practice sometimes encouraged by management. Whereas in most workplaces, workers' substance abuse is seen as a hindrance to productivity and profit, in massage parlors it is an additional means of increasing profits and stabilizing the labor force. This systematized introduction to substance abuse occurs not because of the nature of prostitution per se but due to the criminalization of prostitution and the social stigma placed upon it that guarantees that the work goes on underground and out of reach of any regulations that might protect workers. Owners and management exploit the criminalized status of prostitution and the patriarchal social stigma attached to prostitutes to encourage substance abuse.

MENTAL ILLNESS AND INCARCERATION

Although scientists are debating the role of genetic makeup in predisposition to mental illness, it is undeniable that stress, trauma, and abuse play a significant role in determining the time of emergence and the severity of a mental illness.[15] Anecdotal evidence and observations by Rainbow Center staff suggest that mental illness, understood here in terms of clinical definitions of schizophrenia and paranoia,[16] is common among women who have undergone multiple forms of trauma and abuse. Those who suffer from mental illness in this country are at a high risk for incarceration. Over 10 percent of the nation's incarcerated are known to suffer from schizophrenia, manic depression, or major depression,[17] totaling some 200,000 people on any given day. At Riker's Island in New York City, 15 percent of inmates have serious mental disorders. Mental illness and incarceration are mutually reinforcing, particularly among the poor and those without community resources: Mental illness often results in behavior that the state criminalizes, and incarceration generally adds stress to the lives of mentally ill prisoners, exacerbating their illnesses. Women working in massage parlors who become mentally ill are rarely in contact with family and can end up on the street. Homeless individuals, because they are on the street much of the time and without resources, are subject to much more frequent encounters with law enforcement officials. They thus face a much greater risk of arrest, including for crimes linked to homeless status, such as trespassing, breaking and entering, and theft of food. Individuals who have what our society defines as mental health problems, who are without care and support, often end up in prisons.[18]

POLICING THE BORDER: IMMIGRATION
LAWS AND KOREAN IMMIGRANT PROSTITUTES

U.S. immigration laws exacerbate the circumstances facing Korean women workers in massage parlor prostitution. Undocumented immigration is a deportable offense even if no other crimes have been committed. For documented immigrants, crimes of "moral turpitude" and many drug offenses are grounds for deportation and exclusion from immigration and citizenship. Mental illness also can be grounds for exclusion. In a reversal of previous legislation, current rulings in many states permit certain law enforcement officials and agencies (where a documented immigrant might apply for benefits) to report undocumented or unlawful immigrants to the Immigration and Naturalization Service. As benefits for immigrants are cut back, a woman's prior or current involvement in prostitution or substance abuse may cause her to fear applying for citizenship or for the benefits to which she would be entitled, since many women working in massage parlors are permanent residents of the United States through their marriages with U.S. servicemen. Because prostitution and drug trafficking (many drug laws expose users to trafficking charges) are deportable offenses, women who may seek to leave these areas of employment will be almost completely isolated from structures of support available to citizens.

Repressive and exclusionary mechanisms of the state in the context of globalized economies have created in the United States a class of criminalized and racialized Korean women immigrants. Their experiences suggest that a solution cannot simply emphasize more just or equitable enforcement of existing laws. Such efforts may be helpful and strategic in certain cases, but in the long run they will never address the lack of economic options immigrant women face, nor the forms of criminalization that combine to place groups of people in the position of noncitizen, criminal, and morally corrupt. Efforts must both seek to challenge U.S. military, political, economic, and social dominance in Asia and to transform laws that criminalize women who work as prostitutes or abuse substances. Furthermore, since state institutions play a key role in rendering prostitutes who are immigrant women of color vulnerable to exploitation and abuse in the private sector, both from citizen husbands and from massage parlor owners, we must also seek to strengthen extralegal forms of collective self-defense and empowerment and nurture alternatives to legislative means for change through community organizing. In Kyung's case, things have greatly improved: Today she helps manage the Rainbow Center Thrift Shop, providing key leadership and support for other women. However, she is obliged to take powerful psychotropic medication that has considerable side effects. If the experiences of Korean immigrant women show us how much individual struggle and community support can achieve, they also show us how far we must go to before women are no longer obliged to "choose" between militarized prostitution and hunger, between domestic violence and homelessness, between police raids and violent clients, between mental illness and psychotropic drugs.

NOTES

1. Pseudonyms are used to refer to the women incarcerated or trapped in the sex trade.
2. J. T. Takagi and Hye Jung Park, *The Women Outside* [documentary film] distributed by Third World Newsreel, 1995.
3. Lisa Lowe, *Immigrant Acts* (Durham, N.C.: Duke University Press, 1996), 8.
4. See Lucie Cheng Hirata, "Free, Indentured, Enslaved: Chinese Prostitutes in Nineteenth-Century America," *Signs* 5(Autumn 1979), 3-29.
5. Kim Hyun Sun, *Conditions Facing Prostitutes in U.S. Military Camptowns* (Tongduchon, Korea: Saewoomtuh, 1997).
6. Walden Bello, "From American Lake to a People's Pacific," in Saundra Pollock Sturdevant and Brenda Stoltzfus, eds., *Let the Good Times Roll: Prostitution and the U.S. Military in Asia* (New York: New Press, 1992), 14.
7. Since 1945 the United States has had a dominant influence on South Korea militarily, politically, economically, and culturally and has maintained a constant military presence in South Korea. Some five decades after the armistice that ended the open fighting of the Korean War, 37,000 U.S. troops remain, a legacy of the Cold War that has transformed the lives of Koreans both south and north of the 38th parallel. For a study of prostitution and U.S.-Republic of South Korea security agreements, see Katherine Moon, *Sex Among Allies* (New York: Columbia University Press, 1997).
8. In the 1990s, the prices charged at military bars and clubs climbed steadily, to the point where it was no longer small change for the servicemen. On the contrary, many women migrated to the Korean (clientele) sex industry because they could earn more there than from U.S. soldiers. However, given the recent problems in the national economy, the International Monetary Fund's bail-out, and the drop in value of Korean currency vis-à-vis the dollar, the situation may be changing again. As in other countries, people in Korea with the least resources appear to be bearing the brunt of the restrictions and regulations imposed by the IMF, while the bail-out guarantees loan repayments to foreign banks invested in overleveraged Korean corporations.

9. Uhn Cho, citing UNDP Human Development Report statistics, "Female Labor in Korea: Economically Active But Not Empowered," *Asian Women* (Spring 1996): 2, 57.
10. Note: Korean women married to servicemen should not be assumed to be former prostitutes. The relationship of international marriage to global labor migration is an important matter that space limitations do not permit me to elaborate upon here.
11. Kim Hyun Sun, *Conditions Facing Prostitutes*.
12. Activists around the "comfort women" issue in Korea, in which over 100,000 women, mostly Korean, were forced to serve Japanese soldiers sexually under brutal conditions during World War II, use the term "military sexual slavery." In this case, to continue to use the terms "comfort women" or "comfort troops"—a phrase that the Japanese Imperial Army itself used for the women—is to deny or dim awareness of the kind and degree of sexual and physical exploitation to which the women were subjected.
13. The culture, however, is, as in many Korean small businesses, paternalistic and pseudo-familial, with workers as children.
14. Kim Hyun Sun, *Conditions Facing Prostitutes*.
15. Scholars such as Michel Foucault have argued that mental illness is a socially constructed determination relative to hegemonic constructions of normativity, the behavioral standards of which are imposed by medical, educational, and other institutions. See Michel Foucault, *Madness and Civilization* trans. Richard Howard (New York: Random House, 1965).
16. I retain these definitions as a means of identifying behaviors that may be "natural" reactions to trauma but that in any case expose women to further exploitation or difficulty such as homelessness and incarceration.
17. Fox Butterfield, "Asylum Behind Bars. Prisons Replace Hospitals for the Nation's Mentally Ill" *New York Times,* March 5, 1998, A1.
18. In past decades, there was a far greater rate of placement in mental institutions. While that system was also subject to criticism, the current practice of placing mentally ill individuals in prison seems to be a worse alternative.

FOURTEEN

HIV, AIDS, and Rape in Texas Prisons

BRENDA RODRIGUEZ

State prison systems across the country have created breeding grounds for human immunodeficiency virus (HIV) that expand beyond prison walls and back into the communities. At least 24,200 of the 1.02 million inmates in the United States carry the virus, and 5,100 suffer from acquired immune deficiency syndrome (AIDS)—more than six times the AIDS rate outside prison. The disease is the leading cause of death in Texas prisons, killing 475 inmates since 1992. AIDS deaths started to surpass those from cancer and heart disease in 1990, prompting the state to open separate prison wards to treat infected men and women. Yet prisons in Texas and other states are faced with a greater challenge of dealing with the deadly virus that causes AIDS. Only sixteen states and Washington, D.C. require all inmates to be tested for HIV or AIDS. Texas does not test its inmates, leaving corrections officials in the country's second-largest prison system ignorant of how many inmates are infected with the virus. Voluntary screening shows 1,979 of the 132,400 Texas inmates carry HIV. Experts say the number of infections could be three times higher. Infectious disease clinics at two Texas prisons hold more than five hundred inmates. Other infected prisoners remain integrated in regular cellblocks.[1]

Some inmates enter the prison system already infected, and others contract the virus behind bars through illicit sex, intravenous drug use, and sharing tainted tattoo needles. Prisons try to limit drugs by searching cells and busting abusers when caught in the act. But they are far from stopping the drug trade. In 1996, 295 Texas inmates were prosecuted for drug possession. According to monthly health reports filed by the Texas Department of Criminal Justice, most likely 48 percent of all prisoners diagnosed with HIV or AIDS caught the virus through intravenous drug use. Prison officials in Texas and other states do not know how widespread drug use is behind bars or how many users are exposed to HIV in prison.[2]

The men at the Mark W. Stiles unit in Beaumont call this facility the "death camp." The unit houses the prison system's first hospice, and, for infected inmates, it is where they go to die. In 1996, 99 men died of AIDS complications in the Texas prison system. And, in 1995, 117 died. That compares to 27 deaths from heart disease and 35 from cancer that same year. At the Stiles unit, the AIDS epidemic has "become very real" for the medical staff. "I see these people as somebody's sons. They are paying for their mistakes, but nobody said they had to pay for it with their lives. It's not something we desire to see; so many people so sick. It's a fact of life," said Sally Brown, the prison's former patient-care coordinator. And, as with most male inmates, the men at the Stiles unit don't always like to talk about AIDS. Steve Nesselroth, director of the New York AIDS in Prison Project, said while some men openly discuss their disease, most refuse to talk about the virus and to deal with reality. "Men put up a wall around themselves," Nesselroth said. "It's much less emotional [than with women]."[3]

Inmate Scott Stalcup, thirty, is one of 200 men who live in Building 4—the infectious disease clinic—at the maximum security prison. Another 200 men with HIV are confined in other cellblocks at Stiles. The prison holds 3,000 inmates; more than 400 are HIV positive. "I'm real afraid to die," Stalcup said. "I'm scared to die in a penitentiary. I'm afraid I'm going to die tomorrow and never see my family." The son of a military family stationed in Killeen, Stalcup is serving twenty-five years for armed robbery. He made off with $700 from a deli to finance his cocaine habit. He would have robbed a bank, he says, but it was closed. At the time of his 1997 interview, published in the *San Antonio Express-News*, Stalcup's T-cell count had plummeted to 28, compared with the normal 1,000 for someone HIV-free. Still, he was optimistic about making parole in the year 2007.[4]

A Vietnam veteran and plumber from Houston, forty-eight-year-old Gerald Bill bought hundreds of syringes a month to shoot up heroin after long days at work. He had a modest home, a wife, and two daughters. He lost it all. Bill is serving ten years for possession of drugs and was denied parole in 1997. During a two-year separation from his wife, Bill dated a woman, whom he believes infected him with the virus. "My mama always thought a woman was gonna kill me," he says. "I had a cellie that died of HIV. I was the one that was suffering with him. Every day and night, he was hitting on the walls and hanging from the bed. He was hurting. It scares me. I don't want to end up like that. It could be you."[5]

The hospice at Stiles provides around-the-clock care for inmates until their deaths. It is a separate infirmary at the end of a long hallway decorated by murals painted by prisoners. Patients receive care focused on their spiritual, psychological, and medical needs. Opened January 1, 1997, the hospice is one of several the state expects to place in prisons to handle a growing number of terminally ill inmates. The medical staff at Stiles has trained thirty-five inmates to work with hospice patients— reading to them, writing their letters, and keeping them company. "A lot of them don't have nobody. They are human. Everybody has downfalls," says inmate volunteer Ricky Sterlings, a thirty-four-year-old Fort Worth native who is not HIV-positive. "A lot of people don't see the outcome of this disease. They don't see the effects. It's bad to be locked up and dying." State Senator Michael Moncrief (D-Fort Worth) sponsored legislation in 1995 to start the hospice program. "They [inmates] have the right to die with dignity," Moncrief says. "[The program] is designed to do inside what a hospice does outside the walls."[6]

Men are not the only ones struggling with this disease. Some women of the Texas City Sheltered Housing unit seek out each other for strength in dealing with the virus. Infected women are sent to the unit when their

T-cells are at 500 or lower. The 204-bed facility, which women call the "AIDS center," houses more than 100 patients. Of the 10,061 women prison inmates in Texas, 243 have been diagnosed HIV-positive. In 1996, four women were the only female inmates to die of AIDS complications. Many of the women do not look for sympathy. Instead they form bonds of sisterhood, turning to each other for support. "Women have a broader view of the world. They realize they are part of a family," Nesselroth said. "I cherish when I go into a women's prison. Their openness, their willingness to talk about the problems. They tend to be much more supportive of each other."[7] A comprehensive study sponsored jointly by the National Institute of Justice and Centers for Disease Control concluded that "economic dependency, injection drug use, crack use and associated increases in unsafe sexual practices have placed many women at elevated risk."[8]

Trulena McRinna, thirty-eight, of San Antonio, is infected with AIDS and now only hopes to leave the Texas City unit to be with her children. "I'm one of the healthy AIDS patients. To them [medical staff] on their papers my health has deteriorated, but if you look at me I'm fit as a fiddle," she said. "I try to take care of my body." McRinna arrived at Texas City in March of 1996 from the Mountain View prison in Gatesville and is serving an eight-year sentence for assaulting a police officer and for possession of a stolen check. She has already spent four years in the prison system and has never had a visitor. McRinna, who tested HIV-positive in 1990, once tried to kill a fellow inmate with a broomstick because the other woman spread details about her condition. She believes she was infected by her husband, who was an intravenous drug user. Former inmate Cathy English, forty-two, of Fort Worth, was reunited with her family when she was paroled in March 1997. While at the Texas City unit, English said the unit was her home—she and the other inmates were like sisters: "We are all one big family. We have respect for one another." Like many women, English, who tested positive in March 1996, believes she was infected by her ex-lover, an intravenous drug user. "It was my way of living that brought this on," said English, who is serving a ten-year sentence for possession of cocaine and crack. "I have to live it; I have to accept it. When you know you've done wrong, you have to pay your debt to society."[9]

Across the country, prison administrators rarely discuss or research issues surrounding HIV/AIDS; and few prison systems take steps to protect virus-free inmates. Justice Department officials have not studied transmission of HIV in prison, leaving a critical gap in research that could help wardens control the virus. In August 1997 the agency released its first update in three years on the number of prisoners with HIV and AIDS.[10] An extensive search by the *San Antonio Express-News* for prison AIDS research found only a handful of limited studies, some dated to the 1980s, on HIV transmission. "There are some real problems with the public and education around HIV. It doesn't know and it doesn't care,"[11] says Bob Dorn, spokesman for the Correctional HIV Consortium, a nonprofit organization in California that works with prisons across the country. According to Jackie Walker, AIDS coordinator of the ACLU National Prison Project: "This is the most ignored and underserved population. You really have to educate. Prisons are very interesting institutions, and a lot of them don't want to deal with the real issues."[12]

Sex between men is the most common way to catch HIV, yet prison and state officials note that sex behind bars is illegal. Taboo or not, sex in prison remains widespread, often forced and usually undetected—creating pathways for HIV. "There is something going on, but nobody wants to admit it. Many states are in denial," maintains Nesselroth. "We know [sex] happens. Off the record, any prison official would say that it happens." Stalcup candidly discussed unprotected prison sex. He spent time in administrative segregation in the spring of 1997 after he was caught having sex with another prisoner. "There are no women, so we have to resort," he says. "We want to be open about [sex]." But not all inmates are willing partners. One national study estimated that 131,000 male inmates—about 14 percent of the prison population—are sexually victimized every year.[13]

Don Collins, sixty-one, president of the Los Angeles–based organization "Stop Prisoner Rape," was the victim of frequent sexual assaults during the twenty years he spent in New Jersey prisons for armed robberies. Rape is common, he says, as "an accepted way in the prison culture of expressing rage." A Florida inmate recently told Collins over the phone that an HIV-infected prisoner was regularly having sex with cellmates, without informing his partners that he carries the virus.

Michael Blucker says he got infected with the deadly virus by a cellmate who raped him while in an Illinois prison. He had been in the maximum-security prison only two weeks when he was first choked, stripped, and raped by another inmate. Over the next six months, he became a prison gangster's "punk" and was sexually assaulted so many times he has no idea how many inmates he may have infected. "I was in a position where I feared telling," Blucker says from his Crystal Lake, Illinois, home. "The inmates control the prison, and they control the officers. He [the pimp] sold me to other gang members for cigarettes, alcohol, marijuana joints, or GP— general purposes." Six months after the rape, Blucker said he was sexually assaulted and beaten by inmates in more than fifty cells at Menard Correction Center. He said he did not tell prison officials because he feared the inmates. It took beating and rape by possibly fifteen inmates in a shower to break his code of silence.[15]

Blucker, released from prison in January 1997, filed a federal civil rights suit against employees of the Illinois Department of Corrections, including Director Odie Washington, wardens, assistant wardens, correctional officers, and medical personnel. On August 29, 1997, a jury cleared five staff members at the center. But it deadlocked over whether "deliberate indifference" was shown by Lieutenant Carl Caraway, who heads internal investigators at Menard, and Dr. Nageswasano Vallabhaneni, a psychiatrist employed at the prison. A new trial was expected to be set for them.

It is not uncommon for inmates not to report rapes. Many fear the repercussions, and others are too embarrassed. In Texas, reported rapes are investigated by the Texas Department of Criminal Justice's internal affairs division, and some are referred to district attorneys. In 1996 the state prison system had reported only two sexual assaults. The most reported rapes in the department, from 1993 to 1997, was five. The low number is symptomatic of the prevailing national attitude toward the crime, says Illinois State Representative Cal Skinner (R-Crystal Lake). "Rape in prison has never been a subject," said Skinner. "If you break the laws in Illinois, the punishment is prison. It's not prison and rape." Skinner has proposed legislation to create a program instructing inmates on rape prevention within forty-eight hours of their confinement.[16]

Americans' demand for longer sentences has exposed more inmates to the threat. In Texas, a surge in HIV cases coincided with the prison-building boom, increasing the number of known HIV cases from 615 in 1991 to 1,584 three years later.[17] But most prisoners eventually leave their cells and return to their neighborhoods. Since the true number of HIV-infected inmates is not known, corrections officials also do not know precisely how many are released. And there is little to no follow-up once the infected inmates are freed. Texas paroles at least forty to sixty known HIV carriers every month. They arrive back home with a ten-day supply of medication and the name of a health clinic. Prison officials only hope prisoners who have been released stay in treatment, avoid intravenous drugs, and practice safe sex. "What happens inside the prison walls also impacts what happens outside," says John Miles, special assistant for Corrections and Substance Abuse Activities at the Centers for Disease Control and Prevention. "Sally, John, and Susie are going to come home."[18]

A San Antonio woman, who wanted to remain anonymous, was paroled February 1997 after serving more than a year for possession of drugs. Upon her release she was given the standard supply of AIDS medication and the name of a local clinic. "I try to think that this isn't even happening to me," she said. "All I'm going to do now is get a place and enjoy my children." She tested positive for the virus in 1992 while in the Travis County jail. She says her common-law husband, a drug user, infected her. Her three children were living with her sister in San Antonio at the time. She did not tell Bison officials she was infected when she entered the system. She said many inmates do not and that some infected female inmates have unprotected sex with jail guards and other prisoners. "There are a lot of women who are married that have sex with women. Where I was, there were some officers who messed with the inmates. They need to start testing officers," she said.[19]

While some inmates seek help after their release, others do not. Michelle Wheeler, a San Antonio area supervisor for the State Board of Pardons and Paroles, said an arrest warrant had been issued last spring for a violent HIV-positive parolee who was biting people. He was not showing up for scheduled appointments with his parole officer, she said. Because HIV parolees have no obligation to disclose their condition, parole officers can only hope they are forthcoming. Some inmates released with the virus are assisted through the Texas Department of Health's HIV/STD Medication Program in Austin. The ten-year federally and state-funded effort provides free HIV medication for those who qualify under several income brackets. The cutoff is an annual income of $15,780 or less for a single person, or $26,669 or less for a family of three.

Prisons have dealt with the AIDS epidemic and the cost of treating inmates since the early 1980s, when people still considered it "the gay cancer." The New York state prison system in 1981 reported the first deaths of inmates from AIDS complications. George Prendes, a former New York prisoner who now heads an HIV prison project for inmates, recalled that at the time prison officials ignored the disease and other prisoners burned the cells of victims. In 1983 New York set aside an eleven-bed clinic for HIV inmates at the Sing Sing prison. The same year eighteen inmates died of AIDS-related illnesses. About 9,500 of New York's 70,000 prisoners in 1997 had tested positive for HIV. The state also works with community-based organizations to provide AIDS education, voluntary testing, and discharge planning for inmates. "We do what we think is the appropriate thing," says Jim Flateau, spokesman for the New York Department of Corrections. "It's obviously still a major medical issue for us."[20]

Years of dealing with the deadly virus have brought prisons to the forefront of medical care. "We have really taken a lot of responsibility for their health care," says Dr. Owen Murray, associate director for Texas Correctional Managed Health Care. "It's been something prisons have had to deal with much longer than in the free world." In the last few years the Centers for Disease Control and Prevention in Atlanta have recognized the Texas Department of Criminal Justice for providing the latest in medical treatment to HIV-positive inmates. The department spends $5,600 a year on medications for each HIV-infected prisoner. The money covers the cost of powerful drug cocktails including protease inhibitors, a new and expensive class of medications that have controlled the virus in many HIV carriers. By comparison, AIDS victims on the outside can spend more than $10,000 a year in medical care and up to $24,000 in HIV medications. The Texas prison costs are lower because drugs are bought in bulk and unused prescriptions are reissued. Dr. Charles Bell, head of the HIV and sexually transmitted disease division at the Texas Department of Health, said the medical care inmates received was like having health insurance. "On one hand, taxpayers are paying for this," he said. "But what do you want us to do, let them die? They are human."[21]

While the prison system provides inmates with the newest medications available, it falls short at providing the best education. Many prisoners rely on the word of fellow prisoners to avoid the disease. Misinformation is common, and the results can spread the virus to unsuspecting victims. Francisco Soliz, twenty-five, is a felon serving eight years at the Stiles prison in Beaumont, Texas, for parole violation and unauthorized use of a vehicle. A former dancer at a San Antonio gay club who tested positive for HIV before he entered prison in 1985, Soliz displays his newest prison tattoos: a fanged devil and a large sun with a ghoulish face. He does not worry about spreading the virus, he says, because the inmate tattoo artist told him he keeps his craft clean by using separate inks, one for HIV-positive inmates, one for virus-free inmates. However, the tattoo artist cannot be certain who has the virus and who does not. He could be spreading HIV with every new tattoo. Soliz, the father of a three-year-old daughter, says prison officials simply told him administering tattoos behind bars is against prison rules. "They look at people like us and say we are convicts. I might be here, but I don't consider myself a threat to society," he says. "I'm not ashamed, I know where I come from. I've learned more [about HIV] off of other inmates than the doctors."[22]

Like all Texas inmates, Soliz watched a seven-minute video and received pamphlets on AIDS when he arrived in prison. "Don't have sex with anyone while you are in prison," the narrator beseeches on the video as a cartoon drawing of an inmate in white-and-black striped prison garb displays a book titled *Minding My Own Business in the Big House*. It is the only education Texas inmates receive when they enter the system. Thereafter inmates must specifically request any further education. Criminal justice experts say the Texas approach is insufficient and leaves many inmates at risk. Consider the statements of Richard Tweksbury: "So you hand me a pamphlet during one of the most stressful moments in my life?" asks Tweksbury, professor at the University of Louisville's School of Justice. "Yeah, right. I'm going to read that pamphlet." Videos and pamphlets also warn about drug use and the risk inmates take when sharing hypodermic needles.[23]

Prisons have approached educating inmates about the deadly virus by using peer education, counseling, and literature. Only one program, though, has been hailed as successful in teaching inmates how to protect themselves from HIV—the San Francisco Forensic AIDS Project, where the project's five health workers educate inmates in the city's jails. San Francisco is one of six city, county, and state prison systems in the United States—and the only one in California—to distribute condoms to inmates. "Education on HIV doesn't operate in a vacuum," says Anne Stillwell, director of the Forensic AIDS Project. "People put up all kinds of barriers to this issue. Most correctional agencies have a different agenda, and their focus is not health care. But the programs we do in jail can be done in the prisons."[24]

Of the 2,000 inmates held at various county and city jails in San Francisco, 70 to 80 HIV-infected prisoners see Forensic AIDS counselors every day. The jails spend $360,000 a year on the program. Health workers say it is difficult to track the number of infected inmates in jails because the population changes daily. For many who float in and out of jails, classes offered through the project are a convenient way to learn about HIV and methods of prevention. The classes usually consist of 10 to 20 inmates and are up to two hours long. The project also can be court-ordered to counsel, educate, and test people charged with prostitution. No data exist to measure the project's performance. Jailers say success is measured by people who remain HIV negative. On a visit to one of the city jails, health worker Wolfgang Stuwe came across a student he had taught HIV prevention in the mid-1980s. The student was back in the system, but still HIV-negative—for which Stuwe gave credit to the project.

San Francisco County Sheriff Mike Hennessey, a pioneer in prison reform who makes inmate health care a priority, is given credit for the success of the program. His department was first affected by the virus in the early 1980s, when one of his deputies died of AIDS. Then, one by one, other deputies began to get ill. The department lost ten employees to AIDS in ten years. "It was one of those tragic benefits. . . . We had many gay employees, and [when] one of them died, it put more of a personal and humane face on the epidemic," the sheriff said. "There was a tremendous fear factor. It was something that was new and frightening in jails and prisons." For Hennessey, with the right planning and budget, the project can be copied in state prisons: "It's a matter of whether people who run the system think it's important. There is going to continue to be a lot of infection. All you can do is educate people. It's been a very difficult and emotional problem for our department."[25]

While some believe education is the best way to get a handle on the virus, others suggest more aggressive measures. The American Medical Association ten years ago saw the risks and advised corrections departments to test every inmate for HIV. As of 1995 only seventeen prison systems did so. The federal prison system, with 98,000 inmates, tests every inmate upon release. But federal prisons offer only voluntary screening to those in prison. Texas prison officials say their system does not provide mandatory testing because it is too costly. Screening all inmates also would require more counseling than is available, says Dr. Rosemary Hanicak, an administrator with the Stiles prison infectious disease clinic. According to Dr. Murray, testing everyone is not necessary because at-risk inmates—those most likely to catch HIV—already want to be tested. Based on limited screening in Texas, 1.4 percent of inmates carry HIV.

In Mississippi, prisons require blood tests of all inmates. In 1997, 1,256 of the 14,354 prisoners were HIV-infected. The infection rate of 9 percent is more than ten times higher than that in the general population. Unlike many states, Mississippi takes an aggressive approach to protect virus-free prisoners. Mississippi and Alabama are the only states that segregate those with HIV. And Mississippi allows inmates to buy condoms so they can practice safe sex. Only five other corrections departments in the country distribute condoms: the state prison system in Vermont, and city/county jails in San Francisco, Philadelphia, New York, and Washington, D.C. Texas prison officials say giving condoms to inmates would go against prison rules prohibiting prison sex. "We need to concentrate on education. Condoms are not the answer," says Lannette Lintchicum, associate director of health services for the Texas

Department of Criminal Justice. (Texas incarcerates and treats more than 400 infected men at the Stiles prison and about 100 infected women at the Texas City prison.)[26]

Mississippi prison officials say segregating inmates is the best way to protect virus-free inmates from those who are infected. "We do not mainstream. The benefit is in the health concern of other inmates," says Bill Stiger, a hospital administrator with the Mississippi Department of Corrections. "It's not like the 'Scarlet Letter.' We don't brand on their foreheads 'Unclean.'" Victims' advocates encourage Texas to follow Mississippi's lead. "They should be in a separate lock-up area. You never change someone's sexual habits," says Marinelle Timmons, executive director of the Victim Assistance Center in Houston. "Therapy and education can't change someone's sex preference whether they are homosexuals or predators. We are going to have more victims." The message has not struck a chord with Texas lawmakers. The state has spent $1.5 billion on new prisons since 1991, but AIDS prevention remains a low priority. "AIDS has certainly taken its toll in the free world, as well as that of the confined. It is going to continue to intensify and the population will continue to grow," Senator Michael Moncrief said.[27]

World health officials are prodding governments to control the growing prison epidemic. At the National AIDS Update Conference in March 1997, advocates criticized the level of prison care. "It's 'out of sight, out of mind . . . '" says Dr. Frederick Altice, director of Yale University HIV in Prison Program. "We have got a system that puts drug users in prison instead of rehabilitation. We open the doors, and we drop them off in the same social unrest. The department of corrections has no interest in keeping these people alive. It's too costly."[28]

In April 1997 the United Nations Program on HIV/AIDS (UNAIDS) issued a critical report "AIDS in Prison: A Serious Problem for Society." According to the report, "Prison conditions are often ideal breeding grounds for onward transmission of HIV infection." Describing the situation as urgent in its report to the U.N. Commission on Human Rights, UNAIDS concluded: "It involves the rights to health, security of person, equality before the law and freedom from inhumane and degrading treatment."[29]

NOTES

This chapter is drawn from articles written by the author and published in September 1997 in the *San Antonio Express-News.*

1. Brenda Rodriguez, "AIDS in Prison: Placing Society in Double Jeopardy," *San Antonio Express-News,* September 14, 1997, 1A.
2. Ibid., 14A.
3. Brenda Rodriguez, "For Ill Prisoners, Time at Beaumont's 'Death Camp' Can Be for Life," *San Antonio Express-News,* September 14, 1997, 14A.
4. Ibid.
5. Ibid.
6. Brenda Rodriguez, "Help Limited for Released Prisoners," *San Antonio Express-News,* September 16, 1997, 6A.
7. Brenda Rodriguez, "Sisterhood Forms in Prison AIDS Center," *San Antonio Express-News,* September 15, 1997, 8A.
8. 1994 Update: HIV/AIDS and STDs in Correctional Facilities, pg. 14.
9. Brenda Rodriguez. "Sisterhood Forms in Prison AIDS Center," *San Antonio Express-News,* September 15, 1997.
10. Bureau of Justice Statistics Bulletin "HIV in Prisons and Jails, 1995" (Washington, D.C., August 1997).
11. Brenda Rodriguez, "For Ill Prisoners, Time at Beaumont's 'Death Camp' Can Be for Life," 14A.
12. Ibid.
13. Brenda Rodriguez, "AIDS in Prison: Placing Society in Double Jeopardy," 13A.
14. Brenda Rodriguez, "Rape Contributes to Spread of AIDS," *San Antonio Express-News,* September 15, 1997, 1A.
15. Ibid.
16. Ibid., 8A.
17. Rodriguez, "AIDS in Prison."
18. Ibid.
19. Brenda Rodriguez, "Help Limited for Released Prisoner," *San Antonio Express-News,* September 16, 1997, 7A.
20. Ibid., 6A.
21. Ibid.
22. Rodriguez, "AIDS in Prison," 13A.
23. Ibid.
24. Brenda Rodriguez, "AIDS Education in This Jail Deals with Inmates and Sex," *San Antonio Express-News,* September 17, 1997, 1A.
25. Ibid., 8A.
26. Rodriguez, "AIDS in Prison," 14A.
27. Ibid.
28. Ibid.
29. Ibid.

FIFTEEN

Ritual Killings: Antigay Violence and Reasonable Justice

ANNJANETTE ROSGA[1]

INTRODUCTION: CATALYTIC MOMENTS

The 1998 killing of Matthew Shepard, a gay, white, male college student in Wyoming, produced a surprisingly vocal and widespread demand for more powerful hate crime laws and for a tempering of the antigay rhetoric of conservative Christian churches. *Nightline*, the well-known national news/analysis program, produced a 1998 special television broadcast on the murder, *Beyond Hate*; and Naftali Bendavid, writing for the *Chicago Tribune*, reported that "some think the nation's mood is more conducive than ever for penalizing hate crimes in the strongest possible way."[2] The then-pending federal "hate crimes bill" that would have strengthened a 1968 federal provision criminalizing certain civil rights violations did *not* pass, however, and many argued that Shepard's murder contributed to its failure. Bendavid wrote: "Some of the Kennedy bill's supporters say privately that the killing of Matthew Shepard, the Wyoming gay student, actually hurt the bill's chances. By focusing attention on the gay community's fierce push for the bill, these activists say, the Wyoming incident prompted the religious right to oppose it with equal fervor."[3] Nonetheless, this kind of national public attention to an antigay homicide is notably different from the relative obscurity of numerous very similar crimes, one of which is the subject of this chapter.

On December 15, 1987, in Levittown, Pennsylvania, Anthony Milano was murdered by two men, Frank Chester and Richard Laird, who subsequently were sentenced to death for the crime. At the time, antigay violence organizations reported a number of cases in which such homicides resulted in relatively light sentences. Just under two years prior to Milano's murder, in Kalamazoo, Michigan, a jury acquitted a defendant charged with killing a gay man with a sledgehammer on the grounds that he committed the murder in self-defense against a sexual advance.[4] Months after Chester and Laird were sentenced to death, Judge Jack Hampton in Dallas, Texas, gave a markedly reduced sentence to a man convicted of the premeditated and brutal murders of two gay men and explained his leniency with the following: "I don't much care for queers cruising the streets for teenage boys. . . . I put prostitutes and gays at about the same level, and I'd be hard put to give somebody life for killing a prostitute." Hampton added that he would have given the defendant a harsher sentence if the victims had been "a couple of housewives out shopping."[5]

In this context, the imposition of capital sentences in the Milano case appeared exceptional, even progressive. A death sentence in response to the bias-motivated murder of a gay man—or lesbian— was virtually unheard of in the U.S. criminal justice system at the time. The trial of Chester and Laird was the first to achieve a maximum sentence conviction for a murder explicitly understood to have been antigay, marking the beginning of a shift in how antigay homicides would be treated in the U.S. criminal justice system. Viewed from another angle, a sentence of death for poor and working-class men who have killed is not so unusual.[6] The Milano case, in many ways, had the odd quality of being simultaneously ordinary and extraordinary that marks catalytic moments in a culture. By "catalytic moments" I mean moments in which meaning is most actively constructed and potentially changed. For example, nationwide media coverage of an unprovoked, brutal killing of a white man is not so surprising. When that man has been killed because he was (or was perceived to be) gay, however, anything other than coverage in lesbian and gay newspapers—in 1987 when neither "gay-bashing" nor "hate crimes" had quite become the nationally televised terms they are today—was noteworthy.

Identity categories are essential to this case, just as they are inextricable from all work on hate crimes. The victim, Anthony Milano, was a lower-middle-class, Italian-American gay man of twenty-six, and the men convicted of killing him, Frank Chester and Richard Laird, were both white, heterosexual, working-class men, aged twenty and twenty-four respectively. The murder was understood to have been bias-motivated, even though it was not specifically prosecuted as such.[7] This articulation of the case was made possible by the fact that Anthony Milano's death was disturbing enough, to the right people at the right time, to warrant aggressive criminal justice proceedings, a substantial amount of mainstream local media coverage, and an outcry from that portion of the gay community primarily taken to represent gayness, the "out," white male community.[8]

As it was represented, this case offers a complex example of "repetition with a difference."[9] Both within the trial and out, Milano's ethnicity was clearly marked, while Chester's and Laird's were not. The exact opposite was true of their respective class statuses. (Although Milano's ethnicized whiteness, his Italian heritage, was consistently noted in media representations of the case, whatever potential it may have had to detract from his status as a "good victim" seems to have been neutralized by the equally consistent mention of his family's desire to assimilate successfully into the American middle class.) Media accounts suggest that the trial reiterated characterizations of homosexuals as criminal or sick, and of working-class men as both especially bigoted and inhumanly, inexplicably violent. On the other hand, these same characterizations were applied to different actors than might have been expected in 1988, with the uncommon result that an antigay murder was treated as the most heinous of criminal offenses. By analyzing the kinds of knowledge that were produced about gender, sexuality, criminality, and class through courtroom and media representations of the murder, I attempt to show how narrations of this case both challenged and reinforced the kinds of stories usually told about antigay violence in the United States. What was it about the way this case was narrated that compelled its particular ending?

This semiotic reading of the trial of Milano's killers indicates that specific constructions of masculinity were crucial to its outcome. Furthermore, the trial provides particularly rich examples of how commonsense representations of violence intersect with the sociolegal category hate crime. I will argue that current U.S. academic and popular representations of violence serve to obscure institutional violences of an epistemological nature, specifically, violence exercised by the state. Current ways of understanding violence, I suggest, contribute to the tendency of those working against hate crime to settle for oversimplified formulations of identity that come with its codification in law. The resultant constructions of hate crime permit what Patricia J. Williams has called "this society's most enduring and fatal rationalization, the separation of bias from violence."[10] These constructions are both profoundly dependent upon, and increasingly limited to, strategies that utilize the extant criminal justice system as a tool for social change. I close with some preliminary reflections on how hate crimes might be conceptualized differently to call attention to more complex interactions of violence, identity, and the law.

TRYING TOO HARD TO BE MEN

At about 12:45 on the morning of December 15, 1987, Anthony Milano left his parents' home to go out for a drink at a local bar, where he encountered Frank Chester and Richard Laird. According to testimony given by a bartender who was on duty that night, Chester and Laird had been present for a couple of hours before Milano arrived. The bartender reported that Milano remained at a table alone for half an hour before Laird challenged him to buy them a round of drinks. Eventually Milano did join the two at the bar and paid for one round. At 2:30 A.M., all three men left the bar together. The bartender further testified that Chester and Laird had pressured Milano for a ride and that after hesitating, Milano had agreed to take them home.[11] Nearly twenty-four hours later,

police discovered Milano's body in the woods near an area known as
Venice-Ashby. The coroner placed his time of death at approximately
3:30 A.M.—an hour after the men were seen leaving the bar. The cause
of death was officially recorded as "Extreme blood loss due to multiple
deep throat slashings."[12]

During the course of the evening before Milano's death, Richard
Laird was overheard calling a different man, his opponent in a pool game,
a "pussy" and a "faggot." At least one witness also testified that Laird
said, while Milano was out of hearing range, "I hate fucking faggots!"
and complained to the bartender about people like Milano "trying to
infiltrate us."[13] Finally, Laird and Chester were seen mockingly slow-
dancing in front of Milano. Combined with the details of how Milano
was killed (the attack evinced an intense rage, Milano's head was very
nearly severed from his body), these factors were taken by the Bucks
County District Attorney, the Philadelphia Lesbian and Gay Task Force,
and the editor of the *Philadelphia Gay News* to indicate an antigay
motivation for the murder.

Neither Chester nor Laird denied their presence at the time and
place of Milano's death. Instead, each claimed that after a period of
somewhat aimless driving that ended near the Venice-Ashby woods, he
turned around to find the other first hitting Milano, then slashing his
throat with a knife. Each man said he witnessed this and ran.

The combined trial of Richard Laird and Frank Chester took place
five months later, in May of 1988. Both men were charged with first-
degree murder, kidnapping, conspiracy, and a half-dozen other offenses.
They were convicted and sentenced to death. As of this writing, all of
their appeals have been denied.[14]

What made this trial unique among those that deal explicitly with
"sexualized" violence (violence that is, or is perceived to be, related to
sex or sexual identity) was that the victim was not portrayed as inviting
or provoking violence with his sexuality; nor was the homosexuality of
the victim used to transform him into a perpetrator of violence himself.
Milano was allowed, through discursive constructions of the actual
perpetrators and the murder itself, to *remain* the victim. The "homosexual panic" defense, used in the Kalamazoo case cited earlier, is more
typical of this genre of sexualized violence trials: The victim is said to

have provoked the beating or rape by leading the defendant on or by making unwanted sexual advances.[15] However, because of the ways in which Chester and Laird each chose to describe his own actions on the night of the murder, this approach was effectively foreclosed. Each attorney, in arguing on behalf of his client that the *other* defendant had done "the cutting," could not also plausibly claim Milano had caused his client to panic, for this would have conceded some measure of involvement in the murder. Thus, in one of the extraordinary features of this ordinary trial, Milano was not made to appear responsible for his own death.

In other respects, the story told in court and in the media slipped comfortably back into dominant antigay murder narratives. Not only did this trial not challenge the standard equation of homosexuality with criminality, that link was reinscribed in a complicated combination with class identity. Although neither defense attorney sought to sully Milano's character, the prosecution brought forth testimony designed to prove his essential innocence—thus implicitly countering anticipated juror responses to Milano's homosexuality. Since the district attorney intended to prove that both Chester and Laird had killed Milano, he had to show that their victim was no typical seductively evil homosexual. Had Milano "provoked" his killers, they might have been thrown into an understandable terrified fury—the "natural" response of men threatened with a homosexual advance. They might have been justified in murdering him.

It was the image of Milano as an innocent victim that Lisa DePaulo, then associate editor of *Philadelphia* magazine, picked up for her two-part feature story on the murder, published a year after Milano's death. Her widely read articles were the most detailed and, for many Pennsylvania readers, the only representations of Anthony Milano, Richard Laird, Frank Chester, and each man's family available.

If there is such a thing as a "good homosexual," it was, in DePaulo's depiction, Anthony Milano. She described a tortured young man trying desperately to overcome the touch of an unfortunate and arbitrary hand of nature. Milano's homosexuality (established through interviews with his sister and a former lover) was a bodily threat for which he could not be held responsible: a biological malfunction. Prominent in her account were Milano's qualities of innocence, chief among them his "youth" and religious devotion. Both DePaulo and the prosecutor repeatedly referred to Milano as a "boy," or a "kid," despite the fact that he was twenty-six years old—older than both Chester and Laird at the time of the murder. DePaulo noted Milano's association with women from his family's Mennonite Church who were trying to help him cleanse himself of the sin of homosexuality. She thus indicated both his spiritual sensitivity and his ongoing adolescence (signaled by his internal struggle with sexuality). It helped that Milano had no partner to mourn him in the courtroom. Jurors could picture him as celibate, priestlike.

The narrative position of the threatening, predatory homosexual, then, was left dangerously unfilled. If it was not Milano, then it *could* have been one or both of the men who killed him. Predictably, the defense attorneys took pains to defend their clients' heterosexuality. According to his attorney, Ron Elgart, Richard Laird was "like the primal heterosexual man. Like a caveman. Knock a woman over the head and drag her into his cave. Very confident about his sexuality. Didn't have anything to prove to anybody."[16] Elgart rested his client's defense on this figure of the primal heterosexual man.

The answer to the questions of both guilt and motive seemed to lurk in the possibility that the murderer(s) was guilty *due to* the existence of a suppressed homosexual within. Laird's defense attorney hinted during his questioning that there might be something less than perfectly "straight" about Chester, whom he claimed was the true killer.[17] The prosecutor, District Attorney Alan Rubenstein, also made use of the "suspect homosexual" implication in his examination of Chester on the witness stand, recalling that witnesses said Laird and Chester slow-danced in front of Milano to taunt him.[18]

The working, if invisible, definition of manhood at stake in the Bucks County Courthouse—from which Chester and Laird were disqualified even before they came to trial—was constituted by more than just practicing heterosexuality. It was "classed" as well. When D.A. Rubenstein gave his opening statement, he called upon deeply ingrained notions of what constitutes criminality and violence. "Real" criminality, like violence, is explained by its very inexplicability, its crassness, its affront to reasonable sensibilities. Rubenstein pressed Chester on why his friend would testify against him when they had been on the same side in a fight just days before the murder. By bringing evidence that Chester had been in a fight into the trial—a fight Chester defined as qualitatively different from the murder—Rubenstein suggested to the jury that Chester had a violent nature. He was unable to handle conflict "reasonably," by "talking it out," as, presumably, a more intelligent man would do.

In fact, there were numerous references to Chester and Laird's stupidity in the reports by arresting officers. The detective who arrested Laird wrote in his report: "I commented to Laird that he should have taken off somewhere good, instead of just the Falls Motel. . . . Subject [Laird] was further advised that in the opinion of Detective Wisnewski and the undersigned, in our experience, this was the dumbest homicide we had ever seen, to which Laird nodded his head up and down in an affirmative or agreeing manner."[19]

Rubenstein reportedly made a similar assessment: He was overheard telling Laird before an arraignment hearing "This one was really one of the dumber crimes."[20]

Of course, observations on the lack of wisdom or practicality employed in the committing of a murder have nothing to do with making a determination of who has performed the killing. They do, however, take advantage of widely held stereotypes of working-class men as hoodlums who are unintelligent, violent, and therefore always guilty of something. Further, they are in keeping with years of sociological and other studies that attribute greater prejudice to working-class people.[21] They suggest to the jury that there might be a figure even more deserving of death than a homosexual: a bigot.

The cultural figure of the bigot—best exemplified by the character Archie Bunker from the 1970s television sitcom *All in the Family*—represents what no decent American wants to be.[22] While it is possible for public officials to proclaim the existence of widespread racism—if not homophobia—in the United States, it is often considered an abdication of citizenship to proclaim oneself a "racist" or a "bigot"—except, possibly, in the contrite tone of one attempting to be otherwise. The term has come to signify, in particular, poor and working-class white men. "Bigotry" (indicating bias, prejudgment) is that which the U.S. criminal justice system defines itself against. This is where the connotations of an assertion such as "I'm not a redneck" or of theories that posit recession-threatened workers (read: white working-class males) as the principal carriers of the disease of intolerance become particularly interesting. Thus, negative conceptions of class status in the trial of Chester and Laird were utilized to prove more than guilt; they established the incorrigible barbarism of the offenders.[23]

In an interview nearly two years after the trial, Rubenstein remembered Chester and Laird well as "real macho types" who "thought they were tough" but "underneath, they were basically cowards" and "insecure about their masculinity."[24] DePaulo, too, found this theory compelling. She wrote: "Psychologists who study such things say that in most attacks on homosexuals, the individual is really striking out against himself. His fears, his insecurities, his own doubts about his sexuality. And in some ways, Laird and Chester—with their tattoos, hard drinking, hard talk and tough guy mentality—seemed to be textbook cases: men who were trying, perhaps too hard, to be . . . well, men."[25]

Within the discourse of the trial, then, it was manhood that Chester and Laird fatally failed to achieve. At stake in this courtroom was the reproduction of men. Legitimate manhood, like legitimate power, simultaneously needs no substantiation and deserves to be—must be—defended. Illegitimate manhood asserts itself noisily, thereby revealing its own weakness. It thinks it is manly but is not. It becomes indefensible by its very insistence on self-defense. Implicitly during Chester and Laird's trial, and explicitly in DePaulo's representation of them, the narrative given shape by the pervasive explanatory figures of the "repressed homosexual" and the "bigot," worked to obscure two things. First, it disclaimed the fact that *homosexuality,* especially in combination with a working-class violent nature, was still being posited as the root cause of violent criminality. Second, it simultaneously camouflaged and reinforced the categories of heterosexual masculinity and middle/upper-class "nonviolent," "unbiased" power.

When Charlie Howard was killed in Bangor, Maine, in 1984, the three young men convicted of his murder served only months in a youth detention center. They pushed Howard, whom they had ridiculed for being a transvestite, off a bridge and into a river after he insisted he could not swim. They explained their actions by claiming they did not think

Howard would get hurt. Yet nowhere was the lack of intelligence or foresight of these young men mentioned. Nor were they, according to the chief detective on the case, "ax murderers" (i.e., they were not maniacal, evil, or outside the normal bounds of masculinity). As he elaborated, these boys "came from respectable families who own property in the city of Bangor."[26]

Chester and Laird, on the other hand, both had criminal records. As DePaulo described them, they came from the wrong side of Levittown. Their families and friends were of a different category of "working class" than the first-generation, striving-to-assimilate Milanos. She described their community as that of the wild, hard-living, blue-collar poor. She interviewed their girlfriends and families to learn that Laird had a history of womanizing, drug dealing and assault; he had been in prison. When he came home, she wrote, he tried to "go straight" to support his pregnant wife, but he had a dead-end job and he hung out with a bad crowd. Although Chester almost made it out with a good job in his brother's company, his connection to Laird would not let him go. He succumbed to the world of motorcycles and tattoos. DePaulo portrays two men pulled recklessly toward a destiny of despair. They got drunk, their insecurities got out of hand, and they lost control. They killed someone who did not deserve to die, and worse, they failed even to do it intelligently.

If the families of Laird or Chester owned any property at all, it certainly was not enough to impress county officials with their power or respectability. Their crime, conviction, and sentence revealed the contradictions of a state and society that in another situation—one with a victim less penitent about his sexuality, or murderers less brash about their deed—might not have convicted them of first-degree murder at all.

Bucks County District Attorney Alan Rubenstein brought his arguments to a close with the following: "This is a nightmare, a nightmare come to life. A horrifying killing. . . . We're here because together with the coldness of heart, that's hard to believe, and with an evil intention of mind, that we just sometimes can't comprehend, and with ice water running through their veins, [Laird and Chester] treated [Milano] like a cheap piece of tenderloin and they carved him up."[27]

CONCLUSION: THINKING/WRITING VIOLENCE

Theories of representation emphasize the centrality of available signs (words, images, sounds, and their time- and place-specific connotations) to our ways of experiencing and understanding ourselves and the world. Such theories have proven to be particularly difficult to sustain when the object of attention is, or involves, violence. Bodies, especially dead ones, are often represented as the supreme ground of reality; violence is constituted by its very "unrepresentability." In other words, the various knowledges produced about violence frequently include some reference to it as "excessive," "out-of-control," "unthinkable," "incomprehensible" or "indescribable," despite the fact that violent acts are relentlessly described and represented. Due to what is perceived as its excessive "realness," violence is continually reconstituted as that which can never be fully contained within representation. A conceptual confusion is thus maintained: Representation is separate from "reality"; or, while reality may not be possible to perceive without the lens of representation, it nevertheless exists prior to and apart from representation.

In legal theory in particular, violence has been seen not just as separate from systems of representation (e.g., words, languages, ordered and meaningful, specifically *law*) but as that which requires the use of representation to subdue. Austin Sarat and Thomas Kearns, editors of the collection *Law's Violence,* write: "Violence stands before the law, unruly; it defies the law to protect us from its cruelest consequences. It . . . requires law to traffic in its own brand of force and coercion."[28] Law defines itself against violence, even as it employs violent means. As legal scholar Robert Wolff puts it, law views violence as "the illegitimate or unauthorized use of force to effect decisions against the will or desire of others. Thus murder is an act of violence, but capital punishment by a legitimate state is not."[29] Law, however, is not therefore without meaning, any more than is extralegal violence.

Recognition of the mutual constitution of law and violence, of meaning and force, is difficult to maintain. Even Robert Thornton—an author whose ethnographic account of a police shooting in South Africa attempts to understand violence in terms of how that particular violent event was interpreted and represented—resorts at one point to separating violence as a physical act from violence as productive of meanings. He writes, "Violence itself, raw and unthought, is meaningless. . . ."[30] The bodies of shooting soldiers and their victims *at the instant of the shooting* thus become the blank slates upon which meaning is later inscribed. While I would agree with Thornton that much of the meaning attributed to "unplanned" violent events (presuming we could find a shared satisfactory definition of either "violence" or "unplanned") is generated retrospectively, I think the notion of "meaninglessness" posits a kind of "pure" physical action.

I would argue instead that violence can be more usefully understood as *meaning enacted*. For instance, the ways in which Chester and Laird underwent a gendered transition from being subjects of violence (masculine) to being objects of the violence of the state (insufficiently masculine, if not quite feminine).[31] This case in particular illustrates the complexity of signification attending both violence and masculinity. In this case, not all violence was carried out by fully empowered subjects, nor can it be said that it was all carried out by men. The events-in-action, the body of Milano before, during, and after the killing, the bodies of Chester and Laird, all of these signify, and signify differently, depending on contexts and interpreters. For example, Laird and Chester killed Milano by attempting to cut his head off. Decapitation is an extremely difficult act to carry out and it is hardly meaningless. Katy Doran, the New York City District Attorney's Liaison to the Gay and Lesbian Community, who by virtue of her position had occasion to be familiar with another antigay murder by decapitation, noted the extraordinary symbolism of removing a person's head. This symbolism was of course culturally produced in that place and time (the urban U.S. in 1989), and through the medium of Doran's experience and the cultural terms available to her. She explained to me that "The head contains eyes that see and a mouth that speaks what society demands be hidden. The mouth may also be involved in sexual acts feared and despised by the murderer." Meaning here suffuses the act, it can be "read" from the body, but it is not only the reading that gives the act significance. Acting— something that socially produced bodies do—is itself meaningful.

A separating out of the body frequently occurs in even the most directed attempts to speak of violence and representation. In itself, this is a reminder of how difficult it can be to avoid the conceptual confusion holding reality apart from representation. Since any act of violence itself is always already meaningful, even if that meaning is impossible to establish firmly, it is interesting to ask why violence is so persistently represented as being without, or in excess of, meaning. I believe that to speak of violence as that which exceeds meaning is to permit the denial of community responsibility for that violence. The ideological conception of "violence" as a kind of extremity is inextricable from a production of knowledge about both individual (and categories of) "violent" people—people who are understood to be the "kind" who commit violent acts. Out-of-control violence is that which out-of-control people perpetrate. Such people need to be brought under control by orderly people using orderly physical punishments (punishments that are not, by definition, "violent"). Speaking of violence as that which is "outside" of representation, then, only perpetuates an entire system of meaning in which responsibility for the violence of normative "order" is denied. As a result, nothing other than *individual* accountability can be established for what we do not or cannot understand—for what we define as outside the realm of the meaningful.

In the trial of Anthony Milano's killers, an extreme act of violence was reconstituted as the definitive act of insecure working-class men while execution remained a reasonable act of justice undertaken by a criminal justice system that positions itself above the irrationalities of prejudice and insecurity. Thus, this violent act with profound social and political implications was transformed into the individualized act of two deviant men. Their conviction was won via the mobilization of the very categories of homosexuality, manhood, and class that helped to produce the conditions making Anthony Milano's murder possible. Because hate crime functions as a violent inscription of identity, it is all the more important that we scrutinize the ways identity is used in the service of punishing hate crime.

To insist on contextualizing this violence is not to release Chester or Laird from individual responsibility for their actions. Nor is it to argue that Milano's death is somehow less devastating and unacceptable when placed in relation to the violence of the state. To describe the activities of hegemonic U.S. institutions as "violent" in their production of order is not to deny the urgency of violence against women, gay men, people of color, the homeless, Jews, and other religious "minorities." Any attempt to rank such different kinds of violence seems to me misguided. I simply wish to call attention to the violences that must be relied upon in current criminal justice approaches. Unfortunately, the criminal justice system is now the primary, if not sole, channel through which responses to bias-related violence are being sought.[32]

Instead of a murder committed *on the basis of* sexuality, or race, or gender, it may perhaps be more productive to speak of a sexualized, gendered, or racialized murder. Chester and Laird took part in the enforcement of Milano's gayness, even though their act did not become public for several hours. They (homo)sexualized him in the act of murdering him. While the trial and the media attention their crime received changed the meaning of "gay" in a significant way (gay could mean innocent victim as long as the victim was not sexually active), it also solidly enforced the demarcation of Milano as gay, shifted the evilness of homosexuality onto Laird and Chester, and simultaneously reinforced the categories of "normal" heterosexuality and masculinity. Reconceptualizing incidents of violence as active, formative, meaningful, and comprehensible *processes* may make it more difficult to achieve clarity of blame and intent within the criminal justice system, but still this may be a fruitful direction in which to move.

Chester and Laird *were* held accountable for their actions, but I believe this is precisely due to the fact that they were portrayed as barbaric and inexplicably violent. Their convictions certainly were not won on the basis of an emerging appreciation for the humanity of homosexuals. Perhaps, if we are lucky, the convictions may contribute to the growth of such an appreciation. But the question remains: At what cost? Like an incantation, Rubenstein repeated these words throughout the trial: "For no reason, Ladies and Gentlemen. They killed him for no reason at all." This absence of an explanation, this bewilderment, made Chester and Laird into men who could not be accounted for by their community. As a result, they and not any larger community were held accountable for this murder.

NOTES

1. The author wishes to thank Claire Goodman, Tommi Avicolli, Lisa De Paulo, and Alan Rubenstein for their assistance with research for this chapter. For their helpful

comments on earlier versions of this piece, thanks also go to Ann Snitow, Barbara
Epstein, Joan Scott, Meg Satterthwaite, Lorraine Kenny, Laura Kang, Joseph Dumit,
and Nancy Campbell.

2. Naftali Bendavid, "Hate Crime Bill Stalls," *Chicago Tribune,* October 19, 1998.
3. Op cit. Bendavid in note 2. Introduced by Senator Edward Kennedy (D-Mass), the
   Hate Crimes Prevention Act (HCPA) of 1998 (Senate Bill 1529) would have
   "[amended] the Federal criminal code to set penalties for persons who, whether or not
   acting under color of law, willfully cause bodily injury to any person or, through the
   use of fire, firearm, or explosive device, attempt to cause such injury, because of the
   actual or perceived: (1) race, color, religion, or national origin of any person; and (2)
   religion, gender, sexual orientation, or disability of any person, where in connection
   with the offense, the defendant or the victim travels in interstate or foreign commerce,
   uses a facility or instrumentality of interstate or foreign commerce, or engages in any
   activity affecting interstate or foreign commerce, or where the offense is in or affects
   interstate or foreign commerce." Notably, amendment covers gender, sexual orientation, and disability.
   The HCPA did not pass during the 105th Congressional Session, however. A 1999
   version of the bill, H. R. 1082/S. 622, was introduced in March, and on June 16, 1999,
   a panel of the Senate Judiciary Committee convened a hearing on the problem of "State-
   Sanctioned Discrimination in America." For an update on the status of this and other
   crime bills, consult: <http://thomas.loc.gov/>.
4. National Gay and Lesbian Task Force, *Anti-Gay Violence, Victimization, and Defamation in 1986* (Washington, DC: NGLTF, 1987), 9.
5. Ibid., 24.
6. Studies abound on discrimination in capital sentencing before and after *Furman v.
   Georgia* (the 1972 Supreme Court ruling that all capital punishment statutes then in
   force were unconstitutional, a decision that has since been superseded). For a recent
   review of U.S. administration of the death penalty, see International Commission of
   Jurists, "Administration of the death penalty in the United States," *Human Rights
   Quarterly* 19 (February 1997): 165-213.
7. Milano's murder was not legally prosecuted as a hate crime, since no hate crime law
   existed in Pennsylvania in 1988. However, the anti-gay motivation for the crime was
   made explicit by the prosecution.
8. This community was fortunately well on its way toward being empowered enough to
   demand, and occasionally receive, redress of injustices in 1988. However, in 1989,
   when I first began research on this case, several African American transvestites (who
   may or may not have been gay) had been murdered in Philadelphia. While the
   Philadelphia Gay News reported this, police investigations were scarcely more than
   cursory.
9. See Judith Butler, *Gender Trouble: Feminism and the Subversion of Identity* (New York:
   Routledge, 1990).
10. Patricia J. Williams, *The Alchemy of Race and Rights* (Cambridge, MA: Harvard
    University Press, 1991), 61.
11. *Commonwealth of Pennsylvania v. Frank Chester,* No. 741-01/88, *and Richard Laird,*
    No. 746-01/88. Doylestown, PA (May 16, 1988): 71-96. Testimony of James J.
    Phillips, Jr.
12. Commonwealth of Pennsylvania, Department of Health, Vital Records, Certificate of
    Death for Anthony V. Milano, December 16, 1987.
13. *Commonwealth of Pennsylvania v. Frank Chester, and Richard Laird,* 93.
14. *Commonwealth of Pennsylvania v. Frank Chester, and Richard Laird,* 526 PA. 578, 587
    A. 2D 1367 (1991).

15. The "homosexual panic defense" argues that a defendant should be acquitted for assault, or even murder, on the grounds that he has committed the crime in self-defense against a homosexual advance. The widespread publicity accorded hate crimes against gay men and lesbians has limited the credibility of this defense.

16. Lisa DePaulo, "Killing Anthony, Part II," *Philadelphia* (January 1989): 85-203, 196.

17. *Commonwealth of Pennsylvania v. Frank Chester,* No. 741-01/88, *and Richard Laird,* No. 746-01/88. Doylestown, PA (May 18, 1988): 526 and 560-561.

18. Ibid., 506-507.

19. See Detective Frank Dykes, Bristol Township Police Dept. Homicide Investigation Report, "Arrest/Processing of Richard Laird," Case No. 28078-87, December 22, 1987. (Entered into evidence in *Commonwealth v. Chester and Laird,* 418.)

20. See Detective Robert Potts, Bristol Township Police Dept. Homicide Investigation Report, "Statements of Laird." Case No. 28078-87, December 22, 1987.

21. For research specific to anti-gay prejudice, see Richard Seltzer, "The Social Location of Those Holding Anti-Homosexual Attitudes," *Sex Roles* 26 (1992): 391-98. Speaking of racism, however, D. R. Kinder and D. O. Sears report that prejudice is *not* more prevalent among the working class. "Prejudice and Politics: Symbolic Racism versus Racial Threats to the Good Life," *Journal of Personality and Social Psychology* 40 (1981): 414-431.

22. A more fully developed discussion of this figure of the bigot can be found in AnnJanette Rosga, "Deadly Words: The Entanglement of Speech and Violence in Hate Crime," in *Policing the State: Violence, Identity and Law in Constructions of Hate Crime,* Ph.D. Diss., University of California, Santa Cruz, 1998.

23. Unfortunately, reliable data on the relationship between class status and bias-related violence is lacking. Like many organizations that collect statistics on bias-related attacks, the National Gay and Lesbian Task Force (NGLTF) has not specifically recorded the class status of attackers. Still, Kevin Berrill, the founding direction of NGLTF's Antiviolence Project was willing to offer a generalization from his years in that position: significant numbers of anti-gay attackers are clearly middle to upper class young men. Telephone Interview, March 10, 1992, author's papers.

24. Rubenstein, telephone interview, May 3, 1990, author's papers.

25. DePaulo, "Killing Anthony, Part II," 201. A number of researchers in social psychology and related fields have pursued the link between masculinity and homophobia. In addition to Gregory Herek, "On Heterosexual Masculinity: Some Psychical Conse-quences of the Social Construction of Gender and Sexuality," *American Behavioral Scientist* 29, no. 5 (1986): 563-77; Gregory Herek, "The Social Context of Hate Crimes: Notes on Cultural Heterosexism," in Gregory Herek and Kevin Berrill, eds., *Hate Crimes: Confronting Violence Against Lesbians and Gay Men* (London: Sage, 1992), see, for example: Fiona Hart, "The Construction of Masculinity in Men's Friendships: Misogyny, Heterosexism, and Homophobia," *Resources for Feminist Research* 19, nos. 3-4 (1990): 60-67; Ronald F. Levant et al., "The Male Role: An Investigation of Contemporary Norms," *Journal of Mental Health Counseling* 14, no. 3 (1992): 325-337; and Laura Reiter, "Developmental Origins of Antihomosexual Prejudice in Heterosexual Men and Women," *Clinical Social Work Journal* 19, no. 2 (1991): 163-75.

26. "Candlelight Vigils Protest Killing of Gay Man," *Unitarian Universalist WORLD,* August 15, 1984.

27. *Commonwealth of Pennsylvania v. Frank Chester,* No. 741-01/88, *and Richard Laird,* No. 746-01/88, 638.

28. Austin Sarat and Thomas R. Kearns, "Making Peace with Violence: Robert Cover on Law and Legal Theory," in A. Sarat and T. Kearns, eds., *Law's Violence* (Ann Arbor: University of Michigan Press, 1995), 212-13.

29. Robert Wolff, ed. *The Rule of Law* (New York: Simon and Schuster, 1971), 59.

30. Robert J. Thornton, "The Shooting at Uitenhage, South Africa, 1985: The Context and Interpretation of Violence," *American Ethnologist* 17, no. 2 (May 1990): 218.

31. See Teresa de Lauretis, "The Violence of Rhetoric: Considerations on Representation and Gender," in Nancy Armstrong and Leonard Tennenhouse, eds., *The Violence of Representation: Literature and the History of Violence* (New York: Routledge, 1989), 239-258.

32. I develop this argument in more detail in "Policing the State," *The Georgetown Journal of Gender and Law,* Inaugural Issue (Summer 1999).

I V

POLICING

SIXTEEN

All the Brother Wanted Was a Ride: Lynching and Police Powers in Texas

LARVESTER GAITHER

One of the ingredients of the Anglo-Saxon myth is the claim to moral superiority, but black Americans do not share the morality that is expressed in attacking school buses bringing children to a newly integrated school, in dynamiting churches and blowing to bits little black girls, in conducting medical experiments in which blacks suffering from syphilis are deliberately left untreated. Blacks have fought against those who would oppress them, but they have not organized lynch mobs and carved up the flesh of their victims as souvenirs.

—Herbert Shapiro, *White Violence and Black Response*

In small-town America—where everyone knows everybody—it is not uncommon for folks to offer rides when someone is heading in the same direction. One June 7, 1998, after attending a family get-together earlier in the evening, forty-nine-year-old "African American male suspect" James T. Byrd began his walk home into the nocturnal hours of the morning along Martin Luther King, Jr., Boulevard, a dark and heavily wooded residential area in East Jasper, Texas. At some point, Byrd was offered his ride from three white males riding east in a pickup truck. One of them he apparently knew and, perhaps, might have considered a friend; we may never know their full relationship. What we do know is that after being beaten and battered nearly to death and having his face "minstrelized" with black spray paint, Byrd was brutalized and sadistically tortured by these men.

Chained by both ankles to the back of the pickup truck, he was dragged for three miles along a winding blacktop road through the woods and finally, after suffering indescribable pain, he was murdered. At one point, he was decapitated, and at another, his right arm was ripped apart. Throughout the nightmarish ordeal, other parts of his now-mangled corpse were randomly dismembered—one after the other—so that all one had to do to estimate how far his body had been dragged was to follow the trail of blood and flesh. His killers left parts of his body in front of an African American church. There is no way of imagining how much pain he suffered before his death, but within hours the news had blanketed the national and international media; America as well as other nations once again entered into the ritual of discussing race relations.[1]

Discussing antiblack violence in America too often ends up being a fruitless endeavor, and it is for this reason that I really did not have much to say in response to the news of James T. Byrd's murder. Like millions of others throughout the world, we privately expressed outrage, but further thoughts on ways of expressing our concerns as a community were quickly blurred and distracted by the responses from African American political leadership.

In attempting to reflect on Byrd's murder, however, I have appropriated the language of policing and surveillance—in the above narrative the victim is referred to as a suspect—because this adjective "suspicious" expresses the historical and fundamental status of Africans in American society and partly explains American ambivalence toward the question of black victimization. To be sure, Byrd's violent encounter with three white males takes place against the U.S. historical backdrop of state-sponsored and antiblack violence. Alleged/convicted killers Shawn Berry, John William "Bill" King, and Lawrence Brewer, Jr., were not enlisted as "law enforcement" agents, but their brutal behavior fits well within the historical context of antiblack terror not uncommon among law enforcement officials functioning in a manner similar to neo-Nazi militias.

In recent years, reports of police brutality have become routine. Yet most of the corporate-owned media has focused on hate groups such as the Ku Klux Klan or the Aryan Nation. This has largely obscured police brutality and racism within the criminal justice system. By situating antiblack vigilantism and state-sanctioned violence in the same framework, we can better devise strategies that allow us to move one step closer to, without moving two steps backward from, the solution.

On July 12, 1998, six Houston policemen, based on an informant's tip and without a warrant, stormed into the apartment of Chicano/Hispanic American Pedro Oregón and executed him: They shot him twelve times, nine times in the back. In total, police fired over thirty shots; Oregón fired none. Even while no evidence was presented to a grand jury that Oregón had fired at the policemen, as the officers argued initially, all six policemen were acquitted, except for one who was charged with misdemeanor trespassing. (In 1999, two of the officers, Darrel Strouse and James Willis, received federal indictments.) During a rally for Oregón, several Chicano/Hispanic parents stepped forward to give testimony to the deaths of their children at the hands of police. One elderly man, who spoke little English—he spoke through a translator—stated that his son was "handcuffed and suffocated; the police argued that he had suffocated himself with a plastic device while handcuffed facing the ground. He was killed on a Tuesday yet his body was not allowed to be buried by the family; instead the police buried his body on Saturday." Often it is through these types of testimonies, not mainstream news reports, that we learn about the extent of state-sanctioned violence.

Nevertheless, Amnesty International, a relatively mainstream organization, issued a report on police abuses in New York City and Los Angeles, concluding that it had run amok and out of control.[2] A nationwide study of police brutality and accountability in the United States conducted by Human Rights Watch, another relatively nonradical entity, drew similar conclusions. It stated that "Police officers engage in unjustified shootings, severe beatings, fatal chokings, and unnecessarily rough physical treatment in cities throughout the United States, while their police superiors, city officials, and the Justice Department fail to act decisively to restrain or penalize such acts or even to record the full magnitude of the problem."[3] No more than three months after Byrd's murder, two firefighters and a policeman in New York City participated in a Labor Day Parade float that mocked Byrd's murder. "Black to the Future" was the name of the float, and while nine white men wearing Afro and dreadlock wigs threw watermelons and fried chicken and blasted boom boxes, a mannequin was dragged in the float's wake, apparently symbolizing Byrd. Such reports illustrate the fact that policing and surveillance need not be associated with the state alone, just as mob violence need not be viewed synonymously with vigilantism.

How do we understand the diverse modalities by which antiblack violence expresses itself in order to perceive it in its entirety, and how can we be better prepared to mobilize and organize against it in the twenty-first century? There must be a way to articulate resistance to antiblack violence without ignoring or acquiescing to state-sanctioned violence.

What is commonly known of Byrd's death is mostly imagined, conjectures spurred on by the extraordinary media coverage in the United States and abroad. Fueling media perceptions, in the aftermath of Byrd's murder, people, mostly politicians, said whatever came into their heads. According to the Reverend Jesse Jackson, Sr., "Byrd's death so shocked the country that it has caused all Americans to think about the ills of hate and racism [and] . . . could very well change the state of the nation." NAACP Executive Director Kweisi Mfume commented, "[T]hese cowards should never walk the street again as free men"; and the Reverend Al Sharpton stated, "As Brother Byrd's body was torn, America's spirit was torn, and we need to reweave it with equal protection under the law." Although these types of pronouncements coming from public leaders dominate in political rhetoric, they sharply contradict the reality of Americans attitudes toward race: Most white Americans, polls tell us, believe that racism is not a major problem in the United States. Furthermore, based on this type of rhetoric, this atrocity appears to be an aberration. In addition, they obscure the nature of antiblack vigilantism, which often stems from police measures and fosters the assumption that corrections officers can honestly police themselves. Are we to believe that as pogroms against "nonwhite" peoples escalate, popular empathy will sway in the direction of black victimization, or that harsher and lengthier prison terms will counterbalance antiblack violence? Such comments regarding the murder of James Byrd may have been voiced without much thought; perhaps they even were overlooked by most who heard or read them; nevertheless, they also underscored the inability and, perhaps even unwillingness, of African American leaders to come up with effective strategies for mobilizing resistance to antiblack and state violence. Their blind and narrow predisposition toward the state in thinking of ways to resolve antiblack vigilantism is indeed disquieting.

RACIAL POLICING

It has become fashionable for the dominant media to focus attention on the polarization in attitudes among white and black Americans regarding racism. The majority white population is unaware of (or collectively shares a different reality from) the African American experience of policing; for blacks, police brutality is an everyday reality, given the routine stops and illegal automobile searches by police; for suburban whites, secure and safely isolated from blacks and Latinos, such policing is rare and unfamiliar.

Of course whites do not have the historical experience of being hunted by vigilantes enforcing white supremacy. With the popularity of television shows like *N.Y. Undercover, Law and Order, L.A. Law, Cops,* and *America's Most Wanted,* to name just a few, it is inconceivable that any significant portion of the white population is unaware of black victimization. The question is: How do whites view black victimization?

On one hand, the menacing specter of privatized prison construction and militarization of the nation's police forces reflect the public's growing anxiety, which stems from routine news reporting on crime and violence, and their insecurities in an uncertain economy.[4] On the other hand, it reflects the inability or unwillingness of those representatives whose constituencies would stand to gain from the eradication of the death penalty and the demilitarization and downsizing of the criminal justice system to develop radical critiques of the criminal justice system. Because no new solutions have been offered, the public views black victimization through an ahistorical and highly racialized prism.

RACIAL POLICING AND VIGILANTISM

In hopes of counteracting the escalation of violent criminal activities that run the gamut from social crimes, through hate crimes, to police brutality, civil rights leaders and other black representatives (out of desperation or belief in the rhetoric of "victims rights" groups funded by right-wing philanthropy) call upon the very same state apparatuses that historically have been the most ardent repressors of the political struggles of blacks to police their own communities. (The works of writers Ward Churchill, Jim Vander Wall, and Kenneth O'Reilly all document this fact.) Of course, it is essential to comprehend the historical relationship between legal violence and extralegal vigilante violence against blacks in the United States to gain a deeper understanding of what appears to be a resurgence of police brutality and antiblack vigilantism.

State-approved and antiblack vigilantism historically developed hand in hand, beginning in the early period of colonial America. Slave patrols (also known as "patterollers") emerged at the beginning of the eighteenth century, setting the pattern of policing that people of African descent would experience throughout America. W. Marvin Dulaney, director of the Avery Research Center for African American History at the College of Charleston describes in *Black Police in America* the development of this policing:

> By the middle of the eighteenth century, every southern colony had a slave patrol. Although in some communities all white males were required to serve some time as patterollers, their ranks were usually filled with poor whites. The patrols were authorized to stop, search, whip, maim, and even kill any African slave caught off the plantation without a pass, engaged in illegal activities, or running away. The patterollers policed specific geographic areas in southern communities called "beats." Paramilitary in nature, the slave patrol often

cooperated with the militia in the southern colonies to prevent and suppress slave insurrections. To facilitate the rapid mobilization of the patrol and to ensure that every white man supported its activities in emergencies, colonial governments granted all whites the authority to detain, whip, and even kill slaves suspected of illegal activities or conspiracies. The colonial slave patrol exercised awesome powers which were often abused.[5]

The mandate to police blacks through both the criminal justice system and vigilantism carried over into the nineteenth century, after slavery had been abolished, and later still, into the era of Reconstruction that was dismantled by the southern ruling planter class.[6] Civil War historian William Friedheim's *Freedom's Unfinished Revolution* outlines the shape of post-Reconstruction racism:

Denied land, African Americans became economically dependent, politically disenfranchised, socially segregated, and routinely targeted for acts of chilling and often officially approved violence. From 1890 to 1900, an average of 175 African Americans were lynched each year, many burned or dismembered beyond identification. Public officials in the South did not condemn lynching and did not punish those responsible. By their silence and inaction, but more often by highly visible and vocal encouragement, southern politicians and government leaders endorsed racial violence.[7]

Between 1888 and 1918, a black man was lynched every two or three days. In some cases, thousands of white citizens and law enforcement officers gathered to cheer on the perpetrators. Perpetrators were virtually always listed as "unknown" and hardly ever prosecuted by the criminal justice system. Jerome G. Miller, president of the National Center on Institutions and Alternatives, wrote in his book *Search and Destroy:* "In the 'informal' justice system in the United States, the most extreme punishments and unjust procedures for blacks were never beyond tacit support of a substantial proportion of the white population well into this century. Castration, lynching, and other vigilante-type actions were characteristically reserved for citizens of color and provided the backdrop and collective memory against which the formal criminal justice system functioned when it came to blacks."[8]

Given American history, the murder of James T. Byrd was as shocking to some as it was predictable to others. There are those who stood aghast at the news of Byrd's murder; who felt, or rather hoped, that race relations had improved beyond such acts of terror and murder. Others, however, knowing the anxiety surrounding the possibilities of widespread, violent racial strife understood the historical context for what was reportedly shouted by one of Byrd's assailants: "We're going to start 'The Turner Diaries' early!" *The Turner Diaries,* written by Andrew Macdonald in 1978, and republished by retired university professor William Pierce, has become a widely circulated handbook for thousands of antigovernment, white militia groups.

The Reverend Jackson was right: Byrd's killing sent signals beyond the confines of Texas, affecting the already racially charged climate of American society. But he was right for the wrong reasons.

HATE CRIMES

As noted by the Southern Poverty Law Center's Winter 1999 Intelligence Report, Byrd's murder did not occur in a vacuum. Racially motivated crimes committed in the months prior to Byrd's slaying include Robert J. Neville, Jr., and Michael W. Hall's February abduction and shooting of Amy Robinson in Fort Worth, TX.

Mistaking Robinson, who was white but with dark black hair, for an African American, the men used her for target practice. (Neville was convicted of capital murder in 1998; Hall's trial was set for December 1999.) Little more than a week after Byrd's murder, similar acts of violence against blacks were reported in newspapers across the country. One example was the case of Baron Manning of Belleville, IL, a town near East St. Louis. An act of mock violence similar to the brutal death of Byrd was carried out against the seventeen-year-old Manning, but the local police department, local prosecutors, and national media declared it to be a botched drug deal.[9]

In attempting to construct a rational explanation for the violence committed against Byrd, we also must consider at the same time both the sociopolitical context in which the murder occurred and the experiences and perspectives of those who committed the violent act. Each of the alleged killers was a poverty-stricken veteran of the Texas Department of Corrections (which suggests all had suffered their own kind of victimization and the historical antagonisms between poor whites and blacks).

Why did these men harbor such antiblack white rage? Had the perpetrators been of a more privileged economic class, would they have been treated in the same manner? Would there have been such a rush to judgment by the media and society? Would the public even have heard about the event? Will all of the defendants receive the death penalty if convicted for Byrd's death? How do we who are adamantly opposed to the death penalty maintain such a position in cases like Jasper? A whole medley of issues—hate crime, death penalty, and those of race and class—converged in Jasper, Texas, on June 9, 1998.

America has a long way to go to standardize its definition of "hate crimes." While in 1992 Congress enacted legislation that required police departments throughout the country to make regular reports on crimes believed to fall under the Uniform Crime Reports' definition of "hate crimes." No more than a quarter of the law enforcement agencies have participated in the project. Despite official recognition of various types of hate crime legislation, police agencies throughout the country continue to express uncertainty over how to define hate crimes and appear hesitant to participate fully in the project. U. S. Civil Rights Commission Chair Mary Frances Berry writes in *Black Resistance, White Law*: "Police departments expressed continuing dismay about . . . when to categorize an assault as a hate crime or simply as an assault."[10]

However, more hate crimes are committed against African Americans (in proportion to their population) than against any other ethnic group. Overall, in 1997 there were 331 incidents of reported hate crimes, and African Americans ranked highest as victims, followed by gays and lesbians and Latino Americans respectively. As Byrd's death clearly demonstrated, the state of Texas shares in this country's legacy of racial violence. But what hand does the government have in adding fuel to the fire?

The Uniform Crime Reports provide the most widely cited statistics on hate crime in the United States. Over the past two decades the rates of robbery, rape, and aggravated assault, according to UCR statistics, increased dramatically. These reports greatly influenced the public's perception of violent crime as being completely out of control and provided the rationale for increased repression and policies to get tougher on "criminals." Berry notes that:

> Years of unimpeded, festering racism encouraged racially motivated violence against blacks and police abuse unavenged and unpunished. The justice system, even in cities with black mayors, remained largely unresponsive to the problems of police abuse. The Justice Department's response to police abuse and racially motivated violence during the Carter administration slightly improved over the record of preceding years, but retreat became the byword in the Reagan-Bush years. The Klan, skinheads, and other organizations received attention but not the police abuse or individual intimidation shown to African-Americans seeking housing or education. The result during the Reagan-Bush years was increased racial polarization, hate crimes, and reports of police brutality.[11]

STATE CRIMES:
THE DEATH PENALTY IN TEXAS

In 1998 Governor George W. Bush, Jr., broke a long tradition in Texas of not providing clemency, doing so for Henry Lee Lucas, a convicted serial killer. And there was the spectacle and public outrage around pickax murderer Karla Faye Tucker's execution, which saw reactionary demagogue Pat Robertson joining together with Pope John Paul II to protest. But with few exceptions, state executions occur regularly in Huntsville, Texas, and are met with little organized protest or state intervention. Racism apparent in death penalty statistics for Texas also encounters little opposition.

Outcomes based on race in death penalty cases have a long history in Texas. Historically, the defendant's race played a large role in determining who was executed in the state. Between 1924 and 1972,

361 people were put to death in Texas; 70 percent of them were "nonwhite"; blacks constituted 63 percent of those killed. This statistic reflects the postbellum years in Texas where most—nearly all—lynching victims were black.[12]

Today the state of Texas is responsible for a third of the executions in the United States. If every state had copied Texas in 1993 alone, there would have been 250 executions, one for every business day of the year. In 1997, thirty-seven prisoners were executed in Huntsville. Accordingly, blacks are represented on death row at three and a half times their proportion in the population as a whole.

If, as many are hoping, the murderers of James T. Byrd are convicted and sentenced to death, it will be the first time in the history of Texas, and one of the few times in the history of the United States, that white offenders were sentenced to death for the murder of a black person.

EVADING RACE AND RESPONSIBILITY

When Camille Cosby, wife of entertainer Bill Cosby, made national headlines by suggesting that racism in America provided the context for Russian immigrant Mikail Markhasev's socialization and so was partly responsible for her son's murder, she was accused of condemning all whites and American society in general for the behavior of one individual. "An unfair judgment," many argued. But Cosby's commentary was as instructive as the response it invoked. Nevertheless, the politics of evasion invariably accompany antiblack violence and the response to Cosby was in no way unusual. First, there is the denial and/or obfuscation of the historical context within which the violence occurs. Just as there are those who deny that the Holocaust against Jews, Roma, gays/lesbians, and political dissidents occurred in Germany's Third Reich, there are those today who deny the level of European involvement in the transatlantic slave trade, which resulted in the underdevelopment of the African continent, genocide, and centuries of chattel enslavement of Africans in America.

Elected officials denounced Byrd's killing. A U. S. House of Representatives' resolution, which extended condolences to Byrd's family, was unanimously passed on a 397 to 0 vote. But why should a representative from outside the East Texas district initiate the resolution of condemnation? Texas Representative Sheila Jackson-Lee (D-Houston) introduced the House resolution, not Jim Turner (D-Crockett), in whose district the murder occurred.[13]Turner, who supported the resolution, echoed Martin Luther King, Jr.'s vision that every American be judged not by the color of their skin but by the content of their character, stating "No American is safe until every American treats his neighbor with dignity, regardless of the color of his skin."[14] But Turner failed to specify whom he was talking about, obfuscating racial injustices against blacks.

Another type of evasion occurs in the form of distancing from the crime; downplaying and/or obscuring the climate and legacy of racism that fuels the current antiblack violent behavior. For instance, Jasper's Sheriff Billy Rowles was quoted in the *Houston Chronicle* as saying that "every law enforcement agency within 200 miles has offered to help in the investigation . . . [and that most] of his 14 deputies . . . had to handle routine law enforcement calls during their days off because they [were] so busy with the Byrd investigation."[15] But despite the nature of the crime, the fact that East Texas is widely known to be a focal point for Klan-related activities, that their bodies were tatooed with white supremacist images, that they had been investigated by the Texas Department of Corrections for alleged ties to the Ku Klux Klan, and even despite the sheriff's acknowledgement that they may have had connections with white supremacy groups, Rowles seemed anxious to rule out the racism. As the white sheriff put it, amid hisses and bursts of laughter from African Americans living in Jasper who attended the national press conference, "We have no organized KKK or Aryan Brotherhood groups here in Jasper County."[16]

CONCLUSION

Historically, from the era of slavery to the present, a variety of tactics and strategies have been employed by blacks to protect themselves from antiblack violence. Oftentimes, particularly during the post–civil rights movement, the strategies and tactics have been formulated in response to incidents similar to the atrocity in Jasper, or the Rodney King beating, which sparked a pseudorebellion in Los Angeles and other cities across the United States. Indeed, responses have ranged from armed revolts, to nonviolent protest, to subservient accommodation.[17] But on rare occasions, particularly since the passage of the Civil Rights Act of 1965, the media have projected black responses to violence outside the confines of accomodationism.

Byrd's murder evoked, at least in style if not in substance, these three historical forms of response to white antiblack violence, forms that indicate that African Americans, as a whole, remain uncertain and ambiguous about their political and social status, and for good reason—our status has been and continues to be questionable. There were calls for love, healing, and reconciliation; there were calls for arming the community for self-defense; and finally, there was the call for calm—to let the state and federal authorities handle it. What was conspicuously absent, however, was a radical response that placed the incident in its historical and current political context, that revealed the partnership among racist policing, state executions, and racist violence. African Americans must resolve this ambiguity regarding the question of racial repression in order to create the necessary weapons to address reactionary forms of criminalization and the apparent resurgence of antiblack violence.

Major political and structural changes are needed to address police brutality, the racist application of the death penalty, and the mass incarceration of blacks; such changes also must address vigilantism. These political and structural changes will not come about through humdrum race advisory boards and town hall meetings such as those initiated and managed by President Bill Clinton's "Presidential Race Initiative." In fact, the establishment media will never even entertain such ideas unless there is organized resistance centered on a clear ideological threat to the existing economic, political, and social hegemony.

NOTES

1. White supremacist John William King was convicted of James T. Byrd's murder and sentenced to death in February 1999; Lawrence Brewer, Jr. was convicted and sentenced to death in September 1999. Shawn Berry's trial resulted in conviction but no death penalty.
2. Amnesty International Report, *United States of America: Police Brutality and Excessive Force in New York City Police Department* (Washington, D.C.: AMI, 1996).
3. Human Rights Watch, *Shielded From Justice: Police Brutality and Accountability in the United States* (New York: Human Rights Watch, 1998).

4. See: Peter Cassidy, "'Operation Ghetto Storm': The Rise of Paramilitary Policing," *Covert Action Quarterly* 62 (1997): 20-25; and Reese Erlich, "Prison Labor: Workin' For the Man," *Covert Action Quarterly* 54 (1992): 58-63.

5. W. Marvin Dulaney, *Black Police in America* (Bloomington: Indiana University Press, 1996), 2.

6. See W. E. B. Du Bois, *Black Reconstruction in America* (New York: Harcourt, Brace, 1935); Rayford W. Logan, *The Betrayal of the Negro: From Rutherford B. Hayes to Woodrow Wilson* (New York: Collier Books, 1965); Hans L. Trefousse, *Reconstruction: America's First Effort at Racial Democracy* (Huntington, N.Y.: Robert E. Krieger Publishing, 1979).

7. William Friedheim, *Freedom's Unfinished Revolution* (New York: The New Press, 1996), 281.

8. Jerome Miller, *Search and Destroy: African-American Males in the Criminal Justice System* (New York: Cambridge University Press, 1996), 53.

9. Denise Hollinshed, "3 Allegedly Yelled Racial Epithets as Black Teen Dragged by Vehicle," *Houston Chronicle*, June 14, 1998, 17A.

10. Mary F. Berry, *Black Resistance, White Law: A History of Constitutional Racism in America* (New York: Penguin Books, 1994), 227.

11. Ibid., 243.

12. Richard C. Dieter, *The Future of the Death Penalty in the United States: A Texas-Sized Crisis* (Washington, D.C.: Death Penalty Information Center, 1994), 4-13.

13. Sheila Jackson Lee introduced the Hate Crimes Prevention Act of 1999 (HR77), a bill to enhance federal enforcement of hate crimes. The Texas House passed a Hate Crimes Bill (H.B. 938) named for James T. Byrd, Jr.; the bill failed in committee in the Texas Senate in 1999.

14. Richard Stewart and T. J. Milling, "Trio Charged in Jasper Slaying: Suspects Linked to Hate Groups," *Houston Chronicle*, June 10, 1998, 1A-16A.

15. Richard Stewart and Steve Lash, "FBI Is Leading Investigation of Jasper Case: Local Authorities Welcome Help in Justice for Alleged Hate Crime," *Houston Chronicle*, June 12, 1998, 1A.

16. Stewart, "Trio Charged in Jasper Slaying," 1A-16A.

17. See: Cedric Robinson, *Black Movements in America* (New York: Routledge, 1997).

SEVENTEEN

Surplus Value:
The Political Economy of
Prisons and Policing

DAVID THEO GOLDBERG

The past decade has witnessed massive growth in the United States in both prison construction and levels of incarceration, especially in racially configured terms. These increases, which are related, have occurred at the same time that profound shifts have taken place in the "foundations" of the American political economy. The question is whether these explosions in prison construction and racially driven incarceration are in any way significantly linked with these broader shifts in political economy.

This question is large, and I cannot pretend to do it full justice here. One way into the issues involved is to address a substantially narrower question, but one that is emblematic of the broader concerns: How do we account for the discrepancy between, on one hand, the racially configured criminal suspect rate and, on the other, the racially driven prison rate? In Arizona in 1996, for instance, the criminal suspect rate was something like 17.4 percent not white; nevertheless, 53.3 percent of those incarcerated were people of color. The national figures differ little from those in Arizona (roughly 17 percent and 50 percent respectively).[1] The considerably lower suspicion rate for people of color compared to their incarceration rate is consistent with the now-widespread consensus among researchers that there is not a great deal of explicit discrimination in arrests for crimes.[2] The difference between suspicion and incarceration rates, then, is significant not least because it is so counterintuitive. Why indeed would the rate of incarceration of people of color, particularly black men and women, so outstrip the rate at which people of color are suspected of crimes? A reasonable explanation of this difference, I suggest, implicates precisely that relation among growth in prison construction, levels of racially driven incarceration, and shifts in American political economy, thus revealing the significance about these connections.

One explanation that might be offered for the difference between racial suspicion and incarceration rates is what I call the "No-*nigger*-zone defense." In certain socioeconomically upscale neighborhoods, there is a widespread and widely noted policing sensibility, if not policy, to stop people of color on sight, as their presence in those spaces in which "they do not belong" is deemed "unnatural." There are many examples nationwide. Scottsdale, Arizona, for instance, is the Beverly Hills of Phoenix. A recent civil suit brought by a former "Hispanic" officer on the Scottsdale police force revealed not only the rampant racism facing officers of color on the force, but, equally pressing, it brought to light also the informal but blatant policy of stopping black people on sight in Scottsdale, whether residents or not, and whether engaged in suspicious behavior or not. A captain, a white man, in the Scottsdale department testified at the trial that "nigger" was widely used as a term of reference among the overwhelmingly white officers; he rationalized that usage as no different from its widespread use among predominantly black Cook County police officers in Chicago. Again, police in Chandler, a lower-middle to middle-class city-suburb in the greater Phoenix area, were involved in a two- or three-day roundup with Immigration and Naturalization Service (INS) officers of any person looking Chicano, no matter whether a citizen or residing in the country legally. The policing practice of stopping black people on sight in Beverly Hills and Bel Air has been widely reported. Indeed, if Howard Beach, New York is anything to go by, this police disposition to "suspect people of color" is widespread also in white ethnic working-class neighborhoods.

Now, "stopping black/brown" as a form of surveilling city and suburban space is not at odds with a suspicion rate relatively consistent with demographic percentage. After all, the suspect rate represents the best police response to resolving actual crimes committed and can be matched critically against victims' profile reports.[3] In the face of increasing pressures of policing professionalization and public funding, setting up faked suspects to sustain arrest rates or as a result of prejudice may offer an occasional individual motivation (Mark Fuhrman has hardly faded from memory if his late-night television appearances are anything to go by). But it carries considerable cost as an institutional commitment. Racist expression may assume many forms. That the suspicion or arrest rates for the most part no longer seem to suggest institutional racist bias, as they did not so long ago,[4] does not entail absence of individual or institutional racism in other policing activities— like keeping a neighborhood white or restricting advancement within the force on racial grounds.

The "No-nigger-zone defense," however, clearly implies a greater racially manifested suspect rate, and so it fails to account for the discrepancy we are facing. Indeed, in a society so ripped through with racism, not least in urban police departments, and so marked by the unemployment of black and brown folk—their rate is always at least double that of whites[5]—it's a wonder that the racially fashioned suspect rate is not considerably higher. What all this suggests rather is that there is no naturalized notion of crime, whether in racial terms or more broadly socially. The notion of crime and dispositions toward it are laden with invested social meanings, both in their social production and in their significance. These meanings reflect and resonate with wider social, political, economic, and cultural concerns and with commitments, paranoias, and moral panics.

If the "No-nigger-zone defense" is porous in this play of explanations, consider the "*Coloreds*-only-wanted offense." Here we are concerned with explaining why the racially driven incarceration rate, the well-documented and highly commented upon peopling of prisons by black and brown bodies, is so dramatically high. Accordingly, the question here is how to account for the second part of the discrepancy:

How is it, given the relatively low racially manifested suspect rate, that the racially driven incarceration rate is so large?

I have named these strategies and practices in terms of "niggers" and "coloreds," "defense" and "offense" so as to link them to two not unrelated phenomena: on one hand, to the long-standing tradition of racist culture in America, a culture that the police have been deeply implicated in perpetuating and protecting; on the other hand, to the ways in which sport, war, and their metaphors effect the production and reproduction of broad consent to a deeply racially conceived social order. (I will elaborate on this point toward the end of this chapter.)

The fact that blacks are incarcerated at three to four times their rate in the national population, and that Hispanics are incarcerated at three times their national population rate, is a complex phenomenon that requires a complex response. I want here to address two considerations that factor into the (re)production of this phenomenon: first, the emergence of "the new segregation"—residentially, educationally, and criminally; and second, the political economy of prison building, which requires massive building of prisons actually house people to sustain its development. As I argue below, this is an internal logic of self-perpetuation linked to broader shifts in the reproduction of capital and the social conditions that sustain the promotion and growth of surplus value.

THE NEW SEGREGATION

As institutional design and practice, segregation emerged in the United States in the wake of post–Civil War abolition of slavery and the demise of Reconstruction, marking especially the expansion of urban space first in the South and then, in the wake of massive black migration, northern cities. From 1890 to 1930 the number of black residents in New York surged nearly tenfold, from 36,000 to 328,000; in Chicago, over twenty-fold, from 14,000 to 234,000. Chicago neighborhoods just 10 percent black in 1900 were swept by the cold wind of segregation into neighborhoods 70 percent black just thirty years later.[6]

The dominant picture concerning the racial divide in America is that the civil rights movement and the legislation it effected managed to end de jure segregation. Thus any lingering divide between the social spaces of white and black/brown America is considered to be a function of class formation and the exercise of private preference schemes that government is either helpless to or constitutionally limited from doing anything about; in any case, that divide is likely to disappear as people's socioeconomic status advances "naturally" over time. Failure to advance is rationalized away as a function of the unsuccessful person's nature or culture. Yet this picture fails to account for the deep and resilient racial divisions that continue to mark America largely in black and white.

Thus America remains almost as deeply racially divided residentially, educationally, occupationally, recreationally, and in some ways attitudinally in 1998 as it was in 1968. Starting imperceptibly in the 1950s and gathering speed, blacks and whites were becoming more segregated across and not just within municipal boundaries, living (to use Douglas Massey and Zoltan Hajnal's apt language) not only in different neighborhoods but also in different municipalities. At the very time there was growing expression of desegregation in the public sphere, there was publicly subsidized resegregation in the private. Desegregation never stood a chance. By 1980, blacks living in cities found themselves in municipalities on average 35 percent black; if black and white residents were to be evenly distributed across municipalities, 50 percent of blacks in cities would have had to switch places of residence with whites.[7] The suburban explosion that pulled whites out of the cities transformed the countryside into sprawling suburbs. These suburbs eventually became small self-governing cities, the effect as much of the desire to be politically and fiscally autonomous of deteriorating old and racially identified cities as from some purely administrative rationality.

In 1950 no central cities were overwhelmingly or even largely black. No city with a population larger than 100,000 had a majority black population. Forty years later there were fourteen such cities.[8] Eleven more cities had black populations of between 40 and 50 percent. Among cities larger than 25,000 in 1950 just two had majority black populations; by 1990 that number had exploded to forty.[9] Interestingly, the increase in segregation after mid-century is characteristic only of larger cities with large black populations. There was a noticeable decline in segregation in small cities with small black populations.[10] In the latter cases African Americans found themselves assimilated into dominant white space with little if any noticeable effect on prevailing urban arrangements or culture. By the end of the civil rights era, in contrast, geographic isolation of blacks in larger urban settings—the overwhelming majority of black folk—was nearly complete.

Now resource availability determines educational opportunity, hence jobs, and so by extension quality of housing. Where one lives largely determines where one goes to school, the quality of education one receives, and so the quality of housing one can afford. Segregation accordingly is a totalizing condition: For segregation to be sustained in any one dimension, there has to be segregation in every dimension.

The sociospatial makeup of the contemporary city renders invisible especially the racially defined poor. Similarly, policy priorities and bureaucratic rationality of federal, state, and local administrations restrict the possibilities in addressing the problems (racially) marginalized persons face. Expanding opportunities and social services for the racially marginalized in periods of fiscal conservativism, externally imposed structural constraints, and downsizing imperatives become at best a zero-sum game, if not political and economic suicide for a city. Economic globalization has prompted demographic dislocation and massive migrations not only from country to city but from South and especially East to the West, geographic sites that assume geopolitical significance. A growing share for one group of a fixed if not shrinking racial pie means diminishing returns to other racially defined groups similarly structurally situated.

Segregation within cities concentrates crime—violent crimes, especially homicide—within the spatial confines of the city or neighborhood. So those blacks who kill, kill other black people, for the most part; likewise, those Latinos who kill, kill other Latinos; and so on. In the wealthiest neighborhood of Washington D.C., for instance, which is 88 percent white, there were no murders in the first half of 1996; just a couple of miles apart, in the poorest part of the city, which is 91 percent black, there were thirty murders. The overwhelming majority of homicides take place within ethnic groups. In Texas, for example, 86 percent of Latinos were killed by Latinos. In the final analysis, it is not raw poverty that accounts for the high homicide rates among Latinos and blacks but income inequality—the fact of economic differentials and the related spatial concentration effects, and these have been rising rapidly.[11] The wealthy get protected not only as the poorer do not but at the expense, discomfort, and threat to the safety of those who are impoverished as a result of their racially defined positioning.

The current delimitation of welfare benefits and especially the workfare requirements that are so central to current reform seem to regulate a reserve army of surplus labor that keeps in check the minimum wage rate and thus the wage profile of the low-end service sector. The prison industry likewise has become a form of color-coded segregation, especially of young black and brown men. As prisons are being privatized, prisoners increasingly are being employed at subminimum wage in behalf of profit-producing private businesses. Welfare and prisons, then, have become cornerstones of the New Segregation, locking poor people of color spatially as much as economically into lives of severe limitation. I turn now to the emergence of local political economies centered in part around prisons, viewed in light of this New Segregation.

POLITICAL ECONOMY OF PRISONS

The 1980s closed and the 1990s opened with considerable rhetorical warring over the downsizing of the U.S. military budget. In dollar terms, however, the military budget this past decade has declined less than the rhetoric would lead one to believe: Climbing steadily during the Reagan years, the military budget more than doubled from $133 billion in 1980 to a historical high of $303 billion in Bush's first presidential year, 1989, and then declined modestly through the 1990s to $267 million in 1997. Yet there has been considerable decrease in relative terms as the military budget has shrunk as a percentage of the total U.S. economy. Thus the military share of gross domestic product dropped from a high of 23.6 percent in 1983 to 20.8 percent in 1997, the lowest it had been since 1974.[12] Economic rationalization of the military (in the Weberian sense) at the turn of the decade was a response to the breakup of the Soviet Union and the Soviet bloc in Eastern Europe together with the consequent shift in geopolitical power. This rationalization was really the manifest effect of a deeper and longer shift started under President Ronald Reagan, namely, the shift in military commitment from a primarily manpowered military to one technologically driven, from one fighting wars by those bearing "stars" and mainly "stripes" to one of "star wars." It is against the background of these transitions that bases were targeted for closing and the racially predicated economy of the military industrial complex was scaled back.

This military downscaling, most notably in personnel and the supportive infrastructure, especially troubled the economies of California, the Southwest and South, the Southeast and Northeast, that is, those economies already buffeted by the storm of recession sweeping through these regions. It was racialized in a triple sense. First, a contemporary demographic map of the United States reveals that racial heterogeneity in the country tends overwhelmingly to be concentrated in cities along the two coasts and in the South—the regions hardest hit by the twin storms of recession and downsizing. Second, the lower ranks in the military proper tended to be people of color, and opportunity for military service became scarcer precisely at the moment affirmative action more broadly came under attack and began to be scaled back. Third, now-out-of-work military industrial executives, engineers, and skilled workers in high-paying jobs tended largely to be white. They were the epitome of those angry white males much noted in the first half of the 1990s, culminating in the howl that became the "Contract on America." California suffered the greatest job loss related to base closures between 1988 and 1993—105,000 military and civilian positions in all at seventeen facilities.

Thus at the very moment recession struck at the heart of American political economy, the squeezing of the military industrial complex had a negative multiplier effect both economically and politically. In a sense the Gulf War both marked and papered over the material moment of this shift. It distracted national, indeed, global attention from American economic woes even as it was being used to make a case for the shift from a manpowered military to a technologically fashioned one. Perhaps even more so, it signaled as it fueled the emergent market for virtual war games. At the same time, it covered over, or up, the dramatic economic shifts to the wealthy that the 1980s produced at the expense of the poor. If the futures of wealthy Americans seemed tied dramatically to the stock market, prospects for the poor increasingly lay along a path to prison.

As military bases closed, prisons began to proliferate in precisely those areas economically most affected by militarily motivated slippage.

In a stagnating economy, fiscal "realities" reduced politics to a zero-sum game. The rapid rise in prison appeal and construction was bought at the cost of a long-standing post-1945 commitment to funding higher education. Between 1989 and 1994, 318 new adult prisons opened. In 1994, 41,000 beds were added at $55,000 apiece for a grand total of nearly $2.26 billion. At the same time another 113,000 beds were on the planning table. It has been well documented that more was and is being spent on prisons than on building universities. Between 1987 and 1995 state prison expenditure increased by 30 percent while spending on higher education decreased by 18 percent. In addition, between 1980 and 1994 the prison population nationwide increased by 300 percent while university enrollment decreased by 22 percent. (Here I am suggesting a correlation, or at least some relation, although obviously not a straightforwardly causal one.) California and Florida both now spend more on prisons than on higher education. Relatedly, in 1995 expenditures on police protection in California far outstripped those of other states (by three times that of New York as next largest, for instance). And the incarceration rate of African Americans in prisons nationwide in 1993 was seven times that of whites (1.4 percent of blacks in contrast to 0.207 percent of whites).

Prisons became the growth industry of choice not least because they "killed" three, again racially fashioned, birds soaring in the political economy of America. First, they provided an alternative to the plight of unemployment, especially as a result of industrial downscaling related to the military and the shrinking of educational opportunities available particularly for young people of color. Second, they offered what turned out to be an electorally appealing response to the moral panics about crime felt predominantly among the massively spreading middle classes that are perennially paranoid about losing their newly acquired class status. The prison response was especially pertinent in wake of the explosion in use of crack cocaine in the mid-1980s, predominantly among black and brown men. Thus 88 percent of offenders sentenced for crack offenses in 1995 were African American, 4.1 percent white. (If crack and powdered cocaine were treated alike, the average sentence for the former would be 47 rather than its actual 141 months.) In 1992 nearly 30 percent of state prison admissions were for drug offenses, up fivefold over a ten-year period. While the arrest rate of those deemed not white for drug offenses has long been somewhat higher than that for whites, the difference in arrest rates spiraled during the years of the Reagan administration: For whites between 1980 and 1988 the arrest rate rose slightly, from roughly 0.25 percent of the population to 0.3 percent; for those not white, the arrest rate rose alarmingly, from roughly 0.45 percent of the overall population to a staggering 1.5 percent over the same period.[13] The increase in rates thus more than tripled for the latter while rising just 20 percent for whites. These differentiated rates of increase are all the more telling in view of the fact that whites constitute roughly 70 percent of the U.S. population. And third, the political and economic commitment to prisons consolidated the political conservativism at the center of U.S. politics in the name of keeping America white—which is to say, safe for whites.

These all too brief indications point to a more or less straightforward and conscious link between downsizing the military and upsizing prisons in the political economy of the United States. These changes have been accompanied by the streamlining of educational opportunities to the middle class and wealthy at the expense of the poor. Note that I emphatically am not claiming that the prison industrial complex displaces the military industrial complex as the centerpiece of the U.S. economy. My claim rather is that the self-consciously designed growth in the prison industry picks up—was conceived quite self-consciously to pick up—the slack in the racially driven political economy of America and in the fabrication of its "moral economy." That growth now has become institutionalized, integral to American economic and ideological reproduction.

There does exist some direct evidence of this chaining together of the military, prison, and moral economies of America. In July 1989 then President George Bush established a commission to determine if there were any closing or closed bases suitable for prison usage. In August of that year—just a month after the commission began—a senior official of the Federal Bureau of Prisons wrote the commission laying out the bureau's need for properties with existing structures and facilities of 100 acres or more. The letter went on to argue that "a Federal prison operation can be very beneficial to a local economy, as annual operating expenses run to several million dollars." Prisons, as this astute official was quick to point out, bring to the local economy exactly those sorts of direct and indirect expenditures previously mobilized by military bases. These include not only service industries such as catering, laundry, and supplies; prisons also have economic effects less directly related to prison operation. These include the local infrastructure that supports the lifestyle of prison and prison-related employees—supermarkets, drugstores, gas stations and auto repair shops, doctors, dentists, schools and community colleges, and so on. In some notorious cases prisons also have made available a supply of cheap labor, whether for agriculture, roadwork, street cleaning, or telephone services and credit card collections. In the moral economy, then, prisons are supposed ideologically to represent law and order, work in the face of welfare, discipline rather than delinquency, social control over anarchy.

Total military base acreage converted to prison use far outstripped most other acreage usage—such as the National Guard, parks, hospitals, homeless shelters, the Bureau of Indian Affairs, or at least in one case a satellite campus of my own university. In all, so far as I can tell, though it is well nigh impossible to get a confident read on these figures, at least nine bases were converted to prisons. There is thus a direct substitution effect from the military to the prison industry, from a uniform(ed) economy of one kind to a more or less uniform(ed) economy of another. In addition, so the argument goes, robust economies tend to produce safer environments; prisoners behind barbed wired walls in a local community are better than criminals on the streets of otherwise faded neighborhoods and towns.

So, against the related background of reproduced segregation and rising prison-based economies, we return to the question with which we began: What accounts for the 35 percent differential between racially driven suspicion and racially fashioned imprisonment rates? It cannot be that people of color as a matter of "natural" fact commit more crimes, all else being equal, for from a narrowly crime prevention/detection logic one would expect the suspicion rates to be higher, particularly in light of the racially driven disposition of law enforcement officials "to suspect black." Such an assumption fails *even* on the logic of the most regressive criminological logic.

It follows that a reasonable explanation for the discrepancy between racially driven suspicion and incarceration rates must be a complex version of the "Coloreds-only-need-apply offense." Three considerations at the very least must factor interactively into such an explanation. First, certain crimes committed by blacks are more likely incarcerable in ways other crimes are not. As noted, the rate of drug-related incarceration for blacks far outstrips that for whites, most evident in the differential sentences for crack and powder cocaine.[14] In addition, certain locations not only dispose persons so confined to committing crimes but to being caught, and to larger and longer sentences. The construction of "crime-infested areas" renders those spaces more highly surveilled and policed. Police helicopters regularly patrol South Central Los Angeles but not Santa Monica. South Central, revealingly, becomes characterized for these and other reasons as a "war zone." Similarly, crimes against whites are at least a little more likely to draw prison sentences, and longer terms, than those against people of color, even though African Americans are far more likely to be the victims of violent crimes than any other ethnoracially conceived group in the United States. Thus violent crime victimization rates for African Americans in 1992 were 75 percent higher than those for whites.

Second, young impoverished people of color, especially black and Latino men, are regarded silently as a surplus population. Those unemployed youth of color are considered to have "nothing better to do." So, while approximately 80 percent of all U.S. men of working age are employed full time, only 55 percent of prison inmates were working full time at the time of arrest (at least in "legitimate" formal sector jobs, but isn't that the point in relation to criminalization?). The rate of unemployment for particularly (free) men of color (especially blacks) has always been double that of whites, and in the past two decades the rate of unemployment of young black men across America's inner cities has ranged alarmingly between 25 and 50 percent. In 1996, more than a third of black people between the ages of sixteen and thirty-five were underemployed. Consequently, fully one-third of African Americans, and very nearly that proportion of Hispanics, live in poverty. In light of this, there has been a long-standing concern with "warehousing" those people the society has no other place for.[15] Revealingly, 50 to 75 percent of all state prison inmates are unable to read. Only 33 percent of prisoners nationwide have completed high school in contrast to 85 percent of the general population. Most crimes, especially violent crimes (or at least convictions), are committed by those with no more, and often less, than a high school education.[16] In the zero-sum game of current political economy, the funding of prisons, I have suggested, is at the cost of funding education, especially higher education. Defunded education promotes crime, especially youth crime; crime calls out for prisons; the political economy of prisons reproduces a spiraling prison population. The circle of logic is now self-perpetuating.

Third, and relatedly, those without the capital get prison, not least because not only do they have few other earning options than crime but equally because they likely lack the resources for an adequate defense once arrested. That lack, in a society romanticizing conspicuous consumption, no doubt leads them to consider crime in the first place. Thus more than half of all prison and jail inmates had a reported annual income of less than $10,000 prior to their arrest. The current court challenges to the funding of legal aid services for the poor is but the logical outcome of the relentless post-1970s attack on the rights of the impoverished in America to receive any legal representation, let alone an adequate defense.[17] I attended the community meeting in Phoenix of President Clinton's traveling road show that goes under the name of the Commission on Race. The forum produced a long litany of heartbreaking stories by desperately poor people of all racial characterizations whose rights had been trampled for lack of any legal representation at all. Bereft and stripped of all hope the legal system once had held out for them, they saw this forum as their last opportunity for divine intervention, in the person of the President of the United States. Hope springs almost eternal, and dies hard. The nineteenth-century poorhouse seems to have metamorphosed into the twenty-first-century prison.

Thus the 35 percent differential between racially driven suspicion and racially driven incarceration rates is a cofunction of the economic imperatives of capital and politics, a long history of discursively reproduced racial degradation and segregation, and the all-too-easy policy resolve to set the degraded and socially least popular apart, to hide them by warehousing them in marginal facilities. If prisons are necessary to the political economy of middle America, well, they better be filled, and filled they are. The poor, unemployed, and uneducated will be sentenced to prison more readily than the rich, marginally comfortable, employed, and educated. And in America the poor and uneducated are far more likely black and brown than white.

There has emerged accordingly a carcerality of containment, as author Michael Taussig has suggested in a different context, conjoined with that carcerality of (self-)surveillance Foucault made so theoretically influential. The carcerality of surveillance marking modern states is about controlling (through self-disciplining) the circulation of bodies throughout the social formation. Those deemed threatening to social control, "savage minds" beyond the dictates of this disciplinary logic, were largely to be locked *out*—in the colonies or the outhouse. Some social spaces—some heterotopias, some simply abandoned because seemingly uncontrollable or not worth the cost-benefit balance to bring under control—remain impenetrable to the surveillant gaze. These periphractic spaces, home to "the fabricated savage" the late modern state has made its own by perpetuating, have been *primarily* about keeping the projection of "savagery" contained—locked *in* to the inner city or locked *up* in prison houses. (This, of course, is not to deny respective instances of modern racially driven internment and an array of late modern racially predicated exclusions.) And so it follows that if panoptical carcerality largely defines the logic of modern state control, late-modern racially fashioned regimes enact a new rationality. This rationality is expressed through exterior or surrounding containment, an evacuation for the most part to anarchy of the space of racial others so long as that space is fenced off by a policed cordon[18]—a *cordon sanitaire,* to reference the colonial urban condition in Africa—the boundaries (rather than the interiority) clearly defined and policed, symbolically as much as materially.[19]

This emergent carcerality of containment is probably best represented in relation to the street trade in drugs in abandoned parts of major U.S. cities. Police largely turn a blind eye to street-corner dealing so long as its effects do not too readily spill over into middle or main street America. Little concern is shown for inner city youth either killing for or dying from drugs so long as the anarchic spirit is limited to the inner city, its effects contained largely out of sight. The war on drugs is thus largely a war of position, to twist a well-worn metaphor some. It is a war over place and space, a war to position those black and brown bodies not able to actualize the American Dream through the hyperexploited public sphere of the sports industry. Rather, black and brown bodies are maneuvered in the ongoing racial nightmare into the hypercontained spaces of mean streets preparatory to spending the rest of their usually short lives behind bars.

Accordingly, the sports/war metaphor I started with—defense/ offense—is meant to reflect the deep discursive ordering of the psyche of war in the national imagination, displaced into one of those other foundational poles of U.S. political economy, namely, the business of recreational sports and spectatorship. The war on crime/drugs takes up that space between the rhetorics of war and that of sports as war, furnishing a rationalization—a hiding of—war on young people of color as the surplus value of this society. Impoverished youth of color, then, are seen as surplus in the sense of an unusable commodity, the remainder stock, the detritus of the economy, an inhuman capital capable of producing profit on capital investment only by being treated as alien(able) objects, products to be traded in the marketplace of that new racially fashioned economy of the prison industrial complex. The more value socially, materially, and symbolically these men (and increasingly women) are at the center of creating the less valued they are. Indeed, their value in the former senses is a function of their devaluation in the latter, their devaluation in the latter a necessary condition for their value in the former. So, the more valuable they are, the more worthless; the more civilized if not civilizing the supposed presumption of their incarceration, the more barbarous they are rendered because they are assumed to be; the more economically empowering their imprisonment, the more powerless they are required to be.[20] The "exterior enemy" that fetishistically grounded the moral economy of self-proclaimed superpower status has necessarily, magically given way to the "enemy within" in the face of rapidly shifting alliances and altogether permeable borders.

In closing, I draw a comparison with late-apartheid South Africa. The standing joke about the proto-fascist ruling National Party in the early 1980s went as follows: "So why are the Nationalists spending so much of late on prisons? Because they are investing in their own future." Besides the prophetic nature of the humor (despite the fact that almost no former party leaders are anywhere close to being imprisoned), the building of prisons and incarceration of large numbers of black South Africans said something very basic about the evisceration of freedom for all in South Africa, indeed, one could say for black people and people generally everywhere. Placing imprisonment at the center of national consciousness and as a cornerstone of the national political economy places limits on freedom, predicates freedom on unfreedom, and so delimits freedom at its roots. Thus the political economy of fear and loathing that promotes the prison industrial complex in the United States, that presumes as it at once reproduces surplus values, is one that by necessity restricts freedom in the land of the free and denies courage in the home of the brave. A society that secures itself internally through force in this way—through forced incarceration and forced labor—is one stricken to its roots by anxiety and insecurity. In being so (de)based, it erodes the freedom of us all.

NOTES

An opportunity to present these ideas at the Unfinished Liberation conference at the University of Colorado, Boulder, and to a graduate seminar in the History of Consciousness at the University of California, Santa Cruz, led to their considerable elaboration. I am grateful to Joy James and Angela Y. Davis as well as to the participants in each gathering for these respective opportunities. I thank also my colleagues Peg Bortner and Mona Lynch and my research assistant, Bin Liang, for helping me track down data.

1. Unless otherwise cited, all data in the text is taken from William M. DiMascio with Marc Mauer, *Seeking Justice: Crime and Punishment in America* (New York: Edna McConnell Clark Foundation, 1997).
2. Michael Tonry, *Malign Neglect—Race, Crime, and Punishment in America* (New York: Oxford University Press, 1995), 71 ff.
3. Ibid., 70-74.
4. A spate of high-profile releases from prison of people of color after many years of incarceration over the past few years offers further indication that the racially driven suspicion rate has come under social pressure. Geronimo (ji jaga) Pratt is but one among numerous examples. New evidence, sometimes DNA derived, has proved innocence, suggesting that the racially driven suspicion rate once would have been considerably higher.
5. Tonry, *Malign Neglect,* 79.
6. Douglas Massey and Zoltan Hajnal, "The Changing Geographic Structure of Black-White Segregation in the United States," *Social Science Quarterly* 76, no. 3 (September 1995): 533-34. Arnold Hirsch, "With or Without Jim Crow: Black Residential Segregation in the United States," in Arnold Hirsch and Raymond Mohl, eds., *Urban Policy in Twentieth Century America* (New Brunswick, N.J.: Rutgers University Press, 1993), 65-69.

7. Massey and Hajnal, "The Changing Geographic Structure of Black-White Segregation in the United States," 536-37.

8. Ibid. According to Massey and Hajnal, these included Atlanta, Baltimore, Detroit, Gary (Indiana), New Orleans, and Washington.

9. Ibid., 537.

10. Hirsch, "With or Without Jim Crow," 79.

11. Ramiro Martinez, Jr., "Latinos and Lethal Policy: The Impact of Poverty and Inequality," *Social Problems* 43, no. 2 (May 1996): 131-45.

12. See the Federal Budget Summary, 1945-97.

13. Tonry, *Malign Neglect,*111.

14. Ibid., 81-124.

15. A growing but informal consensus on the social disposition to "warehouse" the racialized poor spans the most unlikely of parties: from Nathan Glazer, "The Renewal of Cities," *Scientific American* 213, no. 3 (1965): 192-203, on one hand, to Coramae Richey Mann, *Unequal Justice: A Question of Color* (Bloomington: Indiana University Press,1993), on the other.

16. David Theo Goldberg, *Racial Subjects: Writing on Race in America* (New York: Routledge, 1997), 173. In general, see William Julius Wilson, *When Work Disappears: The World of the New Urban Poor* (New York: Knopf, 1996).

17. Linda Greenhouse, "High Court Ruling Puts in Doubt $100 Million for Legal Services," *New York Times,* June 16, 1998, A1, 18.

18. Michael Taussig, *The Magic of the State* (New York: Routledge, 1997).

19. David Theo Goldberg, "The New Segregation," *Race and Society* 1, no. 1 (1998), 15-32; and *Racist Culture,* op. cit., 190-192.

20. Karl Marx, "Economic and Philosophical Manuscripts," in *Early Writings* (London: Pelican, 1975).

EIGHTEEN

The Militarization of the Police in the United States

GABRIEL TORRES AND DAVID A. LOVE

Police misconduct, brutality, and murder remains one of the leading human rights challenges facing the United States. If communities hope to reclaim civilian control over the police—and hold the police more accountable to the public—society must address the increased militarization of law enforcement and the normalization of aggressive police practices. As the lines between the police and the army blur, communities across the nation are becoming occupied territories that are subjugated to bold, aggressive, and violent police tactics. Police are waging war in the country against their fellow citizens. The erosion of human rights which accompanies this militarization of law enforcement is real, and something that should concern all of us.

The establishment of the police as a paramilitary force in the United States can be traced to the 1960s and 1970s. Interestingly, up to this point, the National Guard had been used extensively in a military police fashion. National Guards were called upon to quell race riots and enforce desegregation in the civil rights-era South. However, in a more insidious role, they were unleashed upon antiwar protestors on college campuses and occupied the predominantly black and brown inner cities during the rebellions of the 1960s. (Violent actions by local law enforcement in communities of color, it should be noted, often triggered these urban rebellions.) In response to these civil disturbances, large cities created their own paramilitary police units, assuming the role once reserved for the National Guard. The first such force, referred to as a SWAT (Special Weapons and Tactics) team, was assembled in the mid-1960s by former Los Angeles police chief Daryl Gates.

Local paramilitary forces came into being during a time of high-level guerilla warfare in America's streets and were used to wage war against organizations such as the Black Panther Party, the Black Liberation Army, the Symbionese Liberation Army, and the Weather Underground. This state-sponsored domestic warfare often involved raids on the headquarters of these groups, deadly shootouts, and assassinations of targeted leaders within those groups.

WAR ON DRUGS/"TOUGH ON CRIME"

In the 1980s the militarization of the police intensified, and the lines separating local law enforcement and the military were blurred even further. This time the war on drugs—primarily a war against people of color—was used as a pretext for the escalation of terrorism by the state, and used as a justification for more police firepower. The Posse Comitatus Act (which was enacted to ensure that America's military would engage in war while the police would enforce the law) was eroded during the 1980s when new laws allowed the police and the military to operate together: The military could participate with law enforcement in drug interdiction initiatives. At the same time, police forces receive military training from army commando units and Navy Seals as well as surplus weapons and equipment from a post-Cold War military at bargain-basement prices. For example, St. Petersburg,

Florida, recently bought an armored personnel carrier for $1,000 from the military. Furthermore, automatic weapons manufacturers court localities through combat competitions and training camps. Major cities and small towns alike are scurrying about in an effort to acquire new "toys," assault rifles, grenades, tanks, tear gas, military hardware that they do not need and should not have.

The war on drugs feeds on the stereotype of the dangerous, menacing, well-armed drug dealer who is most often perceived as a gang member with a black or brown face. The police's "tough on crime" stance has resulted in the criminalization of people of color, men, women, and children. In the 1960s Malcolm X spoke of the police who come into black communities, "exercising Gestapo tactics, stopping any Black man who is on the sidewalk, whether he is guilty or whether he is innocent. . . . As long as he is Black and a member of the Negro community, the public thinks that the white policeman is justified in going in there and trampling on that man's civil rights and on that man's human rights."[1] Unfortunately, Malcolm's statements are even more relevant today than they were then.

Consider the case of Mrs. Sarah West, an eighty-year-old African American woman in ill health who was thrown to the ground and held at gunpoint while her apartment was ransacked by a dozen narcotics agents from the New York Police Department. The cops left without so much as an apology. The woman still suffers from fatigue and a lack of sleep as a result of the 1996 raid. In 1994, seventy-five-year-old Boston minister Accelyne Williams was chased in his apartment by a SWAT team and died of a heart attack while handcuffed and facedown. The team was looking for drugs and obviously had the wrong address.

It is no wonder that black, brown, and poor communities often feel that the police are an occupying force, existing not only to "serve and protect" but often to contain and terrorize. And many believe that the police do things in these neighborhoods that they would not in more affluent white areas. Consider the aerial bombing on the MOVE headquarters by the Philadelphia police in the 1980s, resulting in the deaths of innocent people. Consider the use of armored tanks by the New York City Police Department to remove squatters from an abandoned apartment building.

Consider the case of North Carolina's "Operation Readi-Rock," a ninja-style paramilitary force that is known to selectively stop and search black people. Some members of the force refer to themselves as "Operation Ghetto Storm," as indicated by a T-shirt that they wear. During one mission, a black community was invaded and 100 people were detained and searched, while whites were allowed to go. In another example of trigger-happy police endangering innocent bystanders, a cleaning woman was shot seven times while running from a bank where she had been held hostage for fifteen hours.

This racial component to aggressive policing, although an important element that cannot be denied, is not the whole story. Without question, African Americans, Latinos, Asian Americans, and other people of color are disproportionately the victims of police brutality, abuse, and misconduct. Similarly, White male officers, with their often-warped racial attitudes and predisposition to brutalize, are disproportionately the offending parties. However, as those of us who deal with this issue can attest, a "blue" mentality pervades police forces across the country. An "us versus them" attitude is fostered among the ranks of the department, and police view the people they "serve" as the enemy. Brutal behavior usually is condoned and often rewarded with commendations or promotions. As a result, many officers of color and female officers will exhibit the same behavior as their white male counterparts—often to impress their superiors or to move ahead in a corrupt, gang-like police structure. Further, whites are mistaken if they assume that they are immune to the kind of police violence visited upon other groups. Whole segments of the population cannot experience such blatant human rights abuses without such abuses overflowing into the general population, the so-called middle America. We are hearing increasingly of abuse and harassment by law enforcement of white Americans, people who believed that it could not happen to them, who believed that it was not *supposed* to happen to *them*.

ZERO TOLERANCE, QUALITY OF LIFE,
AND DISCRIMINATORY POLICING

A political context exists in which we can understand the popularity of police state tactics. Politicians know that the "tough on crime" stance sells well among an insecure electorate. A popular school of law enforcement these days follows the belief that if you control "quality-of-life" crimes such as drinking in public or loitering, you create a sense of order that will prevent more serious crimes such as murder and rape. The New York City Police Department under former Police Commissioner William Bratton and Mayor Rudolph Giuliani (who is regarded in some circles as the de facto police chief) was the first department in the nation to adopt this strategy. Other cities followed suit.

The case of New York (whose police cars bear the motto "Courtesy, Professionalism, and Respect" or "CPR") exposes the inherent problems of this "zero-tolerance" strategy. In Mayor Giuliani's first term of office, murder declined by 50 percent and misdemeanor arrests increased 73 percent. At the same time, police brutality complaints (i.e., those that were reported to the powerless Civilian Complaint Review Board) jumped 62 percent. Meanwhile, the city paid approximately $100 million in taxpayers' revenue to settle police misconduct complaints. Perhaps most revealing are the lost lives of eighty people killed by police during Mayor Giuliani's first term, the majority of whom were black, Latino and Asian youth who died under dubious circumstances. Upon his second inauguration, Giuliani demonstrated his indifference toward the issue of police brutality. At a press conference, he claimed that "only" twenty people were killed by police in 1997, and most of these killings were found to be "justifiable" by a grand jury. Amid an epidemic of police abuse, the mayor states that 93 percent of New York City cops have never discharged their weapon. In a force of over 38,000, about 2,700 officers (some of them, no doubt, racist, trigger-happy, brutal, and mentally unstable) have used their guns.

The use of more violent tactics by the police increases the likelihood of more confrontations between the police and the general public. In fact, the vast majority of police brutality incidents do not involve criminal activity but rather feature an honest, innocent, tax-paying citizen caught in an escalating situation. Many times cops will lash out if they feel that the citizen is questioning their authority.

Despite the glowing reports about the drop in crime due to more aggressive policing, we do not really know that "zero tolerance" leads to a drop in crime. Other factors to consider include the decline in crack cocaine use and the increasing popularity of heroin, community-based programs and initiatives working with gangs and at-risk youths, and changing demographics and economic conditions. Furthermore, even if "zero tolerance" contributes to the decline in crime rates, does that justify the means? Should people have to sacrifice their rights for a more orderly society? Another flaw of the "zero-tolerance" school of policing is that it casts a wide net over the general public and serves to criminalize entire communities. "Zero tolerance" seems to translate into zero tolerance for people of color and the poor. Frequently, youths of color are criminalized as they are picked up for quality-of-life crimes or for not doing anything at all. Sometimes they just "fit the description." Often they are merely guilty of being black while walking. For many young men in major cities such as New York, this is their introduction to the criminal justice system.

THE "PRISON INDUSTRIAL COMPLEX" AND THE WAR AGAINST MEN OF COLOR

Although we are constantly told that crime is decreasing, more prisons are being built everyday. Why is this so? There is a war being waged against youths, particularly black and Latino youths in America. Society has decided that there is a surplus labor force in this country. There are no jobs for this segment of the population. A failing educational system is purposely designed not to prepare these young people for the high-tech information age. So, what do you do with this surplus labor force that has been written off completely?

Meanwhile, as plants are closing in rural white communities, the Angry White Man is getting angrier. In order to keep him happy, you create a new type of factory town, one with a sparkling new prison as the cornerstone of economic activity. Jobs are created because prison guards are needed, as are suppliers for food, clothing, and bedding. Major corporations see that profit is to be made, so they enter into the prison business and trade their stock on Wall Street. The raw materials for these prisons are young people, particularly young men of color, who are warehoused into these "factories" in order to make these institutions functional and profitable for the corporate shareholders.

How does the militarization of the police fit into this? In order to justify the warehousing of whole segments of the population in these prisons, society has to brand them as a criminal element. Brutal and paramilitaristic policing are justified in the eyes of the state because "that is how you must deal with *those* people." Unfortunately, many in the general public (e.g., suburban dwellers) do not care if the rights of other people are violated, as long as the police do not come into *their* neighborhoods and brutalize *them*. In their eyes, the police are the one factor that contains the inner city and protects the rest of the population from the poor, "unruly" black and brown criminal element. They do not realize, however, the dangers that militarized policing poses to the freedoms of all of us. Nor do they understand the consequences to our society if people are subjected to this type of oppression for a prolonged period of time. As Richie Perez of the National Congress for Puerto Rican Rights notes, "[T]he rage in our communities is bubbling, and of course it's going to explode."

SOLUTIONS

There are solutions to the situation just described. Communities throughout this country must dedicate themselves to greater activism around the issue of police brutality and the disturbing trends we are witnessing in law enforcement. Furthermore, communities must have greater control over the police in their neighborhoods and should devise structures of self-policing and monitoring the police.

Moreover, there is a need for effective civilian oversight of local law enforcement: not merely civilian review boards with the power to investigate and subpoena criminal police activity (which is necessary), but bodies that can place limitations on police power and prevent brutality. In order that we acquire and maintain the type of policing that we really want and need, the budget of police departments should be tied to performance, and misconduct incidents, beatings, killings, and civilian complaints should be taken into consideration. The militarization of police can be stopped, but only we can stop it.

NOTES

1. Quote printed in David A. Love, "What's Going On? Rising Tide of Police Brutality," *New York Amsterdam News,* April 26, 1997, 32.

NINETEEN

State Violence, Asian Immigrants, and the "Underclass"

ERIC TANG

The story of policing, detention, and prisons is simultaneously a story of racial and gendered violence. In other words, any discussion of state violence must be viewed within the broader discussion of violence against racial and national minorities, women of color, gays, and lesbians. Yet this is also the age of the neoliberal or neoconservative consensus—a time when bipartisanship shamelessly insists that "there is no racism." (With some regional variation, similar claims are made in reference to gender and sexual discrimination.) Indeed, when today the United States looks for explanations for its tripling prison population, the exponential increase in concentrations of inner city poverty, the hypermilitarization of metropolitan police forces, and the collapse of the welfare state, the public is quickly introduced to a litany of seemingly raceless phrases and terms that it must learn to recite: the "dysfunctional family," a "culture of poverty," and, of course, the "underclass." The underclass is a particular favorite of liberal social scientists and policymakers. A deceptively simple term, it suggests that racism is no longer to blame for social inequities; the real culprits are the individual pathologies, behaviors, and cultures of those who live at the bottom. Racism is out, taking "personal responsibility" is in.

For those of us who know better, "underclass" is merely the racial slur of our time. And, far from being colorless, its color is decidedly "black."[1] To be sure, underclass has become one of those convenient code words: It allows one to conjure up dehumanizing images of black urban life—in the form of the uncontrollably violent black male or the sexually deviant "welfare queen"—without really saying it. In turn, those represented by these images become the prime targets of state violence.

I begin with a discussion of the so-called black underclass because this particular term is quite relevant to a discussion of state violence against Asian immigrants in the contemporary moment. The staying power of the term "underclass" has much to do with the way in which other "nonwhite" groups—particularly Asians—are kept far away from the term. In other words, "underclass" works as an effective justification for state violence against blacks so long as those in power can insist that there is "no Asian underclass." In fact, the words "Asian" and "underclass" often are used in a mutually exclusive manner. In turn, there is utter silence surrounding state violence in Asian immigrant communities.

There are two primary goals here: First, I want to challenge the racist assumptions that justify and naturalize state violence against blacks by exposing the workings of state violence in places where it is least talked about—Asian immigrant communities. Second, I want to encourage Asian community activists to take seriously the question of state violence, avoiding the assumption that it is an exceptional issue for our communities. To emphasize this latter point, I will focus on the particular nature of state violence in Southeast Asian communities.

CONCEALING STATE VIOLENCE
AGAINST ASIAN IMMIGRANTS

As we enter the twenty-first century, capitalism has only accelerated its drive toward an unjust and inhumane social order for this nation.

Without missing a beat, the state has developed sophisticated measures to serve capitalist interests and to discipline the nonwhite working class. Indeed, the state serves as an economic regulator by actively seeking the incarceration of a reserve labor force comprised of predominantly black youths, by issuing city and state ordinances that literally remove poor people of color from public spaces, and by using "workfare" programs to convert welfare recipients into slave laborers at previously unionized worksites. These state practices uphold the needs of the new global assembly line: Just as neo-imperialism has recruited a pool of highly exploitable labor in the Third World for U.S. capital, the prison industrial complex has allowed U.S.-based industries to become "Third Worlded" by relocating manufacturing jobs inside of prisons and by initiating workfare programs. Throughout the nation inmates—the vast majority being people of color—are forced to work as producers for multinational corporations. Here, of course, the economic role of the state is disguised as a crime-fighting effort: "The state isn't doing this to advance capitalist interests but to stop violent crime and welfare fraud." And everyday this crime-fighting charade is played out in the public eye. From the videotaped beating of Rodney King to the hit television series *Cops,* state violence is the primary mode through which images of the black working class are circulated and received these days. The black working class has become a public spectacle for crime and punishment.

At the same time, however, contemporary capitalism has made a point of disguising state violence against Asian immigrant communities. The recent wave of Asian immigrant laborers to the United States is fueled by the same global economic interests that drive the prison industries: the need for highly exploitable or "informal" labor that keeps U.S. manufacturing competitive with the Third World. The new immigrant enclaves of our cities function as veritable "Third Worlds within"—spaces where immigrant workers are forced to labor in sweatshop firms or in the low-wage service economy that caters to the needs of the urban professional class. Keeping this immigrant labor force confined and disciplined requires its own set of violent state practices: police raids of Asian immigrant economies, the literal removal of immigrants from particular areas of the city, and the brutalization and imprisonment of those who transgress the boundaries of the immigrant enclave. These are just a few of the many forms of state violence that pervade working-class Asian immigrant communities in New York City. Yet these acts of state violence—unlike those that target black urban communities—cannot be explained away by the master narrative of crime prevention (save for particular segments of youths that I discuss later). To do so would only subtract from the state's efforts to make the color of crime and state violence decidedly black. What, then, is the appropriate moral panic or social crisis that can be used to justify state violence in Asian communities? How does the state publicly explain its daily police harassment of Asian low-wage workers, vendors, small entrepreneurs, and poor neighborhood residents who live on the borderlands of white residential areas? The answer is simple: It doesn't. State violence against Asian immigrants remains a covert operation, removed from the public spectacle. Much like organized crime, state forces such as the police conceal their violent activity by relying on physical coercion, partnerships with corrupt business owners, and extortion. Add to this a number of vague city ordinances and zoning laws that are arbitrarily enforced in places like Chinatown, and we are confronted with a virtual "underworld" of state violence in Asian communities.

Part of the Committee Against Anti-Asian Violence (CAAAV)'s[2] ongoing mission is to expose and publicly broadcast the crimes of state violence against the Asian immigrant working class. For CAAAV, the terrain of state violence is a strategic site for Asian community organizing because it is here that we may challenge simultaneously the workings of racist violence and capitalism. In other words, by focusing on state violence in Asian immigrant communities, we develop a contemporary analysis on how the state and private capital join forces in their attempt to segregate, discipline, and coerce nonwhite working-class communities. Rarely does the explicit call against racist violence meet the concerns of economic justice in a direct way. Indeed, today's progressive and radical Asian community organizations often are compelled to choose one issue over the other: Either we organize against racist violence or we fight economic exploitation (e.g., low-wage labor and sweatshop conditions), but never both at the same time. CAAAV believes that by entering the realm of state violence against Asian communities, we may find ways to bring these crucial areas of work together.

COMMITTEE AGAINST
ANTI-ASIAN VIOLENCE (CAAAV)

CAAAV is a twelve-year-old organization. Its roots can be traced to the fragments of the Asian American Movement in New York City as they intersected with the small social movement against anti-Asian violence that emerged following the brutal murder of Vincent Chin in 1982 and the state's subsequent refusal to punish his white attackers. During the 1990s, however, CAAAV has focused less on civilian-on-civilian acts of anti-Asian violence—what the government euphemistically calls "hate crimes"—and instead has focused entirely on state violence against Asian immigrant communities. (This is not, however, to suggest that white-civilian attacks on Asians are unrelated to state practices.) To save you from a long-winded discussion on the differences between state violence and hate crimes, allow me simply to fast forward to a snapshot of our work over the past several years.

In Chinatown and in the growing Chinese communities of South Brooklyn, CAAAV has been organizing residents to fight the escalation of police brutality against Chinese immigrants. On a daily basis, Chinese immigrants, particularly those who make their living on the streets as vendors, dollar-van drivers,[3] and delivery people are harassed, beaten, falsely ticketed, and arrested by members of the New York Police Department (NYPD). When CAAAV first began its advocacy program in the mid-1980s, it found that the majority of reported racist attacks against Asians involved the police as primary perpetrators. In fact, CAAAV's first major case involved a Chinese immigrant family whose home had been ransacked by police in an unauthorized raid. During the raid members of the family were beaten and choked, including one woman who was several months pregnant. Similar cases would flood into CAAAV's office in the following years.

By the mid 1990s, as the police state of Mayor Rudolph Giuliani came to power, CAAAV developed the Racial Justice Committee (RJC) to monitor systemic patterns of police abuse and organize community residents to fight for precinct-level reforms and criminal indictments of abusive police officers. RJC's work has focused primarily in Chinatown and Brooklyn, where it publicized patterns of police abuse among those who labor in the "informal economies" of the Chinese enclave. This policing agenda is one that seeks to contain Chinatown as a subeconomy where anything goes, a place where goods are manufactured at slave wages for mainstream markets, where tourism does as it pleases, and where the working-class residents remain confined within designated borders of the enclave. Virtually every Chinatown vendor or small shop owner is routinely ticketed for false violations. (Sometimes these citations do not even correspond with an existing law or regulation.) While the vendor may stand a chance to fight these false tickets in court, the police are well aware that most vendors cannot afford to take a day off from work. Paying the summons turns out to be less expensive than closing shop for a day. Meanwhile, these tickets generate hundreds of thousands of dollars in annual city revenue. In addition to false ticketing, many vendors also are victims of police raids and the illegal confiscation of goods and cash. These raids are meant to encourage vendors to vacate areas marked for future development and tourism. Even low-wage workers who do not operate on the streets of Chinatown—such as those in the restaurant or garment industries—cannot escape the police state. The police operate in partnership with big-business owners who do everything they can to squash unionization and virtually any labor action.

The victims of police abuse are both male and female, young and old. Yet those who experience the brunt of the borderland containment efforts are Chinese youths. Criminalized as gangsters, the police remove a diverse range of Chinese youths—including students, part-time workers, and the unemployed—from public areas without just cause. These removals are invariably accompanied by brutal force, leaving many injured and some hospitalized. In March of 1995, sixteen-year-old Yong Xin Huang was executed by police officer Steven Mizrahi. Evidence from the murder scene revealed that Huang did not struggle with the officer and was shot point-blank in the back of the head. Brooklyn District Attorney Charles Hynes refused to indict Mizrahi. Working closely with the Huang family, CAAAV initiated a citywide justice campaign for Huang, awakening many Asian communities to the reality of police abuse and murder in New York City.

The intersection of economic regulation and racist police violence is not exclusive to working-class Chinese communities. In the early

1990s CAAAV also established an organizing project involving South Asian taxi drivers who face police abuse as part of their overall labor conditions. This project is known as Lease Drivers Coalition (LDC). Since the early 1980s, when Indian and Pakistani drivers began to dominate the yellow cab industry in New York City, patterns of police abuse emerged: Drivers were being stopped by police, given false tickets, and threatened with having their hack licenses taken away. Here too these tickets and suspensions generate close to millions of dollars for the city annually. Most insidious, however, are the acts of physical and mental abuse perpetrated by the police. Countless drivers, including a CAAAV staff organizer, have been beaten and arrested by the police—most of these beatings and arrests happen to those who have a knowledge of their rights and can articulate them in the face of police misconduct. Other drivers have been illegally asked for immigration papers and threatened with deportation.

When Giuliani came into office, one of his immediate proposals was to abolish the Taxi and Limousine Commission (TLC) as the sole regulating body of the taxi industry and to relocate its regulatory powers under the auspices of the NYPD. While his plan did not move forward entirely, Giuliani was successful in securing one of its key elements: taking away street regulation and enforcement from TLC investigators and placing it in the hands of police officers. Today police officers have the exclusive power to enforce TLC regulations on the city streets. It can be said that taxi driving is the only industry in New York City (and perhaps the entire nation) where the workers are directly regulated by a municipal police force. Through LDC, CAAAV has organized Asian drivers to fight police brutality as well as TLC regulations that consistently target low-wage lease drivers[4] in an effort to collect greater revenue for the city. Also, LDC sought to improve industry-wide labor conditions by challenging the exploitative leasing system that denies drivers health insurance, legal contracts, and yet charges them thousands of dollars for their hack licenses.[5]

Immigrant taxi drivers are a mostly male labor force, pointing to the fact that Asian low-wage laborers are segregated not only by nationality but by gender as well. In recent years CAAAV has sought to develop an organizing project specifically among Asian women workers who are not only exploited in the low-wage and informal service industries but who are vulnerable to violent state practices that often fall below the radar of our organizing activities. In 1995 CAAAV developed the Women Workers Project (WWP) with the goal of organizing and advocating for Korean immigrant sex workers. For these women, the state manifests itself in a number of forms: immigration sponsors (often the employers) who use the laws of the Immigration and Naturalization Service (INS) to control women's labor and mobility; the legacy of militarized prostitution that extends itself from U.S. military bases in Asia to the United States (usually through marriage); and local police forces that regulate the sex industry by extorting sex workers and shop owners. In addition to state violence, these women also must contend with the hostility of patriarchal leadership in the Korean community. In an effort to reach these women, CAAAV has advocated for them in court cases, monitored police abuse in the workplace, and organized campaigns seeking justice for workers who have been victims of both state and civilian acts of violence. (For more information on the Women Workers Project and the struggle of Korean immigrant sex workers, see chapter 13.)

SOUTHEAST ASIAN
POVERTY AND STATE VIOLENCE

In the Southeast Asian refugee community of the Bronx, CAAAV has organized around a number of different forms of state violence as they relate to inner city poverty. The Northwest Bronx is home to nearly 20,000 Southeast Asian refugees who fled their homelands in the aftermath of the U.S. invasion of Vietnam and its subsequent bombings of Cambodia. Unlike the Chinatowns and Koreatowns that emerged from the post-1965 immigrant wave, most Southeast Asian communities in the United States lack an "ethnic economy" in the form of restaurants, light manufacturing shops (such as garment sweatshops), and small groceries. Although poverty pervades most ethnic economies, it is often characterized as a "working poverty" where virtually everyone is compelled to work in a sweatshop or small business owned by fellow Chinese or Koreans.

Given that most Southeast Asian refugees were uprooted from an agricultural lifestyle, no significant entrepreneurial segment exists that is capable of stimulating similar ethnic economy jobs—even on the most exploitative basis. Thus unemployment and welfare-dependency rates overwhelm the community. And, as with many communities that face concentrated poverty and unemployment, Southeast Asians are victims of violent state practices in the form of the shrinking welfare state, police repression, and the prison industrial complex.

Southeast Asians, who now constitute over 11 percent of the Asian Pacific American community, maintain the highest welfare-dependency rates of any race or ethnic group per capita in the United States. In California alone the rate of Southeast Asians on welfare has reached levels as high as 86 percent of the state's entire Southeast Asian population. A recent study conducted by CAAAV's Youth Leadership Project revealed that 70 percent of the Southeast Asian community of the Bronx is unemployed while 65 percent receive some type of public assistance. With the passing of the 1996 Federal Personal Responsibility and Work Reconciliation Act (a.k.a. "welfare reform"), many Southeast Asian families have been threatened with cuts to their federally-funded Food Stamps for immigrant children and Supplemental Security Income for the disabled and elderly. These cuts, which target immigrants in particular, have made hunger and homelessness a very real possibility for many Southeast Asian families.

In the midst of this crisis, Giuliani has expanded his Work Experience Program (a.k.a. "workfare"), which forces welfare recipients into hard, manual labor in parks, sanitation jobs, municipal buildings, and city agencies in exchange for their welfare checks. Offering few exemptions, the New York City workfare program—now the largest in the nation—has placed cruel and unreasonable work requirements on the disabled, elderly, and mothers with young children. Southeast Asian welfare recipients who cannot meet the workfare requirements often are forced to remove themselves from welfare rolls. Meanwhile, those who comply with the program find themselves in unsafe work environments that do not accommodate their child care needs, grossly violate the city's own occupational health and safety regulations, pay far below the minimum wage, and offer little or no job-skills training.

As the welfare state collapses, job opportunities for young Southeast Asians are virtually nonexistent, Bronx high schools actively encourage Southeast Asian students to dropout (while those who stay in school become the lab rats for Giuliani's latest experiment: replacing school security guards with armed police officers), and city-funded youth programs shut down on a daily basis. Under these conditions, a minority of Southeast Asian youths turn to crime and gang life while the majority struggle through whatever legal avenues remain. Yet—no matter what choice these young people make—all are susceptible to police harassment and brutality as well as incarceration.

Southeast Asian youths who sit on their front stoops these days can be victims of a random neighborhood drug sweep conducted by the NYPD. During these sweeps, police round up and handcuff any youth who happens to be in the designated hot spot. After illegally searching the captured youth (I use the word "captured" because, despite the handcuffing, the youth has not been officially arrested for a crime) and coming up with absolutely nothing, the police continue the process of detention and questioning for several hours before letting the youth go. During the detention, police officers often take illegal Polaroid snapshots of the youth that are then inserted into so-called Asian mug books. Although the youth has committed no crime and has no prior record, his or her face is now unofficially logged in the criminal justice system. These illegal mug books are used later to facilitate the selection of suspects whenever a crime involving an Asian perpetrator is reported. The Asian mug books are not unique to New York City—in Philadelphia and Orange County, California, valiant community-based struggles have been waged to abolish them.

While organized gang violence in the Bronx has declined in recent years, Giuliani has nonetheless found ways to hype up the appearance of gang life—a sure way to justify increased spending on his police force. Right before his reelection in the fall of 1997, Giuliani released fraudulent reports that the notorious Bloods and Crips gangs had invaded New York City. With the media circus by his side, he rounded up hundreds of black, Latino, and Asian youths suspected of being part of the West Coast gang empires. None of these arrests led to any conclusive ties to the Bloods or Crips. But the media hype was successful in placing fear in the hearts of the city's liberal voting block as well as in justifying a renewed police campaign of harassment that included illegal searches and countless acts of brutality against young people of color.

Finally, many Southeast Asian youths are becoming part of the nation's growing prison population. While in New York City the number of Asian youths in prisons has increased only slightly, states such as California have witnessed an explosion in the number of Southeast Asian inmates, particularly in the municipal jails and boot camps for young offenders. Despite the recent proliferation of Asian American social service organizations, very few groups have developed programs capable of addressing the needs of this Asian prison population. Meanwhile, the efforts of groups willing to work with young Asian prisoners— such as the East Bay Asian Youth Center—often are stifled by the local criminal justice system or, even worse, by conservative and neoliberal Asian American civil rights structures that prefer to ignore the existence of Asian prisoners.

In 1995 CAAAV established the Southeast Asian Youth Leadership Project (YLP) of the Northwest Bronx. Recognizing that state violence in the form of the welfare state, police repression, and the prison industrial complex finds its common target among young people, YLP provides a space for young Southeast Asians to engage community organizing/community building strategies. Most inner-city youth programs are aimed at keeping youths off the streets, out of jails, and in school. While these programs of prevention are certainly important, they often begin with a rather low expectation of what young people living in poverty actually can accomplish. YLP works with a different philosophy: We believe in working with "at-risk" youths by challenging them to combat the economic and state institutions that place them and their families "at risk" to begin with. Currently YLP focuses its organizing activities in three primary areas: resisting the criminalization of youth and the Giuliani police state, abolishing the welfare "reform" measures and the workfare regime, and challenging the corporate development projects in the inner-city. These projects have led only to increased unemployment and environmental hazards, and to a decrease in healthcare and other vital services for community residents.

STRUGGLE WITHOUT EXCEPTIONS

CAAAV's work provides a mere glimpse of the many forms of state violence used to regulate economic relations in diverse Asian communities. Moreover, its work suggests that an anti-state violence agenda is one strategy that can respond coherently to the dual attack of racist violence and economic oppression. Yet, anti-state violence work remains rather marginal in the broader terrain of Asian American activist concerns. Indeed, who would dare suggest that police brutality, the criminalization of sex work, welfare/workfare, and the incarceration of youths emerge as the vanguard issues of our Asian communities? For many, these concerns are merely exceptions to the "core" issues of the contemporary Asian working-class: super-exploitative sweatshop conditions, the plight of the undocumented, the struggle of the poor shop owner who can be won over to working-class interests.

This argument of exceptionalism is often directed at Southeast Asians in particular. Whenever I speak on the conditions in Southeast Asian communities, citing a list of issues that include police brutality, incarceration, unemployment, and welfare dependency, I often receive comments on how unusual these issues seem for any Asian community. The popular assumption is that Southeast Asians represent an exceptional case due to their refugee past: The "unique experience" of war and refugee flight have led to a particular form of Asian inner-city poverty that is strikingly similar to black urban poverty. So too, Southeast Asians struggle with forms of state violence that are rare in most Asian communities, but all too common for blacks. Here the explicit suggestion is that under normal circumstances, issues of state violence belong to the black urban poor.

On one hand, this may be true: A quick glance at the statistics will reveal that blacks make up the majority of the prison population and are the most frequent targets of police abuse. Yet, on the other hand, if we insist that the color of state violence is unequivocally black, then we run the risk of naturalizing notions of black criminality, black pathology—in effect, we reinforce the idea of a black underclass. Indeed, the matter has little to do with whether Southeast Asians pose an exception or not; rather it has to do with the ways in which we—as progressives, radicals, and revolutionaries—also have internalized assumptions about the "character" of black struggle. This may seem a rather subtle point, but I think it is an important one for Asian communities to consider. If Asian community activists fail to talk seriously about state violence in our communities, or if we approach the discussion as mere "visitors," not only do we perpetuate the segregation of struggles under superficial categories—black issues, Asian issues, Latino issues, and so on—but we unwittingly reduce the black community to an undifferentiated mass of people—the ultimate image of ghetto life to which all other nonwhite groups are compared. Moreover, we indirectly participate in the state's conspicuous effort to create the public spectacle of the underclass while hiding the most complex and contradictory workings of state violence.

By refusing to assign a definitive color to the struggle against state violence, I do not mean to minimize its tremendous impact in certain racial communities, nor am I saying that we relinquish our respective ethnoracial, national, gender, and sexual claims against the state for something more universal. I am suggesting, however, that revolutionary change will occur only when we have learned to speak about struggles without exceptions. Certainly, there is much that Southeast Asian communities uniquely share with other nonwhite communities, but this is not because they have somehow transgressed the normal boundaries of Asian issues. Rather, it is because global capitalism now bombards us with new contradictions, new modes of oppressing and segregating poor and working people. Under these conditions, we cannot afford to place any struggle outside of our respective communities.

In closing, I want to relate a story told to me by Dave Kakishibe, director of the East Bay Asian Youth Center. According to Dave, an eruption of Southeast Asian gang violence in the East Oakland area during the mid- to late 1980s prompted the Oakland police to take some affirmative action. With a head nod from the Asian community establishment, the Oakland police began an all-out war against Southeast Asian gangs. In militarized fashion, this program swept Southeast Asian youths off the street by staging frame-ups, making false arrests on trumped-up charges, and, of course, using brutal force. Many of these encounters led to shootouts with police, and some resulted in the cold-blooded police murder of Southeast Asian youths. The tactics used against these youths were a replica of the so-called counterinsurgency tactics that were carried out against the Black Panther Party during the late 1960s and early 1970s. In fact, often they were carried out by the same men. Before retiring from a lifetime of law enforcement, it seems as if these police officials decided to take their final victory lap by exterminating Oakland's new "Southeast Asian peril." But this war against Southeast Asian youths was not so much a final chapter as it was a chance to "come full circle." You see, the counterinsurgency tactics deployed against the urban guerrilla war of the Panthers were adaptations of the counterinsurgency programs used by the U.S. military in the Third World, particularly Vietnam. Here we are presented with a mind-numbing turn of events: The violence used to destroy Southeast Asians abroad was recalibrated to destroy a black "Third World within," which in turn opened the door for destroying America's new urban dwellers— ironically, the children of the Southeast Asian war for which these violent tactics were originally designed.

Almost thirty years ago black, Chicano, and Asian American youths took on the collective title of "Third World People" in an effort to express solidarity and kinship with the revolutionary people of Southeast Asia, Africa, and Latin America. The state, unfortunately, took the analogy one step further by deploying a common militarized agenda for Third World communities abroad and nonwhite communities within the nation-state. Today, however, these two spheres are no longer fully separated by oceans and continents. The Third World masses and the black and Chicano working class now meet on the streets of America's cities. In an age when collective community struggle and the promise of a different society seemed to have vanished, this new racial reality furnishes us with exciting possibilities. Making the most of these possibilities requires that no struggle be rendered misplaced, out of range, or exceptional. The future of working-class unity is before us; we must be courageous enough to claim it.

NOTES

I want to offer my deepest appreciation to Evelyn Hu-DeHart, Joy James, and all the Center for the Studies of Ethnicity and Race in America organizers for inviting me to participate in "Unfinished Liberation," where this work was first presented. I want to thank Jane Bai for reading earlier drafts of this chapter and providing key comments and suggestions.

1. For a historical overview of the "underclass," see Michael Katz, ed., *The Underclass Debate: Views From History* (Princeton, N.J.: Princeton University Press, 1993).

2. In 1998 we changed our name to "CAAAV: Organizing Asian Communities." While the acronym is still kept for reasons of familiarity, we have added the subtitle in an effort to emphasize our focus on community organizing as opposed to hate-crime advocacy.

3. A dollar-van is an informal car service for Chinatown workers. The van takes the workers to and from their homes in Brooklyn. These vans often cost less than public transportation; more importantly, however, they cut travel time in half for women workers who must return home to care for young children.

4. All yellow cabs in New York City are required to have a city-issued medallion. The Taxi & Limousine Commission auctions a set number of these medallions annually. These medallions are very expensive, and most drivers cannot afford them. As such, drivers are compelled to lease the medallions from owners. The lease prices are also very high, forcing the driver to work a twelve-hour shift just to break even. Over the past twenty years, owners in the yellow cab industry have overwhelmingly turned to the leasing system, as opposed to owning a fleet of taxis and hiring a workforce of drivers. The leasing system is attractive to owners who can now evade local and federal labor standards as lease drivers are technically considered "small entrepreneurs" who can set their own work schedules.

5. In February 1998, members of the Lease Drivers Coalition of CAAAV started an independent organization called the New York Taxi Workers Alliance.

TWENTY

The INS and the Criminalization of Immigrant Workers

JULIE A. SU

On August 2, 1995, the discovery of seventy-one garment workers from Thailand forced to work eighteen-hour days in a barbed wire–enclosed apartment compound in a Los Angeles suburb called El Monte sent shock waves across the United States and around the world. The existence of workers hunched over sewing machines in slave-like conditions—where armed guards stood watch; razor wire and inward-pointing iron guard rails helped enforce discipline; and boards, bars, and locks kept the doors and windows inaccessible—exposed in graphic detail the wretched conditions in "Made in the U.S.A." sweatshops. It revealed the extreme exploitation that immigrant workers too often confront in the United States.

The discovery was made in a predawn raid by a multi-agency task force that included the Immigration and Naturalization Service (INS), labor officials, and local police. Rather than liberation for the sixty-seven women and four men, the raid ended in the workers being relocated to another barbed wire–enclosed prison: an INS detention facility.[1] For the next nine days, the Thai workers were dressed in orange prison jumpsuits, their few belongings were taken from them, and again they were denied free access to the outside world. This time, however, their captor was the United States government.

Attorneys and community activists tried to gain access to the workers to inform them of their rights and to advocate for their freedom. Yet the INS continually resisted any effort to allow the workers outside help or counsel. By the time anyone representing the workers' interest was able to speak with them, they had already been told to sign documents making them deportable.

The conditions of detention were deplorable. For the first two nights, the INS locked the immigrant workers in downtown holding tanks, large cells separating the men and the women, without beds, showers, or ventilation. The worker-prisoners curled up on a concrete floor to sleep, sharing one toilet that was set apart from the rest of the cell by a flimsy partition and a large trash can, providing almost no privacy. The odor of bodies pressed too closely together in unbearable heat permeated the detention cell. The INS served food that was inedible. On the third day, the INS transported the workers in an INS bus to the federal detention complex in Terminal Island to sleep. Each time they were shuttled back and forth between their sleeping quarters and their downtown detention facility, the workers were shackled. The workers were treated as if—and made to believe that—it was they who would be punished for the years of slave labor they had endured.

The experience of too many immigrant workers reveals that mistreatment, intimidation, and incarceration occurs as a matter of policy, not by accident. By design, the INS enters a workplace where immigrant workers are being routinely mistreated,[2] rounds up the workers, and imprisons them. Of course, there are variations on this practice. In some cases, workers are detained in their workplace briefly and then summarily deported, thus avoiding a trip to INS prison. In other cases, workers are granted "voluntary departure"—in exchange for an admission that they are in the country illegally, they are given a period of time within which they have to leave. Workplace raids in particular industries—garment manufacturing, restaurant, construction, food processing—where workers are almost exclusively people of color have taken priority status in the interior enforcement activities of the INS. In California, where low-wage immigrant workers are primarily Asian and Latino, INS enforcement reinforces the link between immigrant and criminal and reifies the connection between racial minority and "undesirable." Along with the unprecedented buildup of forces along the U.S.-Mexico border and an aggressive deportation campaign, the INS has sent a tidal wave of fear throughout immigrant worker communities. During the first six months of the 1997-98 fiscal year, the INS reported deporting almost 80,000 people, up 78 percent from the same period in 1997.[3]

This fear does not mean workers stop coming to the United States. In fact, above all else, it means that sweatshops and slave shops are forced farther and farther underground as workers refuse to report violations for fear of retaliation by the INS. INS enforcement through workplaces is particularly insidious because it not only criminalizes immigrant workers—making poverty and the search for opportunity a punishable crime—but it also defends and supports worker exploitation. Immigrant workers, particularly those who are undocumented, are already vulnerable to abuse by employers because of their poverty, desperation for work, and lack of facility with English. By attacking them for their immigration status, the U.S. government ensures that they remain beyond legal protections and justifies their exploitation, thus creating an "underclass" among the poor. Put another way, U.S. government enforcement action and policy has elevated immigration laws above all the laws being broken with respect to low- wage immigrant workers—federal and state minimum wage and overtime, health and safety, workers' compensation, joint liability, anti-harassment, and civil rights protections. INS enforcement in workplaces has turned immigrant workers into criminals and worksites into detention centers.

THE INS AND WORKER EXPLOITATION

Impoverished immigrant workers come to the United States desperate for work. They labor in conditions many believe only exist in "Third World" countries. In the garment industry, Asian and Latino workers labor side by side, sewing garments to be sold in the nation's top retail stores. Yet subminimum wages, no overtime pay, dust and dirt, poor ventilation and insufficient lighting, exposed electrical wiring, unsanitary bathrooms, cockroaches and even rat-infested factories are commonplace. Despite rampant human rights and labor law and health violations, workers are too vulnerable to come forward. One of the most powerful tools at employers' disposal is the threat "If you report me, I'll report *you* to the INS." Employers have made good on this threat both to avoid workers' claims for back wages and to quash worker organizing and unionization efforts.[4] Workers are forced to accept poverty wages and daily harassment as the price they pay to remain and work in this country.

Federal law authorizes the INS to arrest an individual if an INS agent suspects the person is in the country illegally.[5] Both Congress and the judiciary have granted the INS a great deal of discretion. Moreover, the INS maintains almost sole control over detainees. Because immigration enforcement is not considered criminal, immigrants detained on suspicion of being in the country illegally are not granted the same procedural protections as criminal defendants. Thus, many languish in prison for months, sometimes years.[6] INS prisoners endure physical and verbal abuse, including racial slurs and an unknown period of confinement. Often they are taken into detention without any opportunity to communicate with family or friends, and, once there, they have great difficulty gaining legal representation. Anti-immigrant legislation passed in 1996 further cut away at basic due process protections for immigrants and expanded the budget and detention facilities of the INS. Such efforts have made immigrants one of the fastest-growing incarcerated populations in the United States.

SANCTIONED INS
ATTACKS ON IMMIGRANT WORKERS

The United States Supreme Court has upheld the workplace enforcement activities of the INS in a number of cases. The Court has determined that even in cases in which the INS stationed armed and uniformed agents at all exits to a factory while other agents interrogated workers, workers still could have refused to answer their questions and were free to leave, despite the display of physical force by the INS. Therefore, the INS had not made a detention triggering Fourth Amendment standards.[7] Thus, immigrant workers are placed outside constitutional protections. Despite the trappings of criminal arrest and detention that accompany INS treatment of workers, the workers are denied many of the rights afforded criminal defendants. Because immigration-related arrests are considered administrative rather than criminal, workers do not receive Miranda warnings.

In March 1998 the INS launched "Operation Buttonhole," a series of raids in Los Angeles' garment district. Hundreds of garment workers were deported. In a typical raid, INS agents in dark jackets marked "Federal Police" would enter a factory and seal off the exits. One agent would then shout, "Turn off your machines and take out your IDs." Workers were then interrogated by uniformed and plainclothes agents. Those who could not provide proof of legal residency were rounded up, hands cuffed behind their back, into buses destined for the INS station in downtown Los Angeles. In 1997 the INS raided over 200 hotels in the San Diego area in California, arresting forty-two workers in "Operation Clean Sheets."[8] Several hundred other workers left their jobs to avoid discovery. At least one commentator has stated that the reason more workers were not arrested in that operation is that employers were warned prior to the raids and probably gave workers the "opportunity" to quit their jobs to avoid INS detection.[9] Also in 1997, the INS conducted "Operation Rescue" in Phoenix, Arizona, targeting over 400 businesses in the hotel, construction, agricultural, and apparel industries. Over 600 workers were arrested and forced to leave the county as a result of this operation.[10] This is just a small sampling of the numerous examples of the Immigration and Naturalization Service's misguided use of its plenary power to abuse and intimidate workers.

THE INS-EMPLOYER PARTNERSHIP

Many of INS's worksite investigation procedures rely on employer consent. The INS even calls employers before raids to inform them of a planned action and to gain access to the workers, without which they would have to obtain a search warrant. Because the validity of open-ended or "John Doe" search warrants have been questioned by the courts,[11] the INS invariably has chosen the latter of the two legal options by which to gain access to immigrant workers: (1) obtain a specific search warrant, or (2) get employer consent to enter. Gaining employer consent is the method of choice because it is easily obtained and because in the broad workplace sweeps that make up the INS worksite enforcement activity, it is not able to specify individuals whom it reasonably suspects of working without authorization. The only way to get blanket license to interrogate all the workers in one location is to partner with the employer, thus circumventing the warrant requirement. Thus, ironically, employers are turned into the gatekeepers for workers.

Indeed, employers frequently are given a more active role than just opening their doors to the INS. Employers have actually gathered workers together under the guise of a "meeting" so they can be apprehended more easily.[12] Moreover, in May 1998 the INS began requiring that employers be given warnings before raids.[13] Such advance warning gives employers ultimate control over INS access to workers. With the ability to police workers' contact with the INS, employers have a powerful and credible tool with which to exploit their workforce. In fact, garment workers in Los Angeles report that employers regularly alert workers of an upcoming raid once they have received word from the INS. Workers are told to stay home on the day of the raid. Perversely, the employer has simultaneously cooperated with the INS by granting access to its workforce and "saved" the worker from detention and deportation. Who benefits? The employer, whose exploited workers lose a day of work, then return after the INS has left and are even less likely than before to complain about workplace abuse.

HOW EMPLOYER INTERESTS ARE SAFE FROM INS INTERFERENCE

Not only do employers take advantage of the threat the INS poses to workers, but they are also safeguarded from INS sanctions. While failure to have the proper paperwork for its workers may result in small fines,[14] more serious employer sanctions can be levied only if the employer "knowingly" hired an undocumented worker. This standard, however, is very difficult to prove since employers typically claim ignorance, saying they do not have the expertise to differentiate between genuine documents and fraudulent ones.[15] Employers who are fined often negotiate lower settlements. In at least one instance, the INS reduced an employer fine by 40 percent after being pressured by the employer's congressional representative.[16] After the Clinton administration announced its commitment to set up worksite enforcement, there was a 50 percent increase in worksite arrests—that is, incarceration of immigrant workers—but a decrease in employer fines. Fines against employers dropped from $13.2 million for the first half of fiscal year 1996 to $3.8 million for the corresponding period the following year. The INS states projections for the number of people it will deport each fiscal year. Its use of "number of arrests and deportations" to measure the success of its interior enforcement activities belies any attempts by the INS to claim it seeks to punish employers at the same time. While ostensibly meant to deter employers from hiring undocumented individuals, the INS's penalties fall almost solely on workers.

While industries where INS worksite enforcement is concentrated are controlled by corporate interests that subcontract for low-wage immigrant labor, those corporations are completely outside the scope of INS sanctions for using undocumented workers. The INS allows employers (and their corporate contractors) to say "We didn't know" and thereby escape any penalties for employing undocumented workers; the workers themselves are the only ones who are punishable.

THE WORKSITE AS DETENTION CENTER

INS enforcement has a devastating effect on workers' willingness to speak out about abuse and to organize. Out of fear of the INS, workers will not report or bring legal action for subminimum wage payments, long hours without overtime pay, harassment, or the host of other abuses that attend sweatshop work. Any worker who raises her voice in the workplace or tries to organize her fellow workers puts them all in jeopardy of an employer-initiated INS raid. The U.S. government has a responsibility—indeed, a duty—to enforce wage, hour, and safety laws for all workers. By using detention and deportation to undermine labor organizing, the U.S. government not only ignores workers rights abuses, it in fact promotes them.

Immigrant workers in fields, garment factories, restaurants, and hotels, performing everything from agricultural work to apparel production and janitorial service, provide much of the base on which the U.S. economy thrives. Unfortunately, they share in little of the profits or commodities they make possible. Often isolated by language barriers from other workers and from the legal system, fearful of losing their jobs if they speak up, and brutalized by poverty despite long hours of work, full time, year-round, immigrant workers live at the margins of existence. Even where barbed wire and armed guards do not characterize workplaces as they did in the El Monte slave sweatshop, workers labor in *economic* servitude. Still, throughout history, they have continually shown the courage to fight back and to assert their rights. Immigrant workers have mobilized to change their working conditions and to improve their lives.

Increasingly, though, immigrant workers are being silenced by the cooperation between the INS and their exploitative employers. The INS shifts the balance of power, already enormously skewed in favor of the employer, completely away from the worker. INS workplace enforcement turns the worksite into a detention center. This is true not only figuratively—in that workers essentially become afraid of doing anything to disobey their employers—but also literally, through INS raids that post armed guards at each exit and interrogators inside. Workers labor in fear, unable to fight back without risking that they will not only be fired but will lose their ability to work and support themselves altogether.

THE "INS-IZATION" OF GOVERNMENT AGENCIES

Partnerships between government agencies charged with enforcing a variety of laws and the INS are increasingly common. While cities with large immigrant populations have used "no-tell" rules[17] that bar police from inquiring into immigration status or turning over suspects accused of minor violations to the INS, the 1996 legislative war on immigrants expressly voided federal, state, and local rules that kept government agencies from cooperating with the INS. Police in Salt Lake City, Utah, launched an experimental pilot program to deputize local police officers with the authority to enforce immigration laws. While some local law enforcement agencies have refused to cooperate with the INS,[18] others have enthusiastically consulted with INS on how they could do more to enforce immigration laws.[19] INS also uses local law enforcement to assist with workplace raids, typically using them to secure the perimeter of the worksite.

Regardless of whether it works alone or in concert with other police agencies, the INS treats immigrant workers as dangerous and thereby justifies its gross mistreatment of the workers. Garment workers have been handcuffed during workplace arrests and chained to the floor during INS interrogations.[20] According to an INS spokesperson, "handcuffing all suspected illegal immigrants is a standard procedure designed to safeguard the agents and the people in their custody."[21] A similar practice of "detaining first and asking questions later"[22] would seem to be based on an assumption that the workers pose a threat of violence. In at least one reported incident, INS agents inked numbers onto the arrested workers' arms.[23]

The INS also has forged cooperating relationships with other government agencies in order to crack down on immigrant workers. The United States Department of Labor (DOL), ostensibly charged with enforcing federal labor laws, has entered into an agreement with the INS that turns DOL workers into INS agents. This agreement, a Memorandum of Understanding between the two agencies signed in June 1992,[24] gives employers yet another protector. While workers might have looked to the DOL for some relief from their oppressive work conditions, now a sweatshop worker's report of wage and hour violations to the DOL can lead to INS enforcement action—including detention and deportation of workers—without workers having the opportunity to collect the wages owed them. Thus the DOL has been added to the arsenal of weapons sweatshop employers wield against immigrant workers.

These partnerships reveal that the criminalization of immigrant workers occurs not in isolated instances or through the abusive practices of a few rogue government agents. Rather, it is a systematic and concerted policy of the United States. Through these practices, the United States government is at best complicit in, if not actively working in furtherance of, the payment of workers at poverty wages and the rampant disregard of workers' human and civil rights. The ultimate beneficiaries are the corporate interests whose profits are gained off the backs of immigrant workers.

CONCLUSION

For low-wage immigrant workers, too often the protection of labor laws proves illusory. Enforcement of these worker protection laws has been subordinated to enforcement of immigration laws, and government agencies charged with protecting workers from labor law abuses have ceded the ground to the INS.

Immigration law has provided some relief to immigrants whose fear of deportation keeps them in abusive relationships. In such situations, batterers often use the threat of deportation as a way to keep their victims—primarily immigrant women—from escaping or reporting the abuse. The Violence Against Women Act of 1994 gave battered spouses a tool by which they could contemplate leaving their batterers without simultaneously choosing deportation; in other words, so immigration laws would not be a weapon of the perpetrators of domestic violence. While far from a guarantee against INS enforcement, the law at least lessened the vulnerability of battered immigrant women.

This recognition that fear of the INS is a powerful tool of those who want to abuse immigrants has yet to take hold in the parallel world of workers' rights. The INS claims to use factory raids[25] to round up as many undocumented workers as possible with minimal expenditure of resources. This justification for the undeniable harm to workplace rights is simply unconscionable.

By protecting capital, the criminalization of immigrant workers— primarily Asian and Latino immigrants—also preserves racial privilege. The INS has relied on a statistical correlation between racial appearance and undocumented status to justify targeting Latinos and Asians in certain areas of the United States. Undocumented European immigrants are not similarly criminalized. INS enforcement of immigration laws thus is used to engender racial hostility. In many low-wage industries, immigrant workers are considered to be people who have taken jobs away from more "deserving" "American" workers. INS activity also tends to inflame preexisting tension between people of color. In one operation, known as Operation South PAW (Protecting American Workers), the INS targeted over 4,000 undocumented workers from Mexico and Central America in the states of Georgia, Alabama, Tennessee, Arkansas, Florida, and Mississippi.[26] This not-so-subtle attempt to divide Latino immigrants from a large low-wage African American workforce creates and maintains the racial divisions among the poor and working class that prevents the establishment of a broader organized solidarity movement against exploitation. By pitching its workplace enforcement as a way to free up jobs and wages for Americans, the INS pits one low-wage group against another.

At the same time that global economic forces make capital ever-more mobile, anti-immigrant fervor in the United States has made the movement of labor even more restricted. The INS war against immigrant workers creates a wholly exploited and exploitable workforce that serves the interests of corporate profit. While people have been defined as undocumented and therefore "illegal," capital has escaped such characterization. In fact, garment manufacturers and retailers routinely use the threat of taking their work elsewhere to attack workers and workers' advocates demanding better wages and working conditions. In essence, what they are saying is "If I am not allowed to exploit poor people within U.S. borders, I will exploit them elsewhere."

The immigrant worker has been so vilified that the exploitation is often perceived as the natural outgrowth of poverty and border-crossing. The abuse and suffering become invisible, or, when revealed, they seem acceptable. It takes an outrage like the El Monte slave sweatshop to arouse public sentiment, and, even then, real systemic changes are met with harsh resistance. Why?

The attack on immigrants, particularly low-wage immigrant workers, is not just a question of immigration policy. It is also a function of our government's protection of corporate practices and capital. INS workplace raids serve a policing function with respect to capital, allowing profits to be made with impunity and labor costs to remain at inhumanely low levels. Immigrant workers are treated as mere machines to enable corporate profit rather than as human beings with basic rights and protections. They are targeted for the "crime" of poverty and suffer incarceration for the "crime" of working.

NOTES

Special thanks to Christina Ho for her wonderful research assistance.

1. See Karl Schoenberger and Shawn Hubler, "Asian Leaders Call for Release of Thai Workers," *Los Angeles Times,* August 10, 1995, A1; Kenneth B. Noble, "Workers in Sweatshop Raid Start Leaving Detention Site," *New York Times,* August 12, 1995, 6.

2. The exploitation of the Thai workers, while extreme, represents the outer continuum of abuse of workers in the garment industry, where long hours, low pay, wage and hour violations, harmful health and safety conditions, harassment, threats to workers, and degrading treatment are standard. Because of the involuntary servitude experienced by the Thai workers, a criminal action was brought against the family that held them in El Monte. The Thai workers were required to remain in the United States as material witnesses in that criminal prosecution and thus escaped summary deportation. Summary deportation leaves employers who profit from labor law abuses completely off the hook. The Thai workers, along with Latino workers who labored for the same manufacturers and retailers, joined in their own federal civil action against those corporations whose clothes they sewed and were able to collect some of the millions of dollars in back wages owed them. More important, their case has become a powerful tool for other workers, opening the door to manufacturer and retailer liability in the garment industry. See *Bureerong v. Uvawas,* 922 F.Supp. 1450 (C.D. Cal. 1996) and 959 F. Supp. 1231 (C.D. Cal. 1997).

3. Patrick McDonnell, "Immigrant Rights Groups Gather to Protest Abuses," *Los Angeles Times,* June 7, 1998, B3.

4. For example, in January 1997 a workplace with over 100 workers was raided by the INS on the eve of a union vote. See Aurelio Rojas, "Workers Say Firm Aided Big INS Bust," *San Francisco Chronicle,* January 18, 1997, A14. See also Bruce Nichols, "Elusive Target: Houston's Thriving Underground Presents Headache for Regulators," *Dallas Morning News,* November 9, 1997, 1H.

5. 8 U.S.C. 1357(a)(2) (1988).

6. See "Resort to International Human Rights Law in Challenging Conditions in U.S. Immigration Detention Centers," 23 *Brooklyn Journal of International Law* 271 (1997), which documents squalid conditions in detention centers.

7. *INS v. Delgado,* 466 U.S. 210 (1984). Justice Brennan wrote a scathing dissent, criticizing the majority's "studied air of unreality" in issuing its opinion. The Fourth Amendment provides for the right of the people to be free from unreasonable searches and seizures. See the U.S. Constitution, Amendment. IV.

8. "INS cracks down on hotel workers," *San Diego Union-Tribune,* October 1, 1997, B-2.

9. Michael Huspek, "The State; The Gaping Loophole in the Middle of INS Law Enforcement," *Los Angeles Times* (Editorial), October 19, 1997, M6.

10. "INS Raids Send Illegals Out of U. S., Open Jobs," *Arizona Republic,* July 2, 1997, E1.

11. See e.g., Marc Graser, *Aguilar International Molders Allied Workers,* 674 F. Supp. 294 (N.D. Cal. 1987) (holding that a warrant used by INS during a raid was unconstitutional).

12. In January 1997 a raid of a videotape duplication company in the Bay Area was conducted successfully after the employer called the workers to a meeting that was then crashed by almost seventy INS agents. See Rojas, "Workers Say Firm Aided Big INS Bust, Claims Video Company Tried to Stop Union," *San Francisco Chronicle,* January 18, 1997, A14; and Jason Gertzen and Rick Ruggles, "Agency Plans 1-Way Flight for Detainees," *Omaha World Herald,* January 23, 1997, 11SF, which details how workers were requested to report to the lunchroom, where INS agents were waiting to round them up.

13. The justification for such warning was an INS belief that employers had not "knowingly" hired undocumented workers. This procedural requirement was instituted along with requirements that raids be preapproved by INS headquarters or regional offices and that teams must include a community liaison officer when they raid public places such as restaurants. These changes were responses to a brutal Miami raid during which a pregnant woman was shoved to the ground and fainted; one woman was grabbed by the hair, thrown on the ground, and kicked; and over half the workers arrested were found to be documented. See William Branigin, "Criticism Prompts INS to Make New Rules for Work Site Raids," *Washington Post,* May 30, 1998, A2.

14. The INS policy of giving employers three days notice before coming to inspect documents all but eliminates the threat of such fines, giving employers time to assemble any necessary paperwork. Workers have reported that employers will tell them to go acquire documents by the next business day or be fired—of course, without payment for the work they have done thus far.

15. Stanley Ziemba, "25 Workers Arrested in Raid; Undocumented Mexican Laborers Found in Plainfield," *Chicago Tribune* (Metro Southwest), October 22, 1997, 7.

16. Michael Doyle, "Efforts By INS To Levy Fines Falling Short," *Sacramento Bee,* October 5, 1996, A4.

17. Los Angeles adopted the first in 1979, known as Special Order 40. Cities such as Los Angeles and New York feared that INS-police partnerships would prevent immigrants from seeking police protection, reporting crimes, sending their children to school, or requesting health care. See Patrick McDonnell, "Worker Fired for Turning in Illegal Immigrant Reinstated," *Los Angeles Times,* August 15, 1998, A9.

18. Mary Mitchell, "Detention Center Last Stop for Many," *Chicago Sun-Times,* January 19, 1997, 12. From 1989 to 1997, the Chicago police did not turn over to the INS a single person they suspected of being undocumented. "Reaping Abuse for What They Sow; Sweatshops Once Again Commonplace in U. S. Garment Industry," *Washington Post,* February 16, 1997, A1 (discussing Mayor Giuliani's directive to the New York Police).

19. See Betty Beard, "Pilgrimage to Protest Chandler Roundup; Hispanics Organize 22-Mile March," *Arizona Republic,* August 30, 1997, p. EV1 (summary).

20. Mae M. Cheng, "At Work, At Risk/Undocumented Latinos, Especially, Fear INS visit," *Newsday,* June 8,1997, A3.

21. Lisa Leff, "INS Agents Worksite Raids are Dramatic—But Rare," *Washington Post,* June 12, 1994.

22. Ibid.

23. Louis Sahagun, "INS Sweep Puts Wyoming Resort Community on Edge," *Los Angeles Times,* September 13, 1996.

24. Memorandum of Understanding Between INS and Labor Department on Shared Enforcement Responsibilities (June 11, 1992). It provides that the Department of Labor "will be responsible for the prompt referral to INS of all suspected substantive hiring violations, i.e., violations of the provisions against knowingly hiring or continuing to employ unauthorized workers."

25. The INS refuses to use the term "raids," perhaps because of the violent and invasive connotations. The INS instead refers to them as "surveys."

26. Julie Malone, "Clinton orders penalties for companies that hire illegal workers," *Atlanta Journal,* February 14, 1996, 8A.

TWENTY-ONE

The New Surveillance

GARY T. MARX

Popular culture is sometimes far ahead of academic analysis in identifying important social currents. This is true of the hit song "Every Breath You Take," sung by a celebrated rock group known as The Police. This song can be heard to suggest various contemporary surveillance devices. Thus "every breath" you take refers to the breath analyzer; "every move" made to the motion detector; "every bond" broken to the polygraph; "every step" taken to the electronic anklet; "every single day" implies continuous monitoring; "every word" spoken refers to bugs, wiretaps, and mikes; "every night you stay" implies infrared devices; "every vow" broken, voice stress analysis; "every smile" faked, brain wave analysis; "every claim" made suggests computer matching. In totality for the singer these mean *"I'll be watching you."*

From this song we can draw hints of what can be called "the new surveillance." The surveillance component of social control is changing radically. The rationalization of crime control, which began in the nineteenth century, has crossed a critical threshold as a result of broad changes in technology and social organization. Surveillance has become penetrating and intrusive in ways that previously were imagined only in fiction.

The information-gathering powers of the state and private organizations are extending ever deeper into the social fabric. The ethos of social control has expanded from focused and direct coercion used after the fact and against a particular target to anticipatory actions entailing deception, manipulation, planning, and a diffuse panoptic vision.

I shall attempt here to describe some of the major types of this new surveillance, indicate how contemporary forms differ from traditional ones, and consider some undesirable consequences of these changes.

The gigantic data banks made possible by computers raise important surveillance questions. Many basic facts about the computerization of credit, banking, medical, educational, employment, tax, welfare, telephone, and criminal justice records are well known. But beyond the increased amount of information they make available, computers have altered the very nature of surveillance. Record surveillance is routinized, broadened, and deepened, and, for practical purposes, records become eternal. Bits of scattered information that in the past did not threaten the individual's privacy and anonymity are now joined. Organizational memories are extended over time and across space. Observations have a more textured, dimensional quality. Rather than focusing on the discrete individual at one point in time and on static demographic data such as date of birth, surveillance increasingly involves more complex transactional analysis, interrelating persons and events (e.g., the timing of phone calls, travel, bank deposits).[1]

A thriving new computer-based, data-scavenging industry now sells information gleaned from such sources as drivers' licenses; vehicle and voter registration lists; birth, marriage, and death certificates; land deeds, telephone and organizational directories; and census tract records.

Many issues—such as privacy, civil liberties, uses of and control over information, unauthorized access, errors, and the rights of the person about whom information is gathered—are raised by the computer-matching and profiling operations that have come into increased prominence in the recent decades.[2]

Matching involves the comparison of information from two or more distinct data sources. In the United States, more than 500 computer-matching programs are routinely carried out by government at state and federal levels, and the matching done by private interests is far more extensive. Profiling involves an indirect and inductive logic. Often clues are sought that will increase the probability of discovering violations. A number of distinct data items are correlated in order to assess how close an event or person comes to a predetermined model of known violations or violators. Consider the following examples:

- A Massachusetts nursing-home resident lost her eligibility for government medical assistance because of a match of bank and welfare records. The computer match discovered that she had more than the minimum amount welfare recipients are permitted in a savings account. What the computer did not know was that the money was held in trust for a local funeral director, to be used for her burial expenses. Regulations exempt burial contracts from asset calculations.

- The Educational Testing Service uses profiling to help discover cheating. In one year it sent out about 2,000 form letters alleging "copying" to takers of its Scholastic Aptitude Test based partly on computer analysis. A statistical review had "found close agreement of your answers with those on another answer sheet from the same test center. Such agreement is unusual and suggests that copying occurred." Students were told that in two weeks their scores would be canceled and colleges notified, unless they provided "additional information" to prove they had not cheated.

- In New York City, because of computer matching, persons cannot purchase a marriage license or register a deed for a new home if they have outstanding parking tickets.

Some of fiction's imaginary surveillance technology, like the two-way television that George Orwell described, is now reality. According to some observers, video-telephone communication is likely to become more widespread in private homes. One-way video surveillance has expanded rapidly, as anyone who ventures into a shopping mall or uses an electronic bank teller should realize. The interior of many stores is monitored by closed-circuit TV. Often the camera is inside a ceiling globe with complete 360-degree movement and the ability to tape-record. Amber or mirrored surfaces hide where the cameras are aimed.

Among the new techniques that permit intrusions that only recently were in the realm of science fiction, or not even envisioned there, are new or improved lasers; parabolic mikes and other bugs with still more powerful transmitters; subminiature tape recorders; remote camera and videotape systems; means of seeing in the dark, detecting heat or motion; odor, pressure, and contraband sensors; tracking devices; and voice stress analyzers.

Recent decades have seen the increased use of supposedly scientific "inference" or "personal truth technology" based on body clues (i.e., the polygraph, voice stress analysis, the stomach pump, the "passive alcohol detector," and blood, urine, or hair analysis for drugs). These highly diverse forms of detection have at least one thing in common—they seek to verify an implicit or explicit claim put forth by an individual regarding identity, attitudes, and behavior.

"Mini-AWACS" and satellites that can spot a car or a person from afar have been used for surveillance of drug traffickers. The Central Intelligence Agency (CIA) apparently has used satellite photographs for "domestic coverage" to determine the size and activities of antiwar demonstrations and civil disorders. The "starlight scope" light amplifier, developed for the Vietnam War, can be used with a variety of cameras and binoculars. When it amplifies light 85,000 times, it turns night settings into daylight. Unlike the infrared devices developed earlier, it does not give off a telltale glow.

The highly secretive National Security Agency—using 2,000 staffed interception posts throughout the world, plus satellites, aircraft, and ships—monitors all electronic communication from and to the United States. Its computer system permits simultaneous monitoring of about 54,000 telephone calls and cables. The agency is beyond the usual judicial and legislative controls and can disseminate its information to other government agencies without a warrant.[3]

Another surveillance use of the telephone involves the expansion of hot lines for anonymous reporting. One of the largest programs is TIP (Turn-in-a-Pusher). The video equivalent of the old reward posters, a program found in hundreds of communities, is called Crime

Stoppers USA, Inc. It uses televised reenactments ("The Crime of the Week") to encourage witnesses to unsolved crimes to come forward. There are also radio and newspaper versions. Many companies maintain an internal hot line for anonymous reporting. WeTiP, Inc., a nonprofit organization, offers a general, nationwide twenty-four-hour toll-free hot line for reporting suspicious activities. All nineteen federal inspectors-general and some state and local agencies have hot lines for receiving allegations.

The real action, in the future, will be with nonhuman informers: a 400-pound, bulletproof mobile robot "guard" has been developed. It is equipped with a sonar range finder, sonic and infrared sensors, and an odor detector for locating humans. The robot can find its way through a strange building. Should it encounter an intruder, it can say in a stern, synthesized voice, "You have been detected." Another "mobile robotic sentry," resembling a miniature tank, patrols an area and identifies intruders. Users can choose the robot's weaponry and whether human permission (from a remote monitoring station) is needed before it opens fire. But not to worry. The manufacturer assures us that, in the United States, the device will not be "armed with lethal weapons"; or if it is, "there will always be a human requirement in the loop."

Telemetric devices attached to a subject use radio waves to transmit information on the location and/or physiological condition of the wearer and permit continuous remote measurement and control. Such devices, along with new organizational forms based on theories of diversion and deinstitutionalization (i.e., halfway houses and community treatment centers) diffuse the surveillance of the prison into the community.

After over a decade of discussion, telemetric devices are now being used in the criminal justice system. Offenders in many jurisdictions are serving court-supervised sentences that stipulate wearing a monitoring anklet containing an electronic transmitter. The radio signal it emits is picked up by a receiver connected to the telephone in the wearer's home. This receiver relays the signal to a central computer. If the wearer goes beyond 150 feet from this telephone or tries to remove or unplug the device, the computer displays the interruption of the signal. A court officer receives a daily copy of the printout, and offenders must explain any errant behavior.

In other proposed systems subjects are not restricted to their residence; however, their whereabouts are known continuously. The radio signal is fed into a modified missile-tracking device that graphs the wearer's location and can display it on a screen. In some police departments, an automatic car-locator system has been tried to help supervisors know exactly where patrol cars are at all times. There also are various hidden beepers that can be attached to vehicles and other objects to trace their movements.

The Hong Kong government tested an electronic system for monitoring where, when, and how fast a car is driven. A small radio receiver in the car picks up low-frequency signals from wire loops set into streets and then transmits back the car's identification number. The system was presented as an efficient means for applying a road tax to the many cars in Hong Kong's concentrated traffic areas. It can, of course, also be used to enforce speed limits and for surveillance. In the United States, a parking meter recently has been patented that registers inserted coins and then radios police when the time has run out.

Surveillance of workers, whether on assembly lines or in offices or stores, has become much more severe with computerized electronic measures. Factory outputs and mistakes can be counted more easily, and work pace can be controlled, to a degree. Employee theft of expensive components or tools may be deterred by embedded sensors that emit a signal when taken through a barrier. Much has been written about the electronic office, where the data processing machine serves both as a work tool and monitoring device. Productivity and employee behavior thus are carefully watched, and even executives are not exempt. In some major American corporations communication flows (memo circulation, use of internal phone systems) now are closely tracked.

In some offices, workers have to inform the computer when they are going to the bathroom and when they return. Employees may be required to carry an ID card with a magnetic stripe and check in and out as they go to various "stations."

Integrated "management systems" offer visual, audio, and digital information about the behavior of employees and customers. Information may be recorded from cash register entries, voices, motion, or when standing on a mat with a sensor. Audiovisual recording and alarms may be programmed to respond to a large number of "triggering devices."

Means of personal identification have gone far beyond the rather easily faked signature or photo ID. Thus one new employee security-checking procedure involves retinal eye patterns. Before gaining access, or a benefit, a person's eyes are photographed through a set of binoculars, and an enlarged print of the retina pattern is compared to a previous print on file. Retinal patterns are said to be more individual than thumbprints, offering greater certainty of identification.

Finally, undercover practices—those old, traditional means of surveillance and investigation—have changed drastically in form and expanded in scale during the recent decades. The new devices and techniques have enabled police and federal agencies to penetrate criminal, and sometimes noncriminal, milieus in utterly new ways.[4]

In the United States, the federal agency that is most affected by these new methods is the Federal Bureau of Investigation (FBI). In the past, the FBI viewed undercover operations as too risky and costly (for both individuals and the agency's reputation) for use in routine investigations of conventional criminal activity. Now, however, in the words of an agent, "Undercover operations have become the cutting edge of the FBI's efforts to ferret out concealed criminal activity." In the mid-1970s the FBI began using undercover agents in criminal investigations. The number of such investigations has increased steadily, from 53 in 1977, to about 300 each year.

Beyond well-known cases, such as Abscam, the fake consulting firm run jointly by IBM and the FBI that sold "stolen" data to Japanese companies; and the John DeLorean case, police posing as derelicts with exposed wallets or as fences purchasing stolen property, recent cases have involved policewomen posing as prostitutes and then arresting the men who propositioned them; tax agents stationed in banks and businesses posing as prospective buyers or clients to gain information; phony cases entered into the criminal justice system to test if prosecutors and judges would accept bribes, "bait sales" in which undercover agents offer to sell, at a very low price, allegedly stolen goods to merchants or persons they meet in bars; and agents acting as guides for big game hunters and then arresting them for killing protected species or animals out of season.

These examples—and we could add many more—surely make clear that it is a new ball game and that its players are sometimes beyond meaningful restraint.

Although the causes, nature, and consequences of the various new surveillance methods I have described differ from each other, they do share, to varying degrees, nine characteristics that distinguish them from traditional ones.

THE NEW SURVEILLANCE

1. *It transcends distance, darkness, and physical barriers.* As many observers have noted, the historic barriers to the old, Leviathan state lay in the sheer physical impossibility of extending the rulers' ideas and surveillance to the outer regions of vast empires; through closed doors; and into the inner intellectual, emotional, and physical regions of the individual. Technology, however, has gradually made these intrusions easier. Technical impossibility and, to some extent, inefficiency have lost their roles as unplanned protectors of liberty. Sound and video can be transmitted over vast distances; infrared and light-amplifying technologies pierce the dark; intrusive technologies can "see" through doors, suitcases, even fog. Truth-seeking technologies claim to be capable of going beneath surface reality to deeper subterranean truths.

2. *It transcends time;* its records can easily be stored, retrieved, combined, analyzed, and communicated. Surveillance information can be "socially freeze-dried."[5] When stored, it is available for instant analysis many years after the fact and in totally different interpretive contexts. Computer records, video and audio tapes and discs, photos, and various "signatures"—like workers or parts used in mass production—have become increasingly standardized and interchangeable. Information can be converted into a form that makes it portable, easily reproducible, and transferable across vast distances. Thus data sharing, on an immense scale, becomes possible.

3. *It is capital rather than labor intensive.* It has become much less expensive per unit watched, because technical developments

have altered the economics of surveillance dramatically. Information can be sent back to a central source easily. A few persons can monitor a great many things (in contrast to traditional forms, such as the gumshoe tailing a suspect at a discreet distance for many days or manually searching records). The monitor need not literally be attending at the instant of transmission to be able to use it. Economy is further enhanced because persons have become voluntary and involuntary consumers of much of this surveillance—and are participating in their own monitoring. Many of the points that follow relate to these economic changes that facilitate expanded surveillance.

4. *It triggers a shift from targeting a specific suspect to categorical suspicion.* In the technical implementation of Franz Kafka's nightmare, modern society suspects everyone. The camera, the tape recorder, the identity card, the metal detector, the obligatory tax form that must be filled out even if one has no income, and, of course, the computer make all who come within their province reasonable targets for surveillance. The new, softer forms of control are helping to create a society in which people are permanently under suspicion and surveillance. Everyone is assumed to be guilty until proven innocent. As French theorist Michel Foucault observed in *Discipline and Punish*, what is central here is not physical coercion but never-ending "judgements, examinations, and observation."

5. *One of its major concerns is the prevention of violations.* Thus control is extended to ever more features of society and its surroundings. Rather than simply reacting to what is served up around us, anticipatory strategies seek to reduce risk and uncertainty. Publicity about omnipresent and omnipowerful surveillance is used to deter violations. And "target hardening" (e.g., better locks) is used to make committing violations more difficult. Where violations cannot be prevented, the environment may be so structured that violators are either caught in the act or leave strong evidence of their identity and guilt.

6. *It is decentralized and triggers self-policing.* In contrast to the trend of the last century, information can now, in principle,

flow as freely from the center to society's periphery as the reverse. Surveillance is decentralized in the sense that national data resources are available to widely dispersed local officials. (The power of national elites, in turn, also may increase as they obtain instant information of those in the farthest reaches of the network.) Those watched become (willingly and knowingly or not) active participants in their own monitoring, which is often self-activated and automatic. One aspect of this process is that persons are motivated to report themselves to government agencies and large organizations and corporations in return for some benefit or to avoid a penalty; another is the direct triggering of surveillance systems by its subjects when, for instance, a person walks, talks on the telephone, turns on a TV set, checks a book out from the library, or enters or leaves a controlled area.

7. *It either has low visibility or is invisible.* Thus it becomes ever more difficult to ascertain when and whether we are being watched and who is doing the watching. There is a distancing (both socially and geographically) between watchers and watched, and surveillance is increasingly depersonalized. Its instruments are often difficult to discover, either because they are something other than they appear to be or, as with snooping into microwave transmissions, there often are few indications of surveillance. (Contrast this with traditional wire-tapping, which changes electrical currents, or hidden voice analysis with the traditional polygraph, which requires the subject's co-operation.)

8. *It is ever more intensive—probing beneath surfaces, discovering previously inaccessible information.* Like drilling technology boring ever deeper into the earth, today's surveillance can prod ever deeper into physical, social, and personal areas. It hears whispers and penetrates clouds, walls, and windows. It "sees" into the body—and attempts to "see" into the soul, claiming to go beneath ostensible meanings and appearances to real meanings.

9. *It grows ever more extensive—covering not only deeper but larger areas.* Previously unconnected surveillance threads now are

woven into gigantic tapestries of information. Or, in British criminologist Stan Cohen's imagery, the mesh of the fishing net has not only become finer and more pliable, the net itself now is wider.[6] Broad new categories of persons and behavior have become subjects for information collection and analysis, and as the pool of persons watched expands, so does the pool of watchers. Not only might anyone be watched; everyone is also a potential watcher. And the creation of uncertainty about whether surveillance is present is an important strategic element. Mass surveillance has become a reality. The increased number of watchers (whether human or electronic) and self-monitoring devices have recreated, in today's metropolis, some of the dense controls characteristic of the small, closely watched village.

The awesome power to the new surveillance lies in the paradoxical, never before possible combination of decentralized and centralized forms. We are also witnessing an expansion and joining of intensive forms of monitoring traditionally used only in the investigation and surveillance of criminal and espionage suspects, or prisoners, with the shallower forms of categorical monitoring directed at broad populations.

SOME NEGATIVE ASPECTS

The new surveillance has been generally welcomed by those in business, government, and law enforcement. It does have many attractive features. Stirring examples of its effectiveness are readily available. For example, the life of an elderly heart-attack victim who lived alone was saved when her failure to open the refrigerator sent an alarm through her telephone to a centralized monitor; a corrupt judge was caught when he took a bribe from a police agent pretending to be a criminal; serious crimes have been solved as a result of tips received on hot lines. Consider also the ease of obtaining consumer goods with a credit card; the saving of taxpayers' dollars because of computer-matching programs; citizens' increased feeling of safety when video surveillance is installed. Indeed, Americans seem increasingly willing, even eager, to live with intrusive technologies because of the benefits they expect to receive.

Problems concerning errors, data tampering, and misuse can be lessened by government legislation and policies, good program design, and sensitive and intelligent management. Furthermore, in a free market economy, some surveillance can be neutralized (by, e.g., the proliferation of antiradar, debugging, and encryption devices).

My point is not to advance some romantic neo-Luddite worldview or to deny the complexity of the moral judgments and trade-offs involved. Yet in our eagerness to innovate and our infatuation with technical progress and the gimmickry of surveillance, it is easy to miss the time bombs that may be embedded therein. The negative aspects of these new trends have not received sufficient attention.

There is nowhere to run or to hide. A citizen's ability to evade this surveillance is diminishing. There is no escape from the prying eyes and ears and whirring data processing machines of government and business. To participate in the consumer society and the welfare state, we must provide personal information. To venture into a shopping mall, bank, subway, sometimes even a bathroom is to perform before an unknown audience. To apply for a job may mean having to face questioning and psychological testing about intimate details of one's life. Requests for parts of one's personal biography (for birth, marriage, and death certificates, driver's licenses, vehicle and voter registration; information for phone, occupational, educational, and special-interest directories) are invitations to comply with more finely tuned manipulative efforts by a new breed of government and marketing researchers who combine the enormous quantities of available data with the advantages of computerization.

The new surveillance goes beyond merely invading privacy, as this term has been understood; it makes many of the constraints that made privacy possible irrelevant. Traditionally, privacy depended on certain technically or socially inviolate physical, spatial, or temporal barriers— varying from distance, to darkness, to doors, to the right to remain silent. To invade privacy required crossing an intact barrier. With much of the new technology, however, many of these simply cease to be barriers. As we discussed, information becomes accessible without the need to resort to traditional coercive forms of intrusion. There is no longer the need to enter a room surreptitiously to plant a bugging device when a microphone aimed at a window a hundred yards away can accomplish the same end; when microwave phone and computer transmissions can simply be plucked from the air without bothering with direct wire-tapping. Without being opened, mail can be read, purses and briefcases viewed through X rays or sniffed. Alcohol intake can be assessed without a suspect's consent, and voice stress analysis administered without the subject's awareness.

WHAT OF PRIVACY AND AUTONOMY?

In the face of these changes, we must rethink the nature of privacy and create new supports for it. Some of these, ironically, will rely in part on products of the system's technologies (i.e., coded or scrambled communications, antiradar and debugging devices).

The most desirable support of our individual privacy and autonomy surely is public awareness. At this point, less than one state in five has laws requiring binding standards for the collection, maintenance, and dissemination of personal information.

Yet more is at stake than privacy. With these new surveillance methods, some of the positive anonymity involving the right to be left alone and unnoticed, so characteristic of modern society, is diminished. The easy computer bank combining and mining of vast publicly available data to yield precise lists (whether of suspects or targets for sales pitches and solicitations) generate a sense of vulnerability that is very different from the feeling experienced on receipt of junk mail addressed to "occupant." Aside from the annoyance factor, the somewhat "personalized" yet standardized word-processed solicitations can leave one asking "How do they know this about me? How did they find this out? What else to they know? Who are they?" One need not be a Franz Kafka character to feel uneasy.

To mention, briefly, some other major negative aspects of the new surveillance:

It may violate the spirit of the Fourth Amendment, for it can trigger fishing expeditions and searches where there is no specific evidence of wrongdoing. Thus it might transform the presumption of innocence into one of guilt—shifting the burden of proof from the state to the target of surveillance, the accused. There also is a danger of presumption of guilt by association or statistical artifact. And, because of the technical nature of the surveillance and its distancing aspects, the accused may (at least initially) be unable to face the accuser. The legal basis of some of the new surveillance's crime-prevention actions is also questionable.

The system's focus on prevention can entail the risk of sparking violations that would not occur otherwise. And powerful new mechanisms may invite overloading the system. Far more violations may be uncovered and added to the data banks than can be acted upon. This overabundance of violations in turn may lead to the misuse of prosecutorial discretion, the demoralization of control agents, and, perhaps, favoritism and corruption. And, as our examples suggest, the new surveillance has the potential for fostering repression. The system is, invariably, less effective and certain, and more subject to manipulation and error than advocates admit. (Computer matching, for instance, can be no better than the data it is fed, which may be dated or wrong and are often blunt and acontextual. Chemical analysis, which can detect drugs in a person's body, cannot determine how they got there—if a person, for instance, smoked marijuana or simply was around others who did—or whether a drug was taken on or off the job.)

While deterring or discovering some offenders, the routinization of surveillance, ironically, may grant an almost guaranteed means for successful violations and theft to those who gain knowledge of the system and take action to neutralize and exploit it. This suggests that, over time, it seems likely that many of these systems will disproportionately net the marginal, amateur, occasional violator rather than the master criminal.

The proliferation of the new techniques may create a lowest-denominator morality, which may affect even those who will actively protect privacy and autonomy, who thus will use—indiscriminately—the very tactics of those who seek to invade privacy.[7]

The new surveillance increases the power of large organizations (whether governmental or private) over the individual. Individual freedom and liberty prosper when detailed information about a person's life, for the most part, is private. The permanence and accessibility of computerized records mean that we are all tailed by electronic talebearers. As there is the possibility of locking in erroneous or sabotaged data, this may have the unintended consequence of permanent, unjust stigmatization. Thus persons may never cease paying for earlier, or never committed, misdeeds. The issues here go far beyond criminal records and faulty computer banks. As records of education, work, health, housing, civil suits, and the like become ever more important in administering the society, persons may decline needed services (as for mental health), avoid conflictual or controversial action (filing a grievance against a boss or a landlord), and shun taking risks and experimenting for fear of what it will look like on the record. Conformity and uniformity may increase, squashing diversity, innovation, and vitality.

The fragmentation and isolation characteristic of totalitarian societies result not only from the state's banning or absorption of private organizations but because individuals mistrust each other and organizations: In such societies trust, the most sacred and important element of the social bond, is damaged.

To be sure, we are far from such a society, but the direction in which the new surveillance points is clear. Making the means of anonymous denunciation easily available can lead to false and malicious accusations, and efforts to create a "myth of surveillance" may backfire and create a degree of inhibition, fear, and anxiety unbecoming a democratic society. The potential for harm may be so great, should social conditions change, that we must hesitate before creating even apparently justified surveillance systems (i.e., linkages between all federal and state data banks, or a mandatory national identification system). From this perspective, framing the policy debate around how to reform such systems is misguided. The issue, instead, is: Should the system be there to begin with?[8] Once these new surveillance systems are institutionalized and taken for granted in a democratic society, they can be used for harmful ends. With a more repressive government and a more intolerant public— perhaps upset over severe economic downturns, large waves of immigration, social dislocations, or foreign policy setbacks-these devices could easily be used against those with the "wrong" political beliefs, against racial, ethnic, or religious minorities, and against those with lifestyles that offend the majority.

Yet should totalitarianism ever come to the United States, it would more likely be by accretion than by cataclysmic events. As Sinclair Lewis argues in *It Can't Happen Here,* it would come in traditional American guise, with the gradual erosion of liberties.[9]

Voluntary participation, beneficent rationales, changes in cultural definitions and language hide the onerous aspects of the new surveillance. But as Justice Louis D. Brandeis warned: "Experience should teach us to be most on our guard when the government's purposes are beneficent. Men born to freedom are naturally alert to repel invasion of their liberty by evil-minded rulers. The greatest dangers to liberty lurk in insidious encroachment by men of zeal, well-meaning, but without understanding."[10]

The first task of a society that would have liberty and privacy is to guard against the misuse of physical coercion by the state and private parties. The second task is to guard against the softer forms of secret and manipulative control. Because these are often subtle, indirect, invisible, diffuse and deceptive, and shrouded in benign justifications, this is clearly the more difficult task.

NOTES

The text of this chapter originally appeared in *Dissent* (March 1985). For additional information on police surveillance, refer to http://socsci.colorado.edu/~marxg/gary-home.html.

1. David Burnham, *The Rise of the Computer State* (New York: Random House, 1983), offers a useful discussion of this and other salient themes.
2. See, for example, G. Marx and N. Reichman, "Routinizing the Discovery of Secrets: Computers as Informants," *American Behavioral Scientist* (March 1984): 423-452.
3. J. Bramford, *The Puzzle Palace* (New York: Penguin Books, 1983); K. Krajick, "Electronic Surveillance Makes a Comeback," *Police Magazine* (March 1983).
4. For example, see Marx and Reichman, "Routinizing the Discovery of Secrets."
5. See, for example, G. Goodwin and L. Humphreys, "Freeze-Dried Stigma: Cybernetics and Social Control," *Humanity and Society* (November 1982).
6. S. Cohen, "The Punitive City: Notes on the Dispersion of Social Control," *Contemporary Crisis,* no. 3 (1979): 339-63.
7. A large array of control and countercontrol devices, through mail order catalogs and ads in major national periodicals, are now available for the mass market. One large company offers a "secret-connection briefcase," which among other things includes a "pocket-sized tape-recorder detector that lets you know if someone is secretly recording your conversation"; a "micro-miniature hidden bug-detection system, which lets you know if you're being bugged"; a "miniature voice stress analyzer, which lets you know when someone is lying"; a "built-in scrambler for total telephone privacy"; an "incredible 6-hour tape recorder—so small it fits in a cigarette pack." Ready for use—or misuse.
8. See, for example, the thoughtful discussion in J. Rule, D. McAdam, L. Stearns, and D. Uglow, *The Politics of Privacy* (New York: New American Library, 1980).
9. Sinclair Lewis, *It Can't Happen Here* (Garden City, New York: Double Day, 1935).
10. *Olmstead vs. US,* 277 US [Supreme Court] 438 (1927).

POLITICAL REPRESSION AND RESISTANCE

TWENTY-TWO

The Grand Jury: A Tool to Repress and Jail Activists

Margaret Ratner and Michael Ratner

[W]e have witnessed the birth of a new breed of political animal—the kangaroo grand jury—spawned in a dark corner of the Department of Justice, nourished by an administration bent on twisting law enforcement to serve its own political ends, a dangerous modern form of Star Chamber secret inquisition that is trampling the rights of American Citizens from coast to coast.

> —Senator Edward M. Kennedy testifying
> before a House Judiciary Subcommittee, March 1992.

Imagine a country where a prosecutor can subpoena you to a grand jury and ask you anything about your life and thoughts. There are no limits to the scope or breath of the inquiry, and the prosecutor can ask about your friends, for example, or your political affiliations, what you or your friends think of the president, Cuba, Malcom X, Mumia Abu-Jamal, the

Palestinian struggle, independence for Puerto Rico, East Timor, or any other subject. Even your sex life is not off limits.[1] Imagine also that this entire proceeding is secret; only the prosecutors, the grand jurors, a stenographer, and you are present. Not even your attorney is permitted to accompany you. Imagine that after you are subpoenaed, the prosecutor also can subpoena your children, your mother and father, and all of your friends and ask them all about you.

Now, you might think that you had a right not to answer any of these harassing and abusive questions. You might think that you had a Fifth Amendment right not to incriminate yourself; after all, the Constitution does provide you with such a right. But no. You must answer all of the questions. The prosecutor need only promise not to use what he learns against you. What is learned can be used against others, including your friends. And you still can be indicted for the crime about which you testified. To indict, the prosecutor must use independent evidence, incriminating evidence that supposedly comes from an alternative source.

After being granted immunity, if you refuse to answer the questions, if you refuse to name names, if you refuse to discuss your or another's political ideology, you go to jail. You go to jail until you talk. It makes no difference whether you have children or a job or are ill. You go to jail until you talk. You can go to jail for a very long time, sometimes for years.

You might think, "Well, I have nothing to worry about. I am not a criminal and I am not friends with criminals. This cannot happen to me." But you would be wrong. All kinds of people can get caught up in grand jury dragnets. In fact, one of the illegitimate uses of a grand jury is to destroy political movements, intimidate activists, and jail political leadership.

Grand juries often are used as weapons to repress political movements that organize for social change. They were used against the labor movement in the 1900s, the Communists in the 1950s, antiwar activists, Irish nationalists, and Black Panthers in the 1960s and 1970s, and Puerto Rican Independentistas for the last seventy years. Thousands of activists have been subpoenaed and had their lives ruined and their movements weakened.

Grand jury witch hunts similar to those of earlier decades are, at least for the time being, somewhat quiescent. However, this is more an indication of a weakened activist movement than of government forbearance in the use of this repressive tool. Unfortunately, this medieval instrument of repression remains in the government arsenal and will be employed when political activism threatens the status quo.

Recently, however, the use of the grand jury against President Bill Clinton and his friends and acquaintances fit the classic pattern of abuse that, up until now, usually has been directed at the radical left. Every day there was a new criminal justice story involving the president and his sexual scandal: subpoenaed dresses analyzed by the FBI Crime Lab; subpoenas to the president, the Secret Service, his lawyers, his secretary, to name a few in a very long list; leaks to the press; immunity to the twenty-four-year-old with whom the president dallied; immunity to her mother; and the jailing of those like Susan McDougal who refused to talk.[2] And all these items, if you read past the front page in your newspapers, were assumed to be in the name of the grand jury working with the prosecutor, Ken Starr.

We seem to have slept through this whittling away of the Fifth Amendment right to remain silent and our right not to be forced to give evidence against ourselves and our friends. Despite these dramatic changes that have challenged our basic liberty, there is an overriding assumption of regularity—everyone seems to accept the Starr grand jury as just another fact of life. The clear abuse of the grand jury by Starr—his disrespect for the Fifth Amendment, for the attorney-client privilege—is but the most recent chapter in a history of grand jury abuse committed by the executive branch for decades. The only difference during the Starr investigation is that officials of the executive branch are the targets.

As this embarrassing spectacle was played out in the daily press, the federal prosecutor in New York secretly imprisoned a Palestinian physician for more than six months, even though he had not been charged with committing any crimes, for his failure to answer grand jury questions about the Palestine liberation movement. Dr. Abdelhaleem Ashqar, a diabetic, had been on a hunger strike since his imprisonment and had been force-fed by prison officials. Dr. Ashquar explained to the grand jury and the court that he was refusing to testify on the basis of his "long-held and unshakable religious, political and personal beliefs." He said he "would rather die than betray [his] beliefs and commitments to freedom and democracy for Palestine."

Under current law, a subpoenaed witness to grand jury who refuses to testify, as did Dr. Ashquar, is jailed until he or she agrees to cooperate. However, as the jailing is theoretically a form of coercion, and not meant as punishment, Dr. Ashquar could and should have been ordered released by the courts if it appeared that continued incarceration would not cajole him into testifying. A clearer case for release is harder to imagine. Dr. Asquar was willing to die rather than testify. His health was very poor, yet the prosecutor insisted on keeping him in jail, irrespective of his principles, his health, or, more to the point, his life. The court refused to order his release; instead it ordered him force-fed. Finally, after two months of forced feeding—Ashqar was shackled to the bed to prevent him from removing the feeding tubes—the court released him.

The grand jury as we know it today has two basic functions: to determine if there is enough evidence to hold a person for trial on criminal charges, and, through its subpoena power, to serve as an investigative tool of the prosecutor. The first of these functions is all but nonexistent, as the grand jury is now recognized to rubber stamp indictments that a prosecutor places before it. It makes no independent evaluation of whether there is sufficient evidence to support an indictment.[3] The second function, as an investigatory body controlled by the prosecutor, is of much more recent vintage. The grand jury as an investigative tool of the prosecutor continues to expand dangerously out of control, confounding the separation-of-powers doctrine as the grand jury is no longer under the control of the judiciary.

The concept of the grand jury progressed from its early beginnings as a punitive and primitive form of inquisition under King Henry II in the twelfth century to the ideal of a shield against unjust prosecution— a panel of citizens that would review serious charges to determine whether there was sufficient evidence to hold a person for trial. Incorporated into the Bill of Rights to the United States Constitution, it was a notable advance in Western jurisprudence. The drafters of the Constitution were aware that in the past the grand jury had for the most part served the powers-that-be, losing its independence. But they also knew that the grand jury could be a force for justice. In 1765 a grand jury in Boston refused to indict leaders of the Boston Tea Party. Two grand juries in New York refused to indict newspaper publisher John Peter Zenger for criminal libel against the colonial governor. The challenge to the framers of the Constitution was to find a way to keep the grand jury independent.

Keeping the grand jury independent was but one of a number of different ways of insulating against political pressure and ultimately preventing tyranny through checks and balances that were addressed by the Constitution drafters in the separation-of-powers doctrine. Under that doctrine the three parts of government legislative, judicial, and executive—divided the tasks of governing; each had the power to prevent the others from usurping too much power. The grand jury was assigned to the judicial branch to insulate it from pressures from the executive and congressional branches.

Despite all good intentions, the grand jury continued on many occasions to serve partisan purposes. So it was that in Republican strongholds, sedition indictments were brought against Federalists; likewise, similar indictments were brought against Republicans by Federalist grand juries. President Thomas Jefferson used the grand juries to bring sedition charges against his political enemies. Grand juries enforced slavery, indicting people for abolitionist activity and harboring slaves.

For decades the grand jury was used as an arm of the executive branch to repress the development of the labor movement. In the 1880s seventy leaders were charged with inspiring the Haymarket riots in Chicago; in 1884 leaders of the Pullman strike, including Eugene V. Debs, president of the American Railway Union, were indicted for interfering with the U.S. mail. The International Workers of the World (IWW) was a particular target especially during World War I. Hundreds of IWW activists were indicted including its leader Big Bill Haywood. But not only labor union members were indicted by rubber-stamp grand juries. Victims included the anarchists Emma Goldman and Alexander Berkman, black nationalist leader Marcus Garvey, and Black Muslim leader Elijah Muhammad.

The idea of the grand jury as a shield against indictment died hard. In modern times, however, grand juries have been recognized as rubber stamps, agreeing to follow the dictates of the prosecutor in the vast majority of cases.[4] As one commentator notes: "In periods of great turmoil and dissent, when the exploited and oppressed vocally expressed their view, often for the first time, the grand jury, rather than protecting the rights of the dissenters, stood on the side of the rich and powerful, to protect the status quo."[5]

It was not until after World War II that grand jury use of subpoena power increased. At that time the power to require the presence of every person to attend and testify or else assert his/her Fifth Amendment right to silence became prevalent. The tenor of the times encouraged this increased power. The House Un-American Activities Committee made the subpoenaing of Communists, anarchists, and others more acceptable, and so the subpoena power of the grand jury was dusted off as a tool in the war to ferret out the enemy.

A 1954 law, which applied only to national security cases and was promulgated according to President Dwight D. Eisenhower as a "means of breaking the secrecy which is characteristic of traitors," permitted the grand jury with the help and guidance of the prosecutor (part of the executive branch), for the first time in U.S. jurisprudence, to compel the testimony of witnesses. The law apparently avoided offending the Fifth Amendment by granting the witness total immunity from subsequent charges in exchange for waiving the right to remain silent. Shy of using it, the government resorted to compelling testimony under it only three times. The requirement of granting full immunity did operate as a limit on prosecutorial zeal, for a witness who testified could rarely if ever be prosecuted.

Yet the new law still represented a major watering down of the right against self-incrimination. It meant that the protection of individual privacy embodied in the Constitution's Fifth Amendment right to keep one's thoughts inviolable could give way to the prosecutor or government's claimed need for information. By granting immunity, the prosecutor could force the witness to be a snitch on pain of going to jail; it opened the door on the contemporary use of the grand jury as an investigatory tool of repression. In one of the most eloquent statements of the values protected by the privilege against self-incrimination and as an indication of what is lost by forcing individuals to testify on pain of prison, Supreme Court Justice Abraham Goldberg in *Murphy v. Waterfront Commission*[6] outlined some of these values:

> The privilege against self-incrimination "registers an important advance in the development of our liberty"—one of the great landmarks in man's struggle to make himself civilized. . . . It reflects many of our fundamental values and most noble aspirations; our unwillingness to subject those suspected of crime to the cruel trilemma of self-accusation, perjury or contempt; our preference for an accusatorial rather than an inquisitorial system of criminal justice; our fear that self-incrimination statements will be elicited by inhumane treatment and abuses . . . ; our respect for the inviolability of the human personality and the right of each individual "to a private enclave where he may lead a private life. . . ."

The perfection of the grand jury as an investigatory tool under the control of the executive branch occurred early in the administration of President Richard Nixon. Under the guise of needing new and more powerful tools to reach the secret recesses of organized crime, the administration pushed the Organized Crime Control Act through Congress. The law not only allowed the prosecutor to exchange immunity for testimony, it limited the type of immunity offered so that the person compelled to testify could still be indicted for a related crime, albeit not on the basis of his or her compelled words or for that matter any direct fruits therefrom.[7]

The virtually unlimited power of the prosecutor to subpoena witnesses and compel testimony that we are witnessing today was developed under Nixon, a president whose attitude toward his enemies was not unlike that of King Henry II. By employing the new law that limited grants of immunity and compelled jail for refusals to testify, the Justice Department engaged in broad intelligence gathering against the antiwar movement. In the first three years of the 1970s, over one hundred grand juries were convened in eighty-four cities. More than 1,000 people were subpoenaed. The newly formed Internal Security section of the Justice Department took on the job of harassing and investigating people who expressed opposition to the Vietnam War. These subpoenas were used to gather intelligence, to harass, and to incarcerate people.

The government assault on the antiwar movement was widely—and accurately, as it turned out—understood to be a domestic intelligence-gathering operation. It was an important part of its effort to excoriate any person or group that expressed opposition to the Vietnam War. This suppression of dissent met tremendous resistance from the civil liberties and left legal communities as the cases of activists who refused to testify were litigated in the courts.

Prosecutors, knowing that many of the witnesses they sought would not talk, used their subpoenas as a simplified way of jailing protest leaders. Rally organizers were hauled off to grand juries on the eve of mass demonstrations. For example, in 1972 twenty-three leaders of the Vietnam Veterans Against the War were subpoenaed to appear before a grand jury on the day they were to hold a protest at the Democratic convention in Miami.

The abuses were not limited to one or two cases but were endemic. For example, Arthur Kinoy, an outspoken civil rights lawyer, was subpoenaed by a grand jury to testify about his daughter and answer questions about his political associations. Prosecutors claimed that Kinoy's daughter, an antiwar activist, knew the whereabouts of another individual they were investigating. Kinoy charged that the subpoena was intended to intrude on his relationship with his daughter and interfere with his representation of her and other antiwar activists. He avoided jail only because of a ruling by a courageous federal judge.

That federal judge, Constance Baker Motley, upheld Kinoy's challenge to the new limited "use" immunity statute. She found that it was an unconstitutional infringement on his Fifth Amendment rights. The government, afraid at that time of a somewhat liberal Supreme Court, did not appeal and for a moment was pushed back.

Over the next two years, the makeup of the Supreme Court changed. In 1972 the Court, in *Kastigar v. United States,* sanctioned the grant of limited immunity. And just like that, a major legal devaluing of the Fifth Amendment occurred.

Subsequent decisions added more tools to the prosecutor's arsenal: no right to bail pending appeal of a contempt citation; a requirement to give the grand jury physical exemplars such as handwriting and fingerprints, without granting any form of immunity; the ability to incarcerate people for at least two years as a form of compulsion to testify once immunity has been granted; and the limitation of defenses a witness could raise.

The subpoena to Leslie Bacon illustrates many of the abuses that occurred in this period. Bacon, a young woman living in Washington, D.C., was subpoenaed to a Seattle grand jury in April 1971. This was just prior to the planned May Day demonstrations in the capital. She was hustled onto a plane, given no opportunity to contact an attorney, and told the grand jury was investigating the bombing of the Capitol. As she had not committed any crime, she decided to talk. She did not understand the consequences of testifying. Soon the prosecutor, Guy Goodwin, was asking her about her friends, political associations, the organizing of the May Day demonstrations, and a political commune in New York. Bacon finally decided to stop talking. Although she had given the government a lot of information, it wanted more and indicted her for perjury.[8] The Bacon case shows that the government was using the grand jury to gather political intelligence about the antiwar movement and worse; subsequent to her testimony, federal grand juries in New York City, Detroit, and Washington subpoenaed many of those Bacon had named.

The Nixon grand juries were wide-ranging. Journalists, Black Panthers, nuns, feminists, teenagers, academics, supporters of Puerto Rican independence, and pacifists were hauled before grand juries on the flimsiest of excuses and jailed if they refused to talk. Few indictments were ever obtained, and almost no convictions. Rather than a shield to protect the accused, grand juries had become a sword for Nixon to wield against his perceived "enemies," a rubber stamp for prosecutors, and a blatantly political tool that had little to do with justice and everything to do with revenge.

Grand jury abuse and harassment of activists did not end with Nixon's resignation from office. In the 1970s and 1980s Puerto Rican Independentistas and black nationalists have been the primary targets. The government, unable to obtain evidence of criminal activity, has used grand juries both to gather intelligence about these movements and to jail their supporters. Dozens of activists who have insisted on their constitutional right to remain silent have been jailed without any charges or trials.

Until the Fifth Amendment right to silence, the right to not incriminate oneself, is read back into the Constitution, the grand jury will remain an altogether too potent form of repression to exist in a modern democracy. Until that time we may all be its victims.

NOTES

The authors wish to acknowledge their use of information contained in Michael Deutsch, "The Improper Use of the Federal Grand Jury: An Instrument for the Internment of Political Activists," *Criminal Law & Criminology* 75 (1984): 1159. We thank Elizabeth Fink for her help with this chapter.

1. The following is a typical example of the types of questions asked of an antiwar activist in the 1970s:

   I want you to describe for the grand jury every occasion during the year 1970 when you had been in contact with, attended meetings which were conducted by, or attended by, or been any place when any individual spoke whom you knew to be associated with or affiliated with Students for a Democratic Society, the Weatherman, the Communist Party or any other organization advocating revolutionary overthrow of the United States, describing for the grand jury when these incidents occurred, where they occurred, who was present and what was said by all persons there and what you did at the time that you were in these meetings, groups, associations or conversations.

2. Susan McDougal spent eighteen months in jail for civil contempt; she was then tried for criminal contempt, acquitted on one charge and the jury deadlocked on two charges. She was released in 1999.

3. In more than half the cases now presented in federal court, the defendants waive their right to have the grand jury determine whether an indictment should issue and proceed through on information, which is a written accusation by the prosecutor.

4. On occasion, the members of an individual grand jury, taking seriously their role of investigating and shielding, vote to issue subpoenas and to follow or not follow an investigation against the wish of the prosecutor. The government refers to these grand juries as "runaway" grand juries.

5. Deutsch, "The Improper Use of the Federal Grand Jury," 1174.

6. 378 U.S. 52, 55 (1964).

7. At the same time, the law prohibited the granting of "transactional" immunity—the kind conferred on Monica Lewinsky—as unnecessary. "Use" immunity was found to satisfy the Fifth Amendment right against self-incrimination.

8. We had an expression during this period indicating the danger of answering any questions before the grand jury: "It's like eating potato chips; once you start, you can't stop."

TWENTY-THREE

At the Constitution's Edge: Arab Americans and Civil Liberties

HUESSIN IBISH

Like many ethnic minorities, Arab Americans and Arabs living in the United States face harassment and discrimination from bigoted individuals and institutions. But for Arab Americans, problems of discrimination and official or quasi-official political repression are becoming increasingly intertwined. The official repression of Arab American political activity is strongly linked to U.S. policies in the Middle East.

Most Arabs and Arab Americans are at odds with important elements of U.S. Middle East policy, especially with regard to the sanctions against and bombing of Iraq, the denial of Palestinian human and national rights, and the Israeli occupation of Lebanon. Resistance to the expression of these dissenting views forms the basis for much of the political repression currently facing Arabs in the United States. Widespread representations of Arabs in the American mass media as hostile, alien, and dangerous are informed and reinforced by the highly aggressive approach the United States takes to regional politics in the Middle East.

These negative representations and aggressive foreign policies compound one another, producing a vicious cycle of fear and hatred that has provided the necessary backdrop for a serious attack on civil liberties. Politically active Arabs in the United States, especially Palestinians, are now jailed indefinitely, without charge, on the basis of secret evidence. Their property is seized without due process; and, in the form of the "LA 8," seven Pro-Palestinian immigrants persecuted by the Justice Department because of their political beliefs, they are the focus and the cover for a government campaign to severely restrict the political rights of all immigrants.

Notions of a generalized conflict between the Arab World and the United States, or between Islam and the West, which are the source of many of the suspicions that form the basis for discrimination and political repression against Arab Americans, are promoted throughout this society. Films such as *Path to Paradise, True Lies,* and *The Siege* and television programs such as *JAG* paint an image of Arabs as terrorists driven by Islamic fanaticism and irrational anti-Western hatred. Influential academic works, such as political scientist Samuel Huntington's *Clash of Civilizations* and some of the writings of noted scholar of Middle East history Bernard Lewis promote this idea of generalized conflict as the basis for sound scholarship and policy planning. The impression that such a conflict either already exists or is emerging has become so widespread that President Bill Clinton felt the need to state publicly that his bombing attacks on Sudan, Afghanistan, and Iraq in 1998 were in no way representative of the state of relations between the Islamic World and the West, or indicative of an anti-Islamic policy or sentiment. Ironically, such disavowals only serve to reinforce the suspicion that these targets are seen as hostile and are attacked by the United States at least in part because they are Arab and Muslim.

The atmosphere for Arabs in the United States is further poisoned by widespread but insidious "journalism" that is calculated to spread fear and hatred of Arabs and Islam. The most damaging work of this kind has been done by Steven Emerson, a free-lance journalist and so-called "terrorism expert," who has argued that almost all major Arab and Muslim organizations in the United States are fronts for or supporters of "terrorist groups." His 1994 television documentary, *Jihad in*

America, which was widely broadcast by PBS, advanced the dubious and unsubstantiated thesis that there was an extensive fund-raising network in the United States for "Middle Eastern terrorists." Emerson has been quick to point the finger incorrectly at Arabs for any number of tragedies and disasters, publicly blaming Arabs for the bombing of the Federal Building in Oklahoma City and for the crash of TWA Flight 800. In spite of his penchant for false accusation and wild statements, such as his 1994 claim that the aim of pro-Palestinian Muslims in the United States was the "mass murder of all Jews, Christians and moderate Muslims,"[1] Emerson is still called upon as a "terrorism expert" by some of the major American media. Emerson's work is merely the most egregious example of this kind of Arab-bashing, which is by no means unusual in contemporary American journalism.

Against this backdrop, Arab Americans have found themselves at the front lines of an all-out assault on civil liberties by the U.S. government. Long-cherished principles such as the right of the accused to be charged or released, the right to see and test the credibility of evidence and to confront one's accusers, and the exercise of free speech and other rights supposedly protected by the First Amendment are being seriously compromised in the process. Among the more troubling government documents to be uncovered in recent years was a Justice Department contingency plan for the mass arrest of thousands of Arabs in the United States, their detention in concentration camps in Florida and Louisiana, and their possible deportation. This idea has currency not just in the minds of policy planers and government bureaucrats. It has resonated through the culture all the way to Hollywood, where the images of the mass detention of thousands of Arab Americans formed the basis for the 1998 film *The Siege.*

One form of official discrimination against Arabs has been the institution of a system of "profiling" used at U.S. airports and by U.S. airlines around the world as well as by U.S. customs officers. Following the TWA Flight 800 crash, Arab Americans became the targets of unfounded accusations of culpability. Although once again in the rush to judgment, the media, some officials, and "terrorism experts" proved mistaken, the White House Commission on Aviation Safety and Security chaired by Vice-President Al Gore instituted a "profiling" system of airline security that has resulted in the singling out, abuse, and humiliation of Arab American travelers solely based on their national background and ethnicity. The Federal Aviation Administration (FAA) has not been able to point to a single case in which profiling has led to the apprehending or thwarting (i.e. identification and/or arrest) of someone who posed a threat to airport or airplane safety. Again, airport profiling is an instance where a discriminatory approach by the government and popular misconceptions about Arabs reinforce one another. The chief executive officer of Northwest Airlines forcefully made this point when he addressed the National Convention of the American-Arab Anti-Discrimination Committee (ADC) in 1997. In response to complaints that airport profiling had led to discrimination against Arab and Arab American travelers, he candidly stated that even if airline agents were given directives not to discriminate based on ethnicity, their behavior would still be affected by what they see about Arabs in films and on television.

Measures designed to curb, disrupt, or chill Arab American political activity include the criminalization by the Anti-Terrorism and Effective Death Penalty Act of 1996 of certain forms of international fund raising for humanitarian aid. This law makes it a crime to knowingly raise and contribute funds, donate educational and humanitarian aid, or to provide lodging, transportation, or other forms of "material support" to designated foreign "terrorist organizations." U.S. citizens convicted of this new federal crime can face up to ten years in prison, while noncitizens can be deported. This prohibition of support applies to charitable and humanitarian operations by the thirty currently designated groups, at least half of which are Arab or Muslim organizations. Courts in the United States have consistently held that financial contributions to the lawful activities of political organizations are protected by the First Amendment, since such contributions effectively express a political perspective.

The 1996 Anti-Terrorism Act prohibits this form of expression in the case of organizations arbitrarily designated by the Secretary of State, thus creating what can only be described as a political crime or a crime of expression. For example, it is now illegal to donate humanitarian assistance to the extensive network of schools, hospitals, and orphanages run by the resistance movement Hizbullah in southern Lebanon, because Hizbullah has been designated a "terrorist organization" by the State Department. Expressing sympathy for Lebanon's right to be free of Israeli occupation, as demanded in U.N. Security Council Resolution 425, and for Hizbullah's struggle to oust the Israeli occupation forces by supporting its humanitarian work, has become a serious felony. This has occurred in spite of the fact that the U.S. government has recognized the distinction between legitimate resistance and terrorism. Commenting on the activities of Hizbullah in Israeli-occupied southern Lebanon, the U.S. Ambassador to Lebanon David Satterfield said that "We make a distinction between resistance and terrorism, and we do not view this [Lebanese] resistance as terrorism."[2]

The 1996 Anti-Terrorism Act allows the Immigration and Naturalization Service (INS) to use secret evidence against lawful permanent residents of the United States in deportation proceedings. This evidence is withheld from the defendants and their attorneys and is viewed only by the prosecutors and the judges, making an effective defense impossible. The law establishes a new deportation process, to be held in "alien terrorist removal courts." The judges hearing these cases must determine whether an individual is an "alien terrorist," a category that includes any noncitizen who has solicited funds, provided material support to, or solicited persons for membership in any "foreign terrorist organization" on the government's list.

The Illegal Immigration Reform and Immigrant Responsibility Act of 1996 also contains a provision allowing for the use of secret evidence. The law authorizes the INS to use secret evidence in making a determination that an "arriving alien"—that is, any noncitizen seeking admission to the United States—belongs to or has supported a designated "foreign terrorist organization." Any such determination will result in exclusion from the United States. Moreover, the government has made it clear that it intends to use this law against lawful permanent residents who have traveled abroad and are returning home. Once again, political support for a designated organization becomes, in effect, a political crime. Since the passage of the 1996 Anti-Terrorism and Immigration Acts, the INS has begun using secret evidence in many cases, although the full potential for repression in these laws remains largely untapped. As a result at least twenty-five individuals, all of Arab descent or Muslims, are incarcerated without charge on the basis of secret evidence that they are unable to challenge or even evaluate. All of these individuals have resided peacefully in the United States for a number of years. Many have spouses and children who are U.S. citizens. Some have satisfied an immigration judge that they would face certain persecution if returned to their home country. Yet almost all of them remain detained because an INS prosecutor has presented a judge with secret, and therefore unchallenged and untested, evidence alleging that the individual is a "terrorist" or has some "terrorist" affiliation.

In an August 1998 letter to Attorney General Janet Reno and INS Commissioner Doris Meissner, Senators Spencer Abraham (R-Mich.) and Edward Kennedy (D-Mass.), the chair and ranking member of the Senate Subcommittee on Immigration, expressed "grave concerns" about the use of secret evidence. "Some believe that recent actions create the appearance that the INS may be using secret evidence only in cases against Arab immigrants," wrote the senators. "This is especially disturbing since many of these cases appear to be based not on any actions of the immigrants, but rather on their purported associations,"[3] they added.

Perhaps the most notorious case of the use of secret evidence and indefinite detention without trial is that of Dr. Mazen Al-Najjar of Tampa, a Palestinian and former professor at the University of South Florida. In May 1997, following unsubstantiated allegations in Steven Emerson's notorious documentary *Jihad in America* and in articles in the *Tampa Tribune* that a think tank associated with the University of South Florida (USF), the World and Islam Studies Enterprise (WISE), was a front for the Islamic Jihad Organization, Dr. Al-Najjar was arrested. Al-Najjar and his brother-in-law, Professor Sami Al-Arian, were active in WISE. The Federal Bureau of Investigation (FBI) claimed that WISE was in fact a front for Palestinian "terrorists" and accused Dr. Al-Najjar of being a "mid-level operative" in a scheme to fund the Islamic Jihad. The INS took Dr. Al-Najjar into custody and denied him release on bond. An immigration judge ordered him to be held indefinitely on the basis of secret evidence.

Al-Najjar and his wife are both stateless Palestinians not holding citizenship in any country. The judge ordered Dr. Al-Najjar's family to be separated, with him deported to the United Arab Emirates, and his wife to Saudi Arabia, even though neither country has agreed to accept them. The court made no provisions for their three American-born children. A report on the entire matter by former USF President William Reece Smith, Jr., a prominent Tampa attorney, found no indication of a link between Al-Arian, Al-Najjar, their associates, and terrorism. The FBI has not brought forward any evidence of any involvement with any terrorist group or activities against Al-Najjar or Al-Arian, and Al-Arian has been reinstated as an active professor at the University of South Florida. Al-Najjar, on the other hand, remains in jail.

Al-Najjar's case has won sympathy from unusual quarters. On March 20, 1998, the *Miami Herald* reported that "Al-Najjar has been here since May 19, so long that even the guy who runs the place [the INS detention center in Manatee, Florida] feels sorry for him. 'Come on, counselor, get this thing moving,' prison director S. Kent Dodd tells Al-Najjar's lawyer, Luis Coton of Tampa. 'He's been here too long.'"[4] The House Minority Whip, David E. Bonior (D-Mich.), an outspoken opponent of secret evidence, visited Al-Najjar in his jail cell in February 1999. Bonior raised the issue with President Clinton, hand delivering a letter to the president written by Najjar's ten-year-old daughter, Yara. After meeting Al-Najjar, Bonior observed that "Our Bill of Rights specifically grants the right to a public trial and the right to be informed of the nature and cause of the accusation. 'Secret Evidence' makes a mockery of our Constitution, but it is being increasingly being used by the INS and the FBI to harass and incarcerate Muslim and Arab American activists."[5]

On the other hand, Steven Emerson, whose unsupported allegations led to Al-Najjar's arrest, has been quoted as saying that "I feel much more comfortable knowing that Mazen Al-Najjar is in jail and that Sami Al-Arian cannot speak and propagate his message to young students, because it is militant doctrine under a false veneer."[6]

Another noted victim of secret evidence is Nasser Ahmed, a thirty-seven-year-old Egyptian who has been held by the INS in a New York jail since April 1996. Sometime after Ahmed arrived in the United States in 1986, his mosque, Masjid Abu Bakr, was investigated by the FBI, apparently because of its political opposition to the Egyptian government. The FBI found no criminal activity at the mosque. Ahmed again came to the government's attention when he served as a court-appointed paralegal, translating for Sheikh Omar Abdel Rahman during his 1995 trial on charges of conspiracy related to the bombing of the World Trade Center in New York. Shortly thereafter, the INS arrested Ahmad, but then released him on a $15,000 bond. However, the INS arrested Ahmed again in April 1996, after the Rahman trial was over. Ahmed has alleged that the FBI approached him during Rahman's trial and demanded that he work for them covertly. He says that he was threatened with deportation when he refused to cooperate and has speculated that his treatment is a form of retaliation by the government. Ahmed applied for both bond and political asylum.

The INS prosecutor introduced secret evidence that allegedly showed Ahmed associated with a "terrorist organization." At Ahmed's appeal, the judge found that there was "no doubt" that his political beliefs would "likely result in his torture if he is returned to Egypt." Even as the judge questioned the constitutionality of utilizing secret evidence, he found that the secret evidence compelled him to deny the request for political asylum. Because immigration judges cannot rule on the constitutionality of procedures, Ahmed must remain in detention as his attorneys attempt to get a federal court to review his case. Detained for over three years, often in solitary confinement, he remains in jail despite a 1999 order by an immigration judge that he be released.

In another well-known secret evidence case, the INS is holding six Iraqi men in a Los Angeles prison. Ironically it was the U.S. government who brought these men to the United States in the first place. They were among the 6,000 Iraqis brought to the country after a CIA-sponsored uprising in northern Iraq collapsed in 1996. Once they arrived, the six applied for political asylum, which was denied on the basis of secret evidence that supposedly demonstrates that they constitute a "security risk" to the United States and, although brought here by the U.S. government, were charged with entering the U.S. without a valid visa. But as self-declared organizers of a plot against the current Iraqi government, their professed belief that they face certain death if returned to Iraq seems valid. The men are being defended by none other than James Woolsey, former director of the CIA. However, even Woolsey, who has the highest security clearances, was not allowed to see much of the evidence against his clients. On October 8, 1998, Woolsey told a Senate Judiciary Subcommittee that "the INS' procedure in these sorts of cases—uncannily reminiscent of Franz Kafka's *The Trial*—is to collect rumors and unfounded allegations, not investigate them, submit them in camera [i.e., secretly] to the immigration judge, and then demand that the individual in question be held a threat to national security if he does not succeed in refuting the charges of which he is unaware."[7] Woolsey added that some of the secret evidence that later was released showed a clear anti-Arab racist bias, stating that "In ex parte testimony, belatedly declassified, more than one interrogator explicitly expressed bias (e.g., Arabs 'lie an awful lot,' 'there is no guilt in the Arab world') to the immigration court."[8]

Some individuals already have been deported on the basis of such secret evidence. Ali Termos, a thirty-one-year-old Lebanese citizen, was deported from the United States on October 6, 1997, after having been denied bond and held in INS custody a full year. Termos entered the United States on a student exchange visa, which expired, but the INS made no move to ask him to leave the country. Termos was married on June 25, 1996, to a naturalized U.S. citizen and began the process of obtaining lawful permanent resident status. Four months later he was arrested, and rather than releasing him with a small bond, as is normal in cases of spouses of a citizen who have expired visas, the INS held him for questioning by an FBI agent. The agent questioned Termos for two hours about his knowledge of various Islamic religious institutions in Detroit and any possible connection between these groups and "terrorist" organizations such as Hizbullah. Termos acknowledged sending more than $300 to a Hizbullah-run orphanage in southern Lebanon. At the subsequent bond hearing, held one week later, an FBI agent appeared along with the INS prosecutor. This agent presented "confidential information" to the judge to support the government's charge that Termos was a "security risk" and should be denied bond. Termos remained in jail during the entire appeals process and was subsequently deported to Lebanon.

Unlike Termos, Imad Hamad, Midwest Regional Director of ADC, recently won the right to stay in the United States in spite of the use by the INS of secret evidence in its effort to deport him. Hamad, who was never detained by the INS, prevailed in the government's final appeal to the Board of Immigration Appeals against a 1997 order allowing him to adjust his status to that of permanent resident. A stateless Palestinian, Hamad came to the United States as a student in 1980. The INS alleges that while studying in California he attended some rallies and fund-raising events for the Popular Front for the Liberation of Palestine (PFLP). He was placed in deportation proceedings when the INS denied an application for adjustment to permanent residence in 1985. After years of litigation, an immigration judge finally dismissed as unsubstan-tiated the government's allegations that Hamad had engaged in or supported "terrorist activity" and granted Hamad adjustment of status. The INS appealed this decision to the Board of Immigration Appeals. Although they have no authority to rule on constitutional matters, the board's appellate judges defended the use of secret evidence in principle, but found that the secret evidence established no connection between Imad Hamad and any "terrorist" activity or organization.

To date, Hamad is one of the few and perhaps the only immigrant to prevail against secret evidence brought by the INS. While the Board of Immigration Appeals endorsed secret evidence as a prosecutorial tool in its ruling, the fact that the judges found the evidence unconvincing reinforces the view that the government turns to secret evidence when its evidence cannot withstand public scrutiny. Moreover, in June 1998 much of the secret evidence in the Hamad case was declassified and released. Hamad's attorneys found that the "secret evidence" all had been openly used in his original 1989 hearing and that they were fully familiar with it. Here, as in the case of the six Iraqis, "secret evidence" seems synonymous with weak evidence.

The government also has begun to seize property from politically active Arab Americans without due process. On June 10, 1998, federal prosecutors and FBI agents in Chicago seized $1.4 million worth of assets of Mohammad Salah and the Quaranic Literacy Institute, a Chicago-area organization that translates sacred Islamic texts. The assets seized include the house where Salah lives with his family and the Institute's bank accounts. The government claims that the assets were part of a money-laundering operation that funneled money to a "foreign terrorist organization." In this case, the government was not relying on the 1996

Anti-Terrorism Act; instead it was using the civil forfeiture law against Salah and the Quaranic Literacy Institute. This law authorizes the government to seize any assets that are the fruit of a criminal activity or part of a criminal transaction. In Salah's case, the government is alleging that the assets are part of a scheme to fund armed attacks against Israel, thereby violating criminal money-laundering statutes. Civil forfeiture, while frequently used in cases involving illegal drug activity and racketeering, had never before been applied to a group that allegedly was funding political activities abroad. Because forfeiture is technically against the assets, not the person, it is considered to be a civil rather than a criminal action.

Civil forfeiture in politically-charged cases turns the presumption of innocence on its head, since the burden is on the owner to prove that the assets were not part of any illegal activities. In an editorial on June 19, 1998, the *Chicago Tribune* criticized the seizure of Salah's assets as part of a "through-the-looking-glass scenario" that is "not the American way of justice."[9] Even more disturbing is that the case against Salah and the Quaranic Literacy Institute is built almost entirely on a "confession" that Salah allegedly made while imprisoned by the Israeli authorities— a confession the *Tribune* recognized was "without benefit of even the pretense of due process."[10]

The government also has used Arabs in the United States in a test case for restricting the political and First Amendment rights of all immigrants, as exemplified in the ruling by the Supreme Court in the case of *Reno v. American-Arab Anti-Discrimination Committee (ADC)*. The INS had been trying to deport seven Palestinians and a Kenyan on the grounds that they were members or supporters of the PFLP. They were originally arrested on January 26, 1987 by the FBI, under the infamous McCarran-Walter Act, on charges of advocating world communism, which was at that time a crime. These charges were dropped in less than a month, but the eight were then accused, under a different section of the act, of advocating the killing of government officials and the unlawful destruction of property. None of the charges could be sustained in any way, and the FBI turned the individuals, who had become known as the LA 8, over to the INS for deportation. The LA 8 won an injunction preventing the INS from persuing deportation on the

grounds of selective enforcement of the law, since all parties agreed that
they were being singled out for their pro-Palestinian political beliefs. The
government freely admitted that had the LA 8 been citizens, the First
Amendment would have protected their rights to participate in all the
activities for which the government was attempting to deport them.
ADC and the LA 8 won at every step of the way until the case reached
the Supreme Court in October 1998, with all lower courts holding that
immigrants enjoy a constitutional right to free speech and are not to be
subjected to a selective enforcement of the law.

The Clinton administration sought to overturn the injunction
preventing the INS from deporting the LA 8 by using the 1996
Immigration Act, which it interpreted as barring immigrants facing
deportation from access to district courts. Given their unique combination of full discovery and constitutional jurisdiction, district courts are
the best, and in many cases the only, viable forum for the assertion of
constitutional rights. In effect, district courts may be the only way for
immigrants to challenge the manner in which they are being treated in
the course of the effort to deport them. The Supreme Court agreed to
rule on the jurisdictional question but not on the issues in the case. The
Court agreed, by a vote of 8 to 1, that the 1996 law does indeed prevent
immigrants facing deportation from going to district court, thereby
invalidating the LA 8's injunction and opening the way for the INS to
resume deportation proceedings against them.

Yet the Supreme Court went further, ruling by a vote of 5 to 4 that
immigrants facing deportation can almost never raise a claim of selective
enforcement. The Supreme Court authorized the government to use
selective enforcement in deportation cases as it sees fit, ruling that "The
Executive should not have to disclose its 'real' reasons for deeming
nationals of a particular country a special threat—or indeed for simply
wishing to antagonize a particular foreign country by focusing on that
country's nationals. . . ." Thus categories such as race, ethnicity, religion,
political belief, and the like are now established as legitimate grounds for
selective enforcement of the law in cases of deportation.

There is, at present, no clear consensus about exactly what the ruling
will mean for the rights of illegal and legal immigrants. Therefore, all
eyes will be on the INS and the Justice Department to see how they will

enforce this ruling and what they believe it authorizes them to do. How lower courts interpret the Supreme Court's ruling in politically charged deportation cases is also of interest. Much of the Court's language is couched in rhetoric about illegal immigrants, yet two of the LA 8 were fully legal green card holders, while the other six had minor technical violations. Yet the Court did not appear to distinguish in any way between the rights of the legal and the technically "illegal" immigrants among the LA 8; its ruling applied equally to all of the respondents. Hence, it would appear that, in cases of an unsubstantiated accusation of affiliation with a "terrorist organization" or participation in other political crimes that can lead to deportation, there is no distinction between the rights of a legal or a technically illegal immigrant. Professor David Cole, who argued the case on behalf of ADC, commented that "We were blindsided. The Court has effectively denied to all immigrants in this country the right to engage in the same political activities that citizens have an unquestioned First Amendment right to engage in, and they did so after telling us not to address that issue."[11]

As Professor Margaret M. Russell wrote in the *Los Angeles Times*:

> resident aliens face an intolerable Catch-22: If they exercise their 1st Amendment rights, they may be deemed "illegal" and a "special threat." If they seek to challenge INS determinations of their "illegal" status, they will fail because the Supreme Court has decided that "illegal aliens" have no right to challenge politically motivated deportations, and that "illegal aliens" have no right to federal court review of such claims. Herein lies the threat to the liberties of all. If people who came here legally can be declared "illegal" primarily because of the controversy of their political views and then denied the opportunity to appeal such a decision until it is too late to make a difference, what right to speak do we truly possess?[12]

By selecting a group of Arabs in the United States who are supporters of Palestinian national rights and accusing them of being involved in terrorist activity, the government is clearly trying to ensure that concerns about terrorism and fear and distrust of Arabs, Muslims, and Palestinians overshadow the issue of First Amendment rights of immigrants and their protection against selective enforcement of the law. However, a clear sign that this tactic is not working has been the nearly unanimous negative reaction from the press. Major newspapers around the country, including the *New York Times, Washington Post, Los Angeles Times, Orange County Register,* and many others, denounced the ruling as a dangerous violation of First Amendment principles. None of the serious papers that commented on the ruling regarded it as an Arab issue or a question about the fight against terrorism. Rather, they all saw it as a question of civil liberties; they were not distracted from constitutional or human rights issues by the red herring of terrorism, which the government sought to invoke by targeting Palestinians and labeling them "terrorists."

The same equation between politically active Arab Americans and terrorism is being used to keep Arab Americans from participating in the political and policy making processes. On July 12, 1999, House Minority Leader Richard Gephardt's decision to remove Salam Al-Marayati's nomination to serve on the National Commission on Terrorism was a typically disturbing example of the trend. Al-Marayati, Executive Director of the Muslim Public Affairs Council and member of the Los Angeles Human Rights Commission, was appointed to the Commission because of his outstanding reputation as a civil rights leader, but was removed because of objections by pro-Israel groups that he was a "supporter of terrorism." A new litmus test promoted by some pro-Israel groups and designed for blocking Arab American appointments holds that Arab Americans must never have criticized policies of the Israeli government and that the pro-Israel lobby will be the judge of whether they pass this test. It smacks of a new form of anti-Arab McCarthyism. The pattern of this emerging litmus test is consistent: Arab American appointees or government officials are falsely accused of being "supporters of terrorism," quotations by them or their associates criticizing Israeli policies are presented as "evidence," and their removal is demanded. At the time of writing, this pattern had been repeated at least three times in the times in three months, from May through July of 1999.

Mr. Al-Marayati and other the other Arab Americans subjected to this same treatment during this period, including his wife Dr. Leila Al-Marayati who serves on the U.S. Commission on Religious Freedom Abroad and State Department official Joseph Zogby, have all been subjected to blatant character assassination of this type. None of these individuals has ever even remotely condoned terrorism, but all have been critical of Israeli policies. This is the new equation: criticism of Israeli policies by an Arab American equals "support for terrorism." The pro-Israel community has been accustomed and used to a monopoly on discourse about the Middle East, terrorism and other vital issues. Some pro-Israel groups are proving that they will go to extreme ends to maintain this monopoly, including slander and character assassination. Politicians like Rep. Gephardt, who are in a position to stand up to this bullying and insist on the need for serious and critical Arab American and Muslim American involvement in key debates such as foreign and counterterrorism policies, are cravenly caving into this pressure. Thus pro-Israel groups actually become the arbiters of Arab American government appointments.

Since this barrier is being applied solely to Arab American and Muslim American appointees, it also serves as a cover for a very ugly form of ethnic and religious discrimination. No credible or serious Arab American can withstand such an outrageous and unwarranted test, since there is a consensus among Arab Americans, the Arab world, and indeed the international community, that many of the policies of the Israeli government are unacceptable. But now, for Arab Americans at least, policies of the government of Israel would appear to be sacrosanct, above questioning and outside the scope of debate. What emerges is the prospect of the total exclusion of Arab American and Muslim participation in policy making in the United States, especially in debates of greatest concern to these communities and where their contribution is most badly needed. The intended effect of this exclusion is to prevent the critical evaluation by Arab Americans of many one-sided and counter-productive government policies, particularly those relating to the Middle East, and prevent any correction of them.

Politically active Arab Americans are likely to remain on the front lines of the battle over civil liberties and political freedoms in the United States. There is every reason to believe that the government intends to increase, rather than ease, repression and restrictions on organized Arab American political activity, especially in regard to dissenting views on Middle East issues. Yet Arab American activists can be comforted by the thought that in defending their political and civil liberties, they are defending what is best in the American political system, sometimes in spite of itself.

NOTES

1. John Sugg, "Steven Emerson's Crusade," *Extra* (January/February 1999): 17-20.
2. Quoted in *Al-Safir,* December 4, 1998.
3. "U.S. Bars or Expels Suspect Immigrants on Secret Evidence," *New York Times,* August 15, 1998.
4. Martin Merzer, "The Secret War," *The Miami Herald, Tropic Magazine,* March 22, 1998, 12-29.
5. "Bonior Raises Secret Evidence Problem with President Clinton," Press Release, Office of Congressman Bonior, March 4, 1999, author's papers.
6. Martin, "The Secret War."
7. "Prepared Statement of R. James Woolsey before the Senate Judiciary Committee Technology Terrorism and Government Information Subcommittee," Federal News Service Transcript, October 8, 1998, author's papers.
8. Ibid.
9. "A New Brand of American Justice?," *Chicago Tribune,* June 19, 1998.
10. Ibid.
11. "ADC Stunned by Supreme Court Attack on Immigrants' Rights," Press Release, American-Arab Anti-Discrimination Committee, February 24, 1999, author's papers.
12. Margaret M. Russell, "Be Wary of the Court's Protection," *Los Angeles Times,* March 12, 1999.

TWENTY FOUR

Political Incarceration

JOSÉ LÓPEZ

COUNTERINSURGENCY
AND POLITICAL PRISONERS

"The Crisis of Democracy" was a major ruling-class policy statement on domestic affairs, written principally by Samuel Huntington and issued by the Trilateral Commission in 1973. It described the U.S. political crisis of the 1960s and 1970s as being caused by the excessive demands of "ungovernable sectors," black, Chicano, and Native American movements, along with women and youths. In the words of Huntington, "The demands on democratic government grow, while the capacity of democratic governments stagnates. This, it would appear, is the central dilemma of the governability of democracy. . . ." He lamented that society had become too democratic: "There are potentially desirable limits to the indefinite extension of political democracy." The Trilateralist remedy was more authoritarianism to ensure "a more balanced existence."

In the 1960s, as the civil rights and black power movements grew, the number of black political prisoners swelled and the prison struggle became a major part of the black liberation struggle. Political prisoners like George Jackson* stated that prisons are an important tool in the government's effort to contain black people and destroy their freedom.

Although the government refuses to admit it, there are over 100 political prisoners and prisoners of war in U.S. prisons today. They come from the Puerto Rican, Black/New Afrikan, and Native American liberation movements. They include progressive Christians, white anti-imperialists, draft resisters, and grand jury resisters. The movements that these people represent honor, love, and respect them. Yet the government contends that they are criminals or terrorists, and reserves for them, as well as for prisoners showing leadership and political direction, the harshest treatment, which includes the use of "control units" against them.

Control units are designed to totally control the lives of the prisoners in them and to ultimately break the spirit of these prisoners. In the case of political prisoners and prisoners of war, control units are part of a calculated strategy to weaken the movements and intimidate others from taking a stand. The United States Penitentiary at Marion in southern Illinois is the tightest maximum security prison in the country, serving as an experimental laboratory and trendsetter for the whole prison system; the majority of the states had or have control units in operation or under construction.**

At Marion, the Bureau of Prisons (BOP) established the first control unit where prisoners are subjected to sensory deprivation and solitary confinement. In the early years of the prison, officials experimented with the use of drugs on control unit prisoners. For punishment, Marion puts prisoners in "boxcars"—small, enclosed, soundproof boxes. In October 1983 the entire prison was locked down. For many years (as is the case for most control units), prisoners were locked in tiny cells for more than twenty-two hours a day. They were denied contact with each other and forced into total idleness; punished by being shackled naked and spread-eagled to cement beds; denied all contact visits; and deprived of work programs, group educational activities, and congregational religious

---

* Ed.: Author of *Blood in My Eye* and *Soledad Brother,* George Jackson was a field marshal for the Black Panther Party; he was killed by prison guards in 1971.

** Ed.: Colorado's Florence-ADX now exists as the highest security / "lock down" prison in the United States.

worship. Squads of guards in riot gear routinely beat prisoners who broke the rules.

The Bureau of Prisons tries to perpetuate the myth that Marion contains the most violent predatory prisoners in the system. The truth is that the criteria for placement in and out of Marion are intentionally vague. In fact, 80 percent of the men in Marion are eligible for placement in less restrictive prisons. Although some infamous felons are placed there, the prison also houses people sentenced to short terms for victimless crimes, people imprisoned for their political beliefs and activities, and prisoner leaders.

A control unit for women was built at the Lexington Federal Correctional Institute in Kentucky in October 1986. In this behavior modification unit, the Bureau of Prisons used sensory deprivation, extreme isolation, and sexual degradation to control the prisoners. The bureau's director said that the conditions in the unit were necessary to provide adequate security for the women and that their radical politics made them a threat to the community and "escape prone." Other prison officials told the women that their only avenue out of the unit was to renounce their political associations, to repudiate a lifetime of political principle. After a national protest campaign, in October 1987 the bureau announced that it would close the unit, stating that it was not big enough to house all of the female political "terrorists" in the country. In June 1988 three of the prisoners sued the bureau. A federal judge agreed that the bureau had persecuted them for their political beliefs and ruled that they be transferred out of the unit immediately. By August 1988 all of the women had been moved out of the unit and it was closed. In that same month, the bureau opened a new federal prison in Marianna, Florida. It contained a special women's unit that the bureau said would "continue the mission" of the Lexington Control Unit.

WHO IS A POLITICAL PRISONER?

Political prisoners exist as a result of real political and social conflicts in the society. No society is free of contradictions, and therefore no society does not have political prisoners. The absurd position of the U.S. government that it alone has no political prisoners is consistent with its position that there are no legitimate social or political movements in the United States struggling for fundamental change. The strategy of criminalization and isolation of political prisoners, that is, the denial of their existence, in part allows the United States to propagate the lie that U.S. society has achieved social peace and that whatever dissent there is functions solely within the existent bourgeois democratic framework.

Among the political prisoners there is a notable group called prisoners of war. These people are members of oppressed nations who consider their nations to be at war with the United States or building toward such a war. That is, they are members of national liberation struggles who have participated in pursuits similar to political prisoners, except that they have been involved in the use of organized revolutionary violence and/or are members of clandestine organizations that may utilize revolutionary violence. POWs usually take the position, consistent with international law, that U.S. courts have no jurisdiction over them, and therefore they may and often do refuse to participate in legal proceedings, including their own trials. A great deal of international law supports this position, including the Geneva Convention Protocols One and Two and Resolution 1514 of the United Nations General Assembly (passed on December 14, 1960), which states that colonialism is a crime against humanity and that those captured fighting against it are prisoners of war.

Often political prisoners are given longer sentences than other people convicted of similar crimes. When inside prison, many times they are treated worse than prisoners in for nonpolitical crimes. Control unit prisons have been used against them with great vengeance. For example, often male political prisoners are sent to Marion Federal Penitentiary straight from court. This violates the Bureau of Prisons' own regulations, which maintain that prisoners be sent to Marion only after they have been disruptive in another prison. And, finally, the United States has resorted to outright murder, as in the cases of Puerto Rican prisoner of war Angel Rodriguez Cristobal and black revolutionary George Jackson. These repressive acts are designed not so much to punish political prisoners for their actions but to brutalize them and others into turning against their political causes. Simply deny your beliefs and you will be relieved of this burden, they are told. With startling regularity and courage, the vast majority of these prisoners refuse this "option" and remain steadfast, beacons to those of us who believe that a new society must be created.

A BRIEF HISTORICAL OVERVIEW

From the turn of the century until about 1950, there were mass upsurges in political activity, and each was met with repression and imprisonment. From about 1915 to 1920, there was massive repression of the Industrial Workers of the World (the Wobblies). Then came the Palmer raids against the Communist Party and its sympathizers. In the 1940s, many war resisters were sent to prison; in the next decade, more people were imprisoned during the McCarthy period. In 1950, the people of Puerto Rico rose up against the United States in pursuit of their independence, in the Grito de Jayuya. This rebellion was met with massive repression, which in turn was met by attacks against the U.S. government in Washington, D.C., by the Puerto Rican Nationalists. And these attacks in turn resulted in their imprisonment.

Then came the 1960s. The government attacked the Black Liberation Movement, killing approximately thirty Black Panthers and incarcerating dozens upon dozens of black revolutionaries. In the following decade, there was an upsurge in nationalist activity around the question of oppressed nations within the borders of the United States. Several major organizations were formed or reached the height of their activity during this period. These organizations engaged in every aspect of struggle against the United States in efforts to end the hundreds of years of colonial rule over their respective nations and have met with enormous repression. They include: the Provisional Government of the Republic of New Afrika, a black organization founded in 1968 to seek five southern states for a New Afrikan national territory; the Black Liberation Army (BLA), a clandestine political/military organization, which was most active during this period; the American Indian Movement (AIM), which occupied Wounded Knee for seventy-one days in 1973 and demanded sovereignty of its national territories; the Movimiento de Liberación Nacional Puertorriqueño (MLN-PR), founded in 1977, and the Fuerzas Armadas de Liberación Nacional (FALN), founded in 1974, both of which were formed to seek independence for Puerto Rico.

This rise of nationalist organizations coincided with two essential dimensions of imprisonment within the United States. First, the imprisonment rate, which had been constant at about 100 prisoners per every 100,000 population since 1925, began to rise dramatically. This rise, which started in 1972, has resulted in a massive increase of the U.S. prison population.

Second, this period of nationalist activity led to a sharp increase in the number of political prisoners. As these nationalist organizations intensified their struggles, the state intensified its repression and brutality. But it was not only members of oppressed nations who became political prisoners. North American anti-imperialists acted in solidarity with these nationalist struggles and in pursuit of their own visions of a new society. In addition, religious communities began a series of attacks on nuclear weapons that eventually grew into the Ploughshares movement and generated many other North American political prisoners. There are currently over 100 political prisoners, and their sentences are longer than ever before. Whereas in the past, most political prisoners were sentenced to a few years, they are now receiving sentences of thirty years and more, and in some cases as many as several lifetimes! We are thus looking at a situation in which many political people will spend the rest of their lives in prison—unless we do something about it. And, gradually, people are beginning to do something about it.

In the past couple of years, significant efforts have been made to support political prisoners in the United States. These efforts include: the defense work to free Puerto Rican political prisoners and prisoners of war; the work that eventually freed Dhoruba Bin Wahad and the New York 8; the continuing efforts to free Leonard Peltier, the Native American leader; Mumia Abu-Jamal, who is facing the death penalty; and Geronimo ji Jaga (Pratt),* the Black Panther leader who was one of the longest-held political prisoners in the world; and the work of the Ploughshares movement, the antinuclear movement; and the draft resistance movement.

---

* Ed.: Geronimo ji Jaga (Pratt) was released in 1997 after twenty-seven years in prison when a judge ruled that he was convicted based on perjured testimony and police / DA misconduct.

Those of us who are concerned with social justice must be concerned with prisons and political prisoners in this country. We cannot demonstrate and agitate only for the freedom of [apartheid] South African and Salvadoran political prisoners; we also must agitate for the freedom of Leonard Peltier, Susan Rosenberg, and the many others the United States has imprisoned.*

We believe that a fundamental restructuring of society is necessary. In the course of pursuing such a restructuring, some will go to prison. They must be supported—one and all. Political prisoners are not just virtuous and courageous people. They are representatives of movements, and when we fight for political prisoners, we are fighting for those movements. We believe that many progressive people have refused to recognize the importance of political prisoners and that they have made this mistake most often and most intensely when the question of political violence is involved. In the 1960s, many people were willing to defend black revolutionaries who were being framed or attacked, but once they began to fight back, many of their supporters disappeared. Other examples abound.

When Puerto Rican Nationalists rose up against the United States in an effort to gain their independence in 1950 during the Grito de Jayuya, the United States responded with incredible brutality, strafing towns by air, murdering many independentistas, imprisoning over 3,000 of them, and generally repressing the entire nation. In response to this massacre, and in an effort to call international attention to the continuing colonization of Puerto Rico, Oscar Collazo and Griselio Torresola attacked President Harry Truman's residence in Washington, D.C. Torresola was killed during the attack. The Communist Party wrote that its members were shocked by the Puerto Ricans' action and issued a statement condemning all acts of violence and terrorism. They labeled the attack on Truman as an act by "terrorists, deranged men . . . or agents." How interesting, then, that the nation of Puerto Rico regards these men as national heroes.

---

* Ed.: See *Can't Jail the Spirit* or Amnesty International reports for listing of U.S. political prisoners.

When William Morales was captured in 1978, during his trial he became the first person to take a prisoner-of-war position in a U.S. court. He escaped, fled to Mexico, and was arrested by Mexican authorities. He was called a "terrorist" and an "ultra-leftist" by the *Guardian* newspaper, which certainly did not work for his freedom. Yet a mass campaign in Mexico called him a political prisoner and a freedom fighter. In 1988, the Mexican government refused to extradite him; Cuba gave him political asylum. Many progressive people appreciate the fact that Assata Shakur is free.[1] They read *Assata: An Autobiography,* and proclaim her freedom. All of this is, of course, wonderful. What is not so wonderful is that virtually no one has stepped forward to defend Sekou Odinga, Mutulu Shakur, Silvia Baraldini (repatriated as a prisoner to Italy in 1999), and Marilyn Buck, who are in prison for freeing Assata Shakur. In fact, often the left attacks these people for being militarist or ultra-left.

There are dozens of other examples like this, but our purpose here is not to engage in polemics or to attack other organizations. We do not want to minimize the role that others will play in work around political prisoners—we want to maximize the role. But we do think that it must be made clear how the progressive movement in this country traditionally has responded to political prisoners in order to point out how that response must change. One purpose of this chapter is to bring more attention to political incarceration in the United States. We take up this question of political violence because it is here that much division takes place. Amnesty International, for example, will not declare as a political prisoner anyone who has engaged in armed struggle. And, as noted earlier, many others have a similar view. Our position is that we support all political prisoners and demand freedom for all of them. We believe such a position is the only principled one.

The question of political prisoners must always be prominent on the agenda of all of our movements. If we do not stand side by side with our comrades and colleagues when they are taken prisoner, then what does this say to the prisoners and to all those who might dare to struggle in the future? And what does it say to the U.S. government that would so badly like to incarcerate all those whom it perceives to be a threat? Many of us know and understand this, but not enough of us act on this understanding. We hope that you will become involved: Contact prisoners' rights organizations to invite them to speak to your unions, women's groups, churches, house parties; write to political prisoners and POWs; and start your own work around political prisoners.

NOTES

An unedited version of this chapter first appeared as "Prisons as Concentration Camps: It Can't Happen Here—Or Can It?" in *Can't Jail the Spirit* (Chicago: Editorial El Coqui, 1992); this version is excerpted and edited from Elihu Rosenblatt, ed., *Criminal Injustice* (Boston: South End Press, 1996).

1. Assata Shakur was targeted as the alleged leader of the Black Liberation Army and was wounded and arrested in 1973 after a New Jersey State Trooper shot at the occupants in a car in which she was traveling. She was tried seven times, found not guilty six times, and finally convicted and sent to prison for life plus thirty-three years. In 1979 she escaped from the Clinton prison in New Jersey. See Assata Shakur, *Assata: An Autobiography* (Chicago: Lawrence Hill, 1987) and Lennox Hind's introduction to the autobiography.

TWENTY-FIVE

It's Time to Bring Our Political Prisoners Home

DONNA WILLMOTT

Defense of our political prisoners, and a serious campaign to win their release, should be at the heart of our attempt to build a broad movement against increasing state repression. Far from being a peripheral issue taken on by a small circle of loyal supporters, it informs the very nature of the movement we are trying to create. As conditions deteriorate further in this country, there will be new waves of resistance and more political imprisonment. From the nonviolent civil disobedience of those who occupied the School of the Americas in Fort Benning, Georgia, to the militant demonstrations and strikes like those that rocked Puerto Rico in 1998, political imprisonment will be part of the price that will be paid for standing up against injustice.*

More than 100 women and men currently are incarcerated in the United States for their politics, a fact that our government consistently

---

* Ed.: For information on the School of the Americas (SOA) and the incarceration of Christian or faith-based peace activists who have attempted to close it, see Mary A. Fisher, "Teaching Torture," *GQ* (June, 1997).

denies. Many of them are in their second or third decade of incarceration. Most of them are in prison because they were active in the movements of the 1960s and 1970s, when a high tide of liberation movements shaped the world and moved history forward with a vision of a different way we might inhabit this planet.

Leonard Peltier stood up for Native American sovereignty and has been in prison since 1976 for a crime he did not commit at Pine Ridge (South Dakota) reservation.[1] Fifteen Puerto Rican women and men exercised their right to anti-colonial struggle to win independence for their nation. Most had or have been in prison for over eighteen years for "seditious conspiracy," some serving, in effect, life sentences.[2] The New York 3 (Jalil Muntaquin, Herman Bell, and Nuh Washington) survived COINTELPRO's (the counterintelligence program of the Federal Bureau of Investigation) murder of nearly thirty members of the Black Panther Party; went underground; and were captured, framed, and given life sentences for a crime they did not commit.[3] Marilyn Buck acted in solidarity with the black liberation struggle and was convicted of aiding in the escape (in which no one was injured) of Assata Shakur from a New Jersey prison in 1979. She is serving eighty years in prison.

These political prisoners share an understanding of the violently racist, class-based system we live in and the nature of the state that protects it. And they actively resisted what they saw happening before their eyes.

Political prisoners—their trials, the way they conducted themselves while in prison—have had a profound influence on my life from the earliest days of my political involvement. The trials of the Panther 21 in New York City and of Angela Davis in California in the 1970s challenged me to actively support the struggle for black self-determination. At the same time, they demonstrated the lengths to which the state would go in order to crush those who challenge it. But in the dynamic tension between fear of repression and identification with those who stood up to power, the resisters moved me, won my heart. My disaffection and alienation from dominant white culture became a path of militant, collective resistance. Joining an active struggle for justice was an affirmation. I knew the kind of world I wanted for myself and my children as well as for the rest of humanity.

The arrest of the eleven Puerto Rican independentistas in Evanston, Illinois, on April 4, 1980, deeply affected the course of my life. As a member of a colonizing nation who opposed that colonial relationship, I chose to support those who took up arms against it. This led me on a complex journey that included ten years underground and two years in prison, stemming from the "conspiracy to escape" case brought against Puerto Rican independence leader Oscar López, Kojo Bomani, and other political activists.

Before going to the women's prison in Dublin, California, I had known the female political prisoners there only by reputation—four Puerto Ricans, imprisoned for two decades for their actions to win independence for their island: Carmen Valentín, Dylcia Pagán, Lucy and Alicia Rodríguez (all four were released in 1999 through presidential clemency), and three North American anti-imperialists: Marilyn Buck, who is in her nineteenth year of imprisonment, Linda Evans, now in her fifteenth year of incarceration, and Laura Whitehorn, released in August 1999 after years of imprisonment. Even though I had not known them before, I felt an immediate bond based on a shared experience, a shared history. It was a privilege to know them as real people and not only as symbols, because the humanness of the struggle to survive all those years in prison became more real to me. In spite of the differences that exist among them, they are tied by their commitment to a different kind of world and their willingness to give up their freedom in order to make that dream real. They have given up their ability to have a "normal" life with their families and communities, their chance of making it in a system in which they easily could have gained a piece of the pie.

All of the Puerto Rican political prisoners I knew were separated from their young children at the time of their arrest and were unable to raise them. Dylcia did not see her son Guillermo for many years because he was living in Mexico with an adoptive family; he did not become aware of his true identity until he was a teenager. One of my greatest joys while in Dublin was to watch them rebuild their relationship when Guillermo moved to California for two years to be near her. Lucy and Alicia and Carmen all were deprived of the ability to raise their children themselves.

As any incarcerated parent will tell you, separation from one's child is the most difficult part of prison life. Even though my separation from my young daughter was only for a couple of years and I was fortunate to see her often, the loss of that time with her was the most painful part of that experience for me. I am now consciously grateful for things that I had taken for granted before, like putting her to sleep at night or being able to be with her when she is sick.

The other North American women political prisoners at Dublin did not have children at the time of their arrest, but their long sentences have, in all likelihood, denied them the possibility of having children.

It is of enormous significance that there are so many women political prisoners in the United States. When women step out of the bounds set for us by this society and actively pursue our role as agents for social change, we ourselves are changed, and our movements are in turn affected. The women of this generation who are taking their place in the world are not willing to settle for a men-in-control model of activism. They insist on respect and full participation in all processes. Our sisters who are in prison for challenging the state helped break the ground in which that insistence now flowers.

In the case of political prisoners, prison is designed to isolate people not only from their families but from their communities, to lessen their ability to organize and influence. While I was in the company of my sisters inside Dublin I came to appreciate the way they had maintained their core political identity in spite of the isolation; they were not victims but women who had made life-affirming choices. Lucy Rodríguez once told me that when she was arrested, she and her sister Alicia promised each other that no matter how long they were in prison, they would use it "as a crucible," as a way to grow with their people. The independentistas' abiding faith in the Puerto Rican people, their sense that "history will insist itself," carries them through this experience with a strength that moves me deeply.

Of course, long-term incarceration does take a toll on people; it would be foolish to argue that it does not. But it is notable that so many political prisoners have been in prison for decades without breaking, but rather maintaining their commitment and their clarity about who they are and what they stand for.

Prison is designed to break the human spirit; it tears families apart and burdens children with an incalculable loss. Many people in my generation are confronting the issues of aging parents and parental loss.

For political prisoners who are looking at their second or third decade in prison, the loss of parents is especially cruel. Herman Bell, one of the New York 3 who has been in prison for twenty-four years, writes:

> In 1995, when my mother became gravely ill, I was not allowed to visit her sick bed, to hold her hand, to ease her pain. And later that year when she passed away, my keepers gave me a ten-minute phone call to learn of her final words from my siblings. Given these long years of being locked down, having to fight each day of them on one level or another, nothing caused me more pain than the passing of my momma and me being unable to look upon her face or hold her hand one final time. She and I had made big plans for when I got out, going fishing at the reservoir was at the top of our list. . . . She had no direct hand in shaping my politics, but her strength of character, gentle spirit, wisdom and easy laughter had much to do with making me the person I am today, and I miss her so.

The U.S. government's strategy has remained consistent in regard to political prisoners. Like the Latin American governments that "disappeared" their political opponents by killing them, the United States has sought to "disappear" its political prisoners and the history of resistance that they represent. The United States insists that it holds no political prisoners, that they are criminals or terrorists—part and parcel of a mythology that there are no human rights violations here, no social conflict that stems from profound social inequalities.

The collective amnesia that characterizes our national culture allows us to acclaim Nelson Mandela as an international hero while we forget that he spent twenty-seven years in prison for using arms to try to overthrow apartheid—a charge remarkably similar to that of the Puerto Rican independentistas. There is not a country in the world that has not had political prisoners during periods of intense political upheaval, and the defense of political prisoners always has been a critical part of sustaining a resistance. In Ireland, South Africa, Palestine—everywhere in the world where people have struggled for freedom, the demand for the release of political prisoners has been a central demand in the process of resolving those conflicts.

Some of our prisoners were clearly victims of frame-ups, targeted by COINTELPRO for neutralization because of their leadership capabilities, as in the cases of Geronimo ji Jaga (Pratt) and Leonard Peltier. Others were captured while taking actions outside the law to bring about a fundamental change in our society, answering to a higher law, such as United Nations Resolution 1514, which states that colonialism is a crime and that colonial subjects have a right to bear arms to abolish it.

Individual "guilt" or "innocence" of any political prisoner is not the essential issue here. Whatever the particular reason for their incarceration, they are all in prison because of their insistence on speaking truth to power, their refusal to sit by while their people were being destroyed, their willingness to take the risks necessary to bring about profound social change.

The women and men we speak of today represent some of the best qualities in our movements: the kind of courage that allows a village of women and children in Chiapas, Mexico, to form a human chain to turn back military tanks, just a few days after the 1997 massacre in Acteal. The voice from Attica that says "We are men, we are not beasts and we will not be driven as such." The voice that tells us that we need our collective courage to face down a system bent on our destruction. We know that courage and sacrifice in themselves do not a revolution make. But without a willingness to sacrifice, we will never have a chance. This is why we need to claim our prisoners, loud and clear; not to romanticize them or make them larger than life, but to connect them to that part of ourselves that struggles against cynicism and passivity. When one of us acts with integrity and courage, it enables others of us to do the same. Those who refuse to comply with injustice are changed, and so is the movement they are part of.

There is, of course, always a price to this ticket, and our comrades who have spent decades in prison for their politics deserve our deepest respect and support for having paid it. They need to know that we are committed to winning their release, that we are not resigned to their incarceration. When people are willing to risk their individual freedom for our collective freedom, they need to know that they and their families will be supported. We need each other to sustain ourselves through the repression that is an inevitable part of any process of deep and genuine social change.

I was fortunate to be present when Geronimo was welcomed home by the people of Oakland after twenty-seven years in prison for a crime he did not commit. The depth of feeling in the crowd was overwhelming as people came forward to honor this brother who came out of prison with such a strong spirit and a generous heart after doing that kind of hard time. We honored Geronimo, not only as an individual but for what he stands for—a vision of liberation, of a different world for our children. The sweetness of that victory is something we should never forget. It was so long fought for, by Geronimo, his family, his legal team, his supporters, who all refused to give up the fight for his release. This should lead us to strengthen our efforts to demand the release of our other comrades who remain inside. We must not celebrate his release without redoubling our efforts to free Mumia Abu-Jamal, Sundiata Acoli, Oscar López, and all the others who have fought for the freedom of their people. We must not only rejoice in Assata's liberation from prison but also must work to bring home our comrades who are charged with enabling her escape.

Supporting political prisoners is not the easiest of undertakings. Our victories are few and far between. Having a friendship with someone in prison means that you share in their imprisonment, in your own way. It is painful to not be able to do more for people we love and respect who remain inside. Yet the things we gain from supportive relationships with our prisoners are precious. My daughter, who was six when I was released from prison, once said, "Mom, I would never want you to go back to prison, but I guess it was kind of a good thing you were there. If you hadn't gone we never would have Lucy and Ali and Marilyn and all of them in our family." She knows what she loves about these women and knows that her life has been greatly enriched by "having them in our family."

Some may argue that putting a lot of resources into support for political prisoners is not a strategic priority . . . it's too marginal an issue without broad-based support . . . it takes resources away from the "many" who are incarcerated and who do not have movements to defend them. These are not contradictory issues. Demanding freedom for imprisoned comrades should not detract from building opposition to state violence but should inform it. Both political prisoners and social prisoners are products of a repressive system. Political prisoners are in prison precisely because they represent the element of conscious resistance to genocide. They are in prison for fighting against the system that locks up 1.8 million of its members and seems to have no reservations about obliterating those forced into the lowest strata of our society. Social prisoners commit many daily acts of rebellion and refusal. But the political prisoners are among those who most clearly address massive incarceration and the need for collective organizing to abolish the prison industry and police abuses.

There are numerous examples of creative organizing within prisons initiated by political prisoners. Many are AIDS activists in prison. While in Dublin, I was able to participate in a walkathon held on the prison compound to raise money for AIDS service organizations on the outside that served women and children and people of color. The walkathon was organized by PLACE, a prisoner-run support organization founded by Linda Evans, an anti-imperialist prisoner. More than 700 women participated, walking the track for four days, raising more than $5,000. The atmosphere on the prison grounds was transformed: For a brief time, community was being built; we voted with our blistered feet to connect with our communities on the outside. We did not have to be removed, passive, cut off. We were there.

Herman Bell recently helped organize a "Victory Gardens Project." Six thousand pounds of food grown by cooperating farmers was harvested by volunteers ranging in age from eight to eighty. It was then distributed by progressive and New Afrikan groups in the black communities in New York, Boston, and New Jersey. Volunteers from all over the country participated in this project designed to address basic community needs.

Perhaps the most compelling reason to support our political prisoners is this: If the state succeeds in criminalizing them, eventually it can criminalize all who struggle for justice. In defending them, we defend ourselves and our ability to fight for fundamental social change. To defend them does not mean agreeing necessarily with every aspect of the strategies they may have used decades ago; it does mean refusing to allow the state to isolate them from us by defining them as "terrorists." It always amazes me that a government that has one of the bloodiest histories on this planet can succeed in defining people like Alejandrina Torres or Mutulu Shakur as a "terrorist." We all know who respects human life here, and it certainly is not the bombers of Hanoi, Baghdad, and Philadelphia (where police killed eleven MOVE members, including children, in 1985).

There are days when we will feel like Sisyphus with his rock. On days like that I remember the women I can count as my friends who continue to do their time with grace and humor and generous spirits. And I ask myself, if they don't give up in those hell holes, how can we? I have known from my experience how precious solidarity is; how it makes all the difference in the world to know your comrades want you home and claim you as their own. Whether it's a letter, some money for commissary, a place for your family to stay when they come to visit you, driving your child out for a visit—these things are precious beyond words. So is the knowledge that there is a continuing movement for your freedom and that it will have the heart to be there till you're home. This is why Jericho 98, the amnesty for political prisoners campaign, is so important: It gives voice on a national level to a long-felt demand to bring our comrades home.

I'd like to close with a poem by Marilyn Buck, a comrade and friend who is one of the most "stand-up" women I have ever known, a person who takes on her life's work with a full heart and who continues to fill my days with gratitude for her existence on this planet.

> **Thirteen Springs**
> had you planted a tree
> to fill the deep well
> of my absence
> that tree would be thirteen
> springs high
> high enough to soothe
> the relentless sun of my
> incarceration
> strong enough to bear
> the weight of children
> who might have been born
> had I not been seized
> from your life in this acid-washed crypt

of perpetual loss
contained by concrete
reinforcements
and high-wired vigilance

but there is no tree
that stands in my place
to harbor birds and changing winds
perhaps someone will plant
a willow a eucalyptus
or even a redwood
any tree that will
in thirteen years more
bear fruit and provide shelter.

NOTES

1. See Jim Messerschmidt, *The Trial of Leonard Peltier* (Boston: South End Press, 1983).
2. Due to an unprecedented level of public support for their release, eleven of the Puerto Rican political prisoners were granted clemency by President Clinton on September 10, 1999. They were welcomed home as national heroes by thousands of supporters.

    For a list of those released see Dirk Johnson, "Puerto Ricans Clinton Freed Leave Prisons," *New York Times,* September 11, 1999, A1. At least four Puerto Rican independentistas who have been incarcerated for decades still remain in prison, as does the Puerto Rican activist José Solis Jordan who was imprisoned in 1999.
3. For information on COINTELPRO, see Ward Churchill and Jim Vander Wall, *Agents of Repression: The FBI's Secret Wars Against the Black Panther Party and the American Indian Movement* (Boston: South End Press, 1990); for information on U.S. political prisoners see *Can't Jail the Spirit: Political Prisoners in the U.S.* (Chicago: Committee to End the Marion Lockdown, 1998; 4th edition). Current prisoners include: Mondo We Langa (David Rice), Ed Poindexter, Veronza Powers, David Gilbert, Ray Luc Levasseur, Jihad Abdul Mumit, and Tom Manning, as well as members of MOVE.

TWENTY-SIX

Earth First! and the FBI

JUDI BARI

"FOR FBI, BACK TO POLITICAL SABOTAGE?"

On May 24 [1990] a car bomb exploded under my seat as I drove through Oakland, California. The attack followed a series of death threats against me and occurred as I was traveling to organize nonviolent protests with Earth First! against overcutting of the redwood forest in northern California. My injuries are painful and severe, and will leave me permanently crippled.

But the unspeakable terrorism of this ordeal did not end there. The Federal Bureau of Investigation (FBI), working with the Oakland police, immediately concluded that I was responsible for the bombing myself. They attempted to charge me with the assassination attempt that nearly took my life.

Within hours after the bombing, they declared that my passenger, Darryl Cherney, and I were the only suspects. They based this on an FBI agent's statement that since the bomb was on the floor in the back seat of the car, we should have seen it, and therefore we knew we were carrying it. Later they admitted that the bomb was hidden well under the seat and could not have been seen. Nonetheless, Mr. Cherney and I were arrested.

During the next eight weeks, the police and the FBI raided my house twice and even pulled finishing nails from my window trim in a vain attempted to link me to nails found in the bomb. Meanwhile, a local newspaper received a letter claiming credit for the bombing. The letter said that the author wanted to kill me for my political activities and described the bomb in such detail that police had to admit that the writer had personal knowledge of it. But instead of searching for the letter's author, the FBI concluded that the letter writer must be my accomplice, and Mr. Cherney and I remained the only suspects.

While I was in the hospital, too weak to respond, the police and FBI carried on a media campaign against me. Using selected leaks and innuendo, they continued to imply my guilt. Yet the filing of charges against me was delayed twice, then finally dropped on July 18 for lack of evidence. In spite of this, the FBI successfully damaged my reputation and discredited the nonviolent movement I was helping to organize.

Political sabotage of this nature is reminiscent of the activities the FBI engaged in during the 1960s under the name COINTELPRO. This program of covert operations was formally suspended in 1971 after the media revealed that the FBI had deliberately disrupted legitimate movements for social change. Congressional investigations established that the FBI's activities included a ten-year secret war against Dr. Martin Luther King, Jr., and court documents show that agents acted improperly in the murders of members of the Black Panther Party and the American Indian Movement. The FBI agent in charge of investigating my case is Richard W. Held, who worked with COINTELPRO. And although COINTELPRO was formally suspended, a former agent, Wesley Swearingen, has said that its activities continue.[*] The FBI admitted at a news conference that one of its agents, Michael Fain, set up Earth First! activists for arrest in Arizona, and it has been widely reported that the bureau spent more than $2 million to infiltrate and disrupt Earth First! Considering this history, it seems wildly improper for the FBI to be conducting any investigation of the bombing attack on me in Oakland.

---

[*] Ed.: For additional information, see M. Wesley Swearingen, *FBI Secrets: An Agent's Exposé* (Boston: South End Press, 1995).

The reaction of the FBI to the bombing was so improper that a coalition of fifty environmental and women's groups, including the Sierra Club, the Audubon Society, and the National Organization for Women, joined Representative Ron Dellums (D-CA) in calling for a congressional investigation. The House Judiciary subcommittee on civil and constitutional rights, headed by Representative Don Edwards of California (D-CA), has agreed to question the FBI about its handling of the case.

Earth First! is not a terrorist organization, although the FBI has done its best to present us as one. If it can succeed in framing and discrediting us, then domestic dissent is not safe from government sabotage. The right to advocate social change without fear of harassment is the cornerstone of a free society. We cannot allow ourselves to be manipulated by police agencies that have no respect for our democratic principles.

KPFA INTERVIEW:
SURVIVING VIOLENCE

SAMI RIEST: How has the bombing affected Redwood Summer? Are things going on as planned?

JUDI BARI: Well, Redwood Summer is going on the way that it was anticipated, and that's pretty amazing because this bomb blast had a lot of effects on us. It knocked out virtually all of our experienced leadership. It didn't just knock me out. Some of the people who have been working on the issues for years who have also been targeted by death threats as well as I have, have been intimidated from being right up there on the front lines. And then of course there's a lot of support going on for me down here, so people who we had expected to be up there working on Redwood Summer are down here working on support for me, and that even includes our legal team. So what happened is in the absence of our experienced leadership, instead of falling apart, a whole group of people have risen to the occasion. There must be twenty people who have come up and just risen to it and assumed leadership positions and are holding it together.

One thing to me that's very impressive is that most of these people are women. This is the feminization of Earth First! Redwood Summer is an almost entirely women-led action. There are women holding the base camp together, there are women holding the actions together, even the attorney team is women.

SR: It must be fairly frustrating for you to be outside of the main action, when you were one of the main planners in the beginning.

BARI: Yeah, it really is. It's very hard. It's not the way I had planned to spend my summer. I unfortunately recognize the fact that this bombing has galvanized people and increased support for Redwood Summer. People who were thinking about it casually and maybe would and maybe wouldn't, have showed up and were so outraged by the bombing that they vowed to do it. But it sure wasn't any price I had intended to pay, and it's not fun, that's for sure.

SR: So how are you doing, health-wise? Are you feeling like you're recovering well?

BARI: Yeah, actually apparently I'm recovering way ahead of schedule. They just took me out of traction two weeks early. The problem is I'm really in constant pain and it's a long, hard road. Even though I'm out of traction now, not only can I not walk, I can't sit. So it's not like I can just, y'know, jump into a wheelchair and start zipping around. I have a lot of physical therapy to go before I can do anything like that. I can't get a straight answer out of anybody as to how long that's expected to take, or even what exactly is going to be involved. The only thing they'll say is that it's going to be painful, and I think I already know that, 'cause it's been pretty painful so far.

SR: Have you been, in the last while at least, left fairly much alone by the police and the FBI, or are they still coming by?

BARI: I've had no contact from the police at all here. However, they've been up where I live. They've been home harassing my family, and they've raided my house twice and the last time that they raided it they took finishing nails out of the window trim. They're really grasping at straws apparently. I don't think I need to say on KPFA, I think the listeners are perfectly aware of my absolute innocence. I have a twenty-year history as a nonviolent organizer, and I didn't suddenly turn into a bomb thrower. And I'm certainly not stupid enough to put a bomb under my own car seat and blow myself up. I think it's pretty preposterous that I'm being charged with this, that they're saying I'm the only suspect.

This is the second assassination attempt on me in ten months, and that's pretty scary. The last one was really the most violent thing that had ever happened to me in my life. I got run off the road by a logging truck. Karen Silkwood style. The guy just sped up and kept going. My car was moving at the time, and he overtook me and rammed me without hitting his brakes. It was a horrible, violent impact and my car sailed through the air and crashed. But the bombing was twenty times worse. I mean, there's just no describing how awful it felt, and just the horrificness of being blown up by a bomb is not something I can describe in words. And not only having to go through the physical pain and the psychological terror of having this done, but then on top if this, to have somebody trying to frame me and blame me for it and making no effort whatsoever to find out who these assassins are really makes it a lot worse. It really adds a whole other dimension to it, and it's real difficult to go through this.

SR: Do you still fear that someone might try to get you while you're in the hospital here?

BARI: I feel fairly secure here in the hospital. The hospital recognizes my security needs and allows me to have somebody here twenty-four hours a day. I'm too scared to go home. I feel like I need to, because this is really going to be quite an ordeal to recover from this on many levels. And I need to be where my support system is, and that's home. I also have two small children that need their mom. So I feel a very strong need to go home, and I'm scared to death to go home. The police in Mendocino County, over the last year or so, have been encouraging violence against Earth First!ers by refusing to arrest or prosecute people who punch us, shoot at us, and now even bomb us. The message that they've given very clearly in Mendocino County is that it's open season on Earth First!ers, and it's OK to attack Earth First!ers in general and me in particular, and that you won't be apprehended.

I think we were incredibly naive. When I look back over the events leading up to this, it's really surprising to me that I wasn't more careful, and that I didn't realize that something awful was about to happen. I guess this is still white, middle-class privilege. They don't do this to white people. They do this to Black Panthers, they do this to the American Indian Movement, but the idea of using a car bomb on an environmental organizer is fairly unprecedented, and I had never anticipated this level of violence. People in other places certainly live under much greater threats than this. I mean, look at the Salvadorans who continue to fight in spite of the death threats and the death squads. If they can do it, we can do it. But we're going to have to face the way it is now in this movement.

SR: It's interesting. As I look around the room, I can see you're obviously getting a tremendous outburst of support.

BARI: It's been really phenomenal, and I have to say it's kept me going. Last year when I got run off the road by the logging truck, I reached deep down inside myself and found the courage to go on. It wasn't easy. It took me about a month to make the decision that I would go on. And then this year, immediately preceding this bomb blast, I was subjected to a very frightening death threat campaign, and I had to do the same thing. I had to reach down inside myself and find the resources to go on. This time when I reached down inside myself, there wasn't anything there. I wasn't able to go on by myself. I spent a couple of weeks without much of a will to live and acting very passive about the whole thing, and it was the outpouring from the movement that gave me that will to go on.

SR: Are there any other things that you feel you would like to say?

BARI: I guess I'd like to talk a little about what I've learned being here in this hospital bed, because it's a real different experience for me. I've never even sprained an ankle before. I know that they've been reading an old interview with me from *New Settler Magazine* over KPFA, and in that interview one of the things that I talk about is my opinion of men, and that I basically don't have much hope for them based on my experience. I said no matter how far you go with men, eventually you're going to get down to a point where their misogyny is going to show. That had been my personal experience in relationships. One of the things that I've learned in this hospital room is that there is such a thing as nurturing men. There's been some incredible men who've come in here, and I have met enough people now that I have really changed my opinion and I no longer think that there's no hope for men. I think that there is a new kind of man that is coming out in the movement [and] that we can build a new society based on different kinds of relationships with men and women. So my opinion that there's no hope for relationships with men and women has changed based on some of the incredibly nurturing men who have come into my hospital room and helped me and held my hand when I cried and just offered themselves in a way that I thought only women would do. So that's one of the lessons I've learned here.

SR: What about the future, what are your plans? Do you look that far forward or are you just going day to day right now?

BARI: It's really hard. I feel like I'm a public person this summer, whether I want to be or not. So I think it would be futile for me to say I'm going to retreat this summer because especially with the FBI trying to frame me in this case, and my involvement in Redwood Summer, I think it's foolish for me to try to be a private person right now. But I do feel eventually I'm going to have to take a break away from public life and take some time with my children and take some time to heal my body and my spirit from what's been done to me, because in addition to the fact that my body has been broken, if I recover fully at all it will be a very long time I have to live with this constant reminder of this. It's a real change for me having always been strong and all of a sudden to find myself very limited, and at best they say I'm going to be able to eventually walk with a brace in my shoe. To which I reply, you mean I have to wear shoes? But I don't really know the extent of my recovery with Western medicine.

That's another thing I've learned in this hospital is that Western medicine knows how to cut you up and sew you back together, but they don't know a thing about healing. The alternative healing communities have been just as incredible to me as the nurturing men. I mean, the things that I've learned from them is that there are other ways to heal ourselves. The other thing they've taught me is that they consider themselves and their alternative healing methods to be part of the same movement that we're in with our ecological and social justice issues.

So I don't know what the extent of my recovery is, but I know that it's going to be long and difficult, and I think that I'm going to have to take some private time probably in the fall, just to go back and—because in addition to these physical injuries I've been really terrorized to the depths of my soul. It's hard to describe that, but I know it's going to take a long time to get back the confidence that I used to have and it's a really frightening thing to have people try to kill you and it's an even more frightening thing to have them nearly succeed. They actually did nearly succeed. I came really close to dying, and it's going to be a long, hard road back. So I think after the summer you probably won't hear much from me for awhile while I recover. Hopefully after that recovery, I'll be able to come back strong again and be in the movement again.

SR: Well I know most of the people out there listening are really hoping that too.

BARI: Being here and being subjected to this terrorism, I've had to do a lot of soul-searching. It took me awhile even to face it. I was unable to sleep for a long time, because I was afraid to sleep. I was afraid to face what my subconscious had in it. So I've had to do a lot of thinking about violence and nonviolence and terrorism and things like that. I met Brian Willson one week before this happened, and at the time I had a discussion with him and I told him that I considered nonviolence to be the only appropriate tactic in our country at this time, but that I considered it only a tactic.[*] I wasn't a Gandhian who considered

---

[*] Ed.: Peace activist Brian Willson lost his legs at a protest on railroads at Concord, California Naval Weapons Station in 1989. The train, carrying a nuclear weapon, severed the legs of Willson who was lying across the tracks to stop the shipment.

nonviolence to be the only way ever. I would never tell a Salvadoran to use nonviolence only. And Brian gave me an answer that has played out in my mind a thousand times since then. He said, "Your belief in nonviolence as a tactic only will not be enough to sustain you through the hatred you're going to experience this summer." So that one has really gone through me a lot of times. I realize that the person who ran me off the road with the logging truck last summer, I wouldn't have used this word, but I guess that I could say I forgave him in that I saw that he was a victim who took his anger out on the wrong person. I could see that about him. They hauled him out of his truck and made him confront me, and I could see that he was horrified at what he had done. When he saw that my children were in the car too, he kept saying "The children, the children, I didn't see the children." But the person who bombed me was a monster. I've been unable to understand him. I've been unable to understand somebody who would deliberately and coldly, premeditatedly place something like that in my car with the intent to kill me. Knowing who I was and knowing that I have small children and that I'm their sole support, and certainly their emotional support as well as physical support. And what I realized about myself, I never really thought of myself as a Gandhian, I still don't actually because I'm just not that pious. But what I realized is that if you gave me the same bomb, and you gave me the person's car who did this to me, I don't have it in me to do that back to him. What I have discovered is that there's a level of violence, there's a level of terrorism that's really unacceptable to me, and I think that's one of the things that we really need to change in the world. The existence of this kind of violence in the world and this kind of terrorism, this is part of the problem. The same mentality that would level a redwood forest and destroy its ability to regenerate, this is the same mentality that would place this bomb in my car and would do this kind of violence to me. I think that the problem isn't just the economic system, isn't just the social relations, I think that part of the problem is the violence in the society. Violence against humans and violence against the Earth. That's the lesson that this has really taught me.

NOTE

These excerpts are taken from *Timber Wars* (Common Courage Press) by environmental activist Judi Bari. The first section originally appeared in Bari's August 23, 1990, *New York Times* Op-Ed; and the second section stems from an excerpted transcript of a July 5, 1990, KPFA (Pacifica) radio interview, conducted at Highland Hospital in the Bay Area by Sami Riest, while Bari was recovering from injuries sustained in the car bombing. Judi Bari died from breast cancer seven years after the bombing.

CONTRIBUTORS

Judi Bari was a founder of and key organizer in Earth First! and is author of *Timber Wars*.

Joanne Belknap, an associate professor in Sociology and Women's Studies at the University of Colorado-Boulder, researches and teaches about violence against women and girls and female offenders. She is the author of *The Invisible Woman*, an overview of females in the criminal processing system.

Lee Bernstein teaches in the American Studies Program at the University of Colorado-Boulder and is the author of *The Greatest Menace: Organized Crime in Cold War America*.

Angela Y. Davis teaches at the University of California at Santa Cruz in the History of Consciousness program. Her books include *Angela Davis: An Autobiography; Women, Race & Class;* and *Blues Legacies and Black Feminism*.

Juanita Díaz-Cotto is a black, Puerto Rican, lesbian, feminist socialist, editor (under the pseudonym of Juanita Ramos) of *Compañeras: Latina Lesbians (an Anthology)* and author of *Gender, Ethnicity and the State: Latina and Latino Prison Politics*. She is an associate professor of Sociology, Women's Studies, and Latin American and Caribbean Studies at the State University of New York at Binghamton.

Larvester Gaither is editor and publisher of the Houston-based *Gaither Reporter,* a quarterly that focuses on African American politics and literature.

David Theo Goldberg, director and professor of the School of Justice Studies at Arizona State University, is the author of *Racist Culture* and *Racial Subjects*. He is also editor of *Anatomy of Racism* and *Multiculturalism: A Critical Reader* and the coeditor of *Jewish Identity*.

Steven Hawkins is an attorney and the executive director of the National Coalition to Abolish the Death Penalty, based in Washington, D.C.

Hussein Ibish, a doctoral candidate in comparative literature at the University of Massachusetts-Amherst, is communications director for the American-Arab Anti-Discrimination Committee (ADC). As a freelance journalist, he has written extensively on Arab issues and provided commentary on the Middle East for CNN, MSNBC, NPR, and Pacifica.

Joy James is the author of *Resisting State Violence; Transcending the Talented Tenth;* and *Shadowboxing: Representations of Black Feminist Politics,* and the editor of the *Angela Y. Davis Reader.*

José López is the executive director of the Juan Antonio Corretjer Puerto Rican Cultural Center in Chicago and teaches at Northeastern Illinois University and Columbia College.

David A. Love is the producer of Pacifica Radio's daily news magazine, "Democracy Now!" He is also co-producer of the 1997 television documentary "Disorderly Conduct: Are the Police Killing Us?" A regular contributor to the Progressive Media Project, Love has written articles for the *Washington Post* and *Emerge* magazine, and has appeared as a guest commentator on MSNBC and BBC Radio.

Manning Marable is director of the Institute for Research in African American Studies at Columbia University; he is author of numerous publications including *Black Leadership Politics.*

Gary T. Marx is a sociologist who has published numerous articles on policing and surveillance in the United States. He is author of *Undercover: Police Surveillance in America* and coeditor of *Undercover: Police Surveillance in Comparative Perspective.*

Marc Mauer is the assistant director of the Washington, D.C.–based Sentencing Project and author of *Race to Incarcerate.*

Robert Meeropol is the founder and executive director of the Rosenberg Fund for Children, a public foundation that provides for the educational and emotional needs of children whose parents have been targeted due to their progressive activities.

Salim Muwakkil is a senior editor at *In These Times* and a columnist for the *Chicago Tribune.* His work examines the lack of media coverage regarding social services provided by Chicago area gangs that have a political economy primarily based on the drug trade.

Anthony Papa became a renowned artist while serving twelve years of a fifteen to life sentence in New York's Sing Sing prison for a non-violent drug charge. While imprisoned Papa earned degrees in behavioral science, theology, and paralegal studies. His paintings creatively show the impact of arrest, incarceration, and confinement and are currently exhibited in various galleries as well as a number of catalogues and websites.

Margaret Ratner is president of the William Kunstler Fund for Racial Justice, and co-author of the book *Representing Witnesses Before Federal Grand Juries.* She practices criminal law in New York City.

Michael Ratner is a human rights attorney and vice-president of the Center for Constitutional Rights. He is coauthor of *Che Guevara and the FBI* and *International Human Rights Litigation in U.S. Courts.*

Brenda Rodriguez has done extensive reports on HIV, AIDS, and sexual violence in prisons in the Southwest. She is a reporter for *The Dallas Morning News.*

AnnJanette Rosga, an assistant professor of Sociology and Anthropology at Knox College in Galesburg, Illinois, is co-author of a study guide for *Licensed to Kill,* Arthur Dong's documentary about perpetrators of antigay violence.

Luana Ross is an enrolled member of the Salish and Kootenai tribes. Associate professor in Women's Studies and Sociology at the University of Washington, Seattle, her publications include *Inventing the Savage: The Social Construction of Native American Criminality.*

Julie A. Su is a civil rights attorney with the Los Angeles–based Asian Pacific American Legal Center. She represented Thai and Latino workers in the first U.S. federal case for corporate accountability in the garment industry.

Alexandra Suh is a graduate student of English at Columbia University. Her research examines Asian women in local and global contexts. Suh works with the Rainbow Center in Queens, New York.

Eric Tang, a graduate student in American Studies at New York University, directs the Youth Leadership Project of the Committee Against Anti-Asian Violence (CAAAV), which seeks to develop Southeast Asian youths to become organizers for social change.

Gabriel Torres, a long-time community organizer, is a former political prisoner who was active in the Young Lords Party and the Black Liberation Army.

Daniel R. Williams, an attorney for Mumia Abu-Jamal, specializes in criminal and civil rights litigation, including death penalty post-conviction appeals.

Donna Willmott is a former political prisoner incarcerated for her activities in support of the Puerto Rican independence movement. She has been an activist for thirty years and currently works with Legal Services for Prisoners with Children in San Francisco.

Adrien K. Wing is a professor of law at the University of Iowa College of Law where she teaches critical race theory, constitutional law, and comparative law. She is editor of *Critical Race Feminism: A Reader* and author of numerous publications.

SELECTED BIBLIOGRAPHY
OF CITED WORKS

Abu-Jamal, Mumia. *Live from Death Row.* New York: Addison-Wesley, 1995.

Adler, Freda. *Sisters in Crime: The Rise of the New Female Criminal.* New York: McGraw Hill, 1975.

American Correctional Association. *The Female Offender: What Does the Future Hold?* Arlington, VA: Kirby Lithographic Company, 1990.

Amnesty International Report, *United States of America: Police Brutality and Excessive Force in New York City Police Department.* Washington, DC: AMI, 1996.

Amnesty International, Rights for All. *Not Part of My Sentence: Violations of the Human Rights of Women in Custody.* New York: Amnesty International, March 1999.

Amnesty International. *United States of America: The Death Penalty and Juvenile Offenders.* London: Amnesty International, October 1991.

Arnold, R. "Processes of Victimization and Criminalization of Black Women," *Social Justice* 17 no. 3 (fall 1990): 153-166.

Baldus, D. et al. "Race Discrimination and the Death Penalty in the Post-Furman Era: An Empirical and Legal Overview, with Preliminary Findings from Philadelphia." *Cornell Law Review* 83 (September 1998): 1638-1770.

Baskin, Deborah et al. "The Political Economy of Female Violent Street Crime," *Fordham Urban Law Journal* 20 (spring 1993): 401.

Baum, Dan. *Smoke and Mirrors: The War on Drugs and the Failure of Politics.* New York: Little, Brown and Company, 1996.

Beck, Allen J. and Peter M. Brien. "Trends in U.S. Correctional Populations: Recent Findings from the Bureau of Justice Statistics." In Kenneth C. Haas and Geoffrey P. Alpert. *The Dilemmas of Corrections.* Prospect Heights, IL: Waveland Press, 1995.

Belknap, Joanne. *The Invisible Woman: Gender, Crime, And Justice.* Belmont, CA: Wadsworth, 1996.

Bello, Walden. "From American Lake to a People's Pacific." In Saundra Pollock Sturdevant and Brenda Stoltzfus, eds. *Let the Good Times Roll: Prostitution and the U.S. Military in Asia.* New York: New Press, 1992.

Berry, Mary F. *Black Resistance, White Law: A History of Constitutional Racism in America.* New York: Penguin Books, 1994.

Binkley-Jackson, D., V. L. Carter, and G. L. Rolison. "African-American Women in Prison." In B. R. Fletcher, L. D. Shaver and D. B. Moon, eds. *Women Prisoners: A Forgotten Population.* Westport, CT: Praeger, 1993.

Bonilla-Santiago, Gloria. "Legislating Progress for Hispanic Women in New Jersey," *Social Work* 34 no. 3 (May 1989): 270-272.

Boudouris, J. *Prisons and Kids.* College Park, MD: American Correctional Association, 1985.

Bowker, Lee and Malcolm Klein. "Female Participation in Delinquent Gang Activity." *Adolescence* 15 (1980): 509-528.

Bramford, J. *The Puzzle Palace.* New York: Penguin Books, 1983.

Brown, Wendy. *States of Injury: Power and Freedom in Late Modernity.* Princeton, NJ: Princeton University Press, 1995.

Burnham, David. *The Rise of the Computer State.* New York: Random House, 1983.

Burton-Rose, Daniel, Dan Pens, and Paul Wright. *The Celling of America.* Monroe, ME: Common Courage Press, 1998.

Campbell, Anne. "Female Participation in Gangs." In C. Ronald Huff, ed. *Gangs in America.* Newbury Park, CA: Sage Publications, 1990.

Can't Jail the Spirit: Political Prisoners in the U.S., A Collection of Biographies. Chicago: Editorial El Coqui, 1990.

Cardozo-Freeman, I, ed. *Chief: The Life History of Eugene Delorme, Imprisoned Santee Sioux.* Lincoln: University of Nebraska Press, 1993.

Carlen, P. and N. Rodriguez, "Women Under Lock and Key," *The Prison Journal* 63 (1983): 47-65.

Carlen, P. "Women Under Lock and Key." *The Prison Journal* 75 (1995): 186-202.

———. *Women's Imprisonment: A Study In Social Control.* London: Routledge and Kegan Paul, 1983.

Cassidy, Peter. "'Operation Ghetto Storm': The Rise of Paramilitary Policing." *CovertAction Quarterly* 62 (1997): 20-25.

Chandler, Edna Walker. *Women in Prison.* Indianapolis: Bobbs-Merrill, 1973.

Cheng Hirata, Lucie. "Free, Indentured, Enslaved: Chinese Prostitutes in Nineteenth-Century America." *Signs* 5 no. 1 (Autumn 1979): 3-29.

Chesney-Lind, M. "Patriarchy, Prisons, and Jails: A Critical Look at Trends in Women's Incarceration." *The Prison Journal* 71 (1991): 51-67.

Churchill, Ward and Jim Vander Wall. *Agents of Repression: The FBI's Secret Wars Against the Black Panther Party and the American Indian Movement.* Boston: South End Press, 1990.

Cohen, S. "The Punitive City: Notes on the Dispersion of Social Control." *Contemporary Crises* 3 (1979): 339-63.

A Human Rights Watch Report. "Cold Storage: Super-Maximum Security Confinement in Indiana." New York: Human Rights Watch, October 1997.

Curry, G. David et al. "Gang Crime and Law Enforcement Recordkeeping." *National Institute of Justice Research in Brief* (August 1994): 8.

Curry, G. David. "Gang Related Violence." *Clearinghouse Review* (Special Issue 1994): 443, 447.

Deutsch, Michael. "The Improper Use of the Federal Grand Jury: An Instrument for the Internment of Political Activists." *Criminal Law & Criminology* 75 (winter 1984): 1159.

Díaz-Cotto, Juanita. *Gender, Ethnicity, and the State: Latina and Latino Prison Politics.* Albany: State University of New York, 1996.

Dieter, Richard C. *The Death Penalty in Black and White: Who Lives, Who Dies, Who Decides.* Washington, D.C.: The Death Penalty Information Center, 1998.

——. *The Future of the Death Penalty in the United States: A Texas-Sized Crisis.* Washington, DC: Death Penalty Information Center, 1994.

Donziger, Steve, ed. *The Real War on Crime: The Report of the National Criminal Offenders.* New York: Harper Perennial, 1996.

Du Bois, W. E. B. *Black Reconstruction in America.* New York: Harcourt, Brace, 1935.

Dulaney, W. Marvin. *Black Police in America.* Bloomington, IN: Indiana University Press, 1996.

Duran, E. and B. Duran. *Native American Postcolonial Psychology.* Albany: State University of New York Press, 1995.

Erlich, Reese. "Prison Labor: Workin' For the Man." *CovertAction Quarterly* 54 (1992): 58-63.

Faith, Karla. *Unruly Women: The Politics of Confinement and Resistance.* Vancouver, BC: Press Gang Publishers, 1993.

Fischer, Mary A. "Teaching Torture." *GQ* (June 1997): 182-189, 237-240.

Flanagan, L. W. "Meeting the Special Needs of Females in Custody: Maryland's Unique Approach." *Federal Probation* 59 (1995): 49-53.

Flowers, Barri. *The Adolescent Criminal: An Examination of Today's Juvenile Offender.* Jefferson, N.C.: McFarland, 1990.

Foucault, Michel. *Discipline and Punish: The Birth of the Prison.* New York: Vintage, 1979.

Freedman, Estelle. *Their Sisters' Keepers: Women's Prison Reform in America, 1830-1930.* Ann Arbor: University of Michigan, 1981.

Friedheim, William. *Freedom's Unfinished Revolution.* New York: The New Press, 1996.

Garbarino, James. *Raising Children in a Socially Toxic Environment.* San Francisco: Jossey-Bass, 1995.

Giallombardo, Rose. *Society of Women: A Study of a Women's Prison.* New York: John Wiley and Sons, 1966.

Gilfus, M. E. "From Victims to Survivors to Offenders: Women's Routes of Entry and Immersion Into Street Crime." *Women and Criminal Justice* 4 (1992): 63-90.

Gilligan, James. *Violence: Reflections on a National Epidemic.* New York: Random House, 1996.

Glick, R. M. and V. V. Neto, "National Study of Women's Correctional Programs," in B. R. Price and N.J. Sokoloff, eds. *The Criminal Justice System and Women.* New York: Clark and Boardman, 1982.

Goetting, A. and R. M. Howsen, "Women in Prison: A Profile." *The Prison Journal* 63 (1983): 27-46.

Goetting, A. "Racism, Sexism, and Ageism in the Prison Community." *Federal Probation* 49 (1983): 10-22.

Goldberg, David Theo. *Racial Subjects: Writing on Race in America.* New York: Routledge, 1997.

Goldsby, Jacqueline. "The High and Low Tech of It: The Meaning of Lynching and the Death of Emmett Till." *The Yale Journal of Criticism* 9 no. 2 (1996).

Goodwin, G. and L. Humphreys. "Freeze-Dried Stigma: Cybernetics and Social Control." *Humanity and Society* 6 no. 4 (November 1982): 391-408.

T. Gray, L. G. Mays, and M. K. Stohr. "Inmate Needs and Programming in Exclusively Women's Jails." *The Prison Journal* 75 (1995): 186-202.

Grobsmith, E. *Indians in Prison: Incarcerated Native Americans in Nebraska.* Lincoln: University of Nebraska Press, 1994.

Grossmann, M. G. "Two Perspectives on Aboriginal Female Suicides in Custody." *Canadian Journal of Criminology* 34 no. 3 (1992):403-416.

Gwynn, Carolene. "Women and Crime: The Failure of Traditional Theories and the Rise of Feminist Criminology." *Monash University Law Review* 19 (1993): 92.

Hagedorn, John M. "Homeboys, Dope Fiends, Legits, and New Jacks." *Criminology* 32 no. 2 (May 1994).

Haines, Herbert H. *Against Capital Punishment: The Anti-Death Penalty Movement in America, 1972-1994.* New York: Oxford University Press, 1996.

Haney, Craig. "Infamous Punishment: The Psychological Consequences of Isolation." *National Prison Project Journal* (ACLU) (Spring 1993): 23.

Hart, Fiona. "The Construction Of Masculinity In Men's Friendships: Misogyny, Heterosexism, And Homophobia." *Resources For Feminist Research* 19 no. 3-4 (1990): 60-67.

Hawkins, Richard and Geoffrey P. Alpert. *American Prison Systems: Punishment and Justice.* Englewood Cliffs, NJ: Prentice-Hall, 1989.

Heffernan, Esther. *Making it in Prison: The Square, the Cool, and the Life.* New York: John Wiley and Sons, 1972.

Herek, Gregory. "On Heterosexual Masculinity: Some Psychical Consequences of the Social Construction of Gender and Sexuality." *American Behavioral Scientist* 29 no. 5 (1986a): 563-577.

———."The Social Context of Hate Crimes: Notes on Cultural Heterosexism." In Gregory Herek and Kevin Berrill, eds. *Hate Crimes: Confronting Violence Against Lesbians and Gay Men.* London: Sage, 1992.

Hirsch, Arnold. "With or Without Jim Crow: Black Residential Segregation in the United States." In Arnold Hirsch and Raymond Mohl, eds. *Urban Policy in Twentieth Century America.* New Brunswick: Rutgers University Press, 1993.

Human Rights Watch, *Shielded From Justice: Police Brutality and Accountability in the United States.* New York: Human Rights Watch, 1998.

Hyun Sun, Kim. "Conditions Facing Prostitutes in U.S. Military Camptowns." Tongduchon, Korea: Saeumtuh, 1997.

Immarigeon, R. "Women in Prison." *Journal of the National Prison Project,* 11 (1987): 1-5.

Inside the Shadow Government. Declaration of Plaintiffs' Counsel filed by the Christic Institut, U.S. District Court, Miami, Florida, March 31, 1988.

Irwin, John and James Austin. *It's About Time: The Imprisonment Binge.* Belmont, CA: Wadsworth Publishing Co., 1997.

Jacobs, James B. *Stateville: The Penitentiary in Mass Society.* Chicago: University of Chicago Press, 1977.

Johnson, Claire et al. "Prosecuting Gangs: A National Assessment." *National Institute of Justice Research on Brief* (February 1995): 95.

Katz, Michael, ed. *The Underclass Debate: Views From History.* Princeton, NJ: Princeton University Press, 1993.

Klein, Dorie and June Kress. "Any Woman's Blues: A Critical Overview of Women, Crime, and the Criminal Justice System." *Crime & Social Justice* 5 (Spring-Summer 1976): 34-49.

Klein, Malcolm W. *The American Street Gang.* New York: Oxford University Press, 1995.

Kline, S. *Female Offenders: Meeting the Needs of a Neglected Population.* Laurel, MD: American Correctional Association, 1993.

Kruttschnitt, Candace. "Race Relations and the Federal Inmate." *Crime and Delinquency* 29 (October 1983): 577-592.

Lekkerkerker, Eugenia Cornelia. *Reformatories for Women in the United States.* Batavia, Holland: Bij J.B. Wolters' Uitgevers-Maatschappij, 1931.

Leonard, Eileen B. *Women, Crime and Society.* New York: Longman, 1982.

Lewis, Dorothy Otnow. "Neuropsychiatric, Psychoeducational and Family Characteristics of 14 Juveniles Condemned to Death in United States." *American Journal of Psychiatry* 145:5 (May 1988): 584-589.

Lowe, Lisa. *Immigrant Acts.* Durham: Duke University Press, 1996.

Majors, Richard and Janet Mancini Billson. *Cool Pose: The Dilemma of Black Manhood in America.* New York: Lexington Books, 1992.

Mancini, Matthew. *One Dies, Get Another: Convict Leasing in the American South, 1866-1928.* Columbia, South Carolina: University of South Carolina Press, 1996.

Marquart, James W., Sheldon Edland-Olson, Jonathan R. Sorensen. *The Rope, the Chair, and the Needle: Capital Punishment in Texas, 1923-1990.* Austin: The University of Texas Press, 1994.

Martinez Jr., Ramiro. "Latinos and Lethal Policy: The Impact of Poverty and Inequality." *Social Problems* 43 no. 2 (May 1996): 131-45.

Marx, Gary and N. Reichman. "Routinizing the Discovery of Secrets: Computers as Informants." *American Behavioral Scientist* (March 1984): 423-452.

Massey, Douglas and Hajnal Zoltan. "The Changing Geographic Structure of Black-White Segregation in the United States." *Social Science Quarterly* 76 no. 3 (September 1995): 533-4.

Mauer, Marc and Tracy Huling. "Young Black Americans and the Criminal Justice System: Five Years Later." Washington DC: The Sentencing Project, 1995.

Mawby, R. I. "Women in Prison: A British Study." *Crime and Delinquency* 28 (1982): 24-39.

Mello, Michael. *Dead Wrong: A Death Row Lawyer Speaks Out Against Capital Punishment.* Madison: University of Wisconsin Press, 1997.

Merton, Robert. "Social Structure and Anomie." *American Sociological Review* 3 no. 5 (1938): 672-680.

Miller, Jerome G. *Search and Destroy: African American Males in the Criminal Justice System.* Cambridge, U.K.: Cambridge University Press, 1996.

Miller, Walter B. "Lower Class Culture as Generating Milieu of Gang Delinquency," *Journal of Sociology Issues* 14 (1958): 5.

Morris, Ruth R. "Attitudes Toward Delinquency by Delinquents, Non-Delinquents and Their Friends." *British Journal of Criminology* 5 (1965): 249-51.

Myers, Samuel L. Jr. "Crime, Entrepreneurship, and Labor Force Withdrawal." *Contemporary Policy Issues* X no. 2 (April 1992): 84-97.

National Gay and Lesbian Task Force. *Anti-Gay Violence, Victimization, and Defamation in 1986.* Washington, DC: NGLTF, 1987.

O'Shea, Kathleen A. and Beverly R. Fletcher. *Female Offenders: An Annotated Bibliography.* Westport, Ct: Greenwood, 1997.

Oshinsky, David. *Worse Than Slavery: Parchman Farm and the Jim Crow Justice System.* New York: The Free Press, 1996.

Owen, B. and B. Bloom, "Profiling Women Prisoners: Findings From National Surveys and a California Sample." *The Prison Journal* 75 (1995): 165-185.

Owen, Barbara. *"In the Mix": Struggle and Survival in a Women's Prison.* Albany: State University of New York, 1998.

Pollock-Byrne, J. M. *Women, Prison, and Crime.* Pacific Grove, CA: Brooks/ Cole, 1990.

Prendergrast, M. L., J. Wellisch, and G. P. Falkin. "Assessment of Services for Substance-Abusing Women Offenders in Community and Correctional Settings." *The Prison Journal* 75 (1995): 240-256.

Rafter, Nicole Hahn. *Partial Justice: Women in State Prisons, 1800-1935.* Boston: Northeastern University Press, 1985.

Reed, L. R. "Rehabilitation: Contrasting Cultural Perspectives and the Imposition of Church and State." *Journal of Prisoners on Prison* 2 no. 2(1990):3-28.

Reiter, Laura. "Developmental Origins of Antihomosexual Prejudice in Heterosexual Men and Women." *Clinical Social Work Journal* 19 no. 2 (1991): 163-175.

Resnick, J. and N. Shaw, "Prisoners of their sex: Health problems of incarcerated women." In I. P. Robbins, ed. *Prisoners' Rights Sourcebook,* vol. 2. New York: Clark Boardman, 1980. 319-413.

"Resort to International Human Rights Law in Challenging Conditions in U.S. Immigration Detention Centers." *Brooklyn Journal of International Law* 23 (1997): 271.

Rosenblatt, Elihu ed. *Criminal Injustice.* Boston: South End Press, 1996.

Ross, Luana. *Inventing the Savage: The Social Construction of Native American Criminality.* Austin: University of Texas, 1998.

Ross, R. R. and E. A. Fabiano, *Female Offenders: Correctional Afterthoughts.* Jefferson, NC: McFarland, 1986.

Rotman, Edgardo. *Beyond Punishment: A New View on the Rehabilitation of Criminal Offenders.* New York: Greenwood Press, 1990.

Rule, J., D. McAdam, L. Stearns, and D. Uglow. *The Politics of Privacy.* New York: New American Library, 1980.

Sarat, Austin and Thomas R. Kearns. "Making Peace With Violence: Robert Cover on Law and Legal Theory." In A. Sarat and T. Kearns, eds. *Law's Violence.* Ann Arbor: University of Michigan Press, 1995.

Sargent, E., S. Marcus-Mendoza and Yu, C.H. "Abuse and the Woman Prisoner," in eds. B. R Fletcher, Shaver, L.D., and D. B. Moon, *Women prisoners: A Forgotten Population.* Westport, CT: Praeger, 1993.

Sarri, R. "Unequal protection Under the Law: Women and the Criminal Justice System." In Figueira-McDonough and R. Sarri, eds. *The Trapped Woman: Catch-22 in Deviance and Control.* Newbury Park: Sage, 1987.

Seltzer, Richard. "The Social Location of Those Holding Anti-Homosexual Attitudes." *Sex Roles* 26 (1992): 391-98.

Shakur, Assata. *Assata: An Autobiography.* Chicago: Lawrence Hill, 1987.

Shakur, Sanyika. *Monster: The Autobiography of an L.A. Gang Member.* New York: Atlantic Monthly Press, 1993.

Shore, J. H. and S. M. Manson. "Crosscultural Studies of Depression Among American Indians and Alaska Natives." *White Cloud Journal* 2 (1985): 5-11.

Sklar, Morton, ed. *Racial and Ethnic Discrimination in the United States: The Status of Compliance by the U.S. Government with the International Convention on the Elimination of Racial Discrimination.* Washington, D.C.: The Coalition Against Torture and Racial Discrimination, October 1998.

———. *Torture in the United States: The Status of Compliance by the U.S. Government with the International Convention Against Torture and Other Cruel, Inhuman or Degrading Treatment or Punishment.* Washington, D.C.: World Organization Against Torture, October 1998.

Smart, C. *Women, Crime and Criminology: A Feminist Critique.* London: Routledge and Kegan Paul, 1976.

Spergel, Irving A. *The Youth Gang Problem: A Community Approach.* New York: Oxford University Press, 1995.

Spergel, Irving et al. "National Youth Gang Suppression and Intervention Program" *Juvenile Justice Bulletin* 2 (1990): 84.

———. "National Youth Gang Suppression and Intervention Program." *Juvenile Justice Bulletin* 2 Washington, D.C.: U.S. Department of Justice, Office of Juvenile Justice and Delinquency Prevention, 1990.

Streib, V. "Imposing the Death Penalty as Children." In K. Haas, ed. *Challenging Capital Punishment: Legal and Social Science Approaches.* Newbury Park, CA: Sage Publications, 1988.

———. *The Juvenile Death Penalty Today.* (Ada, OH: Claude W., Pettit College of Law 1998). Online: www.law.onu.edu/faculty/streib/juvdeath.htm

Sugar, Fran and Lana Fox. "Nistum Peyako Seht'wawin Iskwewak (First Nations Women): Breaking Chains." *Canadian Journal of Women and Law* 3 no. 2 (1989-1990): 476-77.

Taylor, Carl. *Girls, Gangs, Women and Drugs.* East Lansing, Michigan: Michigan State University Press, 1993.

Thomas, J. "Quiescence in Women's Prison Litigation." *Justice Quarterly* 1 (1984): 253-76.

Thrasher, Frederick. *The Gang: A Study of 1,313 Gangs in Chicago.* Chicago: University of Chicago Press, 1963.

To Heal the Spirit. Directed by B. Barde. 40 min. Why Not Productions, 1990. Videocassette.

Tonry, Michael. *Malign Neglect—Race, Crime, and Punishment in America.* New York: Oxford University Press, 1995.

Trefousse, Hans L. *Reconstruction: Americas First Effort at Racial Democracy.* Huntington, NY: Robert E. Krieger Publishing Company, 1979.

Truman, David R. "The Jet and Sharks are Dead: The State Statutory Responses to Criminal Street Gangs." *Washington University Law Quarterly* 73 (1995): 683, 688.

Turnbull, Robert J. *A Visit to the Philadelphia Prison.* Philadelphia: Budd and Bertran, 1796. On microfiche in *Early American Imprints, 1639-1800.* (American Antiquarian Society).

"Unfinished Liberation: Policing and Imprisonment." Special journal issue, Joy James, ed. *Radical Philosophy Review,* vol. 3, no. 1 (Fall 1999).

U.S. Department of State. *Civil and Political Rights in the United States: Initial Reporting of the United States of America to the U.N. Human Rights Committee under the International Covenant on Civil and Political Rights.* Washington, D.C., July 1994.

United States General Accounting Office. Report to Senate and House Judiciary Committees, *Death Penalty Sentencing: Research Indicates Pattern of Racial Disparities.* Washington, D.C., February 1990.

United States Sentencing Commission, *Cocaine and Federal Sentencing Policy.* Washington, D.C., February 1995.

Vila, Bryan and Cynthia Morris, eds. *Capital Punishment in the United States: A Documentary History.* Westport, CT: Greenwood Press, 1997).

Waldram, J. *The Way of the Pipe: Aboriginal Spirituality and Symbolic Healing in Canadian Prisons.* Peterborough, Ontario: Broadview Press, 1997.

Ward, David and Gene Kassebaum. *Women's Prisons: Sex and Social Structure.* Chicago: Aldine-Atherton, 1965.

Watson, Jane. "Crime and Juvenile Delinquency Prevention Policy: Time for Early Childhood Prevention." *Georgetown Journal on Fighting Poverty* 2 (1995): 245, 251.

Watterson, Kathryn. *Women in Prison.* Boston: Northeastern University, 1996.

Webb, Gary. *Dark Alliance.* New York: Seven Stories Press, 1998.

Whitfield, Stephen J. *A Death in the Delta: The Story of Emmett Till.* New York: Free Press, 1988.

Wilson, N. K. "Styles of Doing Time in a Co-Ed Prison: Masculine and Feminine Alternatives." In J. O. Smykla, ed. *Coed Prison.* New York: Human Services Press, 1980.

Wilson, William Julius. *The Truly Disadvantaged.* Chicago: University of Chicago Press, 1987.

———. *When Work Disappears: The World of the New Urban Poor.* New York: Knopf, 1996.

Wright, Albert Jr. "Young Inmates Need Help, From Inside and Out." *Emerge* (October 1997): 80

INDEX